FRIEDRICH SCHILLER

Poet of Freedom

Schiller Institute

NEW BENJAMIN FRANKLIN HOUSE

New York, N.Y.

1985

Cover Painting: Gerhard Kügelsen
Cover Design: Alan Yue
First Edition 1985
New Benjamin Franklin House
New York, N.Y.

ISBN:933488-44-0

TABLE OF CONTENTS

Foreword

The Schiller Institute, in what will shortly be its one and one-half years of existence, has gained worldwide importance and an even greater influence. It has become the leading symbol for the preservation and renewal of the alliance between the United States and Western Europe. Under its sponsorship, a trade-union movement throughout Ibero-America has come into existence, and a considerable number of developing nations on three continents see in the Institute the only hope that the foreign-policy program formulated by the Schiller Institute for a new just world economic order can be initiated in time.

Why did an institute for republican foreign policy name itself after a poet, in particular Friedrich Schiller? The extraordinary success of the Schiller Institute in the short time since its founding proves that the concepts created and formulated by Schiller have established that higher level of reason on which alone the problems which confront us today can be overcome.

At the previous six international conferences which the Schiller Institute sponsored, his thought has been the starting place from which every specific problem was attacked. It is not without good reason that Schiller is considered throughout the world as the poet of freedom, who not only defined individual freedom of the individual man as an inalienable right, but symbolized national sovereignty in freedom as well. Schiller revealed, in wonderfully beautiful poetic formulations, why there is no contradiction between being simultaneously a passionate patriot and a citizen of the world. From this standpoint, the work of the Schiller Institute up to this point has tremendously contributed to the idea of a community of nations, resting on the absolute precondition of national sovereignty.

It is our intention to newly translate the collected works of Schiller, of which previously only a small number—and those in bad verse—have appeared in English. The present volume is thus only the first of this planned complete edition.

Reading Schiller's poetry, as well as his historical, philosophical, and aesthetic works, has precisely the effect on the sensitive reader of which Schiller informed us in the preface to his drama *Die Braut von Messina* and in other places in his work—to produce in the reader an ennobling power which then continues to exist long after the reading is done.

This is the case because Schiller fulfilled his own ideal concept, namely, to elevate, "jokingly and playfully," the public up to his own level, and he demanded of himself the very highest standard. Schiller's concept of beautiful humanity, of the "beautiful soul" represents the noblest image ever drawn of the potential of human beings. A human being possessing a beautiful soul, is he in whom reason and feeling, duty and passion coalesce, he who does his duty with joy. It is the genius who lawfully extends and creatively restores all limits.

The concept of beauty of character which Schiller gave us, is perhaps what our poor, tormented world most needs. We live today in a time in which ugliness, evil, mediocrity, anxiety, and despair seem to rule. All the more so do we need the grand ideal of the poet who, through his work, demonstrates to us in the powerful language of poetry how a beautiful soul thinks, that we might refresh ourselves through his example.

Helga Zepp-LaRouche
October 20, 1985

Preface on Translation

CHOICE

Canst thou to all give no pleasure through thine own deed
and thine artwork,
Give it well to the few; many 'tis bad to please.

Friedrich Schiller

The purpose of this preface is to identify the method of translation employed in this volume, in contrast to that employed in most previously published translations of Schiller. In so doing, it is first necessary to indicate the general standpoint, which has shaped this project.

Humanity will not survive without a renaissance, precisely because it is only a renaissance, which can defeat the pragmatic philistinism, which currently dooms civilization. Every single renaissance in the past has had as its necessary precondition, the assimilation of the previous high point in human culture. This has invariably entailed the translation of the written works of great minds of such periods, as the necessary point of departure for a new renaissance.

The last such renaissance in human history was the renaissance centered in Weimar, Germany, spearheaded by Friedrich Schiller. Every major development thereafter, whether in the physical sciences, such as the work of Bernhard Riemann and Georg Cantor, or in music, such as the work of Beethoven, traces its inspiration to the poetic genius of Friedrich Schiller.

However, after the Treaty of Vienna in 1815, that renaissance came to an end and has not been significantly advanced upon since. The cultural dark age, which we have experienced since then, has not seen one great American, or any other English language poet, no great composer and a decline in fundamental advances in physical science. The political reality of the 19th and 20th centuries correlates completely with this decline in poetic creation.

The translations in this volume are, therefore, designed, not merely to make Schiller's writings available in English, but also, in this way, to help launch a necessary renaissance in English language poetry, and thereby in music and the physical sciences.

Since the English language has degenerated since the time of Shakespeare and Milton, such an undertaking requires a revival of the language, as it existed at its previous high point. However, more is needed. Since Schiller represented an advance over Shakespeare and Milton, in terms of universal scientific culture, our objective cannot merely be, to imitate the language of an earlier period, but to enrich it, such that it can express the beautiful conceptions developed by Schiller and those which must be expresssed today by a new generation of Schillers, if humanity is to survive.

Therefore, as in all renaissances, what must be rejected from the beginning, is the idea that the English language, as it currently exists, or even as it existed during the time of Shakespeare and Milton, is subject to fixed Aristolelian laws. Just as Schiller improved the German language and introduced forms of poetic expression, which did not previously exist, and as Dante did the same for the Italian language, so today, it is necessary to improve the English language and introduce poetic forms, including especially those pioneered by Schiller in German, into the English language. Any other approach denies the essence of poetry, the principle of willful creation.

To translate Schiller, one must first and foremost aim not to please a contemporary audience, which is only accustomed to the language of a dark age. In such an age, the creative verbal transformations, which characterize poetry, will seem foreign. Such an age is acclimated through the mass media to a language, which places emphasis instead upon objects and therefore, locates reality in the expression of nouns.

All previous translations of Schiller's work into English are flawed, insofar as they reject in one way or another Schiller's own emphasis on verbal transformations, rather than on mere nouns. This is intentional, because, as in the case of British translations of Plato, the best way to prevent the circulation of republican conceptions is for oligarchical representatives, to establish a monopoly over their translation. Just as Plato is deliberately mistranslated by neo-Aristotelians, so Schiller is most often translated by such British oligarchs as Sir Bulwer Lytton.

The most obvious way in which previous translations attempt to destroy the poet's work is through deliberate mistranslation of key conceptions, usually under the guise of poetic license. Such mistranslations have nothing to do with poetry and everything to do with license. One of the most outrageous examples of this is the systematic elimination of the word "beauteous" from all previously published translations of the poem, "To Joy."

Another important example of mistranslation is the attempt to translate into English the word "schwärmer," when no single English word is capable of conveying its meaning. In the translations in this volume, therefore, the German word "schwärmer" has been employed as a new word in English. This word is absolutely crucial to understanding Don Carlos and also the Aesthetical Letters. The word derives from the German verb "schwärmen," which has the same meaning as the English verb "to swarm." A schwärmer is not merely an enthusiast or a dreamer, he is not a zealot or a fanatic. The schwärmer is one, who may be positively motivated by a dream of a better world, but out of self-love, i.e., a desire for immediate gratification, impulsively attempts to implement his dream or vision, as if that could be accomplished, without bringing about a fundamental change in man, by employing the weapon of beautiful art. The schwärmer is one, whose mind "swarms" self-destructively, because he has believed falsely, that the external world could be changed for the good, without transforming the inner emotions of man.

The more insidious way, in which a poem is often destroyed, is, under the guise of making the translation sound more mellifluous, to alter the meter and rhythm of a poem, as if the latter were not consciously selected as integral to the idea of the poem itself.

This latter practice was in fact rationalized on purely racialist grounds by Bulwer Lytton, who wrote, "Every distinct race has its own distinct forms of verse, according to its hereditary associations."

The typical translation of Schiller available prior to publication of this volume is, therefore, neither trustworthy in regard to literal idea content, nor in regard to the meter and rhythm. In translation of a poem, the normal procedure has been to eliminate the alternating line lengths, which characterize all Schiller's poems and to thus end all lines with a stressed syllable. Also, poems written by Schiller in a trochaic rhythm will be transformed into an iambic rhythm. These procedures are usually then accompanied by a willingness to sacrifice the idea content of the poem for the perfect end-rhyme.

As an example of this practice, take the opening two lines of the poem, "The Commencement of the New Century," which are trochaic with alternating line lengths:

> Edler Freund! Wo öffnet sich dem Frieden,
> Wo der Freiheit sich ein Zufluchtsort?

This has been previously translated as follows:

> Where will a place of refuge, noble friend,
> For peace and freedom ever open lie!

As can be seen, the rhythm has been transformed to iambic from trochaic, and the alternating line lengths have been eliminated. The most important line in the poem, the first line, has been changed

entirely by the fact, that it no longer begins with the exclamation—
Noble friend!

The translation in this volume, on the other hand, maintains the
rhythm of the original:

> Noble Friend! Where is to peace imparted,
> Where to liberty a refuge place?

Only a false academic prejudice would prompt one to so distort the
opening lines of this poem, and thus the poem as a whole, when it is
clearly not only desirable, but possible, to translate it in the original
rhythm in English.

In this volume, every effort is made to reproduce the idea content
of both poetry and prose. Since the idea content is inseparable in
poetry from the meter and rhythm with which it is expressed, the
latter are also reproduced. Where a poem is rhymed in the original,
it is rhymed in translation, even if only in the form of a light rhyme,
but not at the cost of the metrical idea.

Since the verbal transformations, which occur in a poem are me-
diated through metaphor, only a literal translation is capable of repro-
ducing the concrete images through which such transformations occur.
To the philistine, literal translation reflects a lack of creative individual
expression in the translator. However, any departure from the literal,
totally aborts the creative process, which is the essence of poetry.

It is one thing to improve in translation upon the work of a bad
poet. But why should one waste one's time in this way? To rationalize
deliberate mistranslations of Schiller, the greatest of poets, as an im-
provement, especially when they abort necessary metaphorical trans-
formations, is the height of arrogant dishonesty.

A good example of this is the word "cannibal," a word which some
might consider ugly, which appears in the seventh stanza of the poem,
"To Joy." Most previous translations eliminate the word cannibal and
thus remove from the poem one of the most powerful metaphorical
representations of the power of joy. The lines in question are as follows:

> Freude sprudelt in Pokalen,
> In der Traube goldnem Blut
> Trinken Sanftmut Kannibalen,
> Die Verzweiflung Heldenmut.

A typical translation is as follows:

> Joy within the goblet flushes,
> For the golden nectar, wine,
> Every fierce emotion hushes,—
> Fills the breast with fire divine.

The translation in this volume, by preserving the literal image of the "cannibals" and also of the "blood" of grape, more completely conveys the transformations, which characterize the realm of joy.

> *Joy* doth bubble from this rummer,
> From the golden blood of grape
> Cannibals imbibe good temper,
> Weak of heart their courage take—

Two additional features of the translations in this volume are important to address:

First, in much of the poetry, including *Don Carlos*, the "thou" form of the familiar second person singular has been employed, as well as many other usages, which by today's standards might be considered archaic. The use of the "thou" form, employed in all great English language writing, including in the King James version of the Bible and in poetry up to the time of Shelley and Keats, is not arbitrary. Its use goes directly to the heart of the inseparability of style and content.

In *Don Carlos*, the character Don Carlos' insistence that Marquis Posa refer to him in the familiar form of "thou" is a crucial expression of the republican conception of the equality of all men. The use of the "thou" form is therefore absolutely necessary to the republican content of the play. It is therefore inconceivable, that this form be regarded as some archaic externality. One recent translation, however, relegates this issue to a mere footnote, rather than employ the "thou" form throughout. One might as well relegate republicanism to a footnote and freedom to a museum-piece.

Second, in regard to the prose translations of especially the *Letters on Don Carlos* and the *Letters on the Aesthetical Education of Man*, the following observation must be made. Schiller was first and foremost a poet. Therefore, one must approach his prose, as if it were a form of poetry, albeit lacking meter, rhythm and rhyme. However, what great prose and poetry have in common is that they stimulate thought through a sequence of verbal actions (ideas).

Besides the problem of mistranslation of particular words, which is a problem in its own right, the major problem with previous prose translations is, that they separate the idea content from the sequence of verbal transformations, which expresses that content. They therefore destroy the idea content.

As in the case of poetry translations, previous translations of Schiller's prose have attempted to "smooth out" the sentences and rearrange them, so as to make them "sound good." Such "sweet sounding" English may lead to tooth decay, but never to beauty.

Part of the problem is, that such translators have "speed readers" as their internalized audience, and therefore feel compelled to eliminate any verbal action, which may require concentration. This is just another example of nominalist chromaticism, similar to a fixation on perfect end-rhymes in poetry, the location of beauty in the beautiful object, rather than in the process of transformation of ugliness.

In this regard, the importance of punctuation should be noted. As in poetry, punctuation in prose helps to order the sequence of verbal actions or modifications. An accurate translation, which reproduces the sequence of such ideas, will necessarily tend to reproduce the punctuation of the original.

The modern reader will tend therefore to react negatively initially to the use of commas in translation of Schiller's prose. But no renaissance in human history was ever created on the basis of reaction. Reaction is the response of those, who have been living in a dark age and either don't know it or don't want to admit it, because they would then have to give up their fixation on the mellifluous and take responsibility for transforming the ugly reality with the weapons of truly beautiful art.

William F. Wertz, Jr.
October 16, 1985

DON CARLOS
INFANTE OF SPAIN

A dramatic poem

DON CARLOS

INFANTE OF SPAIN

A *dramatic poem*

TRANSLATED BY WILLIAM F. WERTZ, JR., DANIEL PLATT,
MURIEL MIRAK AND JOHN SIGERSON

DRAMATIS PERSONÆ

PHILIP II, *King of Spain*

ELIZABETH OF VALOIS, *his spouse*

DON CARLOS, *the Crown Prince*

ALEXANDER FARNESE, *Prince of Parma, nephew of the King*

INFANTA CLARA EUGENIA, *a child of three years*

DUTCHESS OF OLIVAREZ, *Chief Stewardess*

Ladies to the Queen

MARQUISE OF MONDECAR

PRINCESS OF EBOLI

COUNTESS FUENTES

Grandees of Spain

MARQUIS OF POSA, *a Knight of Malta*

DUKE OF ALBA

COUNT OF LERMA, *Chief of the Bodyguard*

DUKE OF FERIA, *Knight of the Fleece*

DUKE OF MEDINA SIDONIA, *Admiral*

DON RAIMOND OF TAXIS, *Chief Postmaster*

DOMINGO, *the Father Confessor of the King*

GRAND INQUISITOR *of the Royal Realm*

PRIOR *of a Carthusian cloister*

PAGE *of the Queen*

DON LUDWIG MERKADO, *physician in ordinary to the Queen*

Various LADIES *and* GRANDEES, PAGES, OFFICERS,
The BODYGUARD *and other non-speaking persons*

3

ACT I

SCENE I—*The royal garden in Aranjuez.* CARLOS, DOMINGO

DOMINGO: The lovely days here in Aranjuez
Are now at end. Your Royal Highness leaves
It with no greater cheerfulness. 'Tis clear
We have been here to no avail. Break off
This enigmatic silence. Open up
Your heart unto your father's heart, my Prince.
Too dearly can the Monarch never buy
His son's repose—his only son's—too dearly.
(CARLOS *looks at the ground and is silent.*)
And were there yet a wish, that Heaven hath
Denied unto the dearest of its sons?
I stood thereby, as in Toledo's walls
Proud Carl receiv'd the homage of them all,
As princes throng'd to kiss his hand, and now
In *one—one single prostrate supplication*
Six kingly realms did lay before his feet—
I stood and saw the youthful, prideful blood
Arise within his cheeks, I saw his breast
Swell up with princely resolution, and
I saw his drunken eye fly through th' assembly,
With rapture dimming—Prince, and then this eye
Confess'd: I am now sated.
(CARLOS *turns away.*)   Prince, this still
And solemn sorrow, that we all have read
Already now for eight moons in your looks,
The riddle of th' entire court, the dread
O' th' kingly realm, hath cost His Majesty
Already many anxious, troubl'd nights,
Your mother many tears already.
        CARLOS (*turns swiftly around*):   Mother?
—O Heaven, pray, let me forget the one,
Who made her thus into my mother!
        DOMINGO: Prince?
        CARLOS (*reflects and passes his hand over his forehead*):
Most rev'rend Lord—I have a great deal of
Misfortune with my mothers. My first deed,
As I beheld a glimpse of this world's light,
Was matricide.
        DOMINGO: Is't possible, kind Prince?
Can this reproach press on your conscience so?
        CARLOS: And my new mother—is it not the case,

That she hath cost me all my father's love?
My father hardly lov'd me. My entire
Desert was yet, to be his only son.
She gave to him a daughter—O who knows,
What slumbers in the hinterground of time?

    DOMINGO: You mock me, Prince. The whole of Spain adores
Its Queen. And you alone should thus regard
Her with such hateful eyes? And at her sight
You should alone hear naught but cleverness?
How, Prince? The fairest woman in the world,
And Queen—and formerly your fiancee?
Impossible, Prince, unbelievable!
Where all do love, Carl cannot hate alone;
So strangely Carlos could not be at odds.
Prince, guard yourself, that she doth ne'er observe,
How very much she doth displease her son.
The news would cause her pain.

    CARLOS: Believe you so?

    DOMINGO: If still Your Highness recollects the last
O' th' tournaments at Saragossa, where
A splinter from a lance did graze our Lord—
The Queen with all her gentlewomen sat
Upon the center rostrum of the palace
And watch'd the fight. At once a cry rang out:
"The King is bleeding!"—People race about,
A muffl'd murmur penetrates to th' ear
O' th' Queen. "The Prince?" she cries and wants, and wants
To dive down from the highest ballustrade.—
"Oh, no! The King himself!" The answer comes—
"So send for doctors!" she retorts, as she
Regains her breath once more.
(*After some silence*)   And so you stand
All lost in thought?

    CARLOS: I wonder at this droll
Confessor to the King, that he is so
Proficient in the art of witty tales.
(*Seriously and darkly*)
Yet none the less I've always heard it said,
That tattle-tales and gesture-peeps have done
More of the evil in this world than e'er
Could dirk or poison in th' assassin's hand.
You could have spar'd yourself the trouble, Lord.
For if it's thanks you want, go to the King.

    DOMINGO: You do quite well, my Prince, to guard yourself
With men—but do discriminate. Do not

Repulse the friend and hypocrite alike.
I mean you well.
  CARLOS: Let not my father come
To notice that. Or else you may be out
Your purple.
  DOMINGO (*starts*): What?
  CARLOS: Indeed. Did not he give
His promise that you'd be the first to get
The purple that would be bestow'd by Spain?
  DOMINGO: You're mocking me, my Prince.
  CARLOS: That God forbid,
That I should mock this terrifying man,
This man who can both canonize my father
And damn him!
  DOMINGO: Prince, I would not thus presume
To forcibly intrude myself into
The venerable secret of your sorrow.
I only ask Your Highness but to bear
In mind, that to th' affrighted conscience doth
The church a refuge open up, whereto
No monarch hath a key, and where misdeeds
Themselves, beneath the seal o' th' sacrament,
Do lie protected—Prince, you know what I
Intend. I've said enough.
  CARLOS: No! Far be it
From me to tempt the bearer of the seal!
  DOMINGO: Prince, this mistrust—You are misjudging your
Most faithful servant.
  CARLOS (*grasps him by the hand*): Rather, then, give up
On me. You are a holy man, the world
Doth know it—yet, to make it plain—for me
You are already overtax'd. Your path,
Most rev'rend Father, is the longest one,
Until you settle down on Peter's chair.
Much knowledge might just weigh you down. Report
That to the King who sent you here.
  DOMINGO: Who sent
Me here?—
  CARLOS: So said I. O, too well, too well
I know, that at this court I am betray'd—
I know a hundred eyes have been engag'd
To watch my ev'ry move, I know full well
King Philip sold his only son unto
The worst among his servants, and that for

Each intercepted syllable of mine
Th'informer gets a far more princely fee
Than he for any good deed ever paid.
I know——O still! No more of this! My heart
Is apt to overflow and I have said
Already far too much.
    DOMINGO: The King intends
To reach Madrid before this evening.
The court assembles even now. Have I
Permission, Prince——
    CARLOS: All right. I'll follow you.
(DOMINGO *goes. After some silence*)
Lamentable King Philip, like thy son
Lamentable——I see thy soul already,
That from suspicion's poison'd snakebite bleeds,
Thy mis'rable inquisitiveness must
Precipitate the fearfulest discov'ries,
And thou wilt rage, when this one thou hast made.

    SCENE II——CARLOS. MARQUIS OF POSA.

    CARLOS: Who comes?——What do I see? O ye good spirits!
My Roderick!
    MARQUIS: My Carlos!
    CARLOS: Can it be?
Is't true? Is't really? Art thou he?——O, th'art!
I press thee to my soul, I feel thine beat
Almightily against mine own. O, now
Is ev'rything all well again. In this
Embrace mine ailing heart is heal'd. For now
I lie upon my Rod'rick's neck.
    MARQUIS: Your ailing,
Your ailing heart? And what is well again?
What is it, that should needs be well again?
You hear, what makes me pause?
    CARLOS: And what doth bring
Thee so unhop'd-for back again from Brussels?
To whom do I owe thanks for this surprise?
To whom? I question still? Forgive the drunk
With joy, high Providence, this blasphemy!
Whom else but thee, Allkindliest? Thou knew'st,
That Carlos was without an angel, thou
Didst send me this one, and I question still?
    MARQUIS: Your pardon, my dear Prince, if I requite

This stormy rapture only with alarm.
'Twas not like this, I did expect to see
Don Philip's son. Upon your sallow cheeks
A most unnat'ral redness doth inflame,
And how your lips do tremble fev'rishly.
What must I then believe, dear Prince?—That's not
The young man, bold as lions, unto whom
A sore oppress'd heroic people sends me—
For now I stand here not as Roderick,
Not as the playmate of the boyish Carlos—
As delegate of all mankind do I
Embrace you—'tis the Flemish provinces,
That weep upon your neck, and solemnly
Assail you with a plea for their salvation.
That land so dear to you is lost, if Alba,
Harsh hangman's helper of fanaticism,
Moves into Brussels with the Spanish laws.
On Emp'ror Carl's own glory-worthy grandson
Doth rest the last hope of this noble land.
'Twill topple, if his lofty heart hath now
Forgot, to beat for all humanity.

    CARLOS: 'Twill topple.

    MARQUIS: Woe is me! What must I hear?

    CARLOS: Thou speak'st of times, that long are pass'd away.
I too have had my dreams of such a Carl,
Whose cheeks turn'd fiery when a man did speak
Of freedom—yet this one is long since buried.
Whom thou dost see here, he's no more the Carl,
That in Alcala took his leave from thee,
Who did presume, in sweet intoxication,
To think that he'd one day create anew
A golden age in Spain—O, the conceit
Was childish, but divinely beautiful!
These dreams are now foreby—

    MARQUIS: These dreams, my Prince!—
So had it been but dreams?

    CARLOS: O let me weep,
Upon thy bosom let me weep hot tears,
Thou only friend. For I have no one—no one—
Upon this earth, so great and wide, I've no one.
So far the scepter of my father reaches,
So far as navigation sends our flags,
There is no place—not one—not one—where I
May shed the burden of my tears, but this.

By everything, O Roderick, that thou
And I in heaven hope to find one day,
Do not expel me hither from this place.
    MARQUIS (*leans over him in speechless emotion*).
    CARLOS: Convince thyself, I were an orphan'd child,
Whom thou in pity pick'd up by the throne.
I know not what my father's call'd—I am
A Monarch's son—O, if it be fulfill'd,
What my heart says to me, if thou from out
Of millions hast been found, to understand
Me, if 'tis true, creating Nature did
Repeat the Roderick in Carlos, and
Upon the morning of our lives, did string
The tender lyre-strings of our souls the same,
If but a tear, that gives me consolation,
Is dearer to thee than my father's favor—
    MARQUIS: O, it is dearer far than all the world.
    CARLOS: So low I've fallen—I've become so poor,
That I must now remind thee of our years
Of early childhood—and that I must beg
Thee to repay the long forgotten debt,
That thou still in thy sailor-suit didst make—
As thou and I, two boys o'th' wildest kind,
Grew up together then so brotherly,
No pain oppress'd me, as to see myself
Eclips'd so by thy spirit—then at last
I boldly chose, to love thee boundlessly,
For I did lack the strength, to be like thee.
Then I began tormenting thee with thousands
Of tender signs and faithful brother-love;
And thou proud heart return'dst them coldly to me.
Oft stood I there, and—yet thou ne'er didst see!
And burning, heavy tearful drops did hang
Upon mine eye, as thou, bypassing me,
Didst press yet humbler children in thine arms.
Why only these? I call'd out mournfully:
Am *I* to thee not also good?—But thou,
Thou knelt'st before me, cold and serious:
That, thou didst say, befits the son o'th' King.
    MARQUIS: O Prince, desist from these so childish tales,
That even now do make me blush with shame.
    CARLOS: This had I not deserv'd of thee. My heart
Thou couldst have scorn'd and torn apart, yet ne'er
Put it away from thee. Three times didst thou

Reject the Prince, three times came he again
As supplicant, to beg for love from thee
And to impose by force his love on thee.
'Twas done by Chance, what Carlos never could.
It happen'd once, that while we were at play
Thy shuttlecock did fly and hit my aunt,
Bohemia's Queen, i'th' eye. She did believe,
That it occurr'd with forethought, and complain'd
Unto the King, with tearful countenance.
All of the youth o' th' palace must appear,
So that the guilty one be nam'd to him.
The King doth vow, the underhanded deed,
And even if 'twere done by his own child,
Most frightfully he'll punish—Then I saw
Thee standing trembling from afar, and now,
Now I stepp'd forth and hurl'd myself to th' feet
O' th' King. I cried out, I, I did it: on
Thy son fulfill thy vengeance.

    MARQUIS: Ah, whereon
You do remind me, Prince!

        CARLOS: 'Twas it: In view
Of all the courtiers, who full of pity
Stood in a circle, was it then perform'd
Upon thy Carl, in manner fit for slaves.
I look'd on thee and did not weep. The pain
Did knock my teeth together, gnashingly;
I did not weep. My regal blood, it flow'd
Most shamefully beneath the ruthless strokes;
I look'd on thee and did not weep—thou cam'st;
And with loud weeping sank'st thou at my feet.
Yes, yes, thou criedst, my pride is overcome.
I will repay thee, when thou art the King.

    MARQUIS (*extends his hand to him*):
And I will do it, Carl. That childish vow
I now as man renew. It shall be paid.
Perhaps my hour will strike as well.

        CARLOS: Now, now—
O do not hesitate—Now hath it struck.
The time hath come, when thou canst settle it.
'Tis love I need—a dreadful secret doth
Lie burning here upon my breast. It should,
It should come out. In thy pale countenance
Will I now read the sentence of my death.
Attend—grow numb—yet do not make reply:

I love my mother.
    MARQUIS: O my God!
    CARLOS: But no!
I'll not have this forbearance. Speak it forth.
Speak, that upon this mighty round of earth
No wretchedness on mine doth border—speak—
What thou can'st say, I have long since divin'd.
The son doth love his mother. Worldly custom,
The ordering of Nature and Rome's laws
Condemn this passion. My pretention strikes
Most frightfully upon my father's rights.
I feel it, and yet still I love. This path
Doth lead alone to madness or the scaffold.
I love bereft of hope—in wickedness—
In mortal fear, at peril to my life—
Yes that I see, and nonetheless I love.
    MARQUIS: The Queen knows of this passion?
    CARLOS: Could I then
Reveal myself to her? She's Philip's wife
And Queen, and this is Spanish soil. Kept on
My guard by my own father's jealousy,
Confin'd on ev'ry side by etiquette,
Could I approach her with no witnesses?
Eight hellish anxious moons hath it been now,
E'er since the King did call me back from school,
So that I am condemn'd to look upon
Her daily and, be silent as the grave.
Eight hellish anxious moons, my Roderick,
This fire hath seeth'd and rag'd within my breast,
A thousand times the dread confession hath
Come forth already here upon my lips,
Yet shy and craven slinks back to my heart.
O Roderick—for just a few brief moments
Alone with her—
    MARQUIS: Ah! And your father, Prince—
    CARLOS: Unhappy man! Why bring him to my mind?
Of all the terrors of the conscience speak,
But speak not of my father to me.
    MARQUIS: Then do you hate your father?
    CARLOS: No! Ah, no!
I do not hate my father—yet a shudd'ring
And evildoer's fearfulness do grip
Me at the mention of this frightful name.
Am I to blame, if in my youthful heart

A servile education trampl'd on
The tender seed of love?—For six years had
I liv'd, when for the first time 'fore mine eyes
The frightful one did come, who, so they told
Me, was my father. 'Twas upon a morn,
That he without e'er hesitating once,
Sign'd four death-warrants. After this I saw
Him only when for some offence he did
Proclaim a punishment for me.—O God!
I feel, that I grow bitter here—Away—
Away, away from here!

MARQUIS: Oh, no, you should—
You should now open up, my Prince. In words
The heavy laden breast relieves itself.

CARLOS: I've often wrestl'd with myself, and oft
At midnight, when my sentries slept, I've thrown
Myself, with scalding show'rs of tears, before
The image of the Blessed Virgin, to
Implore her for a childlike heart—and yet
I did arise unheard. Ah, Roderick!
Reveal to me the wondrous mystery
Of Providence—Why, of a thousand fathers,
Just this one must be *mine*? And why for *him*
Just this son of a thousand better sons?
Two more intolerable opposites
In her circumf'rence, Nature never found.
Why did she wish to force together these,
The two extremities o'th' human race—
Myself and *him*—through such a holy bond?
O frightful lot! Why must it come to pass?
Why should two men, who ever shun each other,
Encounter thus themselves in *one* desire?
Here, Roderick, thou see'st two hostile stars,
That in th' entire long course of time for one
Sole moment in a perpendic'lar course
Do crushingly collide, and then forever
And ever flee from one another.

MARQUIS: I
Foresee a moment of disaster.

CARLOS: I
As well. Like furies from th' abyss the most
Alarming dreams pursue me. Doubtf'lly my
Good spirit grapples with designs most dread;
Through labyrinthine sophistries slinks my

Unhappy acumen, until at last
Before th' abyss's sudden brink it halts—
O Roderick, were I to e'er forget
The father in him—Roderick—I see,
Thy deathly pallid gaze hath understood me—
Were I to e'er forget the father in him,
What would the King then be to me?

      MARQUIS (*after some silence*):   May I
Then dare to ask a favor of my Carlos?
What you're prepar'd to do, just promise me,
You'll nothing undertake without your friend.
You promise this?

      CARLOS: Yes, ev'ry, ev'rything,
Thy love entrusts to me. I throw myself
Entirely in thine arms.

      MARQUIS: As it is said,
Unto the city will the King return.
The time is short. If you do wish to speak
In secret with the Queen, there is no place
Except for Aranjuez where it can come
To pass. The place is calm—the unconstrain'd
Traditions of the country do promote—

      CARLOS: That was my hope. Yet, ah, it was in vain!

      MARQUIS: Not totally. I hasten, to present
Myself to her. If she is still the same
In Spain, as she had been at Henry's court,
Then I'll find open-heartedness. If I
Can read the hopes of Carlos in her glance,
If I find her agreeable to set
This conference—and can her ladies be
Remov'd—

      CARLOS: The most are fond of me.—I've won
The Mondecar especially through her son,
Who serves me as a page.—

      MARQUIS: That's all the better.
So be in the vicinity, my Prince,
T'appear at once upon my given sign.

      CARLOS: That will I—will I—only hurry then!

      MARQUIS: I shall not lose a single moment now.
And so, 'til then, my Prince, farewell!
(*Both depart on different sides.*)

      SCENE III—*The* QUEEN'S *residence in Aranjuez. A simple country
tract, intersected by an avenue, at the end of which can be seen the*

QUEEN'S *villa. The* QUEEN. *The* DUTCHESS OF OLIVAREZ. *The* PRINCESS
OF EBOLI, *and the* MARQUISE OF MONDECAR, *all of whom are coming
up the avenue.*

QUEEN (*to the* MARQUISE):
Ah, *you* I would keep by me, Mondecar!
Those merry eyes of Princess Eboli
Have been tormenting me the morning through.
Behold, she's scarcely able to conceal
Her joy, at leaving country life behind.
    EBOLI: Deny it I cannot, my Queen, that I
Shall be quite pleas'd to see Madrid once more.
    MONDECAR: And not Your Majesty as well? Should you
Still be so loath to leave Aranjuez?
    QUEEN: To leave—this pretty place, at least.
Here I'm as in my world. This little spot
I've long consider'd as my favorite.
Here I am greeted by my rustic nature,
The bosom playmate of my younger years.
And here I can recall my childhood sports,
And my beloved France's air wafts here.
Reproach me not for this. Our hearts all pine
Unto our fatherland.
    EBOLI: How lonely, though,
How dead and dreary here! We might as well
Be in la Trappe.
    QUEEN: I see it otherwise.
I find it lifeless in Madrid. — But what
Doth our fair Dutchess say to this?
    OLIVAREZ: It is
My view, Your Majesty, that it was thus
The custom, since Spain hath been rul'd by kings,
To spend one month here, then one month in Pardo,
And then the winter at the Residence.
    QUEEN: Well, Dutchess, you must know by now, that I
Have always yielded to your arguments.
    MONDECAR: Imagine how, before too long, Madrid
Will spring to life! E'en now the Plaza Mayor
Is being readied for a thrilling bull-fight;
They've promis'd us an auto da fe—
    QUEEN: Promis'd?
I hear this from my gentle Mondecar?
    MONDECAR: Why not? 'Tis only heretics they're burning.
    QUEEN: My Eboli, I trust, thinks otherwise.

EBOLI: I do?—Your Majesty, I beg your pardon,
Could you consider me a poorer Christian,
Than the Marquise Mondecar?
    QUEEN: Ah! I'm
Forgetting, where I am. — To something else. —
O' th' countryside, I do believe, we spake.
The month, methinks, is over ere it started.
So many, many joyful hours I'd promis'd
Myself for this sojourn, and I have not
Discover'd, what I hop'd for. Is it so
With all our hopes? And yet, I cannot find
A wish of mine, the which is unfulfill'd.
OLIVAREZ: But, Princess Eboli, you still have not
Reported, whether Gomez still may hope?
If we may soon be calling you his bride?
    QUEEN: How good of you to touch upon this, Dutchess.
(*To the* PRINCESS)
I have been ask'd, to urge his suit with you.
But how can I do that? The man, to whom
I do award my Eboli, must be
Full worthy of her.
    OLIVAREZ: Yes, and that he is,
Your Majesty—a worthy man, a man,
Whom our most gracious Monarch, as is known,
Hath honor'd with her royal favor.
    QUEEN: Which
Will surely make the man quite happy.—Yet
We wish to know, if he can truly love you
And is of love deserving.—Eboli,
I ask you this.
    EBOLI (*dumbfounded and confus'd, her eyes downcast, finally
falls to the* QUEEN'S *feet*):
                My gen'rous Queen, at least
Can *you* have pity on me. Oh, do not—
For Heaven's sake, do not permit that I
Become a sacrifice.
    QUEEN: A sacrifice?
Enough of this. Stand up. It is, indeed,
A sorry fate, to be a sacrifice.
I do believe you. Now, stand up.—It hath
Been long, since you resolv'd to spurn the Count?
    EBOLI (*rising*): Oh, many months. Prince Carlos, at the time,
Was still attending upper school.
    QUEEN (*starts and looks at her searchingly*):

                              Have you
Review'd your grounds for having done so?
    EBOLI (*with energy*):   Never,
No, never shall I let it come to pass,
My Queen, and for a thousand reasons.
    QUEEN (*quite seriously*):   More
Than one's too many. You could never love him.—
For me that is enough. No more of this.
(*To the other* LADIES)
I haven't seen th'Infanta yet today.
Marquise, bring you her to me.
    OLIVAREZ (*looks at the clock*): The hour
Is not arriv'd, Your Majesty.
    QUEEN: The hour
Is not arriv'd, when I may be a mother?
How very sad! Well, then, do not forget
To tell me, when 'tis come.
(*A page enters and speaks softly to the first* LADY, *who
thereupon turns to the* QUEEN.)
    OLIVAREZ: Your Majesty,
Marquis of Posa—
    QUEEN: Posa?
    OLIVAREZ: Yes. He's come
From France and from the Netherlands and doth
Desire Your Grace, allow him to deliver
Some letters from the Regent Mother's hand.
    QUEEN: Is it permitted?
    OLIVAREZ (*doubtful*):   My instructions ne'er
Provided for the special instance, when
A Catalan Grandee arrives with letters
Dispatch'd from foreign courts, requesting leave
To hand such to the Queen of Spain, whilst she
Is in her garden.
    QUEEN: Well, then, I shall take
The risk upon myself!
    OLIVAREZ: But with Your Majesty's
Permission, I'll withdraw until.—
    QUEEN: You may
Do as you wish, my Dutchess.
(*First* LADY *exits, and the* QUEEN *signals to a page, who
leaves forthwith.*)

    SCENE IV—*The* QUEEN, *the* PRINCESS OF EBOLI, *the* MARQUISE
OF MONDECAR, *and the* MARQUIS OF POSA.

QUEEN: Chevalier,
I welcome you to Spanish soil.
    MARQUIS: Which I
Have ne'er more proudly call'd my fatherland
Than at this moment.—
    QUEEN (*to both* LADIES): The Marquis of Posa,
The same who at the tournament in Reims
Cross'd lances with my father and did lead
My chosen colors thrice to victory—
The finest of his nation, who hath taught me
How glorious 'tis, to be the Spaniards' Queen.
(*Turning to the* MARQUIS)
When last we met i'th' Louvre, Chevalier,
You never dreamt that you would be my guest
Here in Castile.
    MARQUIS: Most surely not, great Queen—
For then I did not dream, that France would lose
The only thing, which made us envy her.
    QUEEN: Proud Spaniard! The only thing?—And this
You venture to a daughter of Valois?
    MARQUIS: I'm free to say it now, Your Majesty—
For now, you're ours.
    QUEEN: Your travellings, I hear,
Have brought you through my native France.— What tidings
Are come from my most honorable mother
And from my much-beloved brothers?
    MARQUIS (*hands her letters*):   Ill
I found the Regent Mother, far remov'd
From ev'ry other worldly joy, save seeing
Her royal daughter happily upon
The Spanish throne.
    QUEEN: And should she not be so,
When my thoughts dwell on sweet remembrances
Of such belov'd relations? Chevalier,
You've visited so many courts, and seen
So many diff'rent countries, diff'ring customs—
And now, I'm told, it is your firm intent,
To settle here within your fatherland?
A greater prince within your silent walls,
Than is King Philip on his mighty throne—
And freer!—A philosopher!—I doubt
Quite strongly, you'll be pleas'd with our Madrid.
'Tis very—peaceful in Madrid.
    MARQUIS: And that

Is more, than all of Europe's other lands
Enjoy at present.
    QUEEN: So I hear.—I must
Admit that all the matters of the world
Could not be further from my mind.
(*To* PRINCESS EBOLI)   Me thinks,
My Princess Eboli, o'er there I spy
A hyacinth in bloom.—You'll bring it me?
(*The* PRINCESS *goes to the indicated place. The* QUEEN
speaks somewhat more softly to the MARQUIS)
If I'm not wrong, my Chevalier, your presence
Hath quicken'd someone else's spirits here
Within my court.
    MARQUIS: I've found a gloomy one—
Whom in this world but something glad—
(*The Princess returns with the blossom.*)
    EBOLI: So! Since
The Chevalier hath seen so many lands,
He'll doubtless have some entertaining things
He can relate to us.
    MARQUIS: Most certainly.
For, after all, to quest for high adventure,
Is knighthood's duty—holiest of all,
To rescue damsels in distress.
    MONDECAR: From giants!
Today there are no giants.
    MARQUIS: Violence
Shall always be a giant to the weak.
    QUEEN: The Chevalier is right. There are still giants.
'Tis just that there are no more valiant knights.
    MARQUIS: Not long ago, on my return to Naples,
I chanc'd to hear a very touching story,
Which holy bonds of friendship prompted me
To take to heart.—If I don't have to fear,
That I might overtire Your Majesty
By telling of this little tale—
    QUEEN: Have I
A choice? The Princess, here, doth nearly burst
With curiosity. So now, proceed.
I am a friend as well of histories.
    MARQUIS: Two noble families from Mirandola,
Grown tired of their long years of jealous feuding,
Bequeath'd to them o'er distant centuries
From warring Ghibellines and Guelphs, decided,

To form a union of eternal peace,
By tender bonds of matrimony seal'd.
And to that purpose, mighty Pietro's nephew,
Fernando, and the heavenly Mathilda,
Colonna's daughter, had been predetermin'd,
To cinch the beauteous knot of unity.
Two hearts more beautiful had ne'er been shap'd
By Nature for each other—never had
The world adjudg'd a choice so fortunate.
His charming bride Fernando had not yet
Beheld save in her portraiture—How did
Fernando tremble, then, to see confirm'd
Before his eyes, what his most fiery hopes
Had scarcely ventured to believe i'th' portrait!
In Padua, where he was shackl'd to
His studies, sat Fernando waiting for
That joyous moment, which would call him forth,
To stammer out his first exalted vows
Of love at his Mathilda's feet.
(*The* QUEEN *grows more attentive. The* MARQUIS, *after a short
silence, proceeds with his narration, which, to the extent
the* QUEEN'S *presence permits it, is directed more toward the*
PRINCESS OF EBOLI.)
                                    But meanwhile,
The passing of his spouse leaves Pietro free
To choose another bride. —with youthful passion
The old man doth devour the voice of rumor,
Which gushes forth in praise of fair Mathilda.
He comes! He sees!—He loves! This new obsession
Drowns out the far more gentle voice of Nature,
The uncle sues to wed his nephew's bride
And 'fore the altar consecrates his theft.
    QUEEN: What doth Fernando do?
    MARQUIS: On wings of love,
Yet unaware of this cruel turn of fate,
He hastens drunk with love to Mirandola.
By starlight doth his speedy steed arrive
Before the gates—A bacchanalian din
Of dances and of drums comes thundering
Towards him from the illuminated palace.
He shyly trembles up the steps, and finds
Himself a stranger at the marriage fest,
Where in the revelry of guests, there sat
Pietro—with an angel at his side—

An angel, whom Fernando recogniz'd,
Who in his dreams had ne'er appear'd so bright.
One glance show'd him, what he had nigh possess'd,
Show'd him, what he had lost forevermore.

    EBOLI: Oh, poor Fernando!

    QUEEN: But, my Chevalier,
That cannot be the story's end?—It needs
An ending.

    MARQUIS: 'Tis not ready yet.

    QUEEN: Did you
Not tell me, that Fernando was your friend?

    MARQUIS: None dearer to my heart.

    QUEEN: But pray, go on,
Continue with your story, Chevalier.

    MARQUIS: It will be very sad—the thought alone
Of telling it renews my pain. Let me
Forego the ending—

(*All lapse into silence.*)

    QUEEN (*turns to* PRINCESS OF EBOLI):

                         Now, most certainly
I may at last embrace my daughter. — Princess,
Bring her to me.

(*The latter withdraws. The* MARQUIS *signals to a page, who hath appear'd in the hinterground, and who immediately disappears. The* QUEEN *breaks open the letters given her by the* MARQUIS, *and seems to be surpris'd. During this time, the* MARQUIS *speaks in an urgent and confidential manner with the* MARQUISE OF MONDECAR.—*The* QUEEN, *having read the letters, turns to the* MARQUIS, *with an inquisitive mien.*)   But you have told us naught
Of fair Mathilda's destiny. Perhaps
She doth not know, how much Fernando suffers?

    MARQUIS: Mathilda's heart is yet a mystery—
But great souls suffer on in silence.

    QUEEN: You look about? Your eyes are seeking someone?

    MARQUIS: I think about, how glad a certain one,
Whom now I cannot name, would feel if standing
Here in my place.

    QUEEN: And who's to blame, that he
Is not so?

    MARQUIS (*interrupting her, with animation*):
        What? May I take liberty
To understand you, as I will?—Would he
Find pardon, if he did appear right now?

QUEEN (*shock'd*):
Now, Marquis? Now? What are you leading to?
　　MARQUIS: May he have hope then—may he?
　　QUEEN (*with increasing confusion*):　　　　Please, Marquis,
You're fright'ning me.—He'd never—
　　MARQUIS　　　　　　　　　Here he is.

SCENE V—*The* QUEEN. CARLOS. (MARQUIS OF POSA *and the*
MARQUISE OF MONDECAR *retreat into the hinterground.*)

　　CARLOS (*thrown down before the* QUEEN):
So is it fin'lly here, the precious moment,
And Carl may dare to touch this cherish'd hand!—
　　QUEEN: What kind of step—and what a culpable,
Adventuresome surprise! Stand up! We are
Discover'd now. My retinue's nearby.
　　CARLOS: I'll not stand up—here will I ever kneel.
Upon this spot I'll lie enchantedly.
I shall take root in this position—
　　QUEEN:　　　　　　　　　Madman!
Unto what boldness doth my favor lead you?
How? Do you know, that 'tis the Queen, that 'tis
The mother, to whom this audacious speech
Is now directed? Do you know, that I—
That I myself of this surprise invasion
Unto the King—
　　CARLOS:　　　And that I then must die!
They'd drag me straight from here onto the scaffold!
One moment, to have liv'd in paradise,
Will not be bought too dearly with my death.
　　QUEEN: And what then of your Queen?
　　CARLOS (*stands up*):　　　　　　　　　God, God! I'll go—
I shall indeed foresake you.—Must I not,
When you demand it *thusly*? Mother! Mother!
How frightfully you play with me! One sign,
One half a glance, one sound from out your mouth
Enjoins me, both to be and pass away.
What do you want, that yet should come to pass?
What can there be beneath this sun, that I
Will not make haste to sacrifice, if you
So wish it?
　　QUEEN: Fly from me.
　　CARLOS:　　　　　O God!
　　QUEEN:　　　　　　　　This one
Thing only, Carl, wherefore I conjure you

With teardrops—Fly from me!—before my ladies—
Before my jailers find you here with me
Together, and then bring the major news
Before your father's ears—

CARLOS: I shall await
My destiny—and be it life or death.
What? Have I concentrated all my hopes
Upon this single moment, which doth grant
You to me without witnesses at last,
That bogus terrors dup'd me at the goal?
No, Queen! The world can move a hundred times,
A thousand times upon its poles before
This favor of coincidence repeats.

QUEEN: And that it should not in eternity.
Unhappy man! What do you want from me?

CARLOS: O Queen, that I have struggl'd, struggl'd, as
No mortal ever struggl'd to this day,
Let God then be my witness—Queen, in vain!
Behind me is my valor. I succumb.

QUEEN: No more of this— for my repose's sake—

CARLOS: You once were mine—in view of all the world
Awarded to me by two mighty thrones,
Conferr'd on me by heaven and by nature,
And Philip, Philip's stolen you from me—

QUEEN: He is your father.

CARLOS: And your husband.

QUEEN: Who
Bequeaths to you the world's most mighty realm.

CARLOS: And *you* as mother—

QUEEN: Mighty God! You rave—

CARLOS: And knows he too how rich he is? Hath he
A feeling heart, to treasure that of yours?
I'll not lament it, no, I shall forget,
How happy past all utterance were I
Become to have your hand—if *he* but is.
But he is not.—That, that is hellish torment!
That he is not and never shall become.
Thou tookst my heaven from me, only to
Annihilate it there in Philip's arms.

QUEEN: Abominable thought!

CARLOS: O yes, I know,
Who was the author of this marriage—and
I know, how Philip loves and how he woo'd.
Who are you then within this realm? Let's hear.

By chance, the Regent? Nevermore! Where *you're*
The Regent, how then could these Albas slaughter?
And how could Flanders bleed for its belief?
Or are you Philip's wife? Impossible!
This I cannot believe. A wife possesses
The husband's heart—to whom doth his belong?
And doth he not, for ev'ry tenderness,
That might escape from him in fev'rish ardor,
Apologize unto his scepter and
To his grey hairs?
     QUEEN: Who told you, that my lot
Be worthy of lament at Philip's side?
     CARLOS: My heart, that strongly feels, how enviable
At my side 'twere.
     QUEEN: Conceited man! If *my*
Own heart now said the opposite to me?
If Philip's deferential tenderness,
Should move me far more intimately than
His haughty son's audacious eloquence?
If an old man's considerate regard—
     CARLOS: Then that is diff'rent—then—yet, then—your pardon.
I did not know it, that you love the King.
     QUEEN: My wish and pleasure is to honor him.
     CARLOS: Then you have never lov'd?
     QUEEN: Peculiar question!
     CARLOS: Then you have *never* lov'd?
     QUEEN: —I love no more.
     CARLOS: Because your heart, because your vow forbids it?
     QUEEN: Depart from me now, Prince, and do not come
For such a conversation e'er again.
     CARLOS: Because your vow, because your heart forbids it?
     QUEEN: Because my duty—Hapless one, whereto
The sad dissection of the destiny
That you and I must both obey?
     CARLOS: We must?
We must obey?
     QUEEN: What? What is it you want
With this most solemn tone?
     CARLOS: So much, that Carlos
Is not dispos'd, to must, where he hath but
To will; that Carlos is not so dispos'd
To stay the one most mis'rable i'th' realm,
When it should cost him but the overthrow
Of laws, and nothing more, to be the one

Most blissful.

    QUEEN: Do I understand you now?
You yet do hope? You venture it, to hope,
Where ev'ry, ev'rything's already lost?

    CARLOS: I give up naught for lost except the dead.

    QUEEN: On me, upon your mother, rest you hopes?—
(*She views him long and penetratingly—then
with dignity and earnestness*)
Why not then? Oh! The new elected King
Can do yet more than that—can extirpate
Decrees of the departed one through fire,
Can fell his images, and what is more—
Who should prevent him?—drag the dead one's mummy
From its repose in the Escurial
Into the light o'th' sun, and strew about
His desecrated dust to the four winds
And last, to consummate it worthily—

    CARLOS: For love of God, do not complete the thought!

    QUEEN: At last he can yet marry with his mother.

    CARLOS: Accursed son!
(*He stands a moment blank and speechless.*)
                             Yes, it is out. Now is
It out—I feel it clear and bright, that which
Should ever, ever dark remain for me.
For me you're gone—gone—gone— forevermore!—
And now the die is cast. You're lost to me.—
Oh, Hell doth lie within this feeling! Hell
Doth lie in yet another feeling, in
Possessing you.—Alas! I grasp it not,
And now my nerves are at the breaking point.

    QUEEN: Lamentable, O precious Carl! I feel—
I feel completely this, the nameless pain,
That storms now in your bosom. Infinite's
Your torment, like your love. Yet infinite
Alike's the glory, this to overcome.
Attain it, youthful hero. The reward
Is worthy of this strong and lofty fighter,
Is worthy of the youth, through whose heart rolls
The virtue of so many regal forbears.
Take courage, noble Prince.—The grandson of
The mighty Carl shall start afresh to struggle,
Where others' children end dejectedly.

    CARLOS: Too late! O god! it is too late!

    QUEEN: To be

A man? O Carl! How great our virtue grows,
When in its exercise our heart doth break!
'Twas high that Prov'dence plac'd you— higher, Prince,
Than millions of your other brothers. She,
In partiality gave to her fav'rite,
What she from others took, and millions ask:
Did he deserve to count in Mother's womb
For more already than we other mortals?
Up, vindicate the equity of Heaven!
Deserve to walk before the rest o' th' world,
And sacrifice, what none have sacrific'd!
    CARLOS: That I can do as well.—to fight for you,
I have a giant's strength, to lose you, none.
    QUEEN: Confess it, Carlos—'tis but spitefulness
And bitterness and pride, that draws your wishes
So fiercely to your mother. That same love,
The heart, you offer wastefully to me,
Belongs to th' realms, that you should rule in days
To come. You see, you squander all the goods
That in your trust your ward hath held for you.
Love is your greatest office. But 'til now
It's stray'd unto your mother.—Bring it now,
O, bring it now to your prospective realms
And feel, instead of daggers of the conscience,
Just how voluptuous 'tis to be God.
Elisabeth was your first love. Be Spain
Your second love! How gladly, my good Carl,
Will I give way to th' loftier Belov'd!
    CARLOS (*throws himself, overwhelm'd with feeling, at her feet*):
How great you are, O Heavenly!—Yes, all
You charge me with, that shall I do!—So be't!
(*He arises.*)
I stand here in th'Almighty's hand and swear—
And swear to you, I swear eternally—
O Heaven! No! Eternal silence only,
Yet not to e'er forget it.
    QUEEN: How could I
Demand of Carlos, what I am myself
Unwilling to perform?
    MARQUIS (*hurries out of the avenue*):
                The King!
    QUEEN: O God!
    MARQUIS: Away, away from out this quarter, Prince!
    QUEEN: 'Tis frightful, his suspicion, should he catch

A glimpse of you—
    CARLOS: I shall remain!
    QUEEN: And who
Will be the victim then?
    CARLOS (*pulls the Marquis by the arm*):
                  Be gone, be gone!
Come, Roderick!
(*He goes and comes back yet another time.*)
           What may I take with me?
    QUEEN: The friendship of your mother.
    CARLOS: Friendship! Mother!
    QUEEN: And from the Netherlands these tears as well.
(*She gives him some letters.* CARL *and the* MARQUIS *depart.
The* QUEEN *looks disquietedly about for her ladies, who are
nowhere to be seen. As she would retreat into the
hinterground, the* KING *appears.*)

SCENE VI—KING. QUEEN. DUKE ALBA. COUNT LERMA. DOM-
INGO. *Some* LADIES *and* GRANDEES, *who stay back in the distance.*

    KING (*looks around in astonishment and is silent a while*):
What do I see! You here! And so alone,
Madame? And not a *single* dame attending?
I am surpris'd—where did your women stay?
    QUEEN: Most gracious husband—
    KING: Why alone?
(*To the retinue*)
          For this
Unpardonable oversight must one
Give me the strictest reckoning. Who hath
The office of attending to the Queen?
Whose orders were to wait on her today?
    QUEEN: O do not fume, my husband—I myself,
I am the guilty one—at my command
The Princess Eboli remov'd herself.
    KING: At your command?
    QUEEN: To call the chambermaid,
Because I yearn'd to see th'Infanta.
    KING: And
You therefore sent away the company?
Yet this excuses but the first o' th' ladies.
Where was the second one?
    MONDECAR (*who meanwhile hath come back and mingl'd with the
remaining* LADIES, *steps forward*):

Your Majesty,
I feel, that I am culpable—
    KING: Therefore
I grant you ten years time far from Madrid,
In order that you may reflect on this.
(*The* MARQUISE *steps back with tearful eyes. General
silence. All bystanders look dismay'd upon the* QUEEN.)
    QUEEN: Marquise, *whom* do you lament?
(*To the* KING)
                                    If I've
Offended, my most gracious husband, then
This kingdom's royal crown, for which I ne'er
Myself have grasp'd, should at the very least·
Protect me from what cause there be to blush.
Is there a law within this regal realm,
That calls a Monarch's daughters into court?
Doth mere coercion guard the wives of Spain?
A witness shields them better than their virtue?
And now forgive me, husband. I am not
Accustom'd to dismiss in tears, those who
With joy have done me service.—Mondecar!
(*She removes her girdle and passes it over to the* MARQUISE.)
It is the King you've anger'd—not myself—
So take you this memento of my favor
And of this hour.—Avoid the realm—It is
In Spain alone that you've transgress'd; within
My France they wipe away such tears with joys.—
Oh, must I be reminded evermore?
(*She leans on the* CHIEF STEWARDESS *and covers her face.*)
There in my France 'twas otherwise.
    KING (*in some agitation*):   Could a
Reproach born of my love afflict you so?
A word afflict you, that the tenderest
Distress did lay upon my lips?
(*He turns to the* GRANDEZZA) Here stand
The vassals of my throne. Did e'er a sleep
Descend upon my eyelids, but I had
Made reckoning upon the evening
Of ev'ry day, just how my people's hearts
Were beating in my farthest latitudes?—
And ought I tremble yet more anxiously
Then for my throne as for my heart's own mate?—
My sword can answer for my populace,
This eye but for this woman's love.

QUEEN: Do I
Deserve this lack of trust, my Sire?
        KING: I'm call'd
The richest man in all the Christen'd world;
The sun doth never set upon my state—
Yet ev'rything another once possess'd,
Will after me be own'd by many more.
This is my own. For what the King doth have,
Belongs to chance—Elisabeth to Philip.
Here is the place, where I am mortal.
        QUEEN: Sire,
You are afeard?
        KING: Yet surely not of these
Grey hairs? When I have once begun to fear,
Then hath my fearing ceas'd.—
(*To the* GRANDEES)   I count the great
Ones of my Court—the first of them is lacking.
Where is Don Carlos, my Infant?
(*No one answers*)   The boy
Don Carl begins, to be a dread to me.
He doth avoid my presence, ever since
He came back from Alcala's upper school.
His blood is hot, why is his gaze so cold?
So calculatedly reserv'd his conduct?
Be watchful. This I recommend.
        DUKE: I am.
So long a heart doth beat within this armor,
Don Philip may in peace lay down to sleep.
As God's own Cherubs stand 'fore paradise,
So stands Duke Alba 'fore the throne.
        LERMA: May I
In humbleness presume to contradict
The wisest of all Kings?—For all too deeply
Do I revere my Monarch's Majesty,
To judge his son so sternly, hastily.
There's much I fear from Carlos' heated blood,
Yet nothing from his heart.
        KING: Count Lerma, you
Discourse quite well, to buy the father's favor;
The Duke will be the mainstay of the King—
No more of this—
(*He turns to his retinue.*)
                        I'll speed now to Madrid.
My royal office calls me. Pestilence

Of heresy contaminates my people,
Rebellion grows within my Netherlands.
'Tis highest time. A horrible example
Should help make converts of the erring ones.
The mighty vow, that all the Kings must pledge
In Christendom, will I fulfill tomorrow.
This crim'nal court should have no parallel;
All of my court is solemnly invited.
(*He leads the* QUEEN *away, the others follow.*)

SCENE VII—DON CARLOS, *holding letters, and* MARQUIS OF POSA,
enter from opposite directions.

CARLOS: I am resolv'd. Now Flanders shall be sav'd.
She wills it so. That is enough for me.
MARQUIS: And not a minute more have we to lose.
I'm told, the Duke of Alba even now
Was nam'd as Governor i'th' Cabinet.
CARLOS: Tomorrow, then, I'll go and ask my father
To grant me audience. I will demand
This office for myself. It is the first
Request I ever dar'd to make of him.
Refuse it he cannot. For some time now
He welcomes not my presence in Madrid.
He'll surely not pass up this golden chance,
To hold me distant! And—my Roderick,
Shall I confess it thee? My hopes go farther.
Perhaps, when face to face I see him, I'll
Enjoy success in winning back his favor.
The voice of Nature hath ne'er yet perturb'd
His ear—So let me test, my Roderick,
Its power when she speaks through mine own lips!
MARQUIS: Now, finally, I hear my Carlos speaking!
Now once again you're totally yourself.

SCENE VIII—*The same.* COUNT LERMA.

LERMA: Just now the King hath quit Aranjuez.
And I am bidden—
CARLOS: Very well, Count Lerma.
I'll catch up with the King.
MARQUIS (*affects to take leave. Rather ceremoniously*):
                      Your Royal Highness
Hath nothing further to entrust to me?

CARLOS: No, nothing, Chevalier. I wish you well
'Til your arrival in Madrid. I trust
You'll have still more to tell me there of Flanders.
(*To* LERMA, *who is still waiting for him*):
I'll follow you forthwith.
(*Exit* COUNT LERMA.)

SCENE IX—DON CARLOS. *The* MARQUIS.

CARLOS: Thy meaning's clear.
I thank thee for it. But such forc'd comport
I can excuse alone by others' presence.
Are we not brothers?—Oh, this silly game
Of rank and status—let it be for now
And ever banish'd from our own alliance!
Imagine, we encounter'd one another
At some mask'd ball, thou in a slave's attire,
And I on whim had donn'd a purple robe.
While carnival endures, we two do play along
With this charade, our comic roles perform
In straight-fac'd seriousness, so not to break
The rabble's sweet delirium. And yet,
Through his disguise thy Carl doth nod to thee,
Whilst thou in passing press'st thy hand in mine,
And we both know our gist.
MARQUIS: Your dream's divine.
But will it never vanish? Is my Carl
So self-assur'd, that he will never scorn
The temptings of unbounded Majesty?
A great day lies ahead for you—a day—
When this heroic spirit—let me warn you—
Might founder 'gainst the stormiest of trials.
Don Philip dies. And Carl ascends the throne
O'th' greatest realm in all of Christendom.—
A giant chasm opens, forcing him
To quit the race of mortals. And today
He's god, who yesterday was but a man.
And now he hath no further weaknesses—
The duties of th'eternal strike him dumb.
Humanity—still now that hallow'd word
Is ringing in his ear—then sells itself
To grovel 'fore its idols. And his breast,
Unrent by passion, feels no sympathy,
His virtue smother'd 'neath his revelry,

Peru delivers gold to feed his follies,
His court procures him devils for his vices,
And, glutted, sleep o'ertakes him in the heaven,
Which his own scheming slaves have spun about him.
So long, his dream's drawn out, he is a god—
And woe to th' madman, who with pity woke him.
But how would Roderick then fare?—His friendship
Is bold and true—but sicken'd majesty
Could never stand its fearsome radiance.
The citizen would irk you with his arrogance,
As would I be by princely pride.

CARLOS: Yes, true
And awful is thy portraiture of monarchs.
Yes, I believe thee.—But debauchery
Alone it was which ope'd their hearts to vice.—
I am still pure, a youth of three-and-twenty.
That treasure which so many thousands 'fore me
Have blindly squander'd in the arms of lust,
The spirit's better half, my potency,
I've hoarded for the future ruler's use.
What, then, could drive thee from my heart, if even
A woman cannot do so?

MARQUIS: I myself.
Could I still love you just as deeply, Carl,
Had I to fear you?

CARLOS: That could never be.
Dost thou need me? Dost thou have any passions
Which must come begging 'fore my throne? Doth gold
Attract thee? As a subject, thou art richer
Than I, a king, shall ever be.—Do honors
Entice thee? Even as a youth, thou hadst
Their measure spent—and thou hast flung them 'way.
So who shall be the other's creditor,
And who of us the debtor be?—So silent?
Doth such temptation make thee quake in fear?
Art thou not confident in thine own self?

MARQUIS: All right. I yield. Here is my hand.
CARLOS: 'Tis mine?
MARQUIS: Forever, and i'th' word's most drastic sense.
CARLOS: Attach'd as true and warm tomorrow to
The King as now today to the Infante?
MARQUIS: I swear it to you.
CARLOS: E'en in times when worms
Of flattery besiege my ill-kept heart—

When these mine eyes have long forgot to weep
The tears which once flow'd free, my ear untouch'd
By all entreaties—wilt thou be for me
A resolute protector of my virtue,
And, powerfully seizing me, invoke
My guiding genius by its own great name?
    MARQUIS: I will.
    CARLOS: And one more bidding! Call me *thou!*
This privilege of closest confidence
Hath always made me env'ous of thy kind.
This brother's *thou* deludes my ear, my heart
With sweet portendings of equality.
—Do not object—I'll guess what thou wilt say.
For thee, 'tis but a little thing, I know—
But I, a monarch's son, do hold it dear.
—Wilt thou be brother to me?
    MARQUIS: Yes—*thy* brother!
    CARLOS: And now, to th' King! I've nothing more to fear—
Thus arm in arm with thee I venture to
Defy the limits of my century!
(*They exit.*)

ACT II

    SCENE I—*In the royal palace of Madrid.* (KING PHILIP *under
a canopy. The* DUKE OF ALBA *at some distance from the King, with
cover'd head.* CARLOS.)

    CARLOS: The realm takes precedence. Most willingly
Doth Carlos to the Minister defer.
He speaks for Spain—I am the son o'th' House.
(*He steps back with a bow.*)
    PHILIP: The Duke remains, and the Infante speaks.
    CARLOS (*turning towards Alba*):
Then I must from *your* generosity
Solicit, Duke, the King as my own gift.
A child—you know—can yield up things diverse
From out his heart unto his father, that
For a third party are not fit. The King
Shall be at liberty to you—I wish
To have my father but for this brief hour.
    PHILIP: Here stands his friend.

CARLOS: Have I deserv'd as well,
To think that I have one of mine i'th' Duke?
PHILIP: Or ever wish'd to earn it?—I am not
Pleas'd by those sons, who hit on better choices,
Than do their fathers.
CARLOS: Can the knightly pride
O'th' Duke of Alba listen to this scene?
As truly as I live, the forward one,
Who unsolicited intrudes between
The son and father without blushing, who
Thus sharply feeling his inconsequence,
Doth stand condemn'd, this role by God—
And were it worth a diadem—I would not play.

PHILIP (*leaves his seat with an angry glance at the Prince*):
Remove you, Duke!
(*The latter goes behind the main door, through which* CARLOS
had come; the King gestures him toward another.)
                        No, in the cabinet,
Until I call you.

SCENE II—KING PHILIP. DON CARLOS.

CARLOS (*goes, as soon as the* DUKE *hath left the room, toward
the* KING *and falls before him in an expression of deepest feeling*):
                        Now once more my father,
You're mine again now, and my best of thanks
For this, your favor—Give your hand, my father! —
O sweetest day!—The rapture of this kiss
Was for so long not granted to your child.
But why do you expel me for so long,
My father, from your heart? What have I done?
PHILIP: Infante, of these arts thy heart knows nothing.
Put them away, I like them not.
CARLOS (*standing*):   That was't!
In that I hear your courtiers—My father!
It is not good, by God! not all is good,
Not everything, a priest doth say, not all
Of what the creatures of a priest do say.
I am not bad, my father—ardent blood
Is my malignity—my crime is youth.
I am not bad, in truth not bad—although
Wild passions often do betray my heart,
My heart is good—
PHILIP: Thy heart is pure, I know't,

Just like thy prayer.

CARLOS: 'Tis now or never!—We're alone.
The anxious barrier of etiquette
Hath fallen 'tween the father and the son.
'Tis now or ne'er! A sunny beam of hope
Doth gleam in me, a sweet presentiment
Flies through my heart—The whole of heaven doth
Bend down with merry bands of angels, and
Completely mov'd, the Thrice-Divine observes
This scene, so great and beautiful—My father!
Forgiveness! *(He falls at his feet.)*

PHILIP: Stand! Release me now!

CARLOS: Forgiveness!

PHILIP: *(wants to tear away from him)*:
This juggler's act is grown too bold—

CARLOS: Too bold,
The love of thine own child?

PHILIP: Complete with tears?
Unworthy spectacle! Depart my sight.

CARLOS: Forgiveness, father! Now or never!

PHILIP: Out,
Depart my sight! Com'st thou bedeck'd with shame
From fighting in my battles, then my arms
Should open, to receive thee.—But like this
I do reject thee!—Coward's guilt alone
Will cleanse itself in such disgraceful springs.
Who blushes not, when he repents, shall ne'er
Be spar'd yet more repentance.

CARLOS: Who is that?
Through what misunderstanding hath this stranger
To mankind gone astray?—Yes tears are the
Eternal attestation of mankind,
His eye is dry, who ne'er was born of woman—
O, you must force the never-moisten'd eyes,
To learn to tear while still there's time, or else,
Or else, in some hard hour, you'll surely wish
You had made up for it.

PHILIP: Believest thou thy father's weighty doubt
Can thus with pretty words be shaken?

CARLOS: Doubt?
This very doubt would I extinguish—would
I hang upon my father's heart, would tug,
Would tug with might upon my father's heart
Until this boulder-solid husk of doubt

At last from this heart drops away.—Who are they,
Who drive me from the favor of my King?
What bids the monk to th' father for the son?
And what will Alba give to compensate
Him for a childless, fortune-forfeit life?
Do you want love?—Within this bosom here
Doth usher forth a spring, more fresh, more fiery,
Than in the turbid, swampy reservoirs,
That Philip's gold must open first.

PHILIP: Presumpt'ous,
Desist! The men, whom thou wouldst dare defame,
These are the proven servants of my choice,
And thou wilt give them honor.

CARLOS: Nevermore!
I sense myself. And what your Albas render,
That Carl can too, and Carl can even more.
What cares a hireling for the kingly realm,
That ne'er shall be his own? What troubles *him*,
If Philip's hairs of grey, should turn to white?
Your Carlos, then, had lov'd you.—I do dread
The thought of sitting, lonely and alone,
Upon a solitary *throne*.

PHILIP (*seiz'd by these words, stands musing and withdrawn.
After a pause.*):   I *am* alone.

CARLOS (*approaches him with warmth and animation*):
So have you been. Don't hate me any more,
I want to give you childlike, fiery love,
But only cease to hate me.—How delightful
And sweet it is, within a beauteous soul
To gloriously sense ourselves, to know,
That our own joy makes red a stranger's cheeks,
That our own fear makes quake a stranger's bosom,
That our own sorrow wets a stranger's eyes!—
How beautiful and splendid, hand in hand
With such a trusty, much-beloved son
To hasten down the rosy path of youth
Again, the dream of life to dream once more!
How great and sweet, within the virtue of his child,
Immortal, never-fading, to endure,
Beneficent for centuries!—How lovely,
To plant, what a dear son will one day reap,
To pile up, what will profit him, and to
Anticipate how high his thanks will flame!
My father, of this earthly paradise

Your monks are wisely silent.

    PHILIP (*not without emotion*): Oh, my son!
My son! Thou dost condemn thyself. Quite charming,
Paint'st thou a bliss, that—thou ne'er gavest me.

    CARLOS: Let the All-Knowing set it right!—Yourself,
You shut me out, as from a father's heart,
Thus from your scepter's heritage. 'Til now,
Until this day—O was that good, was't fair?—
'Til now have I, Spain's princely heir apparent,
A stranger been in Spain, a prisoner
Upon this ground, where one day I'll be lord.
Was that upright, was't gracious? O, how oft,
How oft, my father, did I look down red
With shame, when envoys of the potentates
Abroad, when sheets of news convey'd to me
Late news from court here at Aranjuez!

    PHILIP: Too fiercely roars the blood throughout thy veins,
Destruction only wouldst thou bring.

    CARLOS: Give to
Me, father, to destroy—it fiercely roars
Within my veins—I'm twenty-three years old,
And naught have done for immortality!
I am awake, I sense myself.—My summons
To th' royal throne doth, like a creditor,
Awake me from my slumber, and then all
The lost hours of my youth admonish me
Aloud like debts of honor. It is here,
The great and beauteous moment, which at last,
Demands the int'rest on my ripen'd talents,
World hist'ry calls me, my ancestral fame,
The thund'ring trumpet of the crowd's acclaim.
The time hath come at last, when unto me
Triumphant lists of fame shall open wide.
My King, may I dare speak to the petition,
That hither leads me?

    PHILIP: Yet a supplication?
Reveal it.

    CARLOS: The rebellion in Brabant
Grows threateningly. Rebels' obstinance
Demands a strong and shrewd defense. To tame
The schwärmer' rage, the Duke should lead an army
To Flanders, furnish'd with the sovereign
Authority that issues from the King.
How full of honor is this office, how

Entirely suitable, to thus your son
Initiate in glory's temple!—Me,
My King, to me entrust the army. I'm
Lov'd by the Netherlanders. I make bold
To answer for this faith with my own blood.
  PHILIP: Thou speakest like a dreamer. This high post
Demands a man, and not a youth—
  CARLOS: Demands
A human being only, father, that's
The only thing that Alba ne'er hath been.
  PHILIP: And only terror tames the mutiny,
Compassion were insanity.—Thy soul
Is soft, my son, the Duke is widely fear'd—
Forego thy supplication.
  CARLOS: Send me then
To Flanders with the army, hazard it
On my soft soul. For even now the name
That to the regal son belongs, that would
Go flying 'fore my banners, captures all,
Where Duke of Alba's hangmen but lay waste.
I beg for this upon my knees. It is
The very first petition of my life—
Trust Flanders to me, father—
  PHILIP (*considering the Infante with a penetrating glance*):
          And alike
My finest army to thy power-lust?
The knife to my assassin?
  CARLOS: O my God!
Am I no farther, and is this the fruit
Of this momentous, longest-yearn'd-for hour?
(*After some reflection, with temper'd earnestness*)
Reply to me more gently! Send me *thus*
Not on my way! With this most dire response
Would I not fain to be dismiss'd, would not
Fain be dismiss'd with such a heavy heart.
But use me yet more graciously. It is
My own most pressing want, it is my last,
Most desperate attempt—I cannot grasp,
Can't resolutely bear it like a man,
That you deny me each and ev'rything.—
Let me now take my leave. I go unheard,
Defrauded by a thousand sweeten'd hopes,
Thus I depart your countenance.—Your Alba
And your Domingo will in triumph reign,

Where now your child wept in the dust. The flock
Of courtiers, the tremulous Grandees,
The tribe of sinner-pallid monks was witness,
As you gave me a solemn audience.
Humiliate me not! So mortally,
My father, wound me not, to sacrifice
Me to the scornful insolence o'th' court,
That strangers revel in your favor, while
Your Carlos can entreat for naught. As pledge,
That you would honor me, send me along
To Flanders with your army!
  PHILIP: Do not speak
These words again, or risk thy Monarch's wrath!
  CARLOS: I dare my Monarch's wrath and do entreat
For this last time—entrust to me this Flanders.
I should and must leave Spain. My presence here
Is like a breath beneath the hangman's hand.—
The sky weighs heavy on me o'er Madrid,
Like consciousness of murder. Only a
Quick alteration of the sky can heal me.
If you would save me, send me now forthwith
To Flanders.
  PHILIP (*with forc'd composure*):
     Those who are not well, like thou,
My son, require good care and need to dwell
Beneath the doctor's watchful eye. Thou shalt
Remain in Spain. The Duke shall go to Flanders.
  CARLOS (*beside himself*):
O, now surround me, goodly spirits—
  PHILIP (*taking a step backwards*): Halt!
What is the meaning of this bearing?
  CARLOS (*with quavering voice*): Father,
Is *this* decision irrevocable?
  PHILIP: It issued from the King.
  CARLOS: My suit thus ends.
(*Departs in violent emotion.*)

  SCENE III—(PHILIP *remains standing a while, sunk in melancholy
reflection—finally he takes a number of steps up
and down the hall.* ALBA *draws near with embarrassment.*)

  PHILIP: Be ready for the order any hour
To leave for Brussels.
  ALBA: Everything stands ready,
My King.

PHILIP: Your power of authority
Lies seal'd already in the cabinet.
Now take you leave o'th' Queen, and then present
Yourself to the Infante as you part.
    ALBA: I saw him leaving from this hall just now,
Gesticulating like a man possess'd.
And also your most Royal Majesty
Doth seem beside Himself and deeply mov'd—
Perhaps the content of the talk?
    PHILIP (*after further pacing up and down*):
                          The content
Was Duke of Alba.
(*The* KING *keeps his eyes darkly fix'd on him.*)
                —I would gladly hear
That Carlos *hates* my councillors; yet with
Vexation I discover that he *scorns* them.
    ALBA (*blanches and would depart*).
    PHILIP: No answer now, I'll suffer you, to mend
Your conflict with the Prince.
    ALBA: O Sire!
    PHILIP: Then say
Who was it then who warn'd me at the first
Of my son's black designs? I listen'd then
To *you* and not to *him*. I'll venture now
To put it, Duke, unto the test. Henceforth
Stands Carlos closer to my throne. Depart!

(*The* KING *repairs to the cabinet. The Duke withdraws
through a different door.*)

    SCENE IV—*An anteroom before the Queen's apartment. (Don
Carlos comes through the middle door, in conversation with a Page.
The courtiers, who are to be found in the anteroom, disperse themselves
at his arrival through out the bordering rooms.*)

    CARLOS: A letter sent to me?—Wherefore this key?
And both so furtively deliver'd to me?
Come closer—where hast thou receiv'd these?
    PAGE (*mysteriously*):   As
The lady let be known, she would prefer
To be surmis'd, than be describ'd—
    CARLOS (*starting*):   The lady?
What?—What?—Who art thou then?
    PAGE: A noble page

In service to her Majesty the Queen.
  CARLOS (*startl'd, going to him and presses his hand to the
page's mouth*):
Death covets thee. Refrain! I know enough.
(*He rips the seal hastily open and walks to the outermost end
of the hall to read the letter. Meanwhile, the* DUKE OF ALBA
comes and goes by him into the QUEEN'S *chamber, without being
notic'd by the* PRINCE. CARLOS *begins to tremble violently,
alternately blanching and flushing. After he hath read it, he
stands a long while speechless, eyes staring fixedly at the
letter. — Finally he turns to the* PAGE.)
She gave thee this herself?
  PAGE: With her own hands.
  CARLOS: She gave thee this herself?—O, mock me not!
I have as yet read nothing from her hand,
I must believe in thee, if thou canst swear.
If 'twas a lie, confess it open-hearted
And make no mockery of me!
  PAGE: Of *whom?*
  CARLOS (*looks again into the letter and scrutinizes the page
with a skeptical, searching demeanor. After that he hath made
a pass through the hall*):
Thou still hast parents? Yes? Thy father serves
The King, and is a child o'th' land?
  PAGE: He fell
In battle at St. Quentin, Colonel of
The Duke of Savoy's cavalry, and he
Was call'd Alonzo Count of Henarez.
  CARLOS (*as he takes him by the hand and fixes his eyes
meaningfully on him*):
The King gave thee this letter?
  PAGE (*hurt*):   Gracious Prince,
Do I deserve so much distrust?
  CARLOS (*reads the letter*): "This key doth ope
The rearmost room in the pavilion of
The Queen. The one that's outermost abuts
The one side of a cabinet, wherein
The footsteps of no spy e'er lose their way.
Here love may candidly and loud confess
What she entrusted long to signs alone.
A hearing waits upon the timorous,
And fair reward upon the modest suff'rer."
(*As if awakening from a trance.*)
I am not dreaming—I'm not raving—that

Is my right arm—that is my sword—and these
Are written syllables. It's true and real.
I am belov'd—I am—indeed, I am,
I am belov'd! (*Lurching through the room completely
out of control and his arms thrown up to heaven.*)
    PAGE: So come along, my Prince, I'll lead you there.
    CARLOS: First wait 'til I'm myself again.—Do not
All terrors of this bliss yet quake in me?
Have I so proudly hop'd? Have I allow'd
Myself to ever dream of this? Where is
The man, who learn'd so quickly, to be God?—
Who was I, and who am I now? That is
A diff'rent heaven, and a diff'rent sun,
Than heretofore had been there—She doth love me!
    PAGE (*wants to lead him away*):
Prince, Prince, here's not the place—you do forget—
    CARLOS (*seiz'd by a sudden torpor*):
The King, my father!
(*He lets his arms sink, glances timidly around, and begins
to collect himself.*)   That is terrible—
Yes, quite right, friend. I thank thee, I was not
Myself just now entirely.—That I should
Keep silent *that,* should so much blessedness
Keep wall'd up in this breast, is terrible.
(*Grasping the* PAGE *by the hand and leading him aside.*)
What thou hast seen—hear'st thou?—and hast not seen,
Be sunken like a coffin in thy breast.
Now go! I'll find my way. Now go. They must
Not find us here. Now go—
    PAGE (*wants to leave*).
    CARLOS: Yet halt! yet listen!—
(*The* PAGE *comes back.* CARLOS *lays a hand on his shoulder
and gazes earnestly and solemnly into his face.*)
Thou tak'st along a fearful secret, which,
Just like that potent poison, doth explode
The vessel that conveys it.—Master well
Thy countenance! Thy head hast never once
Experienc'd what now thy bosom guards.
Be like the lifeless speaking tube, that takes
The sound and gives it back and hears it not.
Thou art a boy—be one for evermore,
And travel forth to play the cheerful one—
How well the clever authoress did know,
How to select a messenger of love.

The King will not seek out his serpents *here*.

    PAGE: And I, my Prince, I shall be proud of this
That I myself am richer by one secret
Than is the King himself—

    CARLOS: Thou vain young fool,
That is't, ere which thou must now quake.—If it
Occurs, that we should meet in public, shyly,
Thou shouldst approach me with submission. Let
Thou ne'er be lur'd by vanity to show
How gracious the Infante be to thee.
Thou canst commit no sin more grave, my son,
Than if thou pleasest *me*.—Wouldst thou in future
Confide in me, pronounce no syllable,
Entrust thy message never to the lips;
The universal highway of ideas
Shall not avail thy news! Thou speakest with
Thy eyelash, with thy index finger; and
I'll listen with a glance. The air, the light
Around us, these are Philip's creatures; and
The seemingly deaf walls are in his pay—
Here comes someone—

(*The* QUEEN's *chamber opens, and the* DUKE OF ALBA *steps out.*)
                      Thou must away! Farewell!

    PAGE: Just do not miss the right apartment, Prince! (*Exit.*)
    CARLOS: It is the Duke—Oh no, oh no! All's well!
I'll find the way.

SCENE V—DON CARLOS. DUKE OF ALBA.

    ALBA (*blocking his way*): But two words, gracious Prince.
    CARLOS: Quite right—'tis fine—another time.
(*He wants to leave.*)
    ALBA: The place
Is not the one most seemly, to be sure.
Perhaps Your Royal Highness would be pleas'd
To give me, then, a hearing in your chamber?
    CARLOS: What for? That can occur here, too.—But quickly,
But briefly—
    ALBA: That which leads me hither is,
In truth, to pay Your Highness most
Submissive thanks, for helpful service.—
    CARLOS: Thanks?
To me? What for?—And from the Duke of Alba?
    ALBA: For scarcely had you left the Monarch's room,

When the announcement came to me that I
Should soon depart for Brussels.
    CARLOS: Brussels! So!
    ALBA: How else, my Prince, could I attribute this,
Than to your gracious intercession with
His Majesty the King?
    CARLOS: To me? To me
Not in the least—not, verily, to me.
You journey— journey then with God!
    ALBA: That's all?
That's cause for wonder.—Had Your Highness then
No further mission I should bear to Flanders?
    CARLOS: What else? What there?
    ALBA: Yet, not so long ago
It seem'd as if these countries' fate requir'd
The presence of Don Carlos.
    CARLOS: How is that?
Yet yes—yes right—that was before—that is
Entirely good, right good, so much the better —
    ALBA: I listen with astonishment—
    CARLOS (*without irony*):   You are
A mighty General—who knows it not?
The env'ous must confirm it. I—I am
A younger person. This, too, was the King's
Opinion. And the King is right, quite right.
I realize it now, I am well pleas'd,
And so enough of this. Good luck upon
The way! I can now, as you see, quite simply—
I'm somewhat overburden'd now— the rest
Tomorrow, or whene'er you want, or else
When you come back from Brussels—
    ALBA: How is that?
    CARLOS (*after some silence, as he sees, that the* DUKE *yet remains*):
Good season keep you company.—The trip
Goes through Milan, Lorraine, and Burgundy,
And Germany—and Germany? Quite right,
It was in Germany! They know you there!
It's April now; May—June—and by July,
Quite right, by early August at the latest
You'll be in Brussels. O, I doubt it not,
One will quite soon hear of your victories.
You shall know how to render yourself worthy
Of our most gracious confidence.
    ALBA (*meaningfully*):   Shall I do that

Thus sharply feeling my inconsequence?

CARLOS (*after some silence, with dignity and pride*):
Duke, you are sensitive—and rightfully.
It was, I must confess, not merciful
Of me, to take up arms against you, that
You are incapable of using 'gainst
Me in return.

ALBA: Incapable?—

CARLOS (*smiling as he extends him his hand*): Too bad,
That at this moment I do lack the time
To fight the worthy battle out with Alba.
Another time—

ALBA: Prince, we miscalculate
In very diff'rent ways. You, for example,
You see yourself some twenty years advanc'd,
I see you younger by the same.

CARLOS: Well now?

ALBA: And thereby comes to mind, how many nights
Beside his lovely spouse from Portugal,
Your mother, would the Monarch gladly have
Surrender'd, just to purchase for his Crown
Another arm like *this*? It must have been
Well known to him, just how much easier
It be to propagate more monarchs, than
More monarchies—how much more quickly one
Could fill the world with ample stock of kings
Than furnish kings a world.

CARLOS: 'Tis very true!
But yet, Duke Alba? yet —

ALBA: And how much blood,
The blood of *your* own people must have flow'd,
Before two drops could render *you* the King.

CARLOS: Quite true, by God—and in two words is all
Compress'd, that e'er could set the pride of merit
Against the pride of fortune.—So then, now,
What is the point? Well, Duke of Alba?

ALBA: Woe
To th' tender cradle infant Majesty
That ridicules his nurse! How gently may
He sleep upon the softest pillows of
Our victories! And to be sure, upon
The crown, there glisten only pearls, and not
The wounds, whereby it was achiev'd.—This sword
Hath written Spanish laws for foreign peoples,

It blaz'd a path before the Crucified
And trac'd upon this quarter of the world
A bloody furrow for the seed of faith:
God order'd things in heaven, I on earth—
    CARLOS: God or the devil, carry equal weight!
You were his right arm. I do know it well—
And now no more of this. I beg. I would
Fain guard myself from certain memories.—
I grant my father's choice. My father needs
An Alba; *that* he needs this one, that's not
A circumstance of his that I begrudge.
You are a mighty man—that may be, too;
I almost do believe it. Yet I fear
You came a few millennia too soon.
An Alba, I should say, was just the man,
Who should appear to mark the Final Days!
Then, when the giant insolence of vice
Hath us'd up all of heaven's patience, the
Rich harvest of misdeeds stands in full blade
And doth demand an unexampl'd reaper,
Then *you* do stand upon your place.—O God,
My paradise! My Flanders!—Yet I should
Not think it now. Of this be silent. It
Is said, you took along with you a store
Of sentences of death, sign'd in advance?
This foresight's laudable. Thus one need fear
Chicanery no more.—Alas, my father,
How poorly did I understand thy view!
I thought thee hard, because thou did'st deny
To me a task, wherein thy Albas shine?—
It was the start of thy respect.
    ALBA: O Prince,
This word doth merit—
    CARLOS (*flaring up*): What?
    ALBA: Yet you are sav'd
From *that* as son o'th' King.
    CARLOS (*gripping his sword*): That calls for blood!
Duke, draw your sword!
    ALBA (*coldly*):   'Gainst whom?
    CARLOS (*fiercely pressing him*):   Now draw your sword,
I'll run you through.
    ALBA (*draws*): If that's how it must be,
Then be it—
           (*They fight.*)

SCENE VI—*The* QUEEN. DON CARLOS. DUKE OF ALBA.

QUEEN (*comes from her chamber in dismay*):
                    Naked swords!
(*To the* PRINCE, *indignantly and with commanding voice.*)
                    O Carlos!
CARLOS (*beside himself at the sight of the* QUEEN, *lets his arms
sink, stands motionless and senseless, then he rushes to the* DUKE *and
kisses him*):
Forgiveness! Duke! Be everything forgiven!
(*He throws himself mutely at the* QUEEN'S *feet, then hastily gets up
and speeds away, completely beside himself.*)
    ALBA (*stands there, full of astonishment, without taking his eyes
off him*):
By God, but this is curious!—
    QUEEN (*stands for some moments, doubtful and ill at ease,
then goes slowly toward her chamber, turning around at
the door*):   Duke Alba!
(*The* DUKE *follows her into the chamber.*)

SCENE VII—*An apartment of the* PRINCESS OF EBOLI. (*The* PRIN-
CESS, *beautifully but simply costum'd with an idealiz'd taste, plays the
lute and sings. The* QUEEN'S PAGE *comes upon the scene.*)

    PRINCESS (*springs quickly up*):
He comes!
    PAGE (*hastily*): Are you alone? I'm quite surpris'd
To find him still not here; But yet he must
Appear within an instant.
    PRINCESS: Must he? Well,
Then so he *will*—it hath been so determin'd—
    PAGE: He follows on my heels.—My gracious Princess,
You are belov'd—belov'd, belov'd as you,
No one can be and no one e'er hath been.
And what a scene I look'd upon!
    PRINCESS (*draws him to herself full of impatience*):
                    Make haste!
Thou spak'st with him? Now out with it! What did
He say? How did he act? What were his words?
He seem'd embarrass'd, seem'd perplex'd? Did he
Divine the person, who sent him the key?
Be quick—or did he guess it not? He guess'd
It not at all? He guess'd a false one? Well?
Dost thou have not a word to answer? Pfui,

Pfui, shame on thee: Thou hast ne'er been so wooden,
Hast ne'er been so insufferably slow.

    PAGE: Can I come now to words, Most Gracious One?
I did deliver him the key and note
There in the Queen's own anteroom. He started
And scrutiniz'd me, as I let it slip
That I'd come from a lady's room.

    PRINCESS: He started?
Quite good, quite brave! But onward, tell me more.

    PAGE: I wanted to say more, but then he blanch'd
And tore the letter from my hand and look'd
At me with threats and said, that he knew all.
He read the letter through with consternation,
Then all at once began to quake.

    PRINCESS: Knew all?
That he knew all? Did he say that?

    PAGE: And ask'd
Me three times, four times, if 'twas really you,
If you yourself gave me the letter.

    PRINCESS: If
It was myself? Then did he name my name?

    PAGE: The name—no, that he did not say.—There might
Be spies, he said, that hearken in this place
And prattle to the King.

    PRINCESS (*disturb'd*): Did he say that?

    PAGE: To th' King, he said, 'twould mean amazingly,
Quite powerfully much, especially much,
To gain intelligence about this note.

    PRINCESS: To th' King? And hast thou heard it right? To th' King?
Was that the phrase, which he employ'd?

    PAGE: Yes, 'twas!
He call'd it a most dang'rous secret and
He warn'd me to be fully on my guard
With words and gestures, so the King would not
Develop even slight suspicion.

    PRINCESS (*after some reflection, full of admiration*):
               All
Holds true.—It can't be otherwise—he must
Know of the story.—Inconceivable!
Who could have e'er betray'd it to him?—Who?
I ask again—Who sees so sharp, so deep,
Who other than the falcon-eye of love?
Yet further, travel further forth: he read
The note —

PAGE: The note contain'd a happiness,
He said, before which he would have to quake;
That he himself had never dar'd to dream.
To our dismay the Duke stepp'd in the hall,
And this forc'd us—
    PRINCESS (*vex'd*): But what in all the world
Could bring the Duke there at this time? But where,
Where stays he then? Why doth he tarry? Why
Appears he not? — See'st thou, how falsely thou
Hast been inform'd? How happy had he been
Already in the time, that thou did'st need
To tell me, that he wanted to be so!
    PAGE: The Duke, I am afeard—
    PRINCESS: Again the Duke?
What wants he *here*? Why should this valiant man
Have any business with my silent bliss?
He could have let him be, or sent him on—
To whom i'th' world can't one do that?—O truly!
Thy Prince hath such a sorry expertise
In love, it seem'd, as in the ladies' hearts.
He doth not know, what minutes are—Soft, soft!
I hear him coming. Out! It is the Prince.
        (PAGE *hurries out.*)
Be gone, be gone!—Where do I have my lute?
He ought to catch me by surprise.—My song
Should be a sign to him—

SCENE VIII—*The* PRINCESS *and shortly thereafter* DON CARLOS.

    PRINCESS (*hath thrown herself upon an ottoman and plays*).
    CARLOS (*comes crashing in. He recognizes the* PRINCESS *and stands
there as if struck by thunder*):
                          O God!
Where am I?
    PRINCESS (*lets the lute fall. Facing him*):
            Ah, Prince Carlos? Yes, in truth!
    CARLOS: Where am I? Wretched treachery—I must
Have miss'd the proper cabinet.
    PRINCESS: How well
Carl understands, to bear in mind the rooms,
Where ladies sit unchaperon'd.
    CARLOS: Princess—
Forgive me, Princess—I—I found the door
To th' antechamber open.

PRINCESS: Can that be?
And yet methinks, that I myself did lock it.
    CARLOS: You only thought, you thought it—yet, be sure!
You are mistaken. That you wish'd it lock'd,
Yes, that I'll grant, that I believe—yet lock'd?
It was not lock'd, not verily! I heard
Somebody play upon—a lute, or—was
It not a lute? (*Meanwhile he looks around doubtfully.*)
              'Twas right! It lies there still—
And lute—how God in heaven knows it!—lute,
I love it to the point of madness. I'm
All ears, I know naught of myself, I crash
Into the cabinet, o'th' sweet performer,
Who stirr'd me so divinely, charm'd me with
Such power, to behold her lovely eyes.
    PRINCESS: A kindly curiosity, you ne'er
The less had quickly still'd, as I could prove.
(*After some silence, meaningfully.*)
O, I must value such a modest man,
Who, to preserve a woman from disgrace,
Ensnares himself in such a falsehood.
    CARLOS (*guileless*):   Princess,
I feel myself, that I but worsen things,
Where I would them improve. Excuse me from
A role, which I to carry out am too
Completely, fully spoilt. You sought within
This chamber refuge from the world. Herein
You wanted, unbeheard by any man,
To live the silent wishes of your heart.
I show myself to be disaster's son;
Directly is this lovely dream disturb'd.—
For this my speediest removal—(*He wants to go.*)
    PRINCESS (*surpris'd and disconcerted, yet immediately
compos'd again*):   Prince—
O, that was spiteful.
    CARLOS: Princess—I know well,
What *such* a glance within this cabinet
Should mean, and I admire this virtuous
Embarrassment. O, woe betide the man,
Whom fem'nine blushing doth embolden! I'm
Despondent, when a woman quakes ere me.
    PRINCESS: Is't possible!—A conscience unexampl'd
For a young man and for a Monarch's son!
Yes, Prince—You must indeed remain with me,

Now, I myself request it: so much virtue
Allays the fears of every maid. Yet do you know,
That your abrupt appearance startl'd me
Amid my most beloved aria?
(*She leads him to the sofa and takes up her
lute again.*)
The aria, Prince Carlos, I shall have
To play indeed once more; your punishment
Shall be to hear me play.

CARLOS (*He seats himself, not entirely without duress,
next to the* PRINCESS.):   A punishment,
So much desir'd, as my offense—and truly!
The message was so welcome to me, 'twas
So godly fair, that I for—the third time
Could listen to it.

PRINCESS: What? You've heard it all
Already? That is dreadful, Prince—It was
I do believe, the utterance of love?

CARLOS: And, if I do not err, a happy love—
The text most lovely on this lovely mouth;
Yet surely not so truly said as lovely.

PRINCESS:
Not? Not so true?—And therefore you have doubts?—

CARLOS (*seriously*): I almost doubt, if Carlos and the Princess
Of Eboli can ever understand
Each other, where 'tis love concern'd.
(*The* PRINCESS *is startl'd; he notices it and proceeds on
with a light gallantry.*)
                                        Then who,
Who will believe it of these rosy cheeks,
That passion agitates within this breast?
Doth Princess Eboli run any risk
Of sighing then in vain, unheard? For he
Alone knows love, who loves bereft of hope.

PRINCESS (*with all her previous high spirits*):
O hush! That sounds so frightful.—And 'tis sure,
This fate appears to follow *you* before
All others and in full today—today.
(*Taking him by the hand, with ingratiating interest.*)
Good Prince, you are not happy—you do grieve
By God, you're grieving. Is it possible?
And why this grief, my Prince? At this loud summons
Unto the pleasure of the world, at all
The gifts of lavishly bestowing nature,

And all the claims upon the joys of life?
You— son of a great King and *more*, far more
Than that, already in the princely cradle
Endow'd with gifts that do indeed obscure
The stellar glory of your rank as well?
You—who among the whole stern court of women
Which hath corrupted judges sitting, women,
Who over manly worth and manly fame ·
Pass ostracizing judgment, unoppos'd?
Who, where he but *observ'd*, already conquers,
Enkindles, where he hath stay'd cold, and where
He wants to glow, must play with paradises
And godly bliss bestow—the man, whom Nature
Adorn'd with gifts that could bring happiness
To thousands, though but *few* receive the like,
He should be mis'rable himself? O Heaven,
Thou gav'st him each and everything, so why,
Why then deny to him the very eyes
Whereby he sees his triumphs?

    CARLOS (*who was sunk in deepest distraction the entire time,
is brought suddenly to himself by the silence of the* PRINCESS
and starts up):   Excellent!
Beyond comparison, my Princess! Sing
This passage to me yet again.

    PRINCESS (*views him in astonishment*): But Carlos,
Where were you in the meantime?

    CARLOS (*springs up*):   Yes, by God!
You chide me to the proper time.—I must,
Must leave—must quickly leave.

    PRINCESS (*holding him back*): Where to?

    CARLOS (*in frightful alarm*):   Below
I'th' open air.—Let me be free—my Princess,
It seems to me, as if the world behind me fum'd
Up into flames—

    PRINCESS (*holds him back forcefully*):
                What is the matter? Whence
Comes this most strange, unnatural behavior?
(CARLOS *remains standing and becomes pensive. She seizes
this moment to pull him to herself on the sofa.*)
You need repose, dear Carl—At present doth
Your blood run riot—seat yourself by me—
Away, with these black fever-fantasies!
If openhearted you do ask yourself,
Doth this head know, what weighs upon his heart?

And e'en if it did know—should there then be
From all the knights here at this court not *one*,
From all the ladies none—to help you heal,
To understand you, I would say—not one
From all of them of worth?

   CARLOS (*carelessly, thoughtlessly*): Perhaps the Princess
Of Eboli?

   PRINCESS (*joyfully, hastily*): Indeed?

   CARLOS: Just give me then
A letter—a petition to my father
To recommend me. Give me that! 'Tis said,
You count for much.

   PRINCESS: Who says that? (Ha, 'twas *this*
Suspicion, that hath made thee mute!)

   CARLOS: Most likely
The tale hath made the rounds already. I've
The sudden thought, of going to Brabant,
In order to—to merely earn my spurs.
My father doth not wish that. My good father
Fears that, if I were in command of armies—
My singing might just suffer by it.

   PRINCESS: Carlos!
You're playing false with me. Confess, you would
Escape me by this serpentine evasion.
Look hither now, dissembler! Eye to eye!
Who dreams of only knightly deeds—will *he*,
Confess it now—will *he* forsooth descend
So low as greedily to steal away,
The ribbons, that the ladies have let slip
And—pardon me—(*Meanwhile she, with a light
movement of the fingers, tugs away the ruffle on his
shirt and removes a ribbon-bow that was conceal'd there.*)
       so dearly them to guard?

   CARLOS (*stepping back in amazement*):
Ah, Princess!—No, it goes too far—I am
Betray'd. But you are not deceiv'd.—You are
In league with spirits and with demons.

   PRINCESS: You
Appear astonish'd over this? O'er this?
What should you wager, Prince, that I can call
Back stories to your heart, indeed such stories—
But put me to the test, interrogate me.
And if the jugglings of caprice, a sound,
That's garbl'd when exhal'd i'th' air, a smile,

Eras'd again by sudden gravity,
And if your very gestures, your appearance,
Where your own soul was distant, did themselves
Elude me not, then judge yourself, if I
Did understand, when you'd be understood?
    CARLOS: Well, truly that is much to risk.—The bet
Is taken, Princess. You do promise me
Discoveries within my very heart,
About which I have never known.
    PRINCESS (*somewhat sensitive and serious*):
                        Ne'er, Prince?
Reflect upon it better. Look around.—
This cabinet is not one of the chambers
O'th' Queen, wherein a little masquerade
Might still be found commendable.—You start?
So suddenly you're all aglow? O surely,
Who'd be so clever, so presumptuous,
So idle as to eavesdrop on Don Carlos,
When Carlos thinks himself unheard?—Who saw,
How at the last court ball he left the Queen,
His lady, standing in the midst o'th' dance
And forcefully press'd himself on the nearest pair,
Instead of to his regal dancing partner
To give his hand to Princess Eboli?
An error, Prince, of which the Monarch even,
Took note, for he had only then arriv'd!
    CARLOS (*with an ironic smile*):
So even *he*? Yes, surely, my good Princess,
'Twas not especially for *him*.
    PRINCESS: So little,
As was the scene there in the castle chapel,
Whereof indeed Prince Carlos will himself
Not recollect. You lay absorb'd in prayer
Before the feet of the most Holy Virgin,
When suddenly— could you have help'd—the gowns
Of certain ladies rustl'd at your back.
And then Don Philip's hero-minded son
Began to tremble like a heretic
Before the Holy Office; on pale lips
His poison'd prayer expir'd—i'th' ecstacy
Of passion—such a touching comedy
Was play'd there, Prince—you seize upon the hand,
The cold and holy hand of God's own mother,
And rain down fiery kisses on the marble.

CARLOS: You do me wrong, my Princess. 'Twas devotion.

PRINCESS: Yes, then 'tis something other, Prince— then surely,
It was at that time only fear of losing,
When Carlos sat with me and with the Queen
At playing cards and with such wonderful
Dexterity purloin'd from me this glove—
(CARLOS *springs to his feet in dismay.*)
Which afterwards he was polite enough
To play instead of leading with a card.

CARLOS: O God—God—God! What is it that I've done?

PRINCESS: 'Twas nothing that you will revoke, I hope.
How gladly I was startl'd, as a note
Fell unexpectedly into my fingers,
Which you knew to conceal within the glove.
It was the most exciting romance, Prince,
That—

CARLOS (*interrupting her words hastily*):
    Poetry!—And nothing more.—My brain
Doth oftener send wondrous bubbles up,
Which burst as quickly as they do arise.
That's all it was. Of this, let's speak no more.

PRINCESS (*going from him in astonishment, and observing
him for a time from a distance*):
I am exhausted—all of my attempts
Slide off this serpent-slipp'ry character.
(*She is silent for some moments.*)
Yet why?—Were it colossal manly pride,
Which but, to please itself more sweetly
Requir'd a mask of bashfulness?—Perhaps?
(*She approaches the Prince again and considers him doubtfully.*)
Will *you* at last instruct me, Prince—I stand
Before a chest that's magic'ly lock'd up,
Where I'm deceiv'd by all the keys I try.

CARLOS: As I before yourself.

PRINCESS (*She leaves him quickly, goes silently up and down
the chamber a number of times, and appears to reflect
upon something important. Finally after a great pause,
seriously and solemnly.*): So be it, then—
I must resolve myself this once to talk.
I do elect you as my judge. You are
A noble man—a man, both prince and knight.
I cast myself upon your breast. You will
Be my salvation, Prince, and where I'm lost
Beyond deliv'rance, weep in sympathy.

(*The* PRINCE *draws nearer, with expectant, sympathetic astonishment.*)
A cheeky minion of the Monarch woos
My hand—Rui Gomez, the Count of Silva—
The King consents, the deal's already struck,
And I am sold unto this creature.
     CARLOS (*violently affected*):   Sold?
And once again then sold? and once again
By that most famous merchant in the South?
     PRINCESS: No, first you must hear all. 'Tis not enough,
That I be sacrific'd to politics,
My innocence is waylaid too—There! Here!
This sheet of paper can unmask this saint.
(CARLOS *takes the paper and hangs, full of impatience,
on her explanation, without taking time to read it.*)
Where shall I find salvation, Prince? 'Til now
It was my pride, which did protect my virtue;
Yet now at last—
     CARLOS: At last you fell? You fell?
No, no! For Heaven's sake, no!
     PRINCESS (*proudly and nobly*): Yet through *whom*?
O, paltry sophistry! How weak of these,
Almighty intellects! A woman's favor,
The happiness of love to deem the same
As wares for which one can make bid! It is
The only thing upon this round o'th' earth,
That tolerates no buyer but itself.
Th'inestimable diamond, which I have
To *give away* or, ever unenjoy'd,
Must *bury*—like the mighty merchant, who,
Unmov'd by all the gold of the Rialto,
And in affront to th' Kings, return'd his pearl
Again unto the wealthy sea, too proud,
To part with it for *under* its true worth.
     CARLOS: (*By wondrous God!—The woman's beautiful!*)
     PRINCESS: One calls it fancy—vanity: all one.
I do not *parcel* out my joys. To th' man,
The one, whom I have chosen for myself,
I shall relinquish all for all. I give
Just *once*, but that forever. Only one
My love shall render happy—but this one—
This single one 'twill make into a god.
The soul's enchanting harmony—a kiss—
An hour of love's voluptuous delights—
The high, celestial magic of the beauteous

Are sister colors of a *single* ray,
Are petals of one *single* bloom. I should,
I driven mad! thus give away one petal
Torn from the lovely chalice of its bloom?
Should I defile the lofty majesty,
Of womanhood, the godhead's masterpiece,
To sweeten thus a glutton's evening?

    CARLOS: (*Incredible! How can it be? Madrid*
Had such a maid, and I—I find it out
At first today?)

    PRINCESS: I had this court long since
Forsaken, and this world foresaken, had
Interr'd myself i'th' holy wall; but yet
One single bond doth still remain, a bond,
That binds me to this world almightily.—
Alas, perhaps a phantom! But so dear!
I love, and I am—not belov'd.

    CARLOS (*going to her, full of fire*): You are!
As God in Heaven dwells, 'tis true. I swear't.
You are, beyond expression.

    PRINCESS: You? You swear't?
O, 'twas my angel's voice! Yes, if indeed
'Tis you that swears it, Carl, then I believe,
Then I am so.

    CARLOS (*takes her, full of tenderness, into his arms*):
          O, sweet and soulful maid!
O worship-worthy creature!—Here I stand,
All ears—all eyes—all admiration—all
Delight.—Who had seen thee, who underneath
This heaven had seen thee and still could pride
Himself—that he hath never lov'd?—and yet
Here at King Philip's court? What here? What wouldst
Thou, beauteous angel, here? With clerics and
The regimen that breeds them? That is not
A climate for such flowers!—Would they fain
Pluck them? They would—oh, I believe it gladly—
But no! Not whilst I breathe of life!—I fling
My arm around thee, and within my arms
I'll bear thee through a devil-laden hell!
Yes—let me be thine angel.—

    PRINCESS (*with a glance full of love*): O my Carlos!
How little have I known you! O, how richly
And boundlessly your beauteous heart rewards

The heavy toil of comprehending it!
(*She grasps his hand and would kiss it.*)
    CARLOS (*He pulls it back.*):
Where, Princess, are you now?
    PRINCESS (*with delicacy and grace, as she looks fixedly
at his hand*):   How lovely is
This hand! How rich it is! —Prince, this hand doth
Yet have two costly gifts it may confer—
A diadem and Carlos' heart—and both
Perhaps on *one* mere mortal? On just *one*?
A great and godlike gift!—Well nigh too great
For *one* mere mortal being!—How, my Prince?
If you to a division should resolve?
The queens love poorly - and a woman, who
Can love, is poor at understanding crowns:
'Twere better, Prince, divide it and right now,
Right now—How? Or had you already done so?
You surely had? Oh, then so much the better!
And do I know this happy one?
    CARLOS: Thou shouldst.
To thee, dear maiden, I reveal myself—
To innocence, to Nature unprofan'd
And flawless I reveal myself. Th'art in
This court the worthiest, the one, the first
Who fully comprehends my soul—Yes then!
I won't deny it—I'm in love!
    PRINCESS: Wicked man!
Confession hath become so hard for thee?
Must I be worthy of lament, if thou
Shouldst find me worthy of thy love?
    CARLOS (*starts*):   What? What
Is that?
    PRINCESS: To play a game with me like this!
O truly, Prince, it was not pretty. To
Deny you had the key!
    CARLOS: The key! The key!
(*After a gloomy moment of reflection.*)
Yes—so it was.—I mark it now—my God!
(*His knees give way, he steadies himself on a chair and
hides his face.*)
    PRINCESS (*A long silence from both sides. The* PRINCESS *cries
aloud and falls.*): Abom'nable! What have I done?
    CARLOS (*straightening up, in an eruption of violent anguish*):
                                So deep

To plummet down from all my heavens!—Oh,
That's dreadful!

    PRINCESS (*hiding her face in the pillow*):
                What do I discover? God!

    CARLOS (*himself thrown at her feet*):
I am not guilty, Princess—passion—an
Unfortunate misunderstanding—God!
I am not guilty.

    PRINCESS (*shoves him from herself*): Get you from mine eyes,
For God's sake—

    CARLOS: Nevermore! Shall I leave you
When you're in such a frightful state of shock?

    PRINCESS (*forcefully pushing him away*):
From generosity, from mercy, get
You from mine eyes!—Or would you murder me?
I hate your very sight! Return to me
                      (CARLOS *will go*.)
My letter and my key. Where do you have
The other letter?

    CARLOS: Other letter? What
By other do you mean?

    PRINCESS: That's from the King.

    CARLOS (*startl'd*):
From *whom*?

    PRINCESS: The one you took from me before.

    CARLOS: 'Twas from the King? to whom? to you?

    PRINCESS: O Heaven!
How dreadfully have I ensnar'd myself!
The letter! Out with it! I need it back.

    CARLOS: The King sends letters, and to you?

    PRINCESS: The letter! In
The name of all the saints!

    CARLOS: The one which should
Unmask for me a certain saint—this one?

    PRINCESS: I am undone!—Now give it me!

    CARLOS: The letter—

    PRINCESS (*wringing her hands in despair*):
What have I dar'd so thoughtlessly to do?

    CARLOS: The letter—came it from the King?—Yes, Princess,
That quickly changes all indeed—*This* is
A priceless—weighty—and a precious letter,
That all of Philip's crowns are much too light,
Too unimportant to redeem. *This* letter
I'll keep. (*He departs*.)

PRINCESS (*throws herself in his path*):

>   Great God in Heaven! I am lost!

SCENE IX—*The* PRINCESS *alone.*

(*She stands still stunn'd, beside herself; after he hath gone out, she hurries after him and would call him back*):

PRINCESS: Prince, yet a word. Prince, listen—He is gone!
Yet this as well! He scorns me.—Here I stand
In the most dreadful loneliness—rejected—
Discarded—(*She sinks into an armchair. After a pause.*)

>   No! Displac'd that's all, displac'd

By a competitor. He is in love.
There's no more doubt. He's made it known himself.
Yet *who* is this most happy one?—This much
Is evident—He loves, where he should not.
He dreads discovery. Before the King
His passion slinks away in hiding.—Why
Ere him, who wish'd it most?—Or is it not
The father, that he fears thus in the father?
For when the King's illicit purpose was
Betray'd to him—then did his face light up,
He triumph'd, as a happy man . . . How was't,
That his so rigid virtue here grew dumb?
Here? Even here?—What can he then by this,
What can he have to profit, if the King
Unto the Queen the —
(*She leaves off suddenly, surpris'd by a thought —
At the same time she pulls the ribbon that* CARLOS *had
given her, from her bosom, considers it quickly,
and recognizes it.*)   O I'm going mad!
Now finally, just now—Where were my senses?
My eyes are open now.—They had been long
In love, before the King selected her.
The Prince ne'er saw me without *her.*—So she,
She was intended, where I thought myself
So warmly, truly, boundlessly ador'd?
O, 'tis deception without precedent!
And I've betray'd my weaknesses to her—
(*Silence.*)
That he should love completely void of hope!
I can't believe it.—Hopeless love doth not
Persist in such a battle. Thus to feast,
Where the most lustrous Monarch in the world

Doth pine unheard—Indeed! Such sacrifice
A hopeless love doth never bear. How fiery
Was not his kiss! How fondly press'd he me,
How fondly to his pounding heart!—The test
Was nigh too bold for his romantic faith,
Which should not be requited—He accepts
The key, which, as he is persuaded, had
Been sent unto him by the Queen—he trusts
In this gigantic step of love—he comes,
He really comes!—He credits Philip's wife
With this insane decision.—How can he,
If here great tests do not encourage him?
'Tis clear as day. His suit is heard. She loves!
By heaven, doth this saintly woman feel!
How fine is she! . . . I trembl'd, I myself,
Ere this exalted paragon of virtue.
A higher being she did loom o'er me,
I am eclips'd by her bright radiance.
I grudg'd her beauty its exalted peace,
So free from all the rage of mortal natures.
And this same peace was but a show? She had
Upon both tables wish'd to feast? Had made
Display of virtue's godlike shine and yet
At the same time had dar'd to nibble on
The furtive raptures of depravity?
May she do that? Should this imposture have
Succeeded undetected? Have succeeded,
Since no avenger rises?—No, by God!
I did adore her—This demands revenge!
Then let the King know of the fraud—The King?
(*After some reflection.*)
Yes, right—that is a pathway to his ear. (*She departs.*)

   SCENE X—*A room in the royal palace.* DUKE OF ALBA. FATHER
DOMINGO.

   DOMINGO: What would you say to me?
   ALBA: A most important
Discovery, that I have made today,
Whereof I'd like an explanation.
   DOMINGO: Which
Discovery? Whereof speak you?
   ALBA: Prince Carlos
And I this noon encounter'd one another

I'th' antechamber of the Queen. I am
Offended. Both of us grow hot. The quarrel
Grows somewhat loud. We both reach for our swords.
The Queen at the loud uproar opens up
Her chamber, hurls herself 'twixt us and looks
With a glance of despotic confidence
Upon the Prince.—It was a single glance.—
His arm goes numb—he flies upon my neck —
I feel a burning kiss—and he is vanish'd.

    DOMINGO (*after a silence*):
'Tis quite suspicious.—Duke, you do remind
Me of a matter—Similar ideas,
I do confess, have germinated long
Within my breast.—I shunn'd these dreams—I have
Entrusted them to no one yet. There are
Swords with a double edge, uncertain friends—
I fear these. Hard to differentiate,
Are human beings, harder still to fathom.
Words carelessly let slip are confidants
Offended—so I buried deep my secret,
Until it's brought forth into light by time.
Performing certain services for kings,
Is risky, Duke—a boldly ventur'd shot,
Which, should it miss its target, doth rebound
Upon the marksman.—I would take an oath
Upon the Host, that what I say is true.—
Just one eyewitness, but one word that's snatch'd,
A scrap of paper weighs far heavier
Than my most living sentiment—Accurs'd,
That we stand here on Spanish soil!

    ALBA: Why not
Here on this soil?

    DOMINGO: At any other court
A passion can forget itself. But here
It is admonish'd by our anxious laws.
The Spanish Queens do find it difficult
To sin—I do believe—unfortunately
'Tis *only* there—just *there* alone—where it
Would benefit us to surprise them most.

    ALBA: Then listen further—Carlos went today
Before the King. The audience did last
An hour. He ask'd for the administration
O' th' Netherlands. He ask'd both loud and fierce;
I heard it in the cabinet. His eyes

Were red with weeping, as I met him at
The door. Then he at midday did appear
With looks of triumph on his face. He is
Delighted, that the King doth him prefer.
He thanks him for it. Things stand otherwise,
He says, and better. He could ne'er dissemble.
How shall I reconcile these contradictions?
The Prince exults, receiving such a slight,
And onto me the King confers a favor
With every sign of anger!— What must I
Believe? In truth, this new found dignity
Bears more resemblance to a banishment
Than to a favor.

    DOMINGO: Were it therefore come
To this? To this? A single moment hath
Destroy'd, what we have taken years to build?—
And you so calm? so tranquil?—Do you know
This youth? Can you imagine what awaits
Us, when he comes to pow'r?—The Prince—I'm not
His enemy. But other worries gnaw
Upon my peace, I worry for the Throne,
For God and for his Church.—For the Infante
(*I know him—I can penetrate his soul*)
Doth entertain a dreadful scheme—Toledo—
The raving scheme, that he become the Regent
And then dispense with our most Holy Faith.—
His heart is growing hot for a new virtue,
Which, proud and sure and self-sufficient, will
Come begging to no faith.—He *thinks*! His head
Is fir'd by a peculiar chimera—
He doth revere the people—Duke, were he
A man fit to become our King?

    ALBA: Mere phantoms!
What else? Perhaps 'tis also youthful pride,
That makes him want to play a role.—But hath
He any other choice? 'Twill pass foreby,
Once his turn doth arrive, to take command.

    DOMINGO: I doubt it. He is prideful of his freedom,
Unus'd to the control, wherewith one must
Conform to buy control of others.—Doth
He suit our Throne? His bold gigantic spirit
Will tear apart the sequence of our statecraft.
I've sought in vain, to blunt his rebel spirit
Amid this era of debauchery;

He did surmount the trial.—Dreadful is
This spirit in that body—and soon Philip
Is sixty years of age.

    ALBA: Your vision reaches
Quite far.

    DOMINGO: He and the Queen are of one mind.
Already creeps, conceal'd, in both their breasts
The poison of the innovator; soon
Enough, if it gains ground, 'twill seize the throne.
I know this Valois.—We should be afeard
O'th' total vengeance of this silent foe,
If Philip lets himself be weak. Our luck
Is still propitious. Let us act beforehand.
A *single* snare will capture both.—And now
A hint like this suggested to the King,
Be't proven or unproven—much hath been
Already gain'd, if he but falters. We
Ourselves, we both doubt not. To one convinc'd
Convincing is not difficult. It can
Not fail, that we discover more, if we
Are sure beforehand, that we must discover.

    ALBA: Yet now the question, weightiest of all!
Who takes it on himself, to tell the King?

    DOMINGO: Not you, nor I. So now you shall observe
How long already, full of grand design,
My silent diligence hath driven toward
Its goal. Yet to complete our league, we lack
The third, most weighty personage.—The King
Loves Princess Eboli. I'm nurturing
The passion, which doth profit what I wish.
I am his emissary.—I shall school
Her in our plan.—In this young lady, if
My work succeeds, an ally of our league,
A queen for us should blossom. She herself
Hath call'd me now to meet her in this room.
I hope for ev'rything.—A Spanish maid
Perhaps might break that Valois fleur-de-lis
Within a *single* midnight.

    ALBA: What hear I?
Is it the truth, what I've now heard?—By heaven!
I am surpris'd! Yes that's *the* final stroke!
Dominican, I am amaz'd at thee.
Now have we won—

    DOMINGO: Be quiet! Who doth come?

'Tis she herself.

ALBA: I'll be in the next room,
If one—

DOMINGO: Quite right. I'll call you.

(*The* DUKE OF ALBA *departs.*)

SCENE XI—*The* PRINCESS. DOMINGO.

DOMINGO: I'm at your
Command, my gracious Princess.

PRINCESS (*gazing after the Duke with curiosity*):
                                Are we not
Entirely here alone? You have, I see,
Another witness with you?

DOMINGO: What?

PRINCESS: Who was't,
Who even now has gone from you?

DOMINGO: The Duke
Of Alba, gracious Princess, who doth ask
Permission after me to be admitted.

PRINCESS: Duke Alba? What would he? What can he want?
Perhaps you know it and can tell me?

DOMINGO: I?
And ere I know what meaningful event
Gives me the long withheld good fortune, to
Approach the Princess Eboli anew?

(*Pause, wherein he awaits her answer.*)
Have circumstances come about at last,
Which favor what the King desires? Have I
Hop'd with good grounds, that you would reconcile
Yourself on better thought to a request,
Which only self-will, and caprice rejected?
I come here full of expectation—

PRINCESS: Did
You bring my latest answer to the King?

DOMINGO: I have postpon'd to wound him fatally.
Yet, gracious Princess, there is time. It rests
With you to mitigate it.

PRINCESS: Notify
The King, that I'm awaiting him.

DOMINGO: May I
Accept this for the truth, my lovely Princess?

PRINCESS: Now surely not as jest? By God! You make
Me quite afeard.—What? What have I then done,

If even you—if you yourself grow pale?
    DOMINGO: My Princess, this is so surprising —I
Can hardly grasp it—
    PRINCESS: Yes, most worthy Lord,
Nor should you either. Not for all the world's
Possessions would I, that you comprehended it.
Enough for you, that it is so. Then spare
Yourself the trouble of discerning, whose
Great eloquence to thank for this new turn.
But, to your consolation, this I add:
You have no part in this transgression. Nor
The Church, in truth; although you show'd to me,
That instances were possible, wherein
The Church for higher purposes knew how
To use the *bodies* of its youthful daughters.
But not that either.—Such-like pious reasons,
Are too high for me, rev'rend Lord.—
    DOMINGO: Quite gladly,
Do I retract them, Princess, just as soon
As they became superfluous.
    PRINCESS: Request
On my behalf the Monarch, surely not
Misunderstand *me* in this business. What
I've been, thus am I still. And yet the course
Of things hath in the meantime been transform'd.
As I rejected his proposal with
Such indignation, I believ'd him *happy*
In the possession of the fairest Queen—
Believ'd his faithful spouse was worthy of
My sacrifice. That I believ'd then—then.
But now, now I know better.
    DOMINGO: Princess, further.
I hear, we understand us.
    PRINCESS: 'Tis enough,
She hath been caught. No longer shall I spare her.
The crafty thief hath now been caught. She hath
Betray'd the King, the whole of Spain, and me.
She loves. I know it that she loves. I'll bring
The evidence, the which shall make her tremble.
The King hath been betray'd—oh yes by God!
He shall not be thus unaveng'd. The mask
Of lofty, superhuman self-denial
I'll tear away from her, that all the world
May see and know the sinner's brow. It costs

Me a colossal price, but yet—it doth
Delight me, 'tis my triumph—yet to you
It is a greater still.

    DOMINGO: Now all is ripe.
With your permission, I shall call the Duke.
(*He goes outside.*)

    PRINCESS (*astonish'd*): What is this?

SCENE XII—*The* PRINCESS. DUKE ALBA. DOMINGO.

    DOMINGO (*who leads the* DUKE *in*):   Our intelligence, Duke Alba,
Comes here too late. The Princess Eboli
Reveals to us a secret, that she should
Have come to know from us.

    ALBA: My visit will
So much the less surprise her then. I do
Not trust in *mine* own eyes. Discoveries
Like these require a woman's vision.

    PRINCESS: You
Do speak then of discoveries?—

    DOMINGO: We wish'd
To know, my gracious Princess, in which place
And at which better hour you—

    PRINCESS: That as well!
I shall expect you then tomorrow noon.
I have good grounds, to keep this crim'nal secret
Conceal'd no longer—To withhold it from
The King no longer more.

    ALBA: That was the thing,
Which led me here. The Monarch must know this
At once. Through you, through *you*, my Princess, he
Must know't. Whom else, whom should he sooner trust
Than the severe, the watchful playmate of
His wife?

    DOMINGO: Whom more, than you, and who, so soon
She wants, can rule him absolutely?

    ALBA: I'm
The Prince's stated foe.

    DOMINGO: The very same
Is what the world's come to expect of me.
The Princess Eboli is free. Where *we*
Are forc'd to silence, duties must compel you,
To speak, the duties of your post. The King
Will not escape us, if your hints impress,

And then do we complete the work.

ALBA: Yet soon
Directly now must that occur. The moments
Are precious. Each succeeding hour can bring
The orders to me for departure—

DOMINGO (*turning, after some consideration, to the* PRINCESS):
                                                            If
Some letters were discover'd? Letters surely
From the Infante, intercepted, must
Here have effect.—Let's see—not true?—Indeed.
You sleep of course —methinks—yes, in the same
Bed chamber as the Queen?

PRINCESS: The one right next
To this one.—Yet what should that be to me?

DOMINGO: Had we but someone vers'd in locks—Have you
Observ'd, where she's accustom'd to conceal
Her key to th' privy purse?

PRINCESS (*reflecting*):   That could well lead
To something—Yes— the key were possible
To find, I do believe—

DOMINGO: Now letters would
Have messengers—The retinue o'th' Queen is large—
Who here could help us find a trace!—Gold can
Of course do much—

ALBA: Hath no one ever notic'd
If the Infante hath a confidant?

DOMINGO: Not *one*, in all Madrid not *one*.

ALBA: That's strange.

DOMINGO: In this you may believe me. He doth scorn
The court entirely; I do have my proofs.

ALBA: Yet how? It strikes me even now, as I
Emerg'd from out the bed room of the Queen,
There stood th' Infante with a page of hers;
They spoke in secret—

PRINCESS (*hastily interrupting*): No! Oh no! That was —
That was another matter.

DOMINGO: How can *we*
Know that?—Oh no, the circumstance is suspect—
(*To the* DUKE.)
And did you know the page?

PRINCESS: Such childish tricks!
What should it otherwise have been? Enough,
I know it all.—We'll see us then again,
Before I see the King.—And meanwhile much

May be discover'd.

    DOMINGO (*leading her aside*): And the Monarch may
He hope? I may inform him thus? For sure?
And which most lovely hour will bring at last
Fulfillment of his wishes? That as well?

    PRINCESS: In sev'ral days I shall grow ill; they'll part
Me from the person of the Queen—that is,
As you know well, the custom of the court.
Then I'll remain within my chamber.

    DOMINGO: 'Tis
Successful! Our great game is won. To all
The Queens be bid defiance.—

    PRINCESS: Hearken now!
They're asking after me—The Queen requires
My presence. So farewell. (*She hurries out.*)

SCENE XIII—ALBA. DOMINGO.

DOMINGO (*after a pause, wherein he hath accompanied the* PRIN-
CESS *with his eyes*):
                 These roses, Duke
And your engagements—

    ALBA: And thy God —thus would
I wait the lightning, that should us o'erthow! (*They go.*)

SCENE XIV—*In a Carthusian monastery.* DON CARLOS. *The* PRIOR.

CARLOS (*to the* PRIOR, *as he steps in*):
Already been here then?—That I regret.

    PRIOR: Three times already since this morning early.
He went away an hour ago.—

    CARLOS: But he
Will come again? Did he not leave a word?

    PRIOR: Before midday he promis'd it.

    CARLOS (*at a window, looking out over the region*):
                      Your cloister
Lies far back from the road. There yonder one
Still sees the towers of Madrid.—Quite right,
And here the Manzanares flows.—The landscape
Is, just as I would have it.—Everything
Is still here, as a secret.

    PRIOR: Like the entrance
To th' other life.

CARLOS: Unto your honesty
I have entrusted, rev'rend Lord, that which
I hold most sacred and most dear. No mortal
May know or even but surmise, to *whom*
I have here spoken *secretly*. I have
Quite weighty grounds, to disavow this man,
Whom I await, before the world at large;
Therefore I chose this cloister. Are we here
Secure from traitors and surprises? Do
You still remember, what you swore to me?

PRIOR: Place confidence in us, most gracious Lord.
The King's mistrust will not search through these *graves*.
The ear of curiosity lies only
At doors of passion and of happiness.
The world ends at these walls.

CARLOS: Perhaps you think,
Behind this caution and this fear doth creep
A guilty conscience?

PRIOR: I think nothing.

CARLOS: You
Do err then, pious Father, you in truth
Do err. My secret quakes ere human beings,
But not ere God.

PRIOR: My son, that worries *us*
But little. This asylum stands as open
To th' criminal as to the innocent.
If, what thou dost intend, is good or evil,
If it is righteous or is wicked—that
Thou must decide in thine own heart.

CARLOS (*with warmth*):   What we
Keep secret here, can not disgrace your God.
It is His own most lovely work.—Indeed,
I can reveal it to you.

PRIOR: To what end?
I'd rather you forego it, Prince. The world
And her devices lie a long time seal'd
Away, upon this mighty journey. Why
Reopen it once more before the soon
Appointed hour of my farewell?—It is
But little, one requires for blessedness.—
The bell to Hora rings. I must go pray. (*The* PRIOR *departs.*)

SCENE XV—DON CARLOS. *The* MARQUIS OF POSA *enters.*

CARLOS: Ah, finally, at last—
MARQUIS: O, what a test
For the impatience of a friend! The sun
Hath come up twice and twice gone under, since
My Carlos' fate hath been decided, and
Now for the first time shall I hear it.—Speak,
You're reconcil'd now?
CARLOS: Who?
MARQUIS: Thou and King Philip;
And also Flanders is decided?
CARLOS: That
The Duke shall journey there tomorrow?—That's
Decided, yes.
MARQUIS: That can not be. 'Tis not.
Should all Madrid be so deceiv'd? 'Tis said
Thou had'st a secret audience. The King—
CARLOS: Remain'd unmov'd. We're parted now forever,
And more, than e'er before—
MARQUIS: Thou goest *not*
To Flanders?
CARLOS: No! No! No!
MARQUIS: O, all my hopes!
CARLOS: Aside from that. O, Roderick, since we
Last left each other, what have I liv'd through!
Yet now, before all else thy counsel! I
Must speak with her!
MARQUIS: Thy mother?—No!—Wherefore?
CARLOS: I have a hope.—Thou growest pale? Be calm.
I should and shall be happy.—Yet of this,
Another time. Now counsel me, how I
Can speak to her.—
MARQUIS: What should this mean? On what
Is this new fever dream now bas'd?
CARLOS: No dream!
By glorious God 'tis not!—In truth, in truth!
(*producing the* KING'S *letter to* PRINCESS EBOLI)
It is contain'd within this weighty paper!
The Queen is *free*; before the eyes of men,
As well as free before the eyes of Heaven.
Read here and cease to be astonish'd.
MARQUIS (*opening the letter*):   What?
What do I see? The Monarch's own hand writing?
(*After he hath read it.*)

Whom is this letter sent to?
    CARLOS: To the Princess
Of Eboli.—Two days ago a page
O'th' Queen brings me a letter and a key
From hands that are unknown. Therein it is
Describ'd to me that in the left wing of
The palace, where the Queen resides, there is
A cabinet, in which a lady waits
For me, whom I've long lov'd. I do obey
The hint directly—
    MARQUIS: Madman, thou obey'st?
    CARLOS: I do not recognize the writing—I
Know only *one* such lady. Who but *she*
Would e'er believe herself ador'd by Carlos?
Full of sweet giddiness I fly to th' place;
A godly song, that resonates towards me
From out the room's interior, serves me
As guide.—I open up the chamber door—
And whom do I discover?—Feel my horror!
    MARQUIS: O, I divine it all.
    CARLOS: I was forlorn
Without salvation, Roderick, had I
Not fallen into angel's hands. What an
Unfortunate coincidence! Deceiv'd
By the incautious language of my glances,
She did surrender to the sweet delusion,
She be herself the idol of these glances.
Mov'd by the silent suff'ring of my soul,
Her tender heart in generous imprudence,
Persuades itself to love me in return.
Respect seem'd to impose a silence on me;
She hath th'audacity to break it—lays
Her beaut'ous soul before me bare—
    MARQUIS: So calmly
Relat'st thou that?—The Princess Eboli
Did see through thee. Have no more doubt, she pierc'd
Unto the inmost secret of thy love.
Thou hast abus'd her gravely. She controls
The King.
    CARLOS (*confidently*): But she is virtuous.
    MARQUIS: She is't
From the self-interest of love.—This virtue
I'm quite afeard, I know it well—how little
It reacheth upward to that high ideal,
Which from the soul's maternal soil, conceiv'd

In proud and beauteous gracefulness, doth sprout
Of its free will and with no gard'ner's help
Brings forth the most abundant bloom! It is
A foreign branch which in harsh latitudes
Hath flower'd with a counterfeited South;
A maxim, rearing, call it what thou wilt
An *innocence acquir'd*, that's wrested from
Hot blood through artifices and hard battles,
And credited painstakingly, precisely
To Heaven, which demands it and repays.
Weigh it thyself. Will she be able to
Forgive the Queen now that she knows, a man
Pass'd over her own virtue, won in hard
Fought battle, to consume himself in flames
Of hopeless passion for Don Philip's wife?
    CARLOS: Know'st thou the Princess so exactly?
    MARQUIS: By
No means. I've hardly seen her twice. Yet let
Me say but one more word: It seem'd to me,
She deftly shunn'd exposure to all vice,
She was completely *conscious* of her virtue.
And then I saw the Queen as well. O Carl,
How fully diff'rent, what I have observ'd!
In tranquil glory to which she was born,
With carefree rashness, with the orthodox
Cold calculation of propriety
Unschool'd, from both temerity and fear
Remov'd, she trods the narrow middle-path
Of *properness* with firm, heroic stride
Unwitting of the adoration she compell'd,
Where she ne'er dreamt upon her own acclaim.
And doth my Carl discern here in this mirror,
As well just now his Eboli?—The Princess
Stay'd steadfast for she was in love; love was
Quite lit'rally condition'd on her virtue.
Thou hast her ne'er repaid—she falls.
    CARLOS (*with some vehemence*): No! No!
(*Afterwards he goes back and forth, impetuously.*)
I tell thee, no.—If Roderick but knew,
How excellently it doth suit him thus
To rob his Carl of the most heavenly
Of blisses, faith in human excellence!
    MARQUIS: Deserve I that?—No, fav'rite of my soul,
I would not that, by God in Heaven not!

This Eboli—she were an angel, and
Respectfully, like thou thyself, would I
Cast down myself before her very glory,
Had she—not come to know thy secret.
  CARLOS: See
How idle is thy fear! Doth she have proofs
Beyond the ones that put herself to shame?
And will she purchase with her honor thus
The melancholy pleasure of revenge?
  MARQUIS: In order to retract a blush, have many
Already sacrific'd themselves to shame.
  CARLOS (*rising with vehemence*):
Oh, no, that is too hard, too cruel! She's proud
And noble; I do know her and fear naught.
Thou seek'st in vain to terrify my hopes.
I must speak with my mother.
  MARQUIS: Now? What for?
  CARLOS: I now have nothing left worth saving—I
Must know my fate. Just see to it that I
Can speak to her.
  MARQUIS: And dost thou want to show
This letter to her? Dost thou really?
  CARLOS: Ask
Me of this matter not. The means, the means,
Whereby I'll speak with her!
  MARQUIS (*meaningfully*): Didst thou not say
To me, that thou didst *love* thy mother?—Thou
Art willing then to show this letter to her?
(CARLOS *looks at the ground and is silent.*)
I read, Carl, something in thy countenance—
Completely new to me—and alien
Completely 'til this moment.—Dost thou turn
Thine eyes now from me? *Why* dost thou now turn
Thine eyes from me? So is it true?—Have I
Then really read it right? Now let us see—
(CARLOS *gives him the letter. The* MARQUIS *tears it up.*)
  CARLOS: What? Art thou mad?
(*with a more moderate sensitiveness*)
         Indeed—I must confess—
Upon this letter much did ride for me.
  MARQUIS: So it appear'd. Therefore I tore it up.
(*The* MARQUIS *rests a penetrating glance upon the*
PRINCE, *who views him doubtfully. A long silence.*)
Yet speak—what hath the desecration of

The royal bed to do with thy—thy love?
Was Philip dangerous to thee? What link
Can possibly connect the injur'd duties
O'th' husband to thine own audacious hopes?
He's sinn'd, while thou dost love? Now do I learn
To comprehend thee. O, how poorly have
I come, 'til now, to understand thy love!

    CARLOS: What, Roderick? What think'st thou?

    MARQUIS: Oh, I feel,
From what I must now wean myself. Yes, once,
Once was't quite diff'rent. Then wert thou so rich,
So warm, so rich! A planet had in thy
Wide bosom, space enough to orbit. All
Of that is past, devour'd by *one* desire,
By one small-minded selfish interest.
Thy heart is grown extinct. Not one tear for
The monstrous fate of all the Provinces,
Not even one more tear!—O Carl, how poor
Since thou now lovest no one but *thyself!*

    CARLOS (*throws himself into an armchair.—After a pause,
with barely suppress'd tears.*):
I know, thou hast respect for me no more.

    MARQUIS: Not so, my Carl! I know this surge of feeling.
'Twas error of most laudable emotions.
The Queen belong'd to thee, and thou wert robb'd
Then by the Monarch—yet 'til now thou hast
Been modestly distrustful of thy claims.
Perhaps was Philip worthy of her. Thou
Didst only softly dare, to speak this judgment.
The note decided. *Thou* wert worthiest.
With prideful joy thou sawest then the fate
Of tyranny, convicted of the theft.
Thou didst exult to be the one offended;
For suff'ring wrongs doth flatter mighty souls.
Yet here thy fantasy did go astray.
Thy pride felt *satisfaction*—and thy heart
Allow'd itself to *hope*. I knew it well,
Thou hadst misunderstood thyself this time.

    CARLOS (*mov'd*): No, Roderick, thou art quite wrong. I did
Not think so nobly, not by far, as thou
Wouldst like to make me think.

    MARQUIS: Am I then here
So little known? See, Carl, whenever thou
Hast gone astray, I seek out every time

To guess that virtue from among the hundreds
To which I can impute the flaw. Yet now
We understand us better, be't! Thou shouldst
Now speak to th' Queen, must speak to her.—
 CARLOS (*falling upon his neck*):   O, how
I blush beside thee!
 MARQUIS: Thou dost have my word.
Now leave the rest to me. A wild, a bold
A happy thought soars in my fantasy. —
Thou shalt hear it, Carl, from a fairer mouth.
I press on to the Queen. Perhaps tomorrow
The outcome will be manifest already.
Until then, Carl, forget not, that "a purpose,
Which higher reason hath conceiv'd, that man's
Afflictions urge, ten thousand times defeated,
May never be abandon'd." Hearest thou?
Remember Flanders!
 CARLOS: Ev'rything, that *thou*
And highest virtue bid me do.
 MARQUIS (*goes to a window*): The time
Is up. I hear thy retinue approach. (*They embrace.*)
Again Crown Prince and vassal.
 CARLOS: Thou dost go
At once to town?
 MARQUIS: At once.
 CARLOS: Halt! Yet a word!
How easily forgotten!—A report,
Of greatest import: —"Letters to Brabant
Are open'd by the King." Be on thy guard!
The Royal Post hath secret orders, this
I know—
 MARQUIS: How didst thou learn that?
 CARLOS: Don Raimond
Of Taxis is a friend of mine.
 MARQUIS (*after some silence*): That too!
They'll take the detour over Germany.
(*They depart through different doors.*)

ACT III

SCENE I—*The bedroom of the* KING. (*Upon the night table two burning candles. In the hinterground of the room a few pages upon their knees, fallen asleep. The* KING, *from above half undress'd, stands before the table, one arm bent over the armchair, in a reflecting position. Before him lies a medallion and paper.*)

KING: That formerly she's been a schwärmer—who
Can gainsay? Ne'er could *I* give love to her,
And yet—did she the lack once seem to feel?
Thus 'tis establish'd, she is false.
(*Here he makes a movement, which brings him to himself.
He looks up with astonishment.*) Where was I?
Is none then but the King awake here?—What?
The candles have already burnt? but not
Yet day? I'm finish'd with my slumber. Take
Deliv'ry of it, Nature. Kings have not
The time to repossess forfeited nights;
Now I'm awake and day should dawn.
(*He puts out the candles and opens a window curtain.
Whilst he walks up and down, he observes the sleeping
boys and remains standing for some time silently
before them; thereupon he pulls the bell.*) Perhaps
Someone sleeps in my antechamber too?

SCENE II—*The* KING. COUNT LERMA.

LERMA (*with dismay, as he becomes aware of the* KING):
Doth not Your Majesty feel well?
  KING: There was
A fire i'th' left pavilion. Did you not
Hear the alarm?
  LERMA: Not I, Your Majesty.
  KING: No? How? And therefore had I only dreamt?
That cannot come about by chance. For doth
The Queen not sleep within that very wing?
  LERMA: Indeed, Your Majesty.
  KING: The dream alarms me.
The guards should be redoubl'd there in future,
You hear? as soon as ev'ning comes—but quite,
Quite secretly.—I will not have it, that—
You test me with your glances?

LERMA: I discern
A burning eye, that pleads for slumber. May
I venture to remind Your Majesty
About a precious life, and to remind
You of the people, who the traces of
A sleepless night would read with frightening
Surprise in such demeanor?—Only two
Foreshorten'd morning hours of sleep—
    KING (*with ravag'd looks*):   Of sleep?
Sleep find I in Escurial—So long
The King is sleeping, he foresakes his crown,
The man foresakes his woman's heart—No, no!
It is a calumny—Was't not a woman,
A woman, who did whisper it to me?
The name for woman's calumny. The crime
Is not yet prov'd, 'til by a man confirm'd.
(*To the pages, who in the meantime have awaken'd.*)
Call forth Duke Alba!
(*Pages exit.*)   Step up nearer, Count!
Is't true? (*He remains standing searchingly before the* COUNT.)
          Oh, for a pulse's length to be
Omniscient!—Swear to me, is't true? Have I
Been cheated? Have I? Is it true?
    LERMA: My great,
My best of Kings —
    KING (*drawing back*): A King! And only King,
And King again!—No better answer than
An empty, hollow echo? I do strike
Upon this rock desiring water, water
To quench my burning fever thirst —he gives
Me gold that's glowing.
    LERMA: What were true, my King?
    KING: 'Tis nothing. Nothing. Leave me. Go.
(*The* COUNT *wants to leave, he calls him back once again.*)
                              You're married?
A father? Yes?
    LERMA: Indeed, Your Majesty.
    KING: A married man and yet could risk, to keep
The watch here with your Lord at night? Your hair
Is silver grey and yet you do not blush,
For trusting in your wife's integrity?
O get you home. 'Tis certain that you'll find
Her in your son's incestuous embrace.
Believe Your King, and go—You stand dismay'd?

With meaning do you look at me? for I,
I do myself perchance have greying hair?
Unhappy man, reflect upon it. Queens
Do not defile their virtue. You are now
A dead man, if you doubt —
    LERMA (*with fervor*):   Who can do that?
In every country of my Monarch, who
Is bold enough, to breathe with poisonous
Suspicion on angelic purity?
The very best of Queens so deep —
    KING: The best?
And she is thus your best as well? She hath
Such ardent friends around me here, I find.
That must have cost her very much—much more,
Than it is known to me, that she can give.
You are dismiss'd. Now let the Duke come in.
    LERMA: I hear him in the antechamber—(*About to go.*)
    KING (*with mitigated tone*):   Count —
What you observ'd before, was doubtless true.
My head burns from a sleepless night.—Forget,
What I have said in waking dreams. You hear?
Forget it. I remain your gracious King.
(*He extends his hand to him to kiss.* LERMA *exits and
opens the door for the* DUKE OF ALBA.)

SCENE III—*The* KING *and* DUKE OF ALBA.

    ALBA (*approaches the* KING *with uncertain demeanor*):
An order so astonishing to me —
At this most extraordinary hour?
(*He is startl'd, as he observes the* KING *more closely.*)
And this appearance —
    KING (*hath sat down and seiz'd the medallion on the table.
He looks at the* DUKE *for a long time in silence.*)
                             Is it really true?
I do not have a faithful servant?
    ALBA (*stands still, surpris'd*):
                How?
    KING: I have been mortally offended — It is known
And no one gave me warning!
    ALBA (*with a look of astonishment*): An offense,
Which bears upon my King and which escap'd
Mine eye?

KING (*shows him the letter*):
                                   You recognize this hand?
ALBA: It is
Don Carlos' hand—
    KING (*Pause, wherein he observes the* DUKE *sharply*):
                    Do you suspect then nothing?
'Gainst his ambition have you caution'd me?
Was't only his ambition, this alone,
Should make me quake?
    ALBA: Ambition is a great —
A spacious word, wherein an infinite
Amount can lie.
    KING: And have you nothing special
You can disclose to me?
    ALBA (*after a silence with a reserv'd look*):
                                   Your Majesty
Entrusts the Empire to my vigilance.
I owe the Empire my most secret knowledge
And my intelligence. Whatever else
I do suspect or think or know, belongs
To me alone. These are the consecrated
Possessions, which the auction'd slave, just like
The vassal, hath the privilege to withhold
From every King on earth.—Not everything,
That is so clear to *my* own soul, is ripe
Enough to tell my King. Yet wishes he
To be content, then I must beg, he not
Inquire as master.
    KING (*gives him the letter*): Read.
    ALBA (*reads and turns towards the* KING *alarm'd*):
                                   Who was
The raving one, who plac'd this grievous sheet
Of paper in my Monarch's hand?
    KING: What's that?
You know for whom the content's meant?—The name
Is, as I know, omitted from the paper.
    ALBA (*stepping back disconcerted*):
I was too quick.
    KING: You know?
    ALBA (*after some reflection*): The word is out.
My Lord commands—I may retreat no more —
I'll not deny it—I do know the person.
    KING (*standing up in a frightful movement*):
O help me to devise new means of death,
Ye dreadful God of vengeance! So apparent,

So world-renown'd, so loud is the awareness,
That people, spar'd the trouble of inquiring,
Already guess it at first glance—That is
Too much! I have not known of that! Not that!
I am therefore the last, who finds it out!
The last in all my realm—

    ALBA (*throws himself at the* KING's *feet*):

                                         Yes I confess
My guilt, most gracious Monarch. I'm asham'd
That such a coward's cleverness, which bade
Me to be silent, when my Monarch's honor,
As well as truth and righteousness assail'd
Me loud enough to speak—But since all others
Wish to be silent—since the magic spell
Of beauty binds the tongues of other men,
Though it be risky, I do speak; although
I know, a son's ingratiating protest,
And the seductively enticing charm,
The tearful weeping of a wife—

    KING (*rash and vehement*): Arise.
You have my royal promise—Now arise.
And speak out fearlessly.

    ALBA (*arising*):   Your Majesty
Perhaps you still recall that incident
I'th' garden at Aranjuez. You found
The Queen abandon'd there by each one of
Her ladies—with disrupted look—alone
Within a distant-lying arbor.

    KING: Ha!
What am I hearing? Further!

    ALBA: The Marquise
Of Mondecar was banish'd from the realm,
Since she was generous enough, at once
To sacrifice herself unto her Queen.
Now we've been told—That the Marquise had
Done nothing more, than she had been commanded.—
The Prince had been there.

    KING (*in a frightful passion*): Had been there! Then surely—
    ALBA: The footprints of a man upon the sand,
Which from the left side entrance to that arbor
Departed towards a grotto, where still lay
A handkerchief, which the Infante lack'd,
Arous'd suspicion instantly. A gard'ner
Had come across the Prince there, and that was,

As if computed nearly to the minute,
The time exactly, when Your Majesty
Appear'd within the arbor.

  KING (*recovering from a gloomy thought*):
             And she wept,
When I appear'd to be surpris'd! She made
Me blush before th' entire assembl'd court!
And blush before myself—By God! I stood
Like one convicted ere her very virtue—(*A long and
deep silence. He sits down and covers his face.*)
Indeed, Duke Alba—You are right—That could
Lead me to something terrible.—Now leave
Me for a moment to myself.

  ALBA: My King,
That doth not yet decide in full—

  KING (*seizing after the papers*): Nor that?
And that? And that again? And all of this
Loud harmony of damning evidence?
Oh, it is clearer than the light—What I
Had known a long time in advance—The mischief
Began there in Madrid, when I at first
Receiv'd her from your hands—I still can see
With such a look of horror, ghostly pale,
How she doth dwell upon my greying hair.
It started there, her cheating game!

  ALBA: A bride
Did die unto the Prince in his young mother.
They had indulg'd already in desires,
Each other's fiery feelings understood,
Which her new state did not allow. The fear
Had been o'ercome, the fear, which usually
Attends the first avowal, and more boldly
Seduction spoke in confidential scenes
Of sanction'd reminiscences. United
By harmony of thought and of their years,
By like compulsions anger'd. They obey'd
The boiling of their passions thus more boldly.
Here politics encroach'd upon their fancy;
Is it believable, my Monarch, she
Would grant this pow'r to th' council of the state?
That she restrain'd her lustfulness, to test
The choice o' th' cab'net more attentively?
She was prepar'd for love and she receiv'd—
A diadem.

KING (*offended and with bitterness*):
        You make distinctions quite—
Quite wisely, Duke—I am amaz'd at your
Great eloquence. I thank you.
(*Arising, cold and proud.*)   You are right:
The Queen hath greatly err'd in her concealment
From me of letters of such content—And
In hiding the Infante's culpable
Appearance in the garden from me. From
False kindness she had greatly err'd. I shall
Know how to punish her. (*He pulls on the bell.*)
                Who else is in
The anteroom?—For you, Duke Alba
I have no further need. Withdraw.
    ALBA: Have I
Through my great eagerness dissatisfied
Your Majesty a second time?
    KING (*to a page, who enters*): Now let
Domingo enter.
              (*The page exits.*)
              I forgive you, for
The fact that you for nigh two minutes long
Had *me* made stand in fear of a misdeed
That could have just as well befallen *you*.
(ALBA *withdraws*.)

SCENE IV—*The* KING. DOMINGO.

The KING (*walks back and forth a few times, to collect himself*).
    DOMINGO (*enters a few minutes after the* DUKE, *approaches
the* KING, *whom he observes for some time with solemn
silence*).
How joyfully surpris'd I am to see
Your Majesty so tranquil, so compos'd.
    KING: You are surpris'd—
    DOMINGO: May Providence be thank'd,
My fear was thus unfounded after all!
Now may I hope so much the more.
    KING: Your fear?
What was there to be fear'd?
    DOMINGO: Your Majesty,
I may not hide, that I already know
About a secret—
    KING (*darkly*): Have I then as yet

Express'd the wish, to share this secret with you?
Who came before me so officiously?
Upon my honor, very bold!
  DOMINGO: My Monarch,
The place, the time, when I discover'd it,
The seal, whereunder I discover'd it,
Doth free me at the least of such a guilt.
I'th' stall it was confess'd to me—confess'd
As a misdeed, the which doth weigh upon
The tender conscience of the one who found it,
And from the heaven seeks for grace. Too late
The Princess doth lament a deed, from which
She hath good reason to expect results
Which are most frightful for her Queen.
  KING: Indeed?
That goodly heart—You have surmis'd quite rightly,
The reason why I had you call'd. You shall
Conduct me from this darksome labyrinth,
Wherein I have been cast by my blind zeal.
I look for truth from you. Speak openly
With me. What should I trust and what conclude?
I call upon your Office for the truth.
  DOMINGO: Sire, even had the mildness of my station
Not laid on me indulgence's sweet duty,
Yet would I still beseech Your Majesty,
Beseech you for the sake of your repose,
To stop with this discov'ry—to renounce
Eternally the probing of a secret,
Which never can develop happily.
What is now known, that still can be forgiven.
Just one word from the King—and then the Queen
Hath never err'd. The Monarch's will bestows
Virtue as well as happiness—and only
The ever constant calmness of my King
Can mightily strike down the false reports,
Which slander hath permitted.
  KING: False reports?
About me? and among my people?
  DOMINGO: Lies!
Lies worthy of damnation! I do swear it.
Yet certainly there are some cases where
The people's credence, though 'twere still unprov'd,
Becomes as weighty as the truth.
  KING: By God!

And here precisely 'twere—
    DOMINGO: A goodly name
Is that uniquely, precious good, o'er which
The Queen must be in competition with
A burgher's wife—
    KING: For that though, I would hope,
There is no need to tremble here? (*His glance rests
uncertainly upon* DOMINGO. *After a silence.*)
                                     Chaplain,
I am to hear from you still something worse.
Postpone it not. I do already read it
In your misfortune-bringing countenance.
Let out with it! Be it, whate'er it may!
Let me no longer quiver on this rack.
What do the people think?
    DOMINGO: Sire, once again
The people can be wrong —and surely are.
What they assert, must not affect the King—
But—*that* they dar'd to go so far already,
As to assert this sort of—
    KING: What? Must I
Beg you so long for this one drop of poison?
    DOMINGO: The people still recall to memory
The month that brought Your Royal Majesty
So near to death—and then but thirty weeks
Thereafter they do read o'th' fortunate
Deliv'ry—
(*The* KING *stands up and pulls the bell, the* DUKE OF ALBA
enters. DOMINGO, *taken aback.*)
                       I'm astounded, Sire!
    KING (*walking toward* DUKE ALBA):   Toledo!
You are a man. Protect me from this Priest.
    DOMINGO (*He and* DUKE ALBA *give each other embarrass'd
looks. After a pause*):
If we could possibly have known before
That this report might have become aveng'd
Upon the bringer—
    KING: Bastard do you say?
I had, you say, but from the dead arisen,
When she became a mother?—How? That was
The time, if I'm not otherwise mistaken,
When you were praising Holy Dominic
In all the churches for the lofty wonder
Which he had work'd on me? —What then had been

A wonder, is it now no more? Thus have
You either then or now been false to me.
What is it that you wish, that I should think?
Oh, I see through you. Had the plot been at
That time already ripe—indeed, then was
The Saint depriv'd of credit.
  ALBA: Plot!
  KING: You should
With this unprecedented harmony
Concur now in the very same opinion
And yet not have an understanding? You
Do wish thus to persuade me? Me? Perhaps
I should not have perceiv'd, how eagerly
And greedily you fell upon your prey?
With what a lust you feasted on my pain,
Upon the agitation of my ire?
Should I not see, how full of eagerness
The Duke is burning, to forestall the favor
Which to my son hath been accorded? How
This pious man did gladly fortify
His petty grudge with my ire's giant arm?
I am the bow, is that what you imagine,
Which one need only bend at his own pleasure? —
I have yet my own will as well—and if
I should have doubts, then let me at the least
Begin with you.
  ALBA: Our loyalty did not
Expect this explanation.
  KING: Loyalty!
'Tis loyalty that warns of threat'ning crimes,
Vindictiveness speaks of committed ones.
Let's hear! What did I ever gain through your
Officiousness? If what you charge is true —
What's left to me except the wound of parting?
The sorry triumph of revenge? But no,
You only fear, you give me tottering
Conjectures—on the precipice of hell
You leave me standing and you then take flight.
  DOMINGO: Are other proofs yet possible, when e'en
The eye itself can't be convinc'd?
  KING (*after a great pause, turning seriously and
solemnly towards* DOMINGO): I shall
Convoke the grandees of my kingdom and
Myself shall sit in judgment. Come then forth

Before them all—have you the courage—and
Indict her as a paramour! She shall
Then die the death—without deliv'rance—she
And the Infante shall both die—but—mark you!
If she can clear herself—you die! Will you
Revere the truth through such a sacrifice?
Make up your mind. You won't? You're now struck dumb?
You won't?—That is a liar's zealousness.

    ALBA (*who has stood silently at a distance, cold and calm*):
I will.

    KING (*turns around surpris'd and fixes his eyes on the* DUKE
for some time):
              That's bold! However, it occurs to me,
That you have risk'd your life upon some things
Far less significant in armed battles—
You've risk'd it with a dicing player's rashness
For the absurdity of fame—And what
Is life to you? I shall not give as prize
The royal blood unto a madman, who
Doth hope for nothing more than to give up
A trifling life exaltedly—I spurn
Your sacrifice. Now go—go, and await
I'th' audience room upon my further orders.

                          (*Both exit.*)

    SCENE V—*The* KING *alone.*

    KING: Now give to me a man, good Providence—
Much hast thou given me. Present to me
A human being. Thou—thou art alone,
Because thine eyes do probe what is conceal'd,
I beg thee for a friend, for I am not,
Like thou, all-knowing. The assistants, whom
Thou hast provided me—what they're to me,
Thou knowest. What they do deserve, have they
Receiv'd from me. Their tame depravities,
Controll'd by reins, do serve my purposes,
Just as thy tempests purify the world.
I need the truth—to dig its silent spring
From out the gloomy rubble heap of error,
Is not the lot of Kings. But give to me
That rare man with a pure, an open heart,
With brilliant spirit and impartial eyes,
Who can help me to find it—I do cast

The lots; and let me find among the thousands,
That flutter round the solar disk o'th' Highness,
That man who is unique.
(*He opens a strong box and takes out a writing tablet.
Afterwards for a long time, he hath turn'd over the
pages therein.*)
        These are but names —
Mere names are standing here, and never once
A mention of the service, which they thank
For placement in this tablet—and what is
Forgotten with such ease as gratitude?
But here I read upon this other tablet
Each petty crime precisely noted. How?
That is not good. Is memory of vengeance
In need of this assistance still? (*Reads further.*)
           Count Egmont?
What doth he here?—the vict'ry at Saint Quentin
Was long since lost. I cast him to the dead.
(*He erases this name and writes it on
another tablet. Afterwards, he hath read further.*)
Marquis of Posa?—Posa?—Posa? I
Can hardly still recall this man to mind!
And yet he's doubly underlin'd—a proof,
That I intended him for some great end!
And, was it possible? this man till now
Did shun my very presence? did evade
The very eyes of his monarchal debtor?
By God! within the full range of my states
The only man, who had no need of me!
Were he possess'd by greed or by ambition,
He had appear'd long since before my throne.
Shall I risk it with this odd person? Who
Can do without me, will have truth for me.
(*He exits.*)

    SCENE VI—*The audience room.* DON CARLOS *in conversation
with the* PRINCE OF PARMA. *The* DUKE OF ALBA, FERIA *and* MEDINA
SIDONIA. COUNT OF LERMA *and yet other* GRANDEES *with papers in
their hands. All awaiting the* KING.

    MEDINA SIDONIA (*visibly avoided by all the bystanders, turns
himself towards the* DUKE OF ALBA, *who alone and wrapt
in thought walks back and forth*):
You've spoken just now with Our Lord, my Duke—

How did you find his humor?
 ALBA: Very bad
For you and for your tidings.
 MEDINA SIDONIA: In the fire
Of English guns I found it easier
Than here upon this plaster.
(CARLOS, *who hath look'd on him with quiet sympathy,*
approaches him now and presses his hand.)
         Warmest thanks
For these most gen'rous-hearted tears, my Prince.
You see, how everyone doth flee from me.
Now is my downfall settl'd.
 CARLOS: Hope still for
The best, my friend, both from my father's mercy
And your own innocence.
 MEDINA SIDONIA: I lost a fleet
Like none that e'er appear'd at sea—What is
A head like this one versus seventy
Destroy'd and sunken galleons?—But, Prince—
Five sons, as full of hope as you—that breaks
My heart—

SCENE VII—*The* KING *comes out in full attire. The same people.*

(*All remove their hats and step back on both sides,*
as they form a semi-circle around him. Silence.

 KING (*looking through the entire circle fleetingly*):
    Be cover'd now!
(DON CARLOS *and the* PRINCE OF PARMA *approach first*
and kiss the KING'S *hand. He turns with some*
friendliness to the latter, without wanting to take
note of his son.)
       Your mother, Nephew,
Desires to know, how people in Madrid
Be pleas'd with you.
 PARMA: Let her not ask that sooner
Than the conclusion of my maiden battle.
 KING: Be satisfied. One day it will be your
Turn to succeed, when these old stems are broken.
(*To the* DUKE OF FERIA.)
What do you bring?
 FERIA (*bending a knee before the* KING):
     The Grand Commander of

The Calatrava order died this morning.
His knight's cross is herewith return'd.
    KING (*takes the order and looks around the entire
circle*):   Who will
Be worthiest to wear it after him?
(*He beckons* ALBA *to him, who falls down on one
knee before him and hangs the order on him.*)
Duke, you are my first Gen'ral—be ne'er *more*,
Thus will my favor fail you at no time.
(*He becomes aware of the* DUKE OF MEDINA SIDONIA.)
Look there! My Admiral!
    MEDINA SIDONIA (*approaches wavering and kneels down
before the* KING *with sunken head*):
                      This, my great King,
Is everything, that I do bring back of
The Spanish youth and the Armada.
    KING (*after a long silence*):   God
Is over me—I've sent you to contend
'Gainst men and not 'gainst storms and hidden reefs—
You're welcome in Madrid.
(*He extends his hand to him to kiss.*)
                  And I give thanks,
That in yourself you have preserv'd for me
A worthy servant!—And for this, my grandees,
I credit him, and want his credit known.
(*He beckons him to stand up and to be cover'd—then
he turns himself towards the others.*)
What is there still?
(*To* DON CARLOS *and the* PRINCE OF PARMA.)
                I give you thanks, my Princes.
(*These latter withdraw. The still remaining* GRANDEES
approach and kneeling hand their papers to the KING. *He looks
through them fleetingly and hands them to the* DUKE OF ALBA.)
Lay these 'fore me i'th' cabinet—Am I now done?
(*No one answers.*)
How doth it happen, that among my grandees
A Marquis Posa never shows himself?
I know right well, this Marquis Posa serv'd
Me with renown. Perhaps he lives no more?
Why doth he not appear?
    LERMA: The Chevalier
Hath only recently return'd from travels,
Which he hath undertaken throughout Europe.
He's come just now unto Madrid and waits

Alone upon the public day, to throw
Himself to th' feet of his most Sov'reign Lord.
    ALBA: Marquis of Posa?—Right! That is the same
Daring Maltese, Your Majesty, of whom
Repute proclaim'd the visionary deed.
When at the summons of the Order's master
The knights took up positions on their island,
Which Soliman laid under seige, this youth
Of eighteen disappear'd abruptly from
Alcala's upper school. Though not call'd for
He stood ere La Valette. "This cross was bought
For me," he said; "and now I want to earn it."
He was one of those forty cavaliers
Who held Saint Elmo's castle at high noon
Against Ulucciali, Piali
And Mustafa and Hassem in the face
Of three repeated stormings. When at last
The fort is scal'd and round it all the knights
Are slain, he plunges in the sea and comes
The lone survivor unto La Valette.
But two months afterwards the foe deserts
The island, and the knight comes back again
To end the studies he had once begun.
    FERIA: And 'twas this Marquis Posa also, who
Discover'd afterwards the infamous
Conspiracy in Catalonia
And merely through his skill alone preserv'd
The most important province of the Crown.
    KING: I am amaz'd—What kind of man is this
Who hath done *that*, and of you three, I ask,
Not one is jealous of him?—Certainly!
This man hath most unusual character
Or none at all—Because it is a wonder
I must converse with him.
(*To the* DUKE OF ALBA.)   When mass is over
Bring him to me i'th' cabinet.
(*Exit the* DUKE. *The* KING *calls* FERIA.)
                         And you
Assume my place within the Privy Council.
    FERIA: Today Our Lord is very gracious.
    MEDINA SIDONIA: You
Might say: He is a god! He's one to me.
    FERIA: How well you merit your good luck! I take
The warmest int'rest, Admiral.

ONE OF THE GRANDEES: I too.

A SECOND: I verily as well.

A THIRD: My heart is pounding.
A so deserving General!

THE FIRST: The King
Did not show mercy towards you—only justice.

LERMA (*to* MEDINA SIDONIA *on the way out*):
At once how rich you are through but two words!
(*all exit.*)

SCENE VIII—*The cabinet of the King*. MARQUIS OF POSA *and*
DUKE OF ALBA.

MARQUIS (*as he enters*):
He wants to see me? Me? That cannot be.
You are mistaken in the name.—And what
Then doth he want from me?

ALBA: He wants to meet you.

MARQUIS: From curiosity alone—Oh, then
The wasted moment is a pity—Life
Is gone astonishingly fast.

ALBA: I give
You over to your lucky star. The King
Is plac'd within your hands. Make use, as well
As you are able, of this moment, and
Yourself, you have yourself to blame, if it
Is wasted. (*He withdraws.*)

SCENE IX

THE MARQUIS (*alone*):
               'Twas well spoken, Duke. One must
Make use o'th' moment, which presents itself
But *once*. In very truth, this courtier gives
Me a good lesson—if it's not as well
In his sense good, at least it is in mine.
(*After some walking up and down.*)
But how do I come hither? Were it but
Caprice o'th' temperamental circumstance
Which shows me now my image in *this* mirror?
Among a million others seiz'd on me
Alone, the most unlikely one, and then
Reviv'd me in the mem'ry of the King?
Was this but chance? Perhaps 'twas more—and what

Is chance except the unwrought block of stone,
That takes on life beneath the sculptor's hand?
'Tis Providence provides this chance—But man
Must mould it to his purpose—What a King
May want with me, 'tis all the same! I know,
What I—I should do with the King—And were
It even no more than a spark of truth
With boldness flung into the despot's soul—
How fruitful in the hand of Providence!
So could, what first seem'd so capricious, be
Quite purposeful and rational. Be it
Or not— the same! I'll act on this belief.
(*He makes a few passes through the room and finally
remains standing in calm contemplation before a painting.
The* KING *appears in the adjoining room where he issues
some orders. He then enters, stands quietly at the
door and observes the* MARQUIS *for some time without being observ'd.*)

SCENE X—*The* KING *and* MARQUIS OF POSA.
(*The latter walks towards the* KING, *as soon as he becomes aware of
him, falls before him on one knee, arises and remains standing before
him without any indication of confusion.*)

KING (*examines him with a look of astonishment*):
Have you before now spoken with me?
    MARQUIS: No.
    KING: You did deserve well of my Crown. But why
Did you thus shun my gratitude? Within
My memory are crowded many people.
All-knowing is but One. Thus did it fall
To you, to seek and find your Monarch's eye.
Why therefore did you not do so?
    MARQUIS: It's been
But two days, Sire, since I have come back to
Your Royal Kingdom.
    KING: Nor am I dispos'd,
To stand indebted to my servant — Ask
Some favor of me.
    MARQUIS: I enjoy the laws.
    KING: This right the murderer has too.
    MARQUIS: Much more
The goodly cit'zen! — Sire, I am contented.
    KING (*to himself*):
Much self-esteem and fortitude, by God!

Yet 'twas to be expected — I do like
The Spaniard proud. I gladly would endure
It even if the beaker did foam over —
You did, I hear, resign my service?

  MARQUIS: To
Make place for someone better, I withdrew.

  KING: That gives me sorrow. When such heads stop work,
How much privation for my state — Perhaps
You are afeard, that you will miss the sphere,
Which is most worthy of your spirit.

  MARQUIS: No!
I am quite certain, that the practic'd judge,
In human souls, his subject matter, skill'd,
With first examination will have read,
What use I am to him, what not. I feel
With the most humble gratitude the favor,
Which your most Royal Majesty upon
Me doth confer through such a proud opinion;
Yet — (*He leaves off.*)

  KING: You reflect on it?

  MARQUIS: I am — I must
Confess it, Sire, not presently prepar'd,
To clothe in words that suit your subject,
What I as cit'zen of this world have thought. —
For at the moment, Sire, when I forever
Had broken with the Crown, I thought myself
Releas'd as well from the necessity,
Of giving it the reasons for this step.

  KING: So weak are these your reasons? Do you fear,
Thereby to venture?

  MARQUIS: If I win the time,
Therewith to tire you, Sire—my life at most.
However, I suspend the truth, if you
Deny to me this favor. Then the choice
'Tween your displeasure and contempt is left
To me — If I am forc'd to make the choice,
Then would I rather vanish from your sight
A crim'nal rather than a fool.

  KING (*with an expectant mien*): Well, now?

  MARQUIS:— I can not be the servant of a Prince.
(*The* KING *looks at him with astonishment.*)
I shall not cheat the buyer, Sire.— If you
Do think I merit an appointment, then
You only wish the deeds prescrib'd. You only

Desire my arm and courage in the field,
My head alone in council. Not my deeds,
But the applause, which they find at the throne,
Should be the purpose of my actions. But for me,
For me hath virtue its own worth. The bliss,
Which with my hands the Monarch would implant,
I would create myself, and 'twere my joy
And my own choice, what else were but my duty.
And is that your opinion? Can you bear
Within your own creation strange creators?
Should I reduce myself to be the chisel,
When I could be the artist? I do love
Humanity and in a monarchy
I may love no one but myself.
    KING: This fire
Is laudable. You wish to cause the Good.
How you promote it, can be all the same
To patriots and to the wise. Seek you
That post of all those in my Royal Kingdom,
Which doth empower you, to satisfy
This noble bent.
    MARQUIS: I find none such.
    KING: How so?
    MARQUIS: That which your Majesty would spread abroad
Through these my hands — is that the bliss of man? —
Is that the bliss, that my pure love doth grant
To all mankind? — Before this happiness
Your Majesty would tremble — No! A new
One's been created by Crown policy —
A bliss, which *it's* still rich enough to spread,
And in the heart of mankind new desires,
Which by this happiness are satisfied.
Upon its coins it lets the truth be struck,
The truth, which it can tolerate. All stamps
Which don't resemble this one are rejected.
And yet, is that which profiteth the Crown —
Enough for me? May my fraternal love
Be lent to the enchroachment of my brother?
Know I he's happy — ere he's free to think?
Do not select me, Sire, to circulate
That happiness which *you* have coin'd for us.
I must decline, to circulate these stamps. —
I can not be the servant of a Prince.

KING (*somewhat rashly*):
You are a Protestant.

MARQUIS (*after some reflection*): Sire, your belief
Is mine as well. (*After a pause.*) I am misunderstood.
That was what I did fear the most. You see
The veil thus pull'd away by my own hand
From all the mysteries of Majesty.
Who gives you certainty that what hath ceas'd
To frighten me, yet holy is to me?
I'm dang'rous, for I've thought beyond myself. —
I am not one, my King. My wishes here
Are mouldering. (*Laying his hand upon his breast.*)
                    The rage so ludicrous
For innovation, which doth but increase
The weight of chains it can not fully break,
Will *my* blood ne'er inflame. The century
Is not yet ripe for my ideal. I live
A citizen of those, which are to come.
Can such a picture so disturb your rest? —
Your breath erases it.

KING: Am I the first
To know this side of you.

MARQUIS: This side of me —
Yes!

KING (*Stands up, takes a few steps and remains standing opposite
the* MARQUIS. *To himself.*)
            At the very least this tone is new!
For flatt'ry spends itself. To imitate
Degrades a man who has a head.—Let's once
Put to the test its opposite. Why not?
The unexpected makes for bliss.—If you
Do understand it thus, good, then I'll
Arrange for a new Crown administration —
For your strong spirit —

MARQUIS: Sire, I hear how small,
How low you think the dignity of man,
You see alone i'th' language of a man
Who's free, the artifice of one who flatters,
I think, I know who warrants you thereto.
The people pressure you thereto; *they* have
Freewillingly sold their nobility,
Freewillingly reduc'd themselves to this
Debased state. In terror do they flee
Before the phantom of their inner greatness,
In poverty they please themselves, and they

Adorn their chains with coward's wisdom,
And call it virtue, to sedately bear them.
Thus were you by the world o'ercome. Thus was
It handed down to you by your great father.
How could you possibly in this unhappy
Curtailment — honor mankind?

  KING: Something true
Do I find in these words.

  MARQUIS: But what a pity!
When from the hand of the Creator you
Transform'd mankind into your handiwork
And to this newly moulded creature made
Yourself unto a God—then did you err
In one thing only: You remain'd a man—
A man from the Creator's hand. *You* went
Forth as a mortal man to suffer, to desire;
You needed sympathy—and to a God
One can but sacrifice—and quake—and pray
To Him! Regrettable exchange! Unhappy
Distortion of all nature!—Since you have
Reduc'd all mankind to be but your lyre,
Who then will share your harmony?

  KING: (By God,
He lays hold of my soul!)

  MARQUIS: But yet to you
This sacrifice is meaningless. You are
Unique in this as well —of your own class —
For this price you're a God. —And terrible,
It were if 'twere *not* so — if for this price,
If for the trampl'd happiness of millions,
You had accomplish'd nothing! If the freedom,
Which you have cancell'd, were the only thing,
Which can accomplish your desires?—I pray
You, Sire, dismiss me now. My subject matter
Doth bear me 'way. My heart is full—the charm
Too strong, to stand before the only one
To whom I would be open.

(*The* COUNT OF LERMA *enters and speaks a few words softly with the* KING. *The latter gives him a wave to withdraw and remains sitting in his former position.*)

  KING (*to the* MARQUIS, *after* LERMA *hath departed*):
      Speak on freely!

  MARQUIS: I'm conscious, Sire—of all the worth —

  KING: Conclude!

You still had more to utter to me.
    MARQUIS: Sire!
I just arriv'd from Flanders and Brabant.—
So many rich and blooming provinces!
A people great and vigorous—and also
A people good—and father of this people!
That, thought I, that must be divine! Then did
I stumble on a pile of burnt men's bones —
(*Here falls silent; his eyes rest on the* KING, *who attempts to return
this glance but instead looks to the ground disconcerted
and confus'd.*)
You're right. *You* have to do't. But that you *can*
Do what you realized you must do, hath
Pierc'd me with shuddering astonishment.
O pity, that, convuls'd in his own blood,
The victim is of little use, in singing
Praise to the spirit of his sacrificer.
That only men—not beings higher yet —
Do write the history of the world!—The times
Of Philip gentler centuries do supplant;
Which milder wisdom bring; the welfare of
The citizen will join with Princes' greatness,
The stingy state will covet its own children,
And hard necessity will be humane.
    KING: When, do you think these human centuries
Would come about, had I before the curse
Of present times but trembl'd? Look about
You in this Spain of mine. Here blooms the bliss
Of citizens in ne'er beclouded peace;
And *such a peace* I grant the Flemish people.
    MARQUIS (*quickly*):
The cemetery's peace! And do you hope,
To end, what you have thus begun? You hope
To halt the fully ripen'd transformation
Of Christendom, the universal spring,
That doth renew the form o'th' world? *You* want
Alone in all of Europe—to oppose
The wheel of universal destiny,
Which ceaselessly doth roll in full career?
To fall upon its spokes with human arm?
You will not! Thousands have already fled
From your lands glad and poor. The citizen
Whom you did forfeit for his faith, was your
Most noble one. With open'd mother's arms

Elizabeth receives the fugitives,
And Britain through the skills of our own land
Blooms fruitfully. Grenada lies in waste,
Without the industry of these new Christians.
And Europe sees in glee its enemy
Inflict itself with wounds and bleed to death.
(*The* KING *is mov'd, the* MARQUIS *observes it, and moves
a few steps nearer.*)
You wish to plant for all eternity,
And yet sow death? A work thus gain'd by force
Will not outlive the soul of its creator.
You've labor'd for ingratitude—in vain
Have you with nature wag'd a hardy fight,
In vain have you thus sacrific'd a great
And royal life on projects of destruction.
Much more is man, than you have thought of him.
For he will break the bonds of lengthy slumber
And once again demand his sacred rights.
Alongside *Nero* and *Busiris* will
He cast your name, and—that doth give me pain,
For you were good.
>   KING: Who gave you such assurance
That this is so?
>   MARQUIS (*with fire*): Yes, by Almighty God!
Yes—Yes—I shall repeat it. Give us back
What you have taken from us. As the strong,
With generosity, let human bliss
Stream from your horn of plenty.—Minds mature
Within your worldly structure. Give us back
What you have taken from us. Thus become
Among a million kings, a king.
(*He approaches him boldly, while directing firm and fiery
glances at him.*)
>   O that
The eloquence of all the myriads,
Who do participate in this great hour,
Upon the lips of my own mouth could hover,
To fan into a flame the beam which I
Observe now in these eyes! Abandon this
Unnatural idolatry, which doth
Annihilate us. And become our model
Of truth and the eternal. Never— never
Possess'd a mortal man so much, with which
To make such godly use. All kings in Europe

Do pay their homage to the Spanish name.
Walk at the head of all of Europe's kings.
One pen-stroke from this hand of yours, and new
The world will be created. Give to us
The liberty of thought—(*throwing himself at his feet.*)
    KING (*surpris'd, his face averted and then once again fasten'd
on the* MARQUIS):
                    Peculiar schwärmer!
And yet — arise — I
    MARQUIS: Look about yourself
Upon his glor'ous universe. On freedom
It hath been founded — and how rich it is
Through freedom! He, the great Creator, casts
The worm into a drop of dew and lets,
In e'en the deathly spaces of decay,
Free will enjoy itself — See *your* creation,
How tight and poor! The rustling of a leaf
Afrights the Lord of Christendom — *You* have
To quake before each virtue. *He* — lest freedom's
Delightful presence be disturb'd — *He* rather
Allows the awful multitude of evil
To rage throughout His universe — of Him,
The Artist, one is not aware, discreetly
He veils Himself within th'eternal laws;
Free thinkers see *these*, yet not *Him*. Wherefore
A God? they say; the world is self-sufficient.
No single Christian prayer hath ever prais'd
Him more than this free thinker's blasphemy.
    KING: And is it your desire to undertake
To reproduce this lofty model in
The mortal creatures in my kingdoms?
    MARQUIS: You,
You can do so. Who else can? Dedicate
To your own people's bliss the reigning power,
Which — ah so long — the greatness of the throne
Alone hath serv'd. Restore to all mankind
Its lost nobility. The citizen
Be once again, what he had been before.
The Crown's sole aim — no duty doth him bind
Except his brother's equal, sacred rights.
For once a man, return'd unto himself,
Awakens to a sense of his own worth —
And freedom's proud, exalted virtues thrive —
Then, Sire, when you have made your Royal Realm

The happiest within the world — then it
Is your own duty to subdue the world.
    KING (*after a great silence*):
I let you finish speaking —Otherwise,
I find, than in the heads of other men,
The world in your head is depicted — nor
Shall I subject you to a foreign standard.
I am the first, to whom you have reveal'd
Your soul. I think it, since I know it. For
The sake of this forbearance, such opinions,
To have suppress'd until this very day,
Although with so much fire embrac'd — and for
The sake of this discrete good sense, young man,
I shall forget, that I have learnt of them
And how I came to know of them. Arise.
I shall refute the youth, who overstepp'd
Himself, as an old man and not as King.
I shall because I wish to— Even poison,
I find, can in benignant natures be
Ennobl'd unto something better — But
Escape my Inquisition.—It should give
Me sorrow—
    MARQUIS: Really? Should it?
    KING (*in his appearance lost*): Never have
I such a human being seen.—No! No,
Marquis! You do me too much wrong. I wish
Not to be Nero. That I do not wish—
I wish not to be him towards you. Not all
Of happiness shall wither under me.
For you, yourself shall be permitted to
Remain a man beneath mine eyes.
    MARQUIS (*quickly*):   And Sire,
My fellow citizens? Oh! Not for me
'Twas done, no, not for *my* cause did I wish
To plead. What of your subjects, Sire?—
    KING: And if
You know so well, just how the times to come
Will judge me, let them learn then from you how
I have responded to a human being
When found I one.
    MARQUIS: Oh! Let the most upright
Among the kings be not at *the same* time
The most unjust —There are in your own Flanders
A thousand better men than I. Alone

To *you* —may I thus freely speak, great King? —
You do see freedom now perhaps for the
First time beneath this gentler picture.
     KING (*with mitigated earnestness*): No
More of this subject, my young man. I know,
You will think otherwise, if for the first
Time you do know mankind as I—Yet were
This not the last time I saw you. How do
I set about to bind you to me?
     MARQUIS: Leave
Me, as I am. What were I to you, Sire,
If you corrupted me as well?
     KING: This pride
I can't endure. You are from this day forth
In my employ—and no objections will
I hear! I wish it thus. (*After a pause.*)
                But how? What wish'd
I then. Was it not truth, that I did wish?
And here I find yet something more — You have
Discover'd me upon my throne, Marquis.
But not within my home?
(*Here the* MARQUIS *seems to deliberate.*)
                I understand
You. Yet—were I the most unfortunate
Among all fathers, could I not be blest
As husband?
     MARQUIS: If a son replete with hope,
If the possession of the loveliest
Of wives doth give unto a mortal man
A right upon this name, then, Sire, you are
Through both the happiest.
     KING (*with dark expression*): No! That I'm not!
And that I'm not thus, have I never felt
More deeply than just now —
(*Dwelling with a look of sadness on the* MARQUIS.)
     MARQUIS: The Prince thinks nobly
And well. Ne'er have I found him otherwise.
     KING: But I have—For that which he took from me,
No crown can ever give me compensation—
So virtuous a Queen!
     MARQUIS: Who can presume
To say it, Sire?
     KING: The world! The calumny!
And I myself! The proofs lie here, which quite

Incontrovertibly condemn her; others
Are still available, which make me fear
The utmost terror—Yet, Marquis, it's hard,
It's hard for me, to trust *one* proof alone.
Who charges her?—If *she* — if she should have
Been capable, so deeply to disgrace
Herself, O how much more may I permit
Myself to think an Eboli defames her?
Doth not the Priest hate both my son and her?
And know I not that Alba broods revenge?
My wife's worth more than all of them.

    MARQUIS: And, Sire,
Still something lives within the woman's soul,
That is exalted over all appearance
And over every calumny—It's call'd
A woman's virtue.

    KING: Yes! I say that too.
So low, as they accuse the Queen, to have
Debas'd herself, doth cost alot. So lightly,
As they would fain persuade me, sacred bonds
Of honor are not broken. You, Marquis,
Do know the people. Such a man as you
Have I long needed, you are good and cheerful
And yet you also know mankind. Therefore
I have selected you —

    MARQUIS (*surpris'd and frighten'd*):
                Me, Sire!

    KING: You've stood
Before your Lord and for yourself have ask'd
For nothing—nothing. That is new to me —
You will be just. Your view will not be sway'd
By passion —Press yourself upon my son,
Investigate the heart o' th' Queen. I shall
Send you full pow'r to speak with them in private
And now depart from me. (*He pulls a bell.*)

    MARQUIS: Can I depart
With *one* hope realiz'd? Then is this day
My life's most beautiful.

    KING (*Extends him the hand to kiss*):
                This day is not
A wasted one in mine.
(*The* MARQUIS *rises and leaves. Enter* COUNT LERMA.)
                The cavalier
Will henceforth be admitted unannounc'd.

ACT IV

SCENE I—*The* QUEEN's *chamber. The* QUEEN. *The* DUCHESS
OLIVAREZ. *The* PRINCESS OF EBOLI. *The* COUNTESS FUENTES *and other*
LADIES.

QUEEN (*To the* LADY STEWARDESS, *as she rises*):
Hath not the key been found, then?—Therefore must
The casket forcibly be broken ope,
And be it soon —
(*She notices that* PRINCESS EBOLI *is there, who approaches her
and kisses her hand*)
                    Be welcome, my dear Princess!
Joy fills me now to find your health restor'd —
Though still so pale —
    FUENTES (*a bit insidiously*): 'Tis evil fever's fault,
That most astoundingly assails the nerves.
Is it not true, my Princess?
    QUEEN: I have wish'd
Full much to visit you, my dear.—And yet
I did not dare.
    OLIVAREZ: The Princess Eboli
At least hath felt no lack of company.
    QUEEN: That I believe. What bothers you? You tremble.
    EBOLI: 'Tis nothing — truly not, my Queen. I beg
That I may have your leave, to part—
    QUEEN: Do you
Conceal from us, that you are far more ill
Than you would have us think? For just to stand
Is painful to you. Countess, help you her
To rest herself a while upon this stool.
    EBOLI: The open air doth better suit my spirits. (*She leaves.*)
    QUEEN: Go follow, Countess — what odd change!
(*A* PAGE *enters and speaks with the* DUCHESS, *who then turns to the*
QUEEN)
    OLIVAREZ: Marquis
of Posa cometh here, Your Majesty,
On orders from His Majesty the King.
    QUEEN: I wait on him.

(*The page leaves and returns introducing the* MARQUIS OF POSA)

SCENE II—MARQUIS OF POSA. *The* QUEEN. (*The* MARQUIS *kneels before the* QUEEN, *who motions him to rise*)

QUEEN: What is my master's plea?
May I so openly —
    MARQUIS: My mission sounds
Unto Your Royal Majesty alone.
(*The* LADIES *move off, at a signal from the* QUEEN)

SCENE III

QUEEN (*full of amazement*):
How this? May I believe mine eyes, Marquis?
The King hath sent you to me?
    MARQUIS: Seems it so
Extraordinary to Your Majesty?
To me by no means.
    QUEEN: Now so is the world
Departed from its path. Yourself and he —
I must confess.—
    MARQUIS: That it rings curious?
That may well be. — This present time just now
Is yet with much more wondrous things full rife.
    QUEEN: With greater, not.
    MARQUIS: Suppose, I'd let myself
At last become converted — were it weary,
At Philip's court to play th'eccentric crank?
Eccentric crank!—What doth it mean? He who
Would make himself of use to th' people, must
At first seek to become himself their equal.
Wherefore the ostentatious pomp of sects?
Suppose — Who is from vanity so free,
That for his faith he will not gladly fight?—
Suppose, I were to contemplate, to set
My faith upon the throne?
    QUEEN: No!—No, Marquis.
Not even once in jesting would I e'er
Accuse you of such unripe fantasy.
You are no dreamer, who would undertake,
What can't be brought unto its end.
    MARQUIS: That were
Indeed the question, so I think.

QUEEN: What most
I can accuse you of, Marquis —from you
What near could fill me with surprise, were — were —
 MARQUIS: My ambiguity. May be.
 QUEEN: The least
Dishonesty. The King apparently
Wish'd not to let be known to me through you,
What you shall say unto me.
 MARQUIS: No.
 QUEEN: And can
A goodly cause an evil means ennoble?
Is't so, that — pardon me for this my doubt—
Your noble pride can borrow this employment?
That can I not believe.—
 MARQUIS: Nor *I*, if 'twere
A matter merely how to dupe the King.
But that is not my purpose. Him himself
I plan to serve this time more honestly,
Than he commission'd me to do.
 QUEEN: Therein
Do I know you, and now enough! What doth he?
 MARQUIS: The King? — It seemeth, that I am to have
Full vindication soon by my strict judge.
What I do not here hasten to relate,
Your Majesty doth hasten, as me seems,
Still less, still less to hear. — Yet nonetheless
It must be heard! His Majesty the King
Doth forward to Your Grace the firm request,
That to th'Ambassador of France you grant
No hearing for today. Such was the stuff
Of my commission. It hath been fulfill'd.
 QUEEN: And that is all, Marquis, that you from him
Do have to say?
 MARQUIS: In more or lesser measure,
What can my presence justify.
 QUEEN: I will
Content myself, Marquis, to never learn,
What must perhaps a secret be to me—
 MARQUIS: So *must* it be, my Queen. — And yet, were you
Not *you* yourself, then would I hasten, to
Advise you of some things, and caution you
Against some certain people.—But with you
It is not necessary. Danger may
Flare up and then calm down about you here,

You should not come to know of it. All this
Is not of so much worth, to drive away
The golden slumber from an angel's brow.
Also it was not that, which brought me here.
Prince Carlos—

    QUEEN: How was he when you left him?

    MARQUIS: The only wise man in his time, for whom
It is a crime, to worship truth.—And still
As heart-embolden'd, on *his* love's behalf,
As he who's willing for his own to die.
Not many words I bring you— And yet here,
Here he's himself. (*He gives the* QUEEN *a letter*)

    QUEEN (*after she hath read it*): He says, he'll speak with me.

    MARQUIS: That say I too.

    QUEEN: And will it make him happy,
If he doth see with his own eyes, that I
Am not as well?

    MARQUIS: No. But more active still
'Twill render him, and more decided.

    QUEEN: How?

    MARQUIS: The Duke of Alba hath been nam'd for Flanders.

    QUEEN: Yes, nam'd— so have I heard.

    MARQUIS: The King can ne'er
Withdraw his name. We know the King full well.
Yet it is true: The Prince cannot stay here —
Here absolutely not — and Flanders must
Not be a sacrifice.

    QUEEN: But do you know
How to prevent it?

    MARQUIS: Yes—perhaps. The means
Is near as bad as is the danger. 'Tis
As daring as despair. And yet I don't
Know of another.

    QUEEN: Tell me what it is!

    MARQUIS: To you, and only you, my Queen, may I
Unfold it here. From you, and you alone
Can Carlos hear it, without horror hear it.
The name, 'tis sure, which it will have to bear,
Rings somewhat coarse—

    QUEEN: Rebellion —

    MARQUIS: He should prove
Himself defiant to the King, should make
His way in secrecy to Brussels, where
With open arms the Flemish wait for him.

All Netherlands will break out in revolt,
Upon his sole command. The worthy cause
Will grow much stronger through the Monarch's son.
The Spanish Throne will tremble 'fore his arms!
What in Madrid the father gives him not,
In Brussels will he grant to him.
    QUEEN: Spake you
Today with him, and say you thus?
    MARQUIS: Because
I spake with him.
    QUEEN (*after a pause*): The plan, which you show me
Alarmeth and—enticeth me as well.
I do believe, that you're not wrong. — Th' idea
Is bold, and even therefore, so I think,
It doth entice me. Let the plan mature.
The Prince doth know of it?
    MARQUIS: He should, it was
My plan he hear it first from your own mouth.
    QUEEN: Beyond dispute! Th' idea is grand. But for
The Prince's youth—
    MARQUIS: It hurts him not. There he'll
Discover both an Egmont and an Orange, the
Brave warriors of the Emp'ror Carl, as shrewd
I'th' Cabinet as fearsome on the field.
    QUEEN (*animated*):
No! This idea is grand and fine. — The Prince
Must act. I feel this deeply now. The role,
That he is seen to play here in Madrid,
Doth press me under, in his stead.—To him
I'll promise France; and Savoy too. I am
In full agreement, Marquis, he must act. —
But for this enterprise, is needed gold.
    MARQUIS: That too is ready.—
    QUEEN: There can I advise.
    MARQUIS: So, may I hope that you will speak with him?
    QUEEN: I will consider it.
    MARQUIS: Now Carlos waits
An answer from Your Majesty. — I have
So promis'd him, I'd not return with nothing.
(*Extending his writing tablet to the* QUEEN)
Two lines are for the time enough —
    QUEEN (*after she hath written*)   Will I
See you again?
    MARQUIS: As often as you bid.

QUEEN: As oft — as oft as I command? — Marquis!
How am I to interpret this new freedom?

MARQUIS: As guileless, as *you* ever can. We do
Enjoy it, and that is enough— that is
Sufficient for my Queen.

QUEEN (*changing the subject*):
How much should I rejoice, Marquis, if here
In Europe freedom's refuge might remain!
If it remain through *him*! — Depend upon
My mute participation —

MARQUIS (*fiery*):   O, I knew't,
I knew I would find understanding here —
(COUNTESS OLIVAREZ appears at the door).

QUEEN (*coldly, to the* MARQUIS):
That which comes from my lord, the King, I shall
Revere, as if it were a law. See you,
That you assure him of my full submission!
(*She motions to him with a nod. The* MARQUIS *exits*)

SCENE IV—*Gallery.* DON CARLOS *and* COUNT LERMA

CARLOS: Here are we undisturb'd. What do you have
That you will now disclose?

LERMA: Your Highness had
A friend within this court.

CARLOS (*surpris'd*):   Whom I knew not!—
How so? What mean you thus in telling me?

LERMA: Thus must I beg for your forgiveness, that
I've more reveal'd, than what I should reveal.
To better reassure Your Highness, know
At least I've had it from a loyal hand,
In short, I have it from myself.

CARLOS: Of whom
Then do you speak?

LERMA: Marquis of Posa.

CARLOS: And?

LERMA: If something more, than someone may dare know,
About Your Highness must be known to him,
As I well-nigh do fear—

CARLOS: What do you fear?

LERMA:—The King receiv'd him.

CARLOS: So?

LERMA: For two full hours
And in quite secret colloquy.

CARLOS: Is't so?

LERMA: Of no small moment was the argument.

CARLOS: I do believe 'tis so.

LERMA: I heard, O Prince,
Your name full oft depicted.

CARLOS: 'Tis my hope
It augurs nothing ill.

LERMA: This morning in
The bedroom of His Majesty, the Queen's
Name was discuss'd in tones mysterious.

CARLOS (*steps back with surprise*):
Count Lerma?

LERMA: Then, the Marquis gone away,
I did receive the King's command, henceforth
To let him be admitted unannounc'd.

CARLOS: 'Tis truly much!

LERMA: 'Tis unexampl'd, Prince,
So long methinks, that I do serve the King.

CARLOS: Much! Truly much!—And how? how, did you say,
How was there mention of the Queen?

LERMA (*steps back*):   No, Prince,
Not that! It wars against my duty.

CARLOS: Odd!
The one you do uncover, and the other
You do conceal from me.

LERMA: To you the first,
The second to the King alone was due.

CARLOS:—'Tis just.

LERMA: The Marquis have I always known
To be a man of honor.

CARLOS: Then have you
Quite rightly known him.

LERMA: Each and every virtue
Is spotless—'til the moment brings with it
The proof.

CARLOS: As well before and also after.

LERMA: A great King's favors, so methinks, do cast
It into question. On this golden hook
Have many robust virtues bled to death.

CARLOS: Oh yes!

LERMA: Oft is it prudent, to unveil,
What can not rest conceal'd.

CARLOS: Yes, it is prudent!
But, as you say, you've only known the Marquis

To be a man of honor?
    LERMA: Is he *still*,
The doubt I have doth make him not the worse,
And you, my Prince, will reap a two-fold gain.
(*He gestures to leave*)
    CARLOS (*follows him, mov'd and shakes his hand*)
My gain is three-fold, noble, worthy man.—
I see myself a friend the richer, and
It doth not rob me of the one I had.
(LERMA *exits*)

    SCENE V—MARQUIS OF POSA *passes through the gallery.*
CARLOS.

    MARQUIS: Carl! Carl!
    CARLOS: Who calls? Ah thou! Quite right. I haste
Ahead to th' cloister. Come thou soon! (*He wants to go.*)
    MARQUIS: But two
Short minutes — wait!
    CARLOS: What if we were surpris'd?
    MARQUIS: We shall not be. It hath already pass'd.
The Queen—
    CARLOS: Thou hast been with my father, then?
    MARQUIS: He summon'd me; indeed.
    CARLOS (*full of expectation*):   And now?
    MARQUIS: 'Tis right.
Thou shalt speak with the Queen.
    CARLOS: And, for the King?
What would the King?
    MARQUIS: What, he? Not much.—Desir'd
To find out, who I am.—Obliging for
An uncommission'd friend. What know I more?
He offer'd me some service.
    CARLOS: Which thou didst
Refuse?
    MARQUIS: 'Tis understood.
    CARLOS: How did you part?
    MARQUIS: Quite well.
    CARLOS: Did he not speak to thee of me?
    MARQUIS: Of thee? Why yes, he did. But gen'rally.
(*He pulls out his writing tablet and gives it to the* PRINCE)
Two words writ by the Queen, tomorrow I
Shall learn, the where and how—

CARLOS (*reads quite distractedly, puts the tablet away and moves to exit*):   So thou wilt meet
Me at the Prior's.
    MARQUIS: Wait. Why dost thou haste?
No one is coming.
    CARLOS: (*with forc'd laughter*): Have we then in troth
Exchang'd our roles? Surprisingly today
Thou art so sure.
    MARQUIS: Today? How so, today?
    CARLOS: And what is it the Queen hath writ?
    MARQUIS: Hast thou
Not read it over in a moment?
    CARLOS: I?
Yes. So.
    MARQUIS: What moves thee? What is wrong with thee?
    CARLOS: O
        Angel
O'th' heavens! Yes, I will be—yes, I will—
I will be worthy of thee. Love doth render
Great souls still greater! Be it, what it be.
If *thou* dost so command, then I'll obey. —
She writes, that I should make myself prepar'd
For a great enterprise. What can she mean
By this? Dost thou know nothing?
    MARQUIS: Even if
I knew it, Carl—wert thou of one accord
To hear it said?
    CARLOS: Have I offended thee?
I was distraught. Forgive me, Roderick.
    MARQUIS: Distraught? Whereby?
    CARLOS: By—I don't know myself.
This letter then is mine?
    MARQUIS: Not altogether.
I've come much more to bid, that thou dost give
Me thine.
    CARLOS: Give mine? What for?
    MARQUIS: And all that thou
Now hast, of lesser worth, which by no means
In other hands than ours must ever fall,
Be 't letters or some hasty sketched notes,
That thou dost hold—in short, thou shouldst now give
Me thy portfolio—
    CARLOS: But why?
    MARQUIS: In case

Of all eventualities. Who can
Be safe from rash surprise? No one would seek
Them in my keeping. Give.

  CARLOS (*disquieted*): But this is odd!
Why this all of a sudden—

  MARQUIS: Be quite calm.
I will have intimated nothing thus,
Not anything. It is but cautiousness
Before the danger. Thus I have not meant,
Thus truly not, that thou shouldst be afeard.

  CARLOS (*gives him the portfolio*):
Hold it in trust.

  MARQUIS: I shall.

  CARLOS (*looks at him meaningfully*): O Roderick!
I gave thee much.

  MARQUIS: Not ever more so much,
As I from thee already have—The rest
We'll speak of there, and fare thee well — farewell!
(*He motions to leave.*)

  CARLOS (*fights dubiously with himself—finally he calls him back*)
Give me the letters back again! There's one
From her among them, which she wrote that time,
When I lay deathly ill, there in Alcala.
And at all times, I've held it near my heart.
'Twere hard, to separate me from it now.
Leave me that letter, — only that — the rest
Take all.
(*He takes it out and gives him back the portfolio.*)

  MARQUIS: Unwillingly, I do it Carl.
That letter was the one I sought.

  CARLOS: Farewell!
(*He goes slowly and silently away, he pauses for a moment at the door,
turns around and takes him the letter.*)
Thou hast it now.
(*His hand trembles. Tears well in his eyes, he throws his arms around
the Marquis's neck and buries his head in his breast.*)
    My father were not able?
Not so, my Roderick? *That* can he not? (*He leaves hurriedly*)

  SCENE VI—(MARQUIS *looks after him, astounded.*)

  MARQUIS: 'Twere possible? Were it? Thus had I still
Not known him? Not completely? In his heart
This wrinkle really had eluded me?

Mistrustful of his very friend! O no!
'Tis calumny!—What hath he done to me,
That I accuse him thus o'th' weakest weakness?
What I accuse him of, am I myself—
Surprise—that may be it, that I'd believe.
When had he from his dearest friend expected
This curious reserve?—As well distress!
I cannot save thee from it, Carl, and I
Must longer still keep thy good soul in torment.
The King did trust in the receptacle, to which
He hath deliver'd his most sacred secret,
And trust doth call for gratitude. What were
Mere idle chatter, if my silence brings
To thee no harm? Perhaps doth spare thee? Why
Point out to th' sleeping one the thunder cloud,
Which hangs above his crown? It is enough,
That I do guide it quietly past thee
And, if thou wak'st, the sky's more luminous. (*He exits.*)

SCENE VII—*The King's Cabinet.* (*The* KING *in his chair—near*
him the INFANTA CLARA EUGENIA)

KING (*after a deep silence*):
No! After all she is my daughter—How
Can nature ever lie with such a truth?
This eye of blue indeed is mine! Do I
Not further find myself in every line?
The infant of my love, indeed, thou art. I press
Thee to my heart—thou art my blood.
(*He is startl'd and pauses.*)   My blood!
What worse can I now fear? My very features,
Are they not also *his*?
(*He hath taken the medallion in his hand and looks alternately at the*
picture and to a mirror opposite—finally he throws it on the ground,
gets up quickly and pushes the INFANTA *away*
from himself.)   Away! Away!
In this abyss I perish now.

SCENE VIII—COUNT LERMA. *The* KING.

LERMA: The Queen
Her Majesty is in the antechamber
Just now appear'd.
KING: Just now?

LERMA: And doth request
A gracious audience—
    KING: But now? Just now?
At this most unaccustom'd hour?—No!
I can not hear her now—not now—
    LERMA: But here
Her Majesty herself doth come—(*He leaves.*)

SCENE IX—*The* KING. *The* QUEEN *enters. The* INFANTA. (*The latter runs up to her and clings to her. She kneels down before the* KING, *who stands there, silent and confounded.*)

    QUEEN: My Lord
And husband—here I must—I am constrain'd,
To seek for justice here before your throne.
    KING: For justice?—
    QUEEN: Here within this court I see
I am not held in high enough esteem.
My casket's broken open—
    KING: What?
    QUEEN: And things
Of greatest value to me disappear'd—
    KING: Of greatest value to you—
    QUEEN: In the sense,
The impudence of an unknowing one
Were able to—
    KING: The impudence—the sense—
Yet —rise up now.
    QUEEN: Not sooner, my dear husband,
Than you have bound yourself in solemn promise,
By virtue of your royal arms to give
The culprit o'er to me to make amends,
If not, then to remove me from a court,
Which hides the thief from me—
    KING: Arise I say—
In such position—Rise I say—
    QUEEN (*She rises.*):   That he
Must be a man of rank, I know—for in
The casket pearls and diamonds worth far more
Than millions lay, and he did satisfy
Himself with letters—
    KING: Which, however, I—
    QUEEN: Quite right, my husband. Letters were therein,
And a medallion from th' Infante—

KING: From—
QUEEN: From the Infante, your own son.
KING: To you?
QUEEN: To me.
KING: From the Infante? This you tell
To *me*?
QUEEN: Why should I not tell you, my husband?
KING: With such audacity?
QUEEN: Why your surprise?
I think, you must remember those same letters,
Which with allowance of both princely crowns,
Don Carlos wrote to me in Saint Germain.
Now if the portrait, too, therein enclos'd,
Could taste the freedom which the letters had,
Or whether 'twas rash hope that gave him leave
To take, unauthoriz'd, this daring step—
'Tis something I'll not venture to decide.
Yet if it was imprudence, then 'twas most
Excusable—for this I'll be his surety.
At that time he could not surmise, that it
Were for his very mother—
(*Sees the* KING *is mov'd*)
                              What is this?
What is the matter?
     INFANTA (*who hath found the medallion on the floor and hath
play'd with it, brings it to the* QUEEN):
                         Ah! My mother, look!
A lovely portrait—
     QUEEN: What, my—
(*She recognizes the medallion and stands in speechless paralysis. They
both look at each other with unswerving eyes. After a long silence.*)
                              Truly, Sire!
This means, you use to test your spouse's heart,
Methinks it is quite royal and right noble.—
Yet one more question would I dare to pose.
     KING: To ask is my prerogative.
     QUEEN: At least
Through my mistrust no innocent should suffer.—
If then this act of thievery had been
At your command—
     KING: Yes, 'twas.
     QUEEN: Then I have none
To charge and none to further pity—none
But *you*, for whom *your* wife hath not become

An object worthy of such means as these.

KING: I know *this* kind of talk.—And, yet, Madame,
It should not dupe me for a second time,
As in Aranjuez it dup'd me once.
The Queen, so pure angelical, who then
With dignity herself defended—now
I know her better.

QUEEN: What is this?

KING: Now brief,
And candidly, Madame!—Say, is it true,
Is't true, that you have spoke with no one there?
With no one? Is it really true?

QUEEN: I've spoke
With the Infante. Yes.

KING: Yes?—Now, so is
It clear as day. 'Tis manifest. So bold!
So little doth mine honor hold respect!

QUEEN: What, honor, Sire? If honor was offended,
Then I do fear, one greater is as stake,
Than that Castilian dowry you brought me.

KING: Why did you disavow me?

QUEEN: Sire, because
It hath not been my custom, in the sight
Of courtiers, to have myself be tried
As a delinquent. Truth I'll ne'er deny,
If in the voice of charity and honor
It should be sought.—And was that then the tone,
In which Your Majesty did speak to me
There, in Aranjuez? And is the court
To be compris'd of all grandees assembl'd,
Before which Queens are held up to account
For every private act? I granted to
The Prince the private colloquy, which he
Sought urgently. I did this, my dear husband,
Because I so desir'd—because I do
Not want that custom be my judge o'er things,
That I do hold as faultless—and from you
I did conceal it, for I did not want
To quarrel with Your Majesty about
This liberty before my servants' eyes.

KING: You speak with boldness, Madame, so—

QUEEN: And I
Will add thereto, it is because th' Infante
Hath hardly grounds for joy i'th' equity

Within his father's heart, which he deserves.
    KING: Which he deserves?
    QUEEN: Then why should it be hid,
My Sire?—I love him and do value him,
The dearest of my family, one who
One time was deem'd so worthy, as to bear
A name, more to my liking.—I have not
Yet learn'd to understand, why he should be
Therefore more strange to me than any other,
Because he formerly, more than another
Was dear to me. The maxim of your state,
When it doth tie a knot, which it finds good,
So should it harder be to loosen it.
I will not hate, him whom I should—and since
Howe'er, I am compell'd at last to speak—
I want it not—I will no longer deem
My choice as bound—
    KING: Elizabeth! 'Tis true,
You've seen me in my weaker hours. It is
This memory makes you so bold! You trust
In an omnipotence, which oft enough
You us'd to test my firmness—All the more
Must you now fear! What led me to be weak,
Can now conduct me all the way to madness.
    QUEEN: What have I done, then?
    KING (*takes her hand*):   If indeed 'tis so,
Yet 'tis—and is it not already so?—
If the full, heap'd up measure of your guilt
By only one breath's weight doth make increase—
If I indeed am he, the dupe—
(*He releases her hand*)   I can
Yet triumph over this last weakness too.
I can and will—Then woe to me and you,
Elizabeth!
    QUEEN: What is it I have done?
    KING: For aught I care, then let blood flow—
    QUEEN: What, is
It come to this—O God!
    KING: No longer do
I know myself—I honor no tradition,
Nor any voice of nature, and not one
Of any treaties binding nations—
    QUEEN: O,
How much I pity you, Your Majesty—

KING (*beside himself*): You pity me! A paramour's compassion—

INFANTA (*clings frighten'd to her mother*):

The King doth rage, my lovely mother weeps.

KING (*grabs the child roughly from her mother*).

QUEEN (*with gentleness and dignity, but in a trembling voice*):

This child I must protect from cruelty.

Come with me, my dear daughter.

(*She takes her in her arm.*)   If the King

No longer will acknowledge thee, then I

Will seek beyond the Pyrenees for surety,

To have our interests look'd after. (*She wants to leave.*)

KING (*startl'd*):   Queen?

QUEEN: I can no more—it is too much—

(*She tries to reach the door and falls with the child to the floor at the threshold.*)

KING (*running toward her in dismay*):

God! What is this?—

INFANTA (*screaming with terror*): Alas! My mother bleeds!

(*She rushes out.*)

KING (*anxiously trying to revive her*):

O, horrible occurrence! Blood! Deserve

I then so harsh a punishment? Arise!

Come to your senses! Stand up now! They come!

They will surprise us here—Arise! Shall my

Whole court feast eyes on such a spectacle?

Must I implore you to arise?

(*She rises to her feet, supported by the King.*)

SCENE X—*The same.* ALBA, DOMINGO *enter, shock'd.* LADIES *follow.*

KING: The Queen

Be brought into her rooms. She is not well.

(*The* QUEEN *leaves, accompanied by the ladies.* ALBA *and* DOMINGO *draw nearer.*)

ALBA: The Queen in tears, and blood upon her face—

KING: The devils, who have led me to this deed,

Do rest astonish'd.

ALBA, DOMINGO: We?

KING: Who said enough

To me, to bring me to the point of madness;

But to convince me, nothing.

ALBA: We did give,

What we did have—

KING: Let hell then thank you for it.
I have committed something I regret. Was that
The voice of guilty conscience that did speak?
    MARQUIS OF POSA (*still offstage*):
I wish to see the Monarch?

    SCENE XI—MARQUIS OF POSA. *The same.*

    KING (*jumping up vividly at this voice and moving a few steps
toward the* MARQUIS):
                          Ah! That's he!
I bid you welcome, Marquis—Your good office, Duke,
Is needed here no longer. Leave us.
(ALBA *and* DOMINGO *look at each other in dumb amazement and leave.*)

    SCENE XII—*The* KING *and the* MARQUIS OF POSA.

    MARQUIS: Sire!
To that old man, who march'd for you toward death
In twenty battles, must it be quite hard
To see himself so sent away!
    KING: It fits
You *so* to think, and *so* for *me* to do.
What you've become for me in these few hours,
Was *he* within a generation not.
I will not deal in secret with my satisfaction;
The clear impression of my kingly favor
Should shine both bright and wide upon your brow.
I want to see him envied, whom I chose
To be my friend.
    MARQUIS: And then, too, if alone
The cloak of darkness were to give him pow'r,
To be thus worthy of the name?
    KING: What do
You bring to me?
    MARQUIS: As I travers'd the hall,
I heard of certain rumors horrible,
Which I dare not believe—A sharp exchange
Of words—then, blood— and then, the Queen—
    KING: Come you from there?
    MARQUIS: It should astonish me,
If the report had not been wrong, and if
Meanwhile, perhaps, had something happen'd to
Your Majesty.—Discoveries of great

Importance I have made, which fully change
The sense of the affair.

    KING: And?

    MARQUIS: I did find
The chance, to take the Prince's portefeuille,
Which in it did contain some papers here,
And, 'tis my hope, they may throw light—

(*He gives* CARLOS' *portfolio to the* KING.)

    KING (*going through the papers eagerly*): A note
Writ by the Emp'ror, by my father—What?
I don't recall that I have heard of it?

(*He reads it through, puts it aside, and hurries to the other papers.*)
Designs of fortresses—and here some thoughts
Writ down from Tacitus—And what then have
We here?—It is a hand that I should know!
It is the writing of a dame.

(*He reads carefully, now loudly, now softly.*)

                        "This key—
The rearmost room in the pavilion of
The Queen"—Aha! And what is this?—"Here love
May candidly—a hearing—fair reward".—
The treachery of Satan! Now I know
'Tis hers. It is her hand!

    MARQUIS: Is it the hand
Of her, the Queen's? Impossible—

    KING: The Princess
Of Eboli—

    MARQUIS: So were it true, the word
I heard from Henarez's page, he who
Bore us the letter and the key.

    KING (*taking the* MARQUIS' *hand, passionately mov'd*):

                              Marquis!
I see myself in horrifying hands!
This woman—I must now confess—Marquis,
This woman broke into the Queen's own casket,
From her the soonest warning came—Who knows,
How much thereof the monk may know—
I know a youngster's prank hath me deceiv'd.

    MARQUIS: Then were it yet more happy.

    KING: Marquis! Marquis!
I do begin to fear, that I o'erstepp'd
The limits with my wife—

    MARQUIS: E'en if between
The Prince and Queen there may have been

Some secret understandings that have pass'd,
For sure they were of far—far other content
Than that of which they're charg'd. I have sure news,
The Prince's wish, to journey on to Flanders,
'Twas given birth from out the Queen's own head.
 KING: I thought it all the time.
 MARQUIS: The Queen's ambitious—
Dare I say more?—With sensitivity
And in her own proud hope she sees herself
Deceiv'd, excluded from her share o'th' throne.
The Prince, in his rash youth, did offer up
Himself to her far-sighted plan—her heart—
I am in doubt, that she can love.
 KING: Before
Her diplomatic plans I tremble not.
 MARQUIS: If she is lov'd?—or if we have to fear
From the Infante nothing worse? It seems
To me this question's worth investigation.
Much stronger vigilance, I think, is needed—
 KING: You are responsible to me for him.—
 MARQUIS (*after brief reflection*):
Yet if Your Majesty doth deem me able,
To fill this post, so must I beg, it *wholly*
And limitless deliver'd to my hands.
 KING: It shall occur.
 MARQUIS: And least of all I want,
To be disturb'd by not one single aide,
Though be his name renown'd, in undertakings
I could find necessary.
 KING: Not by one.
I promise you. You were my guardian angel.
How thankful am I to you, for that you
Have made me debtor for this hint!
(*To* LERMA, *who enter'd during the last exchange of words*)
            How did
You leave the Queen?
 LERMA: Exhausted from her swoon.
(*He looks at the* MARQUIS *ambiguously and leaves.*)
 MARQUIS (*after a pause, to the* KING)
One note of caution more it seems is needed.
The Prince, I am afeard, can still be warned.
He hath full many goodly friends.—Perhaps
Connexions with the rebels there in Ghent.
And fear may lead him to some desperate

Decisions—thus do I advise you, now
To take precautions, so that this event
Is met with speedy means.
     KING: You are quite right.
But how—
     MARQUIS: A secret warrant for arrest,
The which Your Majesty to me consign'd,
That I, at danger's notice, might avail—
And—
(*as the* KING *seems to be pensive*)
        It remains a secret of the state
Until—
     KING (*going to his writing desk and writing the arrest order*):
        The Kingdom is at stake—All means
Extraordinary doth the danger want—
Here 'tis, Marquis.—I need not recommend
Your care.
     MARQUIS (*He receives the mandate.*):
        'Tis for th' extremest case, my King.
     KING (*puts a hand on his shoulder*):
Now go, my dear Marquis.—Becalm my heart
And to my nights bring back again sweet sleep.
(*Both exit to different sides.*)

     SCENE XIII—*Gallery.* CARLOS *enters in great anxiety.* COUNT
LERMA *encounters him.*

     CARLOS: 'Tis you I seek.
     LERMA: And I seek you.
     CARLOS: Is't true?
By God in Heaven, is it true?
     LERMA: What then?
     CARLOS: That he his dagger 'gainst her drew? that she
Was taken bleeding from his chamber forth?
Now, by all saints! I beg you, answer me!
What am I to believe? Was't true?
     LERMA: She fell
Into a swoon and graz'd herself i'th' fall.
'Twas nothing else.
     CARLOS: There was no danger else.
Naught else? Upon your honor, Count?
     LERMA: Not for
The Queen—though all the more for you.
     CARLOS: But for

My mother, none! O now, let God be thank'd!
A terrible report did reach my ear,
The King doth rave against both child and mother,
And some things very secret be disclos'd.

LERMA: This last may well be true.—

CARLOS: Be true! And how?

LERMA: My Prince, today I gave to you *a* warning,
Which you have held in scorn. The second one
Use better!

CARLOS: What?

LERMA: If I am not mistaken,
I saw, some days ago, my Prince, a portefeuille,
Of sky-blue velvet, interwove with gold,
Held in your hand—

CARLOS (*somewhat startl'd*): I own one such. Yes—Well?—

LERMA: And on the cover, I believe, it hath
A silhouette, all trimm'd with pearls—

CARLOS: Quite right.

LERMA: As I quite unexpectedly did step
Within the cab'net of the King, I thought
I saw the same held fast within his hand,
And near him, standing, the Marquis of Posa—

CARLOS (*after a short, numb'd silence, impetuously*):
This is not true.

LERMA (*sensitively*): Then sure I am a traitor.

CARLOS (*looking at him at length*):
Yes, that you are.

LERMA: Ah! I forgive it you.

CARLOS (*moves up and down in terrible agitation
and in the end stands before him*)
What harm hath he done thee? What harm to thee
Would come from bonds full innocent, which thou
With hellish industry do haste with zeal
To rend asunder?

LERMA: Prince, I do respect
The pain, which maketh you unjust.

CARLOS: O, God!
God!—God! Protect me from suspicion!

LERMA: I
Do well remember what the King's words were:
How many thanks, he said, as I approach'd,
How grateful am I to you for this news!

CARLOS: Oh, peace! oh, peace!

LERMA: The Duke of Alba must

Have fallen—and that from Prince Ruy Gomez
The great seal hath been taken and bestow'd
Upon the Marquis—

    CARLOS (*lost in deepest meditation*): And from *me* he hid it!
Why hid he it from *me*?

    LERMA: The whole court doth
Gape at him as almighty minister,
Or as a fav'rite without bounds—

    CARLOS: He lov'd
Me, lov'd me much. I was as dear to him
As was his very soul. Oh, that I know—
A thousand tests have proven that to me.
Should not then millions, not his fatherland,
Be dearer to him far more than just *one*?
His bosom was too spacious for *one* friend,
And Carlos' luck too meager for his love.
He made me victim of his virtue. So
Can I upbraid him for it?—Yes, 'tis certain!
Now is it certain. I have lost him now.
(*He moves sidewards and covers his face.*)

    LERMA (*after some silence*):
My exc'llent Prince, what can I do for you?

    CARLOS (*without looking at him*):
Go to the King and there betray me too.
I have no more that I can give away.

    LERMA: Will you just wait to see what may ensue?

    CARLOS (*leans on a bannister and stares ahead of himself*):
I've lost him. Oh! Now I am quite forlorn!

    LERMA (*approaches him with sympathizing emotion*):
Do you not want to think of your salvation?

    CARLOS: Of my salvation?—My good man!

    LERMA: And yet,
Yet is there no one more who makes you tremble?

    CARLOS (*rising*): My God! You do admonish me!—My mother!
The letter, which I gave him back! at first
I wanted not to yield, and yet I did!
(*He moves up and down, violently wringing his hands.*)
Wherefore hath *she* deserv'd as much from him?
He should have spar'd her. Lerma, shouldn't he?
(*Rashly decided*)
I must to her—I have to give her warning,
I must prepare her—Lerma, dearest Lerma—
Whom shall I send? Have I then no one more?
Let God be prais'd! I've *one* friend still—and here

It cannot worsen further. (*Leaves rapidly*)

    LERMA (*follows him and calls after him*) Prince! Where to? (*Exits*)

SCENE XIV—*One of the* QUEEN'S *Rooms. The* QUEEN. ALBA.
DOMINGO.

    ALBA: If we may have the privilege, great Queen—

    QUEEN: In what way can I serve you.

    DOMINGO: Most sincere
Concern for your most royal Majesty's
Exalted personage permits us not,
To hold our tongues in idleness ere an
Event, which threatens your security.

    ALBA: We hasten, with our timely warning to
Defeat a plot, which is against you play'd—

    DOMINGO: And our warm zeal—and our best service
To lay at the feet of Your Majesty.

    QUEEN (*looks at them in wonder*):
Most Rev'rend Lord, and you, my noble Duke,
You verily engender my surprise.
For such devotion had I never dream't
Would come from Duke of Alba and Domingo.
I know, how I must value you.—You speak
About a plot, that is to threaten me.
May I discover, who——

    ALBA: We beg of you,
Be on your guard against a Marquis Posa,
Who for his Majesty the King, doth make
Some secret business.

    QUEEN: It pleaseth me
To hear, the King hath made so good a choice.
The praises to the Marquis as a man,
Both great and good, have long since reach'd my ear.
The highest favor never was so justly
Bestow'd.—

    DOMINGO: Bestow'd so justly? We know better.

    ALBA: Since long no secret hath it been, whereto
This man hath let himself be us'd.

    QUEEN: How so?
What were that then? You raise my expectations.

    DOMINGO:—Is it so long ago, Your Majesty
Last check'd into your casket?

    QUEEN: What?

    DOMINGO: And found

You nothing precious missing there within?

    QUEEN: How so? And why? What I am missing, my
Whole court doth know.—But Marquis Posa? How
Comes Marquis Posa in connection to this?

    ALBA: Quite near, your Majesty—in that the Prince
Doth also miss some papers of importance,
Which have indeed been seen this very morning
Within the King's hands—when the Chevalier
Had had a secret audience.

    QUEEN (*after some reflection*): How strange,
By God! Extremely singular! I find
An enemy, of whom I never dream't,
And then in turn two friends, I never can
Recall I had possess'd.—But verily
(*as she fixes a penetrating glance on both of them*)
I must confess, that I did run the risk,
Of blaming you for that misservice, that
My Lord prepar'd for me.

    ALBA: Of blaming us?

    QUEEN: Yes, you.

    DOMINGO: O Duke of Alba! Us!

    QUEEN (*her eyes still firmly directed at them*): How sweet
It is to me, to be aware so soon
Of my own hastiness—Besides I had
Decided, to implore His Majesty
This very day, to put before me my
Accuser. All the better! I can call
Upon Duke Alba's evidence.

    ALBA: On me?
But do you mean that seriously?

    QUEEN: Why not?

    DOMINGO: In order to defeat all services,
That we in secret have for you—

    QUEEN: In secret?
(*With pride and seriousness*)
Yet would I really like to know, Duke Alba,
What should your Monarch's wife have to arrange
With you, or likewise, priest, with you, the which
Her husband may not know.——Now am I guilty
Or am I innocent?

    DOMINGO: Why, what a question!

    ALBA: But, if the King were not so just? If now,
At least, he were not so?

    QUEEN: Why, in that case,

I must await, until he's thus become—
He's blest, who gains, when he it hath become!
(*She curtsies to them and exits; they leave through
another side.*)

SCENE XV—PRINCESS EBOLI'S *Room.* PRINCESS OF EBOLI.
CARLOS.

EBOLI: So is it true, the extraordinary news,
That doth already fill the court?
CARLOS (*enters*):   Fear not,
Princess! I'll be as gentle as a child.
EBOLI: Prince—this surprise.
CARLOS: Are you offended still?
Still?
EBOLI: Prince!
CARLOS (*more pressingly*): Are you offended still? I beg
You, tell me if you are.
EBOLI: What should that be?
You seem to have forgotten, Prince—what seek
You from me?
CARLOS (*taking her hand impetuously*):
              Canst thou hate forever, Maid?
Will injur'd love ne'er pardon make?
EBOLI (*tries to free herself*):   Whereon
Will you remind me, Prince?
CARLOS: On thy great goodness
And my ingratitude—Ah! I do know
It well! Severely I've offended thee,
O Maid, have rent thy gentle heart, have press'd
Teardrops from these angelic eyes—alas!
And I am not here now, to seek repentance.
EBOLI: Prince, leave me—I—
CARLOS: I have come here, because
Thou art a gentle Maid, because I count
Upon thy beautiful and goodly soul.
See, Maiden, see, I've no more friends upon
This world but thee alone. Once wert thou good
To me—Thou wilt not ever hate and wilt
Not be implacable.
EBOLI (*turns her face away*): Oh peace! No more,
For Heaven's sake, O Prince—
CARLOS: Thou shalt allow

Me to remind thee of the golden times—
Allow me to remind thee of thy love,
That love of thine, o Maid, against which I
Did thus unworthily offend. Allow
Me to make worthy now, what I'd been once
To thee, what thy heart's dreams have render'd me—
But once—but just—just *once* again place me,
As I at that time was, before thy soul
And offer to this shadow, what thou me,
Canst never more forever offer me!

    EBOLI: O Carl! How cruelly do you play with me!

    CARLOS: Be greater than thy sex! Forgive offense,
Do, what 'fore thee no woman ever did—
And what no woman after thee will do.
I ask of thee a thing unheard—Let me
Speak two words with my mother! (*He throws himself down before her.*)

    SCENE XVI—*The same.* MARQUIS OF POSA *rushes, behind him two officers of the royal bodyguard.*

    MARQUIS (*breathless, beside himself, stepping between them*): What hath he
Confess'd? Believe him not.

    CARLOS (*still on his knees, with rais'd voice*):

                          By all that you

Do hold as holy—

    MARQUIS (*interrupting him vehemently*)

                               He doth rave—lend not

The raving man your ear.

    CARLOS (*louder, more pressingly*): It is a question
Of life and death. Conduct me to her!

    MARQUIS (*wrenches the* PRINCESS *violently away from him*): I
Will murder you, if you do hear him.
(*To one of the officers*)   Count
Of Cordua! In the name of the Monarch.
(*He shows the arrest warrant.*)
The Prince is now your prisoner.
(CARLOS *stands rigid, as if struck by lightning. The* PRINCESS *cries out in terror and tries to flee, the officers stand astonish'd. A long, deep pause. The* MARQUIS *is seen trembling violently and is at pains to maintain his composure. To the* PRINCE)

                               I beg

Of you your rapier.—Princess Eboli

Stay here; and
(*To the* OFFICER) *you're* responsible to see,
His Highness speaks to no one—none at all—
Not to yourself, on peril of your head!
(*He says something in a low voice to the* OFFICER, *then turns
to the other.*)
I cast myself unto the Monarch's feet,
To render him account—
(*To* CARLOS)   And to you too—
Await for me, my Prince—within the hour.
(CARLOS *allows himself to be led away without giving signs of con-
sciousness—Only as he passes does he let a dying glance fall upon the*
MARQUIS, *who covers his face. The* PRINCESS *tries once more to flee;
the* MARQUIS *leads her back by the arm.*

SCENE XVII—PRINCESS OF EBOLI. MARQUIS OF POSA.

EBOLI: I beg you for the sake of Heaven, let
Me leave this place.
    MARQUIS (*leads her fully forward, with dreadful earnestness*):
                        What hath he said to thee,
Unhappy creature?
    EBOLI: Nothing—Leave me—Nothing—
    MARQUIS (*holds her back by force. More earnestly*):
How much hast thou discover'd? Here there is
No more escape. Thou wilt not tell it to
Another soul upon this world.
    EBOLI (*looks at him terrified in the face*): Great God!
What do you mean by this? You surely do
Not want to murder me?
    MARQUIS (*draws a dagger*): In fact, I'm quite
Dispos'd to it. Now make it brief!
    EBOLI: Me? Me?
O thou, eternal mercy! What have I
Then done?
    MARQUIS (*looking heavenward, the dagger held to her breast*):
            There is still time. The poison still
Hath not yet overflow'd these lips. Now I
Do dash to bits the vessel, and all rests,
Just as it's been.—The destiny of Spain
And of one woman's life!—
(*He stands irresolutely still in this position.*)
    EBOLI (*hath sunk down beside him and looks at him
firmly in the face*):   Now? Why delay?

I beg no mercy of you—No! I have
Deserv'd to die, and that I will.
    MARQUIS (*lets his hand fall slowly. After brief reflection*):
It were
As cowardly, as barbarous. No, no!
May God be prais'd!—There's yet another means!
(*He lets the dagger fall and hurries out. The* PRINCESS *rushes out another door.*)

    SCENE XVIII—*A Room of the* QUEEN'S. *The* QUEEN *to* COUNTESS
FUENTES

    QUEEN: What is this clamor in the palace? Each
New turmoil, Countess, frightens me today.
O, do look into it and tell me then,
What it doth mean!
(*The* COUNTESS FUENTES *leaves, and the* PRINCESS OF EBOLI *enters agitated.*)

    SCENE XIX—QUEEN. PRINCESS OF EBOLI.

    EBOLI (*breathless, pale and alter'd, sunk down before the* QUEEN):
My Queen! Help, help! He's been
Imprison'd.
    QUEEN: Who?
    EBOLI: The Marquis Posa took
Him prisoner, on orders of the King.
    QUEEN: But whom? Whom did he take?
    EBOLI: The Prince.
    QUEEN: Thou ravest?
    EBOLI: Just now they're leading him away.
    QUEEN: And who
Arrested him?
    EBOLI: The Marquis Posa.
    QUEEN: Now!
May God be prais'd, it was the Marquis, who
Did take him prisoner!
    EBOLI: That you do say
So calmly, Queen? so coldly? O my God!
You do not think—you do not know—
    QUEEN: Why he
Was taken captive?—Due to some misstep,
I do suspect, which was quite nat'ral to
The youth's impetuous character.

EBOLI: No, no!
I know the cause much better—No—O Queen!
Derang'd and most satanic act! For him
Salvation is no more! He dies!
    QUEEN: He dies?
    EBOLI: And here, his murderess am I!
    QUEEN: He dies!
Thou lunatic, dost thou reflect?
    EBOLI: And why—
Why he doth die!—O if I could have known,
That it would come to this!
    QUEEN (*takes her gently by the hand*): O Princess! You
Have not yet your composure—Gather up
Your spirits first, that you may then more calmly,
Relate, and not in gruesome images,
Which send a shiver through my innermost.
What do you know? What is it that occurr'd?
    EBOLI: O not this condescension as from heaven,
Not this your goodness, Queen! Like flames in hell
They smite my conscience with their burning fire.
I am not worthy, to direct my gaze,
Defil'd, upon your glory high above.
Crush underfoot this miserable wretch,
Whom shame, remorse and self-contempt have strewn
Contrite, here cringing at your feet.
    QUEEN: Poor wretch!
What have you to confess to me?
    EBOLI: O Angel
Of light! Great Saint. Still now you do not know,
Nor have the faintest notion of the devil,
On whom so full of love you've smil'd—Today
You'll learn to know her. I—I was the thief,
Who robb'd you—
    QUEEN: You?
    EBOLI: And handed over all
Those letters to the Monarch.
    QUEEN: You?
    EBOLI: Who had
The impudence, to charge against you—
    QUEEN: You,
You could—
    EBOLI: Vendetta—love—insanity—
I hated you and I lov'd the Infante—
    QUEEN: Because you lov'd him—?

EBOLI: 'Cause I told it him
And found no love return'd.

QUEEN (*after a pause*):   O everything
Is now unriddl'd for me!—Now arise!
You lov'd him—I've already pardon'd you.
It hath already been forgotten.—Rise.
(*She extends her the arm.*)

EBOLI: No! No! One horrible confession still
Remains. Not sooner, my great Queen—

QUEEN (*attentive*):   What more
Am I constrain'd to hear? Speak you—

EBOLI: The King—
Seduction—O, you look away—I read
Rejection in your countenance—That crime,
Which I accus'd you of—'tis I that did
Commit it.
(*She presses her burning face to the floor. The* QUEEN *leaves. Great
pause. A few minutes later, the* DUCHESS OF OLIVAREZ *comes out of
the cabinet, into which the* QUEEN *had gone, and finds the* PRINCESS
*lying in the same position. She approaches her silently. On hearing
her, the latter sits up and rises like a madwoman, when she realizes
the* QUEEN *is no longer there.*)

SCENE XX—PRINCESS OF EBOLI. DUCHESS OF OLIVAREZ.

EBOLI: God! She hath abandon'd me!
Now all is lost.

OLIVAREZ (*approaches nearer to her*):
                                   Princess of Eboli—

EBOLI: I know, the reason, Duchess, why you're come.
The Queen hath sent you in here, to announce
My sentence to me.—Quickly, then!

OLIVAREZ: I have
The order from Her Majesty, to take
Possession of your cross and of your keys.

EBOLI (*takes a gold cross of a religious order from her bosom
and hands it to the Duchess*):
Just *once* more will it be allow'd to me,
That I may kiss the best Queen's hand?

OLIVAREZ: Within
Saint Mary's cloister 'twill be told to you,
What is o'er you decided.

EBOLI (*under a flood of tears*): Shall I see
The Queen no more?

OLIVAREZ (*embraces her with face averted*):
                    May you live happily!
(*She exits quickly. The* PRINCESS *follows her to the door of the cabinet,
which is immediately lock'd after the* DUCHESS. *She remains motionless
and in silence on her knees for a few minutes, then she gets up with
a start and rushes off hiding her face.*)

SCENE XXI—*The* QUEEN. MARQUIS OF POSA.

QUEEN: Ah, finally, Marquis. 'Tis good you're come!
MARQUIS (*pale, with ravag'd face, trembling voice and throughout
the whole scene in solemn, deep commotion*):
Your Majesty is here alone? Can none
In these adjacent chambers overhear us?
    QUEEN: No one—but why? What do you bring?
(*Meanwhile she looks at him more closely and recoils in horror.*)
                                              And how
So fully chang'd? What is it? You do make
Me tremble, Marquis—all your features seem
Disfigur'd, like a dying man's—
    MARQUIS: You know
Already, I suppose—
    QUEEN: That Carl's been jail'd,
In fact through you, they add—So really is
It true? I would believe it from no man
But only you.
    MARQUIS: Indeed 'tis true.
    QUEEN: Through you?
MARQUIS: Through me.
QUEEN (*looks at him perplex'd for a few moments*):
                    I do respect your deeds, e'en if
I comprehend their meaning not.—But for
This once forgive a woman's fears. I fear,
You play a daring game.
    MARQUIS: 'Tis one that I
Have lost.
    QUEEN: O God in Heav'n!
    MARQUIS: Be you, my Queen,
Entirely calm! For *him*, is all arrang'd.
I have already lost it for *myself*.
    QUEEN: What is it I am hearing! God!
    MARQUIS: Then who,
Who did command, that I should stake my all
Upon one doubtful toss? My all? So daring,

So fully confident should play with Heav'n?
Who is the man, who is so self-esteem'd,
To take the heavy helm of Chance in hand,
And yet not the All-knowing One to be?
O, it is fair!—Yet why must it be now
Of me? This instant is as costly, as
Is one man's life! And who doth know, if from
The judge's stingy hand the final tears
For me have not already fallen?
            QUEEN: From
The judge's hand?—What solemn tones! I do
Not understand the meaning of these words,
But they do frighten me—
            MARQUIS: He hath been sav'd!
What price he is, is all the same! Yet for
Today alone. Few moments are still his.
He should be sparing. In this very night
He must depart Madrid.
            QUEEN: This very night?
            MARQUIS: All measures are prepar'd. Within that same
Carthusian cloister, which in times long past
Had been the sanctuary of our friendship,
The news is waiting for him. Here's in bills,
What fortune's given to me in this world.
That which is lacking, *you* will add thereto.
Indeed had I still much within my heart
For Carl, still much, that he must know; and yet
I surely lack the leisure to conclude
In person everything with him.—Tonight
You speak with him, therefore I turn to you—
            QUEEN: But, for the sake of my tranquillity,
Marquis, explain yourself more clearly. Speak
Not with me in such terrifying riddles—
What is it hath occurr'd?
            MARQUIS: I have still one
Confession of the greatest weight to make;
I place it in your hands. To me was given
A joy, that only very few do know:
I lov'd a Prince's son.—My heart, to but
A sole one consecrated, did embrace
The world entire!—Within my Carlos' soul
Did I create a paradise for millions.
O, beautiful were those my dreams.—Yet it
Pleas'd Providence, to summon me away

Before my time from this my beauteous planting.
Soon will he have his Roderick no more,
The friend makes way for the beloved. Here,
Here—here—upon this holy altar, I
Do lay upon the heart of you, his Queen,
My final precious testament, so he
May find it here, when I no longer am—
(*He turns his face away, tears smother his voice.*)
   QUEEN: This is the language of a dying man.
I trust, it is but from your blood's excitement—
Or doth there lie some meaning in this speech?
   MARQUIS (*hath tried to collect himself and continues in a firm voice*):
Say to the Prince, he should recall the oath,
That we within those former schwärmerish days
Have sworn together on the parted Host.
Mine I have kept, and have been faithful to
It unto death—now it is up to him,
To keep his own—
   QUEEN: To death?
   MARQUIS: Then must he make—
O, tell you it to him! the vision true,
The daring vision of a new born state,
The godlike birth of friendship! Let him lay
The first hand on this rough unshapen'd stone.
And if he doth complete it or succumbs—
'Tis one to him! But let him lend his hand.
When centuries have flown on by, once more
Will Providence repeat a Prince's son,
Like him, upon a throne, like his, and with
The same enthusiasm will inflame
Her cherish'd newest darling. Tell you him,
That he should hold in high esteem his dreams
Of youth, if he will be a man one day,
And that he should not open up the heart
Of these most tender godly flowers to
Reputed better reason's deadly insect—
That he not stray, e'en if the voice of wisdom
Speak out from muddy depths its calumny
Against enthusiasm, heaven's daughter.
I've told him this before—
   QUEEN: How so, Marquis
And whither leads—
   MARQUIS: And tell him, that I place

The weight of mankind's fortune on his soul,
That dying I demand of him—demand!
And was thereto quite justified. It would
Have been within my power, to bring forth
A new tomorrow over all this realm.
The King had given me his heart. He call'd
Me as his son—And I command his seal,
And all his Albas are no more.
(*He pauses and looks at the* QUEEN *a few moments in silence.*)
                                        You weep—
O, I do know these tears, most beauteous soul!
'Tis joy doth make them flow. But 'tis foreby,
It is foreby. 'Twas Carl or I. The choice
Was quick and dreadful. One of us was lost,
And I will be this *one*—far better I—
Ask not to know beyond that more.
    QUEEN: Now, now
At last do I begin, to understand—
Unhappy man, what have you done?
    MARQUIS: But two
Short ev'ning hours given o'er, to save
One shining summer's day. The King I do
Renounce. What can I be to him?—In this
Parch'd earth no rose of mine can further bloom—
The destiny of Europe ripens now
In my great friend! Let him have Spain.—It bleeds
Until then under Philip's hand!—But woe,
Woe be to me and him, should I repent.
Perhaps I've chosen what is worse!—No, no!
I know my Carlos.—That would never be,
And *you*, my Queen, are surety.
(*After some silence*)
                                        I saw
It bud, this love, and saw the hapless passion
Take root within his heart—I had the might,
To fight it then. But I did not. I fed
This love, which 'twas to me not hapless then.
The world may judge in other ways. But I
Do not repent. My heart doth not accuse
Me. I saw life, where they saw only death—
Within this hopeless flame I early glimps'd
The golden beam of hope. To excellence
I wanted to conduct him, elevate
Him to the highest form of Beauty: But

Mortality denied to me an image,
And language bore no word—to *this*
I did refer him—every care of mine
Was spent to illustrate his love to him.

    QUEEN: Marquis, your friend fulfill'd you so, that you've
Forgotten me o'er him. Did you in earnest
Believe me free of ev'ry woman's frailty,
When you had made me be his angel, and
Had added virtue to his weaponry?
But you did not consider well, how much
It is our heart doth hazard, when we do
Ennoble passion with such names as these.

    MARQUIS: For every woman, save for *one* alone.
On *one* I swear my oath—Or else should you,
You be asham'd of the most noble longing,
To be creator of heroic virtue?
And what then should King Philip care, if his
Transfiguration in th' Escurial
Ignites the painter, who doth stand 'fore it,
With feelings of eternity? And doth
The sweetest harmony, that slumbers in
The lyre, belong to him, its buyer, who
With deafest ears doth guard it? He hath bought
The right, to smash the lyre to bits, but not
The art, of calling forth its silver tones
And in the bliss of song to melt away.
Sagacious men find Truth doth lie at hand,
A feeling heart finds Beauty. And the two
Belong to one another. This belief
No craven prejudice should lay to waste.
Now promise me, that you will love him always,
By human fear, by faulty heroism
Be tempted ne'er to vain renunciation,
To love him ever and unchangingly,
Will you make me this promise?—Queen—Will you
Make me this promise on my hand?

    QUEEN: My heart,
I promise you, will ever and alone
Be judge of this my love.

    MARQUIS (*draws back his hand*): Now I can die
In peace—My work is now complete.
(*He bows to the* QUEEN *and wants to go.*)

    QUEEN (*accompanies him silently with her eyes*): You go,
Marquis without yet having said to me,

When we—how soon—we'll meet again?
    MARQUIS (*comes back again, his face averted*):
                              Of course!
We'll meet again.
    QUEEN: I understood you, Posa—
I understood you very well.—Why have
You done this to me?
    MARQUIS: He or I.
    QUEEN: No! No!
You plung'd yourself into this deed, which you
Deem lofty. But deny it not! I know
You, you have long been thirsting for it—May
A thousand hearts be broken, what is it
To you, so long your pride is satisfied.
O, now—now do I learn to understand you!
You only vied for admiration.
    MARQUIS (*shaken, to himself*): No!
Thereon was I not quite expecting—
    QUEEN (*after a silence*):   Marquis!
Is no salvation possible?
    MARQUIS: None.
    QUEEN: None?
Reflect on it! None possible? Not e'en
Through me?
    MARQUIS: Not e'en through you.
    QUEEN: You only half
Know me—I do have courage.
    MARQUIS: I know that.
    QUEEN: And no salvation?
    MARQUIS: None at all.
    QUEEN (*moves away from him and covers her face*):
                       Then go!
I shall esteem no man again.
    MARQUIS (*thrown down before her in profound emotion*):
                My Queen!
—O God! yet life is beautiful.
(*He springs up and rushes out quickly. The* QUEEN *withdraws into her cabinet.*)

    SCENE XXII—*Antechamber of the* KING. DUKE OF ALBA *and* DOMINGO *walk up and down, silently and separately.* COUNT LERMA *comes out of the* KING'S *cabinet, then* DON RAIMOND OF TAXIS, *the Master of the Post.*

LERMA: Hath the Marquis still not made his appearance?

ALBA: Not yet.

(LERMA *wants to go back into the cabinet.*)

TAXIS (*enters*):   Count Lerma, please announce me now.

LERMA: The King receiveth no one—

TAXIS: Say to him,
I *must* now speak to him—The matter is
Of utmost import to His Majesty.
Make haste! It will not bear delay.

(LERMA *goes into the cabinet.*)

ALBA (*goes to the Postmaster*): Dear Taxis,
Let patience be your custom! You will not
Speak to the King—

TAXIS: No? And why not?

ALBA: You should
Have taken care, to gain permission from
The Cavalier of Posa, who doth make
Both son and father prisoners of his.

TAXIS: Of Posa? What? Indeed! He is the same,
From whose hand I receiv'd this letter—

ALBA: Letter?
What letter's that?

TAXIS: The one I was suppos'd
To send to Brussels—

ALBA (*attentively*): Brussels?

TAXIS: Which I'm just
Now bringing to the King—

ALBA: To Brussels! Have you heard
That, Chaplain? Brussels!

DOMINGO (*enters*):   This is very suspect.

TAXIS: How anxiously, and how confusedly
It was commended to me!

DOMINGO: Anxiously?
Aha!

ALBA: To whom is it address'd?

TAXIS: 'Tis to the Prince
Of Nassau and of Orange.

ALBA: Unto William?—
O Chaplain! This is treachery.

DOMINGO: What else
Then could it be?—Of course, this letter must
Be handed to the King this very instant.
What merit on your part, most worthy man,
To be so strict in service to your King!

TAXIS: Most Rev'rend Lord, I only did my duty.

ALBA: You did it well.

LERMA (*comes out of the cabinet. To the* POSTMASTER):
                         The King will speak with you.

(TAXIS *goes in.*)
And still the Marquis is not here?

DOMINGO: They're searching
In every place for him.

ALBA: How odd and strange.
The Prince a prisoner of state, the King
Himself uncertain as to why?

DOMINGO: He was
Not even here, to give account to him?

ALBA: How did the King receive it then?

LERMA: The King
Spake no word yet.

(*Noise in the cabinet*)

ALBA: What was that? Still!

TAXIS (*from the cabinet*):   Count Lerma!

(*Both go in*)

ALBA (*to* DOMINGO): What is afoot?

DOMINGO: With such a tone of fear?
Perhaps this intercepted letter?—I
Suspect no good, my Duke.

ALBA: He sends for Lerma!
Yet he must know, that you and I are in
The antechamber—

DOMINGO: Now our time's foreby.

ALBA: Am I no longer then the same, for whom
All doors once sprang wide ope? How everything
About me hath been chang'd—how strange—

DOMINGO (*hath quietly near'd the door to the cabinet and
stands before it listening*):
                         Hark!

ALBA (*after a pause*): All
Is deadly silent. You can hear them breathe.

DOMINGO: The double tapestry doth suffocate
The sound.

ALBA: Away! They come.

DOMINGO (*leaves the door*): I feel so solemn,
So fearful, just as if the moment should
Determine a great fate.

SCENE XXIII—PRINCE OF PARMA, DUKE OF FERIA, MEDINA SI-DONIA, *and still more* GRANDEES *enter. Others as in the foregoing scene.*

PARMA: Now doth the King
Receive?
ALBA: No.
PARMA: No? Who is with him?
FERIA: Marquis
Of Posa, doubtless?
ALBA: They are waiting for
Him even now.
PARMA: This very moment we
Have just arriv'd from Saragossa. All
Throughout Madrid the terror flies. Is it
Then true?
DOMINGO: Alas, it is!
FERIA: 'Tis true? He hath
Been plac'd in custody by the Maltese?
ALBA: So is't.
PARMA: But why? What hath then happen'd?
ALBA: Why?
That no one knows except His Majesty
And Marquis Posa.
PARMA: With no consultation
O' th' Cortes of his kingdom?
FERIA: Woe to him,
Who did partake in this offense of state.
ALBA: Woe be to him! I cry it too.
MEDINA SIDONIA: And I.
THE OTHER GRANDEES: So do we all.
ALBA: Who follows me into
The cabinet?—I'll throw myself down at
The Monarch's feet.
LERMA (*rushes out of the cabinet*): Duke Alba!
DOMINGO: Finally!
May God be prais'd!
(*Alba hurries in*)
LERMA (*breathless, deeply agitated*):
                          If the Maltese arrives,
Our Lord will now not be alone, and he
Will have him summon'd—
DOMINGO (*to* LERMA, *as all the others gather around him, in curious expectation*):   Count, what is occurring?

You are as pale as is a corpse.
    LERMA (*trying to rush away*): O this
Is devilish!
    PARMA and FERIA: What, then? What, then?
    MEDINA SIDONIA: What is
The Monarch doing?
    DOMINGO (*at the same time*): Devilish? What then?
    LERMA: The King hath wept.
    DOMINGO: Hath wept?
    ALL (*all at once, in an embarrass'd stupor*):
                                  The King hath wept?
(*A bell is heard in the cabinet.* COUNT LERMA *hurries in.*)
    DOMINGO (*after him, trying to hold him back*):
Count, one more word— Forgive me—He's away!
And here we stand bound up in chains of terror.

    SCENE XXIV—PRINCESS OF EBOLI. FERIA. MEDINA SIDONIA.
PARMA. DOMINGO *and other* GRANDEES.

    EBOLI (*in haste, beside herself*):
Where is the King? Where? I must speak to him.
(*To* FERIA)
You, Duke, conduct me unto him.
    FERIA: The King
Hath weighty matters to prevent him. None
Will be receiv'd. Hath he already sign'd
The terrifying sentence? He is now
Betray'd. I have the proof to bring to him,
That he's betray'd.
    DOMINGO (*gives her a meaningful nod from afar*):
                  The Princess Eboli!
    EBOLI (*walks up to him*):
You're here too? Priest? Right good! I need you now.
You shall confirm it for me.
(*She seizes his hand and tries to lead him into the cabinet.*)
    DOMINGO: I?—Are you
Beside yourself, my Princess?
    FERIA: Stay behind.
The King will not give you a hearing now.
    EBOLI: He must hear me. Truth must he hear—the truth!
And were he ten times God!
    DOMINGO: Away! Away!
You hazard everything. Remain behind.
    EBOLI: Man, tremble thou before thy idol's wrath.

For I have nothing left to hazard.
(*As she tries to go into the cabinet, rushes out*)
    DUKE ALBA (*His eyes sparkling, triumph is in his gait. He hurries over to* DOMINGO *and embraces him.*)
                                       Let
Resound in all the churches a Te Deum.
The victory is ours.
    DOMINGO: Ours?
    ALBA (*to* DOMINGO *and the rest of the* GRANDEES)
                        Now let's go
To see the Lord! More you will hear from me anon.

ACT V

A room in the royal palace, separated by a wrought iron door from a large forecourt, in which guards walk up and down.

      SCENE I—CARLOS *sitting at a table, his head plac'd forward on his arms, as if he slumber'd. In the hinterground of the room some* OFFICERS, *who are lock'd in with him.* MARQUIS OF POSA *enters, without being observ'd by him, and speaks softly with the* OFFICERS, *who immediately withdraw. He himself steps quite near to* CARLOS *and considers him silently and sadly for a few moments. Finally he makes a motion which awakes the latter from his stupor.*

    CARLOS (*arises, becomes aware of the* MARQUIS *and starts back frighten'd. Then he looks at him a while with large, staring eyes and strokes his forehead with his hand, as if he wanted to recall something*).
    MARQUIS: Carl, it is I.
    CARLOS (*gives him his hand*): Thou com'st to me e'en now?
That's truly beautiful of thee.
    MARQUIS: I did
Believe, thou could'st make use here of thy friend.
    CARLOS: Indeed? Did'st thou suppose that really? See!
I'm pleas'd—I'm pleas'd unspeakably. Alas!
I knew it well, that thou wert true to me.
    MARQUIS: I have deserv'd it too of thee.
    CARLOS: Not true?
O, we do understand us fully. Thus
I like it well. This mildness, this forebearance
Becomes great souls like thou and I. If it

Should be, that one of my demands was quite
Presumpt'ous and unjust, must thou deny
To me on that account the just one too?
Severe can virtue be, yet never gruesome,
Inhuman never—It hath cost thee much!
O yes, methinks, I know right well, how much
Thy gentle heart hath bled, when thou adorn'dst
Thy sacrifice before the altar.
  MARQUIS: Carlos!
How mean'st thou that?
  CARLOS: Thou wilt thyself fulfill,
What I should have and never could—*Thou* wilt
Bestow the golden days upon the Spaniards,
Which they have hop'd from me in vain. For me
'Tis over now—forever over. Thou
Hast recogniz'd that—O this frightful love
Hath snatch'd away beyond recall all of
The early blossoms of my spirit. I
Am dead to all thy noble hopes. The King
Is led to thee by Providence or Chance—
My secret is the price, and he is thine—
Now thou art able to become his angel.
For me there is no rescue more—perhaps
For Spain—Ah, here is nothing to condemn,
Naught, naught except my furious delusion,
Not to have realiz'd until this day,
That thou—art just as great as thou art gentle.
  MARQUIS: No! That, that I have not foreseen—have not
Foreseen, that a friend's generosity
Could be more skillfully inventive than
My worldly-clever care. My edifice
Collapses—I forgot thy heart.
  CARLOS: Indeed, had it been possible for thee,
To save *her* from this fate—behold, that I
Had thank'd thee inexpressibly. Could I
Then bear it not alone? Must she then be
The second sacrifice?—Enough of that!
I will not burden thee with a reproach.
What is the Queen to *thee*? And lovest *thou*
The Queen? Should thy strict virtue have to ask
The narrow-minded worries of my love?
Forgive me—I have been unjust.
  MARQUIS: Thou art.
Yet—not because of this reproach. If I

Deserve this one, then I deserve them all—
And then I would not stand before thee *thus*.
(*He takes out his portefeuille.*)
Here are some of the letters back again,
Which thou hast given me for keeping. Take
Them.

    CARLOS (*looks with amazement first at the letters, then at the* MARQUIS):
              What?
    MARQUIS: I give them to thee once again,
Because they may be safer now within
Thy custody than mine.
    CARLOS: How can that be?
The King hath never read them then? receiv'd
Them never once before his eyes?
    MARQUIS: *These* letters?
    CARLOS: Thou did'st not show him all of them?
    MARQUIS: Who told
Thee, that I show'd him *one*?
    CARLOS (*extremely astonish'd*): Is't possible?
Count Lerma.
    MARQUIS: *He* told thee?—Now everything,
Yes, everything becomes quite clear! Who could
Have e'er foreseen?—So was it Lerma?—No,
That man hath never learnt to lie. Quite right,
The other letters lie before the King.
    CARLOS (*looks at him for a long time with speechless astonishment*):
But why am I now here?
    MARQUIS: As a precaution,
If thou should'st for a second time attempt
Perhaps, to choose an Eboli to be
Thy confidante—
    CARLOS (*as if awaken'd from a dream*):
              Ha! Now finally!
I see now—everything grows light—
    MARQUIS (*goes to the door*):   Who comes?

SCENE II—DUKE ALBA. *The former.*

    ALBA (*approaches the* PRINCE *respectfully, turning his back to the* MARQUIS *throughout the entire scene*):
Prince, you are free. The King dispatch'd me, to
Announce it to you.
(*Carlos looks surpris'd at the* MARQUIS. *All are silent.*)

                    At the same time, Prince,
I deem myself quite fortunate, that I
May be the first, who hath the honor—
        CARLOS (*observes both with extreme astonishment. After a pause
to the* DUKE):
                                        I
Am made a prisoner and then set free,
Without my being made aware, wherefore
I have been both.
        ALBA: It was by error, Prince,
As much I know, to which someone—a base
Deceiver hath the Monarch carried hence.
        CARLOS: However is it order'd by the King,
That I do find myself here now?
        ALBA: Yes, through
An error of His Majesty.
        CARLOS: That makes
Me truly sorry—Surely if the King
Doth err, it doth befit the King, in his
Own person to correct the wrong again.
(*He seeks the* MARQUIS' *eyes and observes a proud look of disparagement
towards the* DUKE.)
They call me here Don Philip's son. The eyes
Of calumny and curiosity
Do rest on me. And what His Majesty
From duty's done, I would not seem to thank
Your favor. Otherwise I am prepar'd,
To place myself before the Cortes' court.
I won't receive my sword from such a hand.
        ALBA: The King will never hesitate, Your Highness,
To grant this just demand to you, if you
Will only grant permission, to allow
Me to accomp'ny you to him.
        CARLOS: I shall
Remain here, 'til the King or his Madrid
Conducts me from this dungeon. Take
This answer to him.
(ALBA *withdraws. One sees him still for a time tarry in the forecourt
and issue orders.*)

SCENE III—CARLOS *and* MARQUIS OF POSA.

        CARLOS (*after the* DUKE *hath gone, full of expectation and aston-
ishment to the* MARQUIS): What is that? Explain

It to me. Art thou then not Minister?
    MARQUIS: I have been one, as thou can'st see.
(*walking up to him with great emotion*)   O Carl,
It hath work'd out. It hath. It hath succeeded.
Now is it done. Prais'd be Almighty God,
Who hath let it succeed.
    CARLOS: Succeed? How's that?
I do not comprehend thy words.
    MARQUIS (*seizes his hand*):   Thou hast
Been rescued, Carl—art free—and I— (*He leaves off.*)
    CARLOS: And thou?
    MARQUIS: And I—I press thee to my bosom now
For the first time with full and total right;
I purchas'd it indeed with ev'rything,
With ev'rything, that's dear to me—O Carl
How sweet, how great this moment is! I am
Contented with myself.
    CARLOS: What sudden change
I see upon thy features? I've ne'er seen
Thee so before. Thy breast doth elevate
Itself more proudly, and thy glances gleam.
    MARQUIS: We must take our departure, Carl. Fear not.
O be a man. Whatever thou wilt hear,
Carl, promise me, not by excessive pain
Unworthy of great souls, to aggravate
This separation—Thou hast lost me, Carl—
For many years—A fool would say it is
Forever.
(CARLOS *draws back his hand, looks at him fixedly and doth not answer.*)
        Be a man. I've reckon'd much
On thee, and I have not avoided, to
Endure the dreadful hour, which they do term
In fear the *final* one. Indeed, should I
Confess it to thee, Carl? I have thereon
Enjoy'd myself—Now come, let us sit down—
I feel exhausted and quite weak.
(*He moves near to Carlos, who is still in a state of dead numbness and
involuntarily allows himself to be drawn down by him.*)
             Where art thou?
Thou dost not answer me?—I will be brief.
The day thereafter, we had seen us last
At the Carthusian monast'ry, the King
Requir'd my presence. The result thou know'st,
All of Madrid doth know. Yet thou dost not

Know, that thy secret's been betray'd to him,
That letters, in the casket of the Queen
Are found, the which have witness'd versus thee,
That I from his own mouth discover this
And that—I was his confidant.
(*He pauses, to hear* CARLOS' *answer; the latter persists in his silence.*)
                              Yes, Carl!
I broke my loyalty with mine own lips.
I guided the intrigue myself, that brought
About thy ruin. Much too loud thy deed
Already spake. It was too late to clear
Thee of it. To assure myself of his
Revenge was all, 'twas left to me—and so
I did become thy foe, to serve thee better.
Dost thou not hear?
    CARLOS: I hear. Go on. Go on.
    MARQUIS: Until now am I without guilt. But soon
I was betray'd by unaccustom'd beams
Of this new royal favor. Rumor of
It rush'd unto thee, as I had foreseen.
But I, corrupted by false tenderness,
Deceiv'd by proud delusion, to conclude
This daring venture without thee, have kept
Conceal'd my dang'rous secret from our friendship.
That was great hastiness! Severely have
I err'd. I'm conscious of it. Madness was
My confidence. Forgive me—it was bas'd
Upon thy friendship's everlastingness.
(*Here he becomes silent.* CARLOS *passes from
his petrifaction over into spirited motion.*)
That which I fear'd, doth now occur. They made
Thee tremble 'fore fictitious dangers. Here
The Queen lies in her blood—the frightfulness
Of the reverberating palace—Lerma's
Unfortunate officiousness—and last
My own incomprehensible reserve,
All storm thy startl'd heart—Thou waverest—
And giv'st me up for lost—But far too noble
Thyself, to doubt thy friend's integrity,
Bedeck'st thou his apostasy with greatness,
Now first thou hazardest to call him faithless,
Because thou may'st revere him even faithless.
Foresaken by the only one, thou throw'st
Thyself i' th' arms of Princess Eboli—

Unhappy man! into a devil's arms;
For this one 'twas, who thee betray'd.
(CARLOS *arises.*)   I see
Thee hasten off. A bad presentiment
Flies through my heart. I follow thee. Too late
Thou lie'st before her feet. Already the
Confession flows across thy lips. For thee
There is no rescue more—

    CARLOS: No! No! She was
Bestirr'd. Thou art mistaken. Sure was she
Bestirr'd.

    MARQUIS: Here turns it night before my senses!
Naught—naught—no remedy—no help—at all
In nature's whole circumference! Despair
Makes me a fury and a beast—I place
The dagger on a woman's breast—But now—
Now falls a beam of sunlight on my soul.
"If I did but mislead the King? If I
Succeeded, to appear the guilty one?
A likelihood or not! For him enough,
Apparently enough for Philip, since
'Tis evil! Be it so! I'll venture it.
Perhaps a thunderbolt, which unforeseen
Doth strike, may make the tyrant hesitate—
What want I more. He stops to think and Carl
Hath won the time, to flee unto Brabant."

    CARLOS: And that—that had'st thou then perform'd?
    MARQUIS: I write
To William, Prince of Orange, that I've lov'd
The Queen, and that I have succeeded in
Escaping the suspicion of the King,
Through the distrust, which falsely clung to thee—
That I discover'd through the King himself
The means, to freely near the Queen. I add
Thereto, that I'm afeard to be detected,
That thou, advis'd about my passion, hast
Rush'd quickly to the Princess Eboli,
Perhaps by means of her to warn the Queen—
That I have thee imprison'd here and now,
Since everything is doubtless lost, be willing,
To hurl myself towards Brussels—This same letter—

    CARLOS (*interrupts his words terrified*):
Hast thou indeed not trusted to the post?
Thou know'st, all letters to Brabant and Flanders—

MARQUIS: Are handed over to the King—So as
Affairs now stand, already Taxis hath
Perform'd his duty.

CARLOS: God! So am I lost!

MARQUIS: Thou? Wherefore thou?

CARLOS: Unhappy man, and thou
Art lost together with me. This immense
Deceit my father can not pardon thee.
No! This he pardons nevermore!

MARQUIS: Deceit?
Thou art distraught. Reflect thee. Who tells him,
That it hath been deceit?

CARLOS (*looks at him fixedly in the face*):
                    And *who*, ask'st thou?
I do myself. (*He wants to leave.*)

MARQUIS: Thou ravest. Stay behind.

CARLOS: Away! Away! for God's sake. Hold me not.
Whilst I stay here, already doth he hire
Assassins.

MARQUIS: All the nobler is the time.
We still have much to tell each other.

CARLOS: What?
Ere he still everything—
(*He wants again to go. The* MARQUIS *takes him by the arm and
looks at him meaningfully.*)

MARQUIS: Now listen, Carlos—
Was I so hasty, and so scrupulous,
When thou had'st shed thy blood for me—a boy?

CARLOS (*remains standing before him mov'd and full of
admiration*):
O blessed Providence!

MARQUIS: Preserve thyself
For Flanders' sake. The kingdom is thy calling.
To die for thee was that of mine.

CARLOS (*walks up to him and takes him by the hand,
full of the most ardent feeling*):
                    No! No!
He will—he cannot possibly resist!
Cannot resist so much sublimity!—
I'll lead thee to him. Arm in arm we shall
Walk up to him. And Father, I will say
To him, a friend hath done this for his friend.
He will be mov'd. Believe me, he is not
Without humanity, my father. Yes!

Indeed, he will be mov'd. His eyes will overflow
With warmest tears and he will pardon thee
And me—
(A *shot is fir'd through the barr'd doors.* CARLOS *springs up.*)
        Aha! For whom was that intended?
    MARQUIS: I do believe—for me.
    CARLOS: O heavenly
Kind-heartedness!
    MARQUIS (*with a breaking voice*):
                         He's very quick—the King—
I hop'd—for longer—Think of thine escape—
Hear'st thou?—of thine escape—Thy mother knows
Of everything—I can no more—
(CARLOS *remains lying as if dead besides the corpse. After some time
the* KING *enters, accompanied by many* GRANDEES *and recoils at this
sight. A general and deep pause. The* GRANDEES *place themselves in
a half circle around both of them and look alternately on the* KING *and
his son. The latter still lies without any signs of life.—The* KING
observes him with thoughtful silence.)

    SCENE IV—*The* KING. CARLOS. *The* DUKES OF ALBA, FERIA *and*
MEDINA SIDONIA. *The* PRINCE OF PARMA. COUNT LERMA. DOMINGO
and many GRANDEES.

    KING (*with benevolent tone*): Thy prayer,
Hath been accorded, my Infant. Here am
I, I myself, with all the grandees of
My kingdom to proclaim thee free.
(CARLOS *looks up and glances around, like one, who hath awaken'd
from a dream. His eyes first fasten on the* KING, *then on the dead one.
He doth not answer.*)
                       Receive
Thy sword again. We have behav'd too rashly.
(*He approaches him, extends him his hand and helps him to rise.*)
My son's not in his rightful place. Arise.
And come into thy father's arms.
    CARLOS (*receives the* KING'S *arms unconsciously—but suddenly
remembers himself, pauses and looks at him more exactly*):
                         Thy smell
Is murder. I cannot embrace thee now.
(*He pushes him back, all the* GRANDEES *are in commotion.*)
No! Stand not so bewilder'd there! What have
I done that is so monstrous then? Impugn'd

The Heaven's own anointed? Do not fear.
I will not lay a hand on him. Do you
Not see the brand upon his forehead? God
Hath branded him.

    KING (*starting to leave quickly*):
                   Now follow me, my grandees.

    CARLOS: Whereto? Not from this place, my Sire—
(*He holds him forcibly with both hands and with the one manages to seize the sword, which the King hath brought. It comes out of its sheath.*)

    KING: A sword
Is drawn upon thy father?

    ALL THE GRANDEES PRESENT (*draw theirs*):
                            Regicide!

    CARLOS (*the KING firmly in the one hand, the naked sword in the other*):
Now sheathe your swords. What do you want? Believe
You, I be raving mad? No, I'm not mad.
Were I, then *you* did not do well, to thus
Remind me that his life doth hover on
The point of this my sword. I pray, you stand
Far off. For constitutions, such as mine,
Want to be flatter'd—therefore keep away.
What I must settle with this King, doth not
Concern your oath of fealty. Just look,
At how his fingers bleed! Look at him well!
You see? O look you here as well. *This* hath
He done, the noble Artist!

    KING (*to the GRANDEES, who anxiously want to press around him*):
                    Everyone
Step back. Why do you tremble? Are we not
A son and father? I will yet await,
For what disgraceful action nature—

    CARLOS: Nature?
I know of none. Now murder is the watchword.
The bonds of humankind are sever'd. Thou
Thyself hast rent them, Sire, throughout thy realm.
Shall I respect, what thou disdain'st?—O see!
See here! No murder hath yet been committed
Except today—Is there no God? What? May
In His creation Kings thus wreak such havoc?
I ask again, is there no God? As long as mothers
Have given birth, there's only *one*— just *one*
Who died so undeservedly—Know'st thou

What thou hast done? O no, he knows it not,
Knows not, that he hath stolen from this world
A life, that was more noble and important
And far more precious than was he with all
His century.

    KING (*with lenient tone*): If I've been all too rash,
Befits it thee, *for* whom I have been so,
To say that I'm responsible?

    CARLOS: How's that?
Is't possible? You never guess'd, just who
This dead man was to me—O tell him then—
Help his Omniscience solve the weighty riddle.
The dead one was my friend—And do you want
To know wherefore he died? He died for me.

    KING: Ha! My suspicion!

    CARLOS: Bleeding one, forgive,
That I do desecrate it ere such ears!
But this great judge of human nature shall
Sink down for shame, that his grey wisdom was
Outwitted by a youth's sagacity.
Yes, Sire! For we were brothers! Brothers through
A nobler bond, than nature ever forg'd.
His beauteous course of life was love. His love
For me his great and beauteous death. And he
Was *mine*, as *you* have bragg'd of his regard,
And as his jesting eloquence made sport
With your most prideful giant intellect.
You fancied you could master him—and were
A pliant instrument of his exalted plans.
That I have been imprison'd, was a plan
Drawn from his friendship. Then to rescue me,
He wrote the note to Orange—O my God!
It was the first time in his life he lied!
To rescue me, he threw himself toward death,
Which he did suffer. You may have bestow'd
On him your favor—but he died for me.
Your heart and friendship did you force on him,
Your scepter was the plaything of his hands;
He threw it down and died for me!

(*The* KING *stands motionless, his gaze fix'd on the floor. All grandees look upon him abash'd and fearful.*)

                      And was
It possible? You lent belief unto

This clumsy lie? How meanly must he think
Of you, that he did undertake, to gain
With you by means of this crude jugglery!
You dar'd to court him for his friendship, and
You did succumb before this easy test!
O, no—no, that was naught for you. That was
No man for you! That knew he well himself,
As he rejected you with all your crowns.
This fine string instrument was shatter'd in
Your metal hand. You could do nothing else,
But murder him.

    ALBA (*hath until now not let the* KING *out of his sight and hath observ'd the commotion with obvious uneasiness, which works on his face. Now he timidly approaches him.*):
                       Sire—not this deathly silence.
Look round yourself. And speak with us.
    CARLOS: You weren't
Indifferent to him. You long had had
His sympathy. Perhaps! He had still made
You happy. His full heart was rich enough
To satisfy yourself with its abundance.
The splinters of his mighty spirit would
Have render'd you a god. And you have robb'd
Your very self—Now what
Will you then offer, to replace a soul,
Like this one was?
(*A deep silence. Many of the* GRANDEES *look away or cover their faces with their mantles.*)
O, you who stand assembl'd here and with alarm
And with astonishment grow dumb—do not
Condemn the youth, who hath employ'd this speech
Against his father and the King—Look hither!
For my sake hath he died! Do you have tears?
Flows blood, not molten brass, within your veins?
Look hither and condemn me not!
(*He turns to the King with more composure and self-possession.*)
                            Perhaps
You are awaiting, how this most unnat'ral story
Will terminate?—Here is my sword. You are
My king once more. Do you suppose, that I
Am trembling 'fore your vengeance? You can kill
Me too, as you have kill'd this noblest one.
My life is forfeit. That I know. Now what
Is life to me? I here renounce all that,

Which is awaiting me upon this world.
Go seek you for a son among unknowns—
There lie my kingdoms—
(*He sinks down upon the corpse and takes no more part in the following.
Meanwhile one hears a confus'd din of voices from the distance and a
thronging of many people. There is a deep silence surrounding the*
KING. *His eyes run through the entire circle, but no one meets his
glances.*

KING: Now? Doth no one want
To answer?—Every glance upon the floor—
Each face is veil'd! My sentence is pronounc'd.
Upon these silent countenances do
I read what is proclaim'd. My subjects have
Condemn'd me.
(*The former silence. The tumult comes nearer and grows louder.
A murmur runs through the standing* GRANDEES, *they give embarrass'd
nods to one another. Count Lerma finally touches the Duke of Alba
softly.*)

LERMA: Truly! 'Tis a storm!
ALBA (*softly*):   So fear I.
LERMA: They're rising up. They're coming now.

SCENE V—*An* OFFICER *of the bodyguard. The former.*

OFFICER (*urgently*):   Rebellion!
Where is the King?
(*He works his way through the crowd and presses forward to the* KING.)
                All of Madrid in arms!
The raging soldiers and the mob surround
The palace by the thousands. Word is spread,
Prince Carlos, hath been taken prisoner,
His life's in danger. And the people want
To see him living or all of Madrid
They'll let go up in flames.

ALL THE GRANDEES (*in motion*):
                    Preserve! Preserve
The King!

ALBA (*to the* KING, *who stands calm and unmov'd*):
        You must take refuge, Sire—There is
A danger—We are not aware as yet,
Who arm'd the rabble—

KING (*awakes from his stupor, stands erect and strides with majesty
among them*):   Doth my throne still stand?

Am I still Monarch of this country?—No.
I am no longer. These poltroons do weep,
Made feeble by a boy. They only wait
Upon the watchword, to desert from me.
I am betray'd by rebels.
    ALBA: Sire, o what
A horrifying fantasy!
    KING: O'er there!
There fling yourself below! Before the budding,
The youthful Monarch fling yourself below!—
I'm nothing more—an impotent old man!
    ALBA: Now is it come to this!—Ye Spaniards!
(*All press around the* KING *and kneel before him with drawn swords.*
CARLOS *remains alone and deserted by all besides the corpse.*)
    KING (*tears off his mantle and throws it from himself*):
                                 Clothe
Him with this royal finery—Upon
My trampl'd body bear him—
(*He remains unconscious in the arms of* ALBA *and* LERMA.)
    LERMA: Help! O God!
    FERIA: God! What a mischance!
    LERMA: He is from himself—
    ALBA (*leaves the* KING *in the hands of* LERMA *and* FERIA):
Bring him to bed. And in the meanwhile I
Shall give peace to Madrid.
(*He exits. The* KING *is carried off and all the* GRANDEES *accompany
him.*)

    SCENE VI—CARLOS *remains behind with the corpse. After a few
moments* LUDWIG MERKADO *appears, looks about timidly and stands
for a time silently behind the* PRINCE, *who doth not notice him.*

    MERKADO: I have
Been sent here by Her Majesty the Queen.
(CARLOS *looks away again and gives him no answer.*)
Merkado is my name—I am the doctor
Unto Her Majesty—and here is my
Authority.
(*He shows the* PRINCE *a signet ring—the latter persists in his silence.*)
        The Queen desires full much,
To speak with you this very day—important
Affairs—
    CARLOS: There's nothing more important to
Me in this world.

MERKADO: A message, she did say,
That the Marquis of Posa left—
    CARLOS (*arises quickly*):   What's that?
Directly. (*He wants to go with him.*)
    MERKADO: No! Not now, most gracious Prince.
You must await the night. All entrances
Are mann'd and every guard is doubl'd there.
It is impossible, to set a foot
Into this wing o' th' palace unobserv'd.
You would be risking ev'rything—
    CARLOS: And yet—
    MERKADO: But one means, Prince, at best is still at hand—
The Queen hath thought it out. She lays
It out to you—Yet it is bold and strange
And hazardous.
    CARLOS: That is?
    MERKADO: There long hath been
A legend, as you are aware, that says
At midnight in the arched corridors
O' th' royal citadel, in monk's attire,
The Emperor's departed spirit walks.
The mob believes in this report, the guards
Take up these posts with but the greatest dread.
And if you are decided, to make use
Of this disguise, you will be able to
Come freely and unharm'd through all the guards
Right to the Queen's apartment, which this key
Will then unlock. This holy figure will
Protect you from attack. And yet upon
The spot, Prince, your decision must be made.
The necessary garb, the mask you'll find
Within your chamber. I must haste, to bring
Her Majesty your answer.
    CARLOS: And the time?
    MERKADO: The time is twelve o'clock.
    CARLOS: Inform her, that
She may expect me.

(MERKADO exits.)

SCENE VII—CARLOS. COUNT LERMA.

LERMA: Save yourself, my Prince.
The King doth rage against you. An attempt

Upon your freedom—if not on your life.
Do not interrogate me further. I
Have stolen off, to give you warning. Flee
Without delay.
  CARLOS: I am within the hands
Of the Almighty.
  LERMA: As the Queen reveal'd
To me just now, you ought to leave Madrid
This very day and flee to Brussels. You
Must not postpone it, truly not! Revolt
Will aid your flight. With this intention hath
The Queen effected it. Now they will not
Make bold, to practice violence on you.
In the Carthusian cloister doth the post
Await on you, and here are weapons, if
You should be subject to attack—
(*He gives him a dagger and pocket pistols.*)
  CARLOS: Thanks, Thanks,
Count Lerma!
  LERMA: This affair of yours today
Hath mov'd my inmost soul. Like this no friend
Loves any more! All patriots do weep
For you. More now I venture not to say.
  CARLOS: Count Lerma! This departed one describ'd
You as a noble man.
  LERMA: Once more, my Prince!
A pleasant trip. More beauteous times will come;
However, I shall then no longer be.
Receive my homage even here.
(*He falls on one knee before him.*)
  CARLOS (*wants to prevent him. Very mov'd*):
      Not thus—
Not thus, my Count—You're moving me—I would
Not like to be so weak—
  LERMA (*kisses his hand with feeling*):
     My children's King!
O surely will my children be allow'd
To die for you. That I may not. Recall
Me in my children.—Now return in peace
To Spain. And be a human being on
King Philip's throne. For you have come
To know affliction also. Undertake
No bloody act against your father! Yes
Indeed no bloody act, my Prince! King Philip

The Second forc'd your elder father to
Yield up the throne—This Philip quakes today
Before his very son! *Thereon* give thought,
My Prince—and so may Heaven be your guide!
(*He exits quickly.* CARLOS *is about, to hasten away in another direction,
turns suddenly around and throws himself down before the corpse of
the* MARQUIS, *which he once again clasps in his arms. Then he leaves
the room quickly.*)

SCENE VIII—*The* KING'S *Antechamber.* DUKE OF ALBA *and* DUKE
OF FERIA *enter in conversation.*

ALBA: The city is at peace. How did you leave
The King?
FERIA: In the most dreadful frame of mind.
He's lock'd himself within. And whatsoe'er
May come about, he will allow no one
To come before his sight. The treachery
Of the Marquis hath all at once transform'd
His total nature. We don't recognize
Him any more.
ALBA: I must to him. This time
I can't be sparing to him. An important
Discov'ry, which is made just now—
FERIA: A new
Discov'ry?
ALBA: A Carthusian monk, who stole
Into the Prince's chamber secretly
And with suspicious curiosity
Inquir'd about the Marquis Posa's death,
Was notic'd by my guards. They seiz'd him straight.
They question'd him. Urg'd by the fear of death
He made confession, that he bore along
With him some papers of great worth, the which
The dead one had commanded him, to give
Into the Prince's hand—if he himself
Had not appear'd to him once more before
The sun went under.
FERIA: Now?
ALBA: The letters read,
That Carlos 'tween the mid of night and morn
Should leave Madrid.
FERIA: What's that?
ALBA: And that a ship

At Cadiz lies prepar'd to sail, to bring
Him bound for Vlessingen, and that the states
O' th' Netherlands are waiting but for him,
To cast away the Spanish fetters.
    FERIA: Ha!
What is that then?
    ALBA: Yet other letters say,
That Soliman's already put a fleet
To sea from Rhodes—in order to attack
The Spanish Monarch on the Midland Sea,
According to the terms of the alliance.
    FERIA: Is't possible?
    ALBA: Just now these letters teach
Me to know well the journeys, the Maltese
Made recently through all of Europe. 'Twas
No less, than to equip all northern powers
With arms in aid of Flemish liberty.
    FERIA: So that was it!
    ALBA: These letters finally
Are follow'd by a detail'd plan o'th' war,
Which ought to separate the Netherlands
Forever from the Spanish Monarchy.
Naught, naught is overlook'd, the power and
Resistance reckon'd, ev'ry source, all powers
O' th' land precisely indicated, all
The maxims, which are to be follow'd, all
The treaties, which are to be made. The plan
Is devilish, but truly— godly.
    FERIA: What an impenetrable traitor!
    ALBA: Yet
There's ref'rence made within this letter to
A secret conference, the which the Prince
Should bring about the ev'ning of his flight
Together with his mother.
    FERIA: How? That were
Indeed today.
    ALBA: This midnight. Also I've
Already given orders for this case.
You see, that it is pressing, not a moment
Is to be lost—Now open up the chamber
O' th' Monarch.
    FERIA: No! All entrance is forbidden.
    ALBA: I'll open it myself—the growing danger
Doth justify this boldness—

(*As he goes towards the door, it is open'd, and the King comes out.*)

FERIA: Ha! 'Tis he!

SCENE IX—KING *to the preceding.* (*All are startl'd at his appearance, fall back and respectfully let him pass through their midst. He comes in a waking dream, like a sleep-walker.—His dress and his figure still show the disorder, wherein the previous fainting had plac'd him. With slow strides he walks past the present* GRANDEES, *looks fixedly at every one, without recognizing a single one. Finally he remains standing thoughtfully, his eyes sunk to the earth, until his agitation gradually becomes audible.*)

KING: Give this dead one to me again. I must
Have him again.
    DOMINGO (*softly to the* DUKE OF ALBA):
                    Now you must speak to him.
    KING (*as above*):
He thought of me as small and died. I must
Have him again. He must think otherwise
About me.
    ALBA (*approaches with fear*):
            Sire—
    KING: Who's speaking here?
(*He looks long around the entire circle.*)
                                    Have they
Forgotten, who I am? Why not upon
The knees before me, creatures? I am still
The King. Submission do I want to see.
Doth everyone ignore me, since that *one*
Look'd down on me?
    ALBA: Naught more of him, my King!
Another foe, more meaningful than he,
Arises in your Kingdom's heart.—
    FERIA: Prince Carlos—
    KING: He had a friend, who hath now pass'd away
In death for him—for him! With me he had
A kingly realm divided!—O how he
Look'd down upon me! One doth not look down
So haughtily from thrones. Was it not clear,
How much he had in mind with *such* a conquest?
What he had lost, his pain confess'd. Thus will
He weep for nothing transient.—That he still liv'd!
I'd give an India for that. O comfortless

Omnipotence, which cannot even stretch
Its arm into the grave, to rectify
A little overhaste with human life!
The dead do not arise again. Who dares
To say to me, that I am happy? In
The grave dwells one, who doth deny respect
To me. What do I care about the living?
A spirit, *one* free man arose in all
This century—Just one—and he scorn'd me
And died.

    ALBA: Thus do we live in vain! Let us
Go to our graves, ye Spaniards. Even while
In death this man doth rob us of the heart
O' th' Monarch!

    KING (*He sits down, the head supported on his arm.*)
               Had he died this way for me!
I've held him very dear, quite dear. He was
As precious to me as a son. In this
Young man a new, more beauteous morning rose
For me. Who knows, what I had plann'd for him!
He was the first whom I have lov'd. All Europe
Condemn me! Europe may condemn me then.
I have deserv'd his gratitude.

    DOMINGO: Through what
Enchantment—

    KING: And this sacrifice was made
For whom? The boy, my son? O nevermore.
That I do not believe. A Posa doth
Not perish for a boy. The scanty flame
Of friendship doth not fill a Posa's heart.
That beats for all mankind. His bent was for
The world with all its coming generations.
To satisfy it he did find a throne—
And let it pass? Should Posa then forgive
Himself for this high treason to his own
Humanity? O no. I know him better.
He sacrifices Philip not for Carlos, but
The old man for the young one, his own pupil.
The father's setting sun can compensate
No longer for the new day's work. That's sav'd
For the approaching rising of his son—O, it
Is clear! They wait for my departure.

    ALBA: Read
The full corroboration in these letters.

KING (*arises*): It could be he miscalculated. Still,
Still I exist. I'm thankful, Nature. I
Feel youthful strength throughout my sinews. I
Shall make a laughing stock of him. And let
His virtue have been but a dreamer's fancy.
He shall have died just like a fool. His fall
Shall crush his friend and all his century!
Let's see, how well they can dispense with me.
The world is still upon an ev'ning mine.
I shall employ, this evening, so that
No planter after me should reap for ten
Full generations on this scene of fire.
He sacrific'd me to humanity,
His idol; let humanity atone
For him!—And now—I shall begin now with
His puppet.
(*To the* DUKE OF ALBA)
                              What was it with the Infante?
Repeat. What do these letters teach to me?
    ALBA: These letters, Sire, contain the legacy
Of Marquis Posa to Prince Carlos.

    KING (*runs through the papers, whereby he is observ'd sharply
by all those standing around. After he hath read for a time, he puts
them aside and walks silently throughout the room.*)

                                 Call
The Cardinal Inquisitor to me.
I beg him, to bestow on me an hour.
(*One of the* GRANDEES *goes out. The* KING *takes up the papers once
more, reads forth and again puts them aside.*)
In this same night as well?
    TAXIS: At two o'clock
The post should stop at the Carthusian cloister.
    ALBA: And people, whom I have dispatch'd, observ'd
Assorted travel gear, on which the arms
O' th' crown are stamp'd, transported to the cloister.
    FERIA: And also it hath been reported that
In the Queen's name large sums are being rais'd
Among the Moorish agents, for revolt
In Brussels.
    KING: Where was the Infante left?
    ALBA: By the Maltese's corpse.
    KING: Is there still light i' th' room
O' th' Queen?

ALBA: There everything is silent now.
As well she hath dismiss'd her chambermaids
Much earlier, than it hath been her wont.
The Dutchess of Arcos, who was the last
To leave her room, left her already in
Profoundest sleep.
(*An officer of the bodyguard enters, draws the* DUKE OF FERIA
*to the side and speaks softly with him. The latter turns
disconcerted to the* DUKE OF ALBA, *others press around and
a murmur arises.*)
     FERIA, TAXIS, DOMINGO (*together*):
                         Peculiar!
     KING: What is it?
     FERIA: A report, my Sire, the which
Is hardly to believe—
     DOMINGO: Two Swiss, who have
Just now come from their posts, report—it is
Too ludicrous, to give it credit.
     KING: Now?
     ALBA: That in the left wing of the palace they
Beheld the spirit of the Emperor
And with stout-hearted, solemn strides it pass'd
Besides them. Even now this same report's
Confirm'd by all the guards, who through the whole
Pavilion stand dispers'd, and they do add
Thereto, the apparition disappear'd
Into the Queen's apartments.
     KING: In what form
Did he appear?
     OFFICER: In the same garments, that
He wore in those last days in Justi as
A monk of Saint Geronimo.
     KING: A monk?
And had the guards then been acquainted with
Him while he was alive? For how else did
They know, that 'twas the Emperor?
     OFFICER: That it
Must be the Emperor, the scepter show'd,
That he bore in his hands.
     DOMINGO: And also he
Hath been observ'd much oftener, so goes
The tale, in this same form.
     KING: Hath no one tried
To speak to him?

OFFICER: No one was bold enough.
The guards all said their prayers and let him pass
Respectfully straight through their midst.
    KING: And in the chamber
O' th' Queen the apparition disappear'd?
    OFFICER: I' th' antechamber of the Queen.
(*General silence*)
    KING (*turns around quickly*):   *What* say you?
    ALBA: Sire, we are dumb.
    KING (*after some reflection to the Officer*):
                       Let all my guards report
In arms and barricade each entrance to
That wing. I am desirous, to engage
In conversation with this spirit.
(*The* OFFICER *exits. Directly thereon a* PAGE)
    PAGE: Sire!
The Cardinal Inquisitor.
    KING (*to those present*): Now leave us.
(*The* CARDINAL GRAND INQUISITOR, *an old man of ninety years and blind, supported on a staff and led by two Dominicans. As he walks through their rows, all the* GRANDEES *throw themselves down before him and touch the hem of his garment. He bestows his blessing on them. They all withdraw.*)

SCENE X—*The* KING *and the* GRAND INQUISITOR (*A long silence.*)

    GRAND INQUISITOR: Stand
I 'fore the King?
    KING: Indeed.
    GRAND INQUISITOR: I was't no more
Suspecting.
    KING: Now do I renew a scene
Of bygone years. Infante Philip doth
Take counsel from his master.
    GRAND INQUISITOR: Counsel ne'er
Did need my pupil Carl, your worthy father.
    KING: So much the happier was he. I have
Committed murder, Card'nal, and no peace —
    GRAND INQUISITOR:
And for what reason have you murder'd?
    KING: A
Deceit, which is unparallel'd —
    GRAND INQUISITOR: I know't.
    KING: What do you know? Through whom? Since when?

GRAND INQUISITOR: For years,
What *you* have known since set the sun.
    KING (*with astonishment*):   You had
Already known about this man?
    GRAND INQUISITOR: His life
Lies from commencement to conclusion in
The Holy Register of Santa Casa.
    KING: And walk'd he freely round?
    GRAND INQUISITOR: The rope, upon
Which he did hang, was long, but would not break.
    KING: Indeed, he was outside my kingdom's borders.
    GRAND INQUISITOR: Where'er he would be, I was too.
    KING (*walking up and down indignantly*):   One knew,
Within whose hands I was — Why did one fail,
To mention it to me?
    GRAND INQUISITOR: This question I
Turn back upon you — Why didn't *you* inquire,
Since you did throw yourself in this man's arms?
You knew him well! *One* look unmask'd to you
The heretic.—What power'd you, to wrest
The victim from the Holy Office. Plays
One *thus* with us? When Majesty degrades
Itself to taking stolen goods — to reach accord
Behind our backs with our worst enemies,
What will become of us? May *one* find pardon,
By which right would a hundred thousand then
Be sacrific'd?
    KING: He too is sacrific'd.
    GRAND INQUISITOR:
No! He's been murder'd — fameless! wantonly! — The blood,
That should have flow'd with glory in our honor,
Was shed by an assassin's hand. The man
Was ours — What authoriz'd you, to encroach
Upon the Order's holy property?
For he was here to die through us. God gave
Him for the pressing need o'th' course of time,
In solemn desecration of his spirit
To make a show of ostentatious reason.
That was my well-consider'd plan. Now lies
It stretch'd undone, the work of many years!
We have been robb'd, and you have not a thing
But bloody hands.

KING: My passion carried me
Away. Forgive me.
    GRAND INQUISITOR: Passion?—You respond
To me Infante Philip thus? Have I
Alone become an aged man?—Your passion!
(*With indignant shaking of the head.*)
Grant liberty of conscience in your realms,
When thou art walking in thy chains.
    KING: I am
A novice still in matters such as these.
Have patience with me.
    GRAND INQUISITOR: No! I'm not contented
With you. — To think that you would slander your
Entire foregoing course of Regency! Where was
That Philip then, whose steadfast soul was like
The polar star i'th' heaven, that unchang'd
And endless round itself doth drive? Was an
Entirety of the past behind you sunk?
Was instantan'ously the world no more
The same, when you extended him the hand?
Was poison no more poison? Hath the wall
'Twixt good and evil, truth and falsehood fallen?
What is a purpose? What is constancy,
What manly honor, if a sixty year
Long rule within a tepid minute like
A woman's fickle temper melts away.
    KING: I look'd into his eyes—Be lenient towards
Me for my relapse into mortal frailty.
The world hath that one avenue the less
Into thy heart. Thine eyes have been effac'd.
    GRAND INQUISITOR:
What should this man have been to you? What is
There new that he could have display'd to you,
For which you weren't prepar'd? Know you so little
The minds of schwärmers and of innovators?
The boastful language of the world reformer
Rang in your ear so unfamiliar? If
The edifice of your conviction from
Mere words doth fall — with what expression, must
I question, did you sign the bloody sentence
Upon the hundred thousand feeble souls,
Who climb'd the pile of wood for nothing worse.

KING: I did desire to find a man. For these
Domingos —
    GRAND INQUISITOR: Why desire a man? For you
Men are mere numbers, nothing more. Must I
With my now grey hair'd student hear repeated
The elements o'th' art of monarchy?
The God o'th' earth must now unlearn the need
For what can be refus'd to him—If *you*
Are whimpering for sympathy, have you
Not granted that the world is of your kind?
And what rights have you, I would like to know,
Which you can point to as above your kind?
    KING (*throws himself into the armchair*):
I am a little man, I feel't—Thou ask'st
O'th' creature, what but the Creator doth.
    GRAND INQUISITOR:
No, Sire. One doth deceive me not. You are
Seen through — You wanted to escape from us.
The Order's heavy chains did weigh you down;
You wanted to be free, unique.
(*He leaves off. The King is silent.*)
We are aveng'd —Be thankful to the Church,
Which is content to punish like a mother.
The choice, which one doth let you blindly make
Was your chastisement. You have been appris'd.
And now return to us. If I had not
Stood now before you — by the living God!
You would be standing 'fore me thus tomorrow.
    KING: Forbear this language! Priest, restrain thyself!
I bear it not. I can not listen to you
Address me in these tones.
    GRAND INQUISITOR: Why do you call
The shade of Samuel up? I have bestow'd
Two Kings upon the Spanish throne and hop'd,
To leave a firmly grounded work behind.
I see the fruit of all my lifetime lost,
Don Philip shakes my edifice himself.
And now, my Sire — wherefore have I been call'd?
What should I do here? I am not inclin'd
To visit here again.
    KING: Yet one more task,
The last one—then may'st thou depart in peace.
The past shall disappear, and peace shall be
Concluded 'tween us—We are reconcil'd?

GRAND INQUISITOR: If Philip humbly bows himself.

KING (*after a pause*):   My son
Doth plot rebellion.

GRAND INQUISITOR: What have you resolv'd?

KING: On nothing or on all.

GRAND INQUISITOR: And what is all?

KING: I'll let him flee, if I cannot
Decide to let him die.

GRAND INQUISITOR: Well, Sire?

KING: Canst thou create for me a new faith, which
Defends the bloody murder of a child?

GRAND INQUISITOR: To expiate eternal righteousness,
The Son of God died on the tree.

KING: Wilt thou
Implant this viewpoint throughout all of Europe?

GRAND INQUISITOR: As far, as one reveres the cross.

KING: I give
Offense 'gainst Nature — dost thou also wish
To still this mighty voice?

GRAND INQUISITOR: Before the Faith
No voice of nature is of worth.

KING: I place
My Judge's Office in thy hands — Can I
Fall back entirely into line?

GRAND INQUISITOR: Give him
To me.

KING: He is my only son—for whom
Have I amass'd?

GRAND INQUISITOR: Far better putrefaction
Than freedom.

KING (*stands up*): We are one. Now come.

GRAND INQUISITOR: Where to?

KING: To take the sacrifice from mine own hand.
(*He leads him away.*)

LAST SCENE—*Room of the* QUEEN. CARLOS. *The* QUEEN. *In
the end the* KING *with his retinue.*

CARLOS (*in a monk's robe, a mask before his face, which he just
now removes, under his arm a naked sword. It is completely dark.
He nears a door, which is open'd. The* QUEEN *comes out, in her night
clothes, with a burning light. CARLOS kneels before her.*):
Elizabeth!

QUEEN (*lingering with quiet sadness upon his face*):
     Thus do we meet again?
CARLOS: Thus do we meet again! (*Silence*)
QUEEN (*seeks to compose herself*): Arise! We do not wish
To weaken one another, Carlos. Not
Through fruitless tears will the great dead
One best be honor'd. Tears may want to flow
For lesser suffering! He sacrific'd
Himself for *you*! With his most precious life
He purchas'd that of yours—And had this blood
Then flow'd forth for a chimera?—O Carlos!
I've pledg'd myself responsible for you.
Upon my surety he departed hence
More joyously. Will you now make me out
A liar?
     CARLOS (*with spirit*):
     I will build a monument
To him, like hath become no Monarch yet—
And over where his ashes rest will bloom
A paradise!
     QUEEN: So have I wanted you!
That was the noble meaning of his death!
He chose me as the executor of
His final wishes. I remind you. I
Shall hold to the fulfillment of this vow.
—And yet another legacy bequeath'd
The dying one into my hand—I gave
My word to him—and—why should I keep still?
He handed me his Carl—I will defy
Appearances—I will not tremble more
Before mankind, I will be bold for once
Just like a friend. My heart should speak. He said
Our love was virtue? I believe him and
My heart no longer will—
     CARLOS: Don't finish, Queen—
I've lain within a long and heavy dream.
I was in love—And now I am awake.
Forgotten be the past! Here are your letters
Return'd. Destroy those which are mine. You need
Fear no more agitation from me. 'Tis
Foreby. A purer fire hath purified
My being. All my passion dwells within
The graves o'th' dead. No mortal appetites
Divide this bosom more.

(*After a silence taking her hand*)
                                 I came, to take
My leave—O Mother, finally I see,
There is a higher good, more to be wish'd
For, than possessing thee—Just one short night
Hath lent wings to the sluggish progress of
My years, matur'd me early to a man.
I have no further labor for this life
Except the memory of him! Foreby
Are all my harvests—
(*He approaches the* QUEEN, *who covers her face.*)
                                 Mother, have you naught
To say to me?
     QUEEN: Pay no attention to
My teardrops, Carl—I can do nothing else—
Yet do believe me, I do wonder at you.
     CARLOS: You were the only confidante of
Our league—And by *this* name you shall remain
The dearest one in all the world to me.
I can so little grant my friendship to you
As yesterday I could bestow my love
Upon another woman. Holy shall
The regal widow be to me, if I
Be led by Providence unto this throne.
(*The* KING, *accompanied by the* GRAND INQUISITOR *and his* GRANDEES,
appears in the hinterground, without being observ'd.)
Now I leave Spain and see my father not
Again—No, never in this life again.
I value him no longer. Nature is
Extinct within my breast—Be you again
A wife to him. He hath already lost
A son. You must return unto your duties.
I hasten now, to save from tyrant's hand
My people long oppress'd. Madrid shall see
Me only as the King or never more.
And now unto the last farewell! (*He kisses her.*)
     QUEEN: O Carl!
What do you make of me?—I may not dare
To soar to such a height of manly greatness;
But I can comprehend and wonder at you.
     CARLOS: Am I not strong, Elizabeth? I hold
You now within my arms and waver not.
Just yesterday the terror of close death
Would not have torn me from this place.

(*He leaves her.*)
That is foreby. Now I defy each fate
Of mortal man. I held you in my arms
And waver'd not—Still! Did you not hear something?
(*A clock strikes.*)

    QUEEN: Naught do I hear except the dreadful bell,
Which to our separation tolls.

    CARLOS: Good night then, Mother.
From Ghent you shall receive a letter first
From me, which should proclaim the secret of
Our intercourse aloud. I go, to meet
Don Philip now upon the open field.
Henceforth, I wish, that there be nothing more
Conceal'd between us. *You* need not avoid
The eye o' th' world—Let this be here my last
Deceit.
(*He wants to reach for the mask. The* KING *stands between them.*)

    KING: It is thy last one!
(*The* QUEEN *collapses in a swoon.*)

    CARLOS (*rushes to her and takes her in his arms*):

                                   Is she dead?

O Heaven and Earth!

    KING (*cold and quietly to the* GRAND INQUISITOR):
                         Now Cardinal! I've done
The part that's mine. Perform the part that's yours. (*He exits.*)

End.

LETTERS ON
DON CARLOS

LETTERS ON

DON CARLOS

TRANSLATED BY WILLIAM F. WERTZ, JR.

First Letter

You inform me, dear friend, that the judgments to date of Don Carlos have given you yet little satisfaction, and think therefor, that the greatest part of the same be gone astray from the actual viewpoint of the author. It seems to you still quite possible, to save certain daring passages, which the critic declared untenable; many doubts, which have been aroused thereagainst, you find in the coherence of the play—where not fully answered, yet foreseen and taken into consideration. In most of these objections you would far less admire the sagacity of the judges than the self-satisfaction, with which they express the such as lofty discoveries, without letting themselves be disturbed by the most natural thought, that transgressions, which fall at once upon the eye of the most weaksighted, may have been visible, as well to the author, who among his readers seldom is the least informed, and that they have thus less to do with the matter itself than with the *grounds*, which thereby decided it. These grounds can by all means be insufficient, can be based upon a one-sided mode of presentation: but it would have been the concern of the judge, to show this insufficiency, this one-sidedness, if he indeed wants to acquire a value in the eyes of the one, on whom he forces himself as judge or to whom he offers himself as counsellor.

But, dear friend, what doth it matter in the end to the author, whether his judge hath had a profession or not? How much or little acuteness he hath demonstrated? He may decide that within himself. Bad for the author and his work, if he lets the effect of the same depend upon the *gift of divination* and *equity* of his critics, if he made the impression of the same dependent upon qualities, which unite themselves only in very few heads. It is one of the most deficient conditions, in which a work of art can find itself, if it hath been placed at the caprice of the spectator, what interpretation he wants to make thereof, and if it requires assistance, to move him to the right standpoint. If you wanted to indicate to me, that that of mine found itself in this condition, then you have said something very bad thereof, and you induce me, to examine it once again more exactly from this viewpoint. It would depend therefore, methinks, above all thereon, to investigate, whether everything is contained in the play, that is of service to the comprehension of the same, and whether it is stated in so clear terms, that it was easy to the reader, to apprehend it. May it therefore please you, dear friend, that I entertain you for a time with this subject. The play is become more distant to me, I find myself now as it were in the middle between the artist and his spectator, whereby it becomes perhaps possible to me, to unite the former's entrusted acquaintance with his subject with the impartiality of the latter.

I can in general—and I find it necessary, to say this in advance— I can be countered, that I have excited other expectations in the first acts, than I fulfilled in the last. St. Real's novel, perhaps even mine own statements thereon in the first issue of the Thalia, may have directed the reader to a standpoint, from which it can now no longer be considered. Namely during the time, that I worked it out, which was a rather long time because of many interruptions, hath—much in myself changed. In the different fortunes, which during this time have occurred in respect to my mode of thinking and feeling, even this work had necessarily to take part. What had fettered me above all in starting the same, this effect made thereafter already weaker and in the end only scarcely extant. New ideas, which in the meantime sprang up within me, supplanted the earlier; Carlos himself had fallen in my favor, perhaps from no other reason, than because I had sprung too far ahead of him in years, and for an opposite reason had Marquis Posa taken his place. Thus it then came to be, that I brought with me an entirely different heart to the fourth and fifth acts. But the first three acts were in the hands of the public, the outline of the whole was no longer to be reversed—I would have had therefore to either suppress the play entirely (and for that the smallest part of my readers would have indeed thanked me), or I had to adapt the second half to the first, as well as I could. If this hath not happened overall in the most fortunate mode, then it serves me as some consolation, that a more gifted hand than that of mine would not have succeeded much better. The main fault was, I had borne the play too long; a dramatic work however can and should be only the bloom of a single summer. Also the plan was too vastly designed for the limits and rules of a dramatic work. This plan for example required, that Marquis Posa bore the most unlimited confidence of Philip; but the economy of the play permitted me only a single scene to bring about this extraordinary effect.

With my friend these disclosures will perhaps justify me, but not with art. They may in the meantime only terminate the many declamations, wherewith a storm hath been run against me from this side by critics.

Second Letter

The character of Marquis Posa hath been deemed almost universally to be too ideal; in how far this contention hath a basis, will be then best shown, if one hath traced back the characteristic mode of action of this man to its true content. I have here, as you see, to do with two opposing parties. To those, who want to have him banished from the class of natural beings altogether, must it therefore be set forth, in how far he coheres with human nature, in how far his inner convictions like his actions flow from his quite human instincts and are grounded in the chain of external circumstances; to those, who give him the name of a divine man, I need only call attention to some of his weaknesses, which are absolutely human. The inner convictions, which the Marquis expresses, the philosophy, which guides him, the favorite feelings, which inspire his soul, so much as they elevate themselves also above daily life, it can, looked upon as bare conceptions, indeed not be, which banished him rightfully from the class of natural beings. For what can not be conceived to be present in a human head, and what offspring of the brain can not mature to passion in the glowing heart? Even his actions it can not be, which, so seldom as this also may occur, have found in history itself their like; for the self-sacrifice of the Marquis for his friend hath little or nothing over the heroic death of a Curtius, Regulus and others. The erroneous and impossible had to lie therefore either in the contradiction of his inner convictions with that era or in their powerlessness and their lack of vitality, to truly kindle such actions. Therefore, the objections, which are made against the naturalness of this character, I can not otherwise understand, than that in Philip the Second's century no man could have thought so as Marquis Posa,—that thoughts of this kind do not so easily, as occurs here, go over into will and deed,—and that an ideal schwärmerei is not realized with such consistency, is not wont to be accompanied by such energy in action.

What one raises as an objection to this character in respect to the age, in which I cause him to appear, seems to me to speak much more *for* rather than *against* him. After the example of all great heads he arises betwixt darkness and light, a salient isolated appearance. The point of time, where he emerges, is universal ferment of minds, struggle of prejudice with reason, anarchy of opinions, dawning of the truth— at all times the hour of birth of extraordinary men. The ideas of freedom and human nobility, which a fortunate accident, perhaps a favorable education brought forth in this purely-organized responsive soul, astound it through their novelty and have an effect upon it with all the power of the unfamiliar and the surprising; even the mysterious, under which they were probably communicated to it, must have heightened the strength of their impression. They have through a long-eroding use not yet the triviality, which makes in these days their impression so blunt; their great stamp hath been effaced neither by the twaddle of the schools nor by wit of worldly people. His soul feels itself in these ideas as it were as in a new and beautiful region, which works upon it with all its blinding light and enchants it into the most lovely dream. The opposite misery of slavery and of superstition draws it ever firmer and firmer to this favorite world; the most beautiful dreams of freedom are dreamt yes in the dungeon. Tell me yourself, my friend—the boldest ideal of a republic of men, universal toleration and freedom of conscience, where could it better and where more naturally be born to the world than in the proximity of Philip II and his Inquisition?

All the principles and favorite feelings of the Marquis revolve around *republican* virtue. Even his self-sacrifice for his friend evidences this, for the capacity for self-sacrfice is the substance of all republican virtue.

The point of time, wherein he appeared, was precisely that, wherein the discourse on human rights and freedom of conscience was stronger than ever. The preceding Reformation had brought these ideas for the first time into circulation, and the unrests in Flanders maintained them in practice. His external independence, his position as a Knight of Malta itself gave him the happy leisure, to brood this speculative schwärmerei to ripeness.

In the era and in the state, wherein the Marquis appears, and in the external conditions, which surround him, lies not therefore the basis, wherefore he would not have been capable of this philosophy, would not have been able to be devoted to it with schwärmerisch attachment.

If history is rich in examples, that one can neglect everything earthly for *opinions*, if one attacheth power to the most baseless delusion, to take in the minds of men to such a degree, that they are made capable of every self-sacrifice; so were it peculiar, to deny this power to the *truth*. In a point of time moreover, which is so rich as that in examples, that men risk property and life for dogmas, which of themselves have so little inspiring, should, methinks, a character not attract notice, who risks something similiar for the most sublime of all ideas; for one would have to assume, that truth be less capable, to bestir the heart of man, than delusion. The Marquis is announced moreover as a hero. Already in early youth he hath furnished proof with his sword of a valor, which he shall manifest hereafter in a more serious matter. Inspiring truths and a soul-elevating philosophy must, methinks, become something quite different in a hero's soul than in the brain of one educated in the schools or in the worn out heart of an effeminate man of the world.

There are above all two actions of the Marquis, to which one, as you inform me, hath taken offense. His conduct towards the King in the tenth scene of the third act and his self-sacrifice for his friend. But it could be, that the candor, with which he puts forth his inner convictions to the King, would come less on account of his courage than of his exact knowledge of that one's character, and with reduced danger the primary objection to this scene would accordingly also be removed. Thereon another time, when I entertain you about Philip II; now I had merely to do with Posa's self-sacrifice for the Prince, whereon I will communicate a few ideas to you in the next letter.

Third Letter

You wished recently to have found in Don Carlos the proof, that *passionate friendship* could be just as moving a subject for the tragedy as *passionate love*, and my answer, that I had held the picture of such a friendship in reserve for the future, surprised you. Therefore do you also assume, like most of my readers, as absolute, that it hath been *schwärmerisch friendship*, which I have set as my aim in the relationship between Carlos and Marquis Posa? And from this standpoint have you consequently considered hitherto both of these characters and perhaps the whole drama? But what, dear friend, if you had attributed truly too much to me with this *friendship*? If from the entire context it appeared clearly, that it had *not* been this aim and also absolutely could not be? If the character of the Marquis, as it thus results from the totality of his actions, were not to agree completely with such a friendship, and if precisely from his most beautiful actions, which one ascribes to its account, were furnished the best proof of the contrary?

The first announcement of the relationship between both of these could have been misleading; but this also only apparently, and a modest attention to the contrasting conduct of both would have sufficed, to remove the error. Thereby, that the poet sets out from their youthful friendship, hath he given away nothing of his higher plan, on the contrary, this could have been spun from no better thread. The relation, in which both appear together, was a reminiscence of their earlier academic years. Harmony of feeling, a like loving passion for the great and the beautiful, a like enthusiasm for truth, freedom and virtue had knitted them in that time to one another. A character like Posa's, which thereafter thus, as it occurs in the play, develops, must have begun early, to acquire this lively emotional power by practice on a fruitful subject: a benevolence, that should subsequently extend over humanity as a whole, had to have begun from a more narrow bond. This creative and fiery spirit had to have a subject soon, upon which it worked; could a more beautiful one be offered to him than a delicate and lively-feeling Prince's son, receptive to his pourings forth, rushing towards him of his own free will? But also already in this earlier time the seriousness of this character is visible in a few traits; already here Posa is the colder, the later friend, and his heart, now already too far embracing, to draw itself together for a single being, must be conquered through a severe sacrifice.

> Then I began tormenting thee with thousands
> Of tender signs and faithful brother-love;
> And thou proud heart return'dst them coldly to me.
> ——— My heart
> Thou couldst have scorn'd and torn apart, yet ne'er
> Put it away from thee. Three times didst thou
> Reject the Prince, three times came he again
> As supplicant, to beg for love from thee, etc.
> ——— My regal blood, it flow'd
> Most shamefully beneath the ruthless strokes.
> So high a price I paid for my self-will,
> To be belov'd by Roderick.

Here already are a few hints given, how little the attachment of the Marquis to the Prince is grounded upon *personal* agreement. Early thinks he of him as a *King's son*, early this idea thrusts itself between his heart and his entreating friend. Carlos opens his arms to him; the young world citizen kneels down before him. Feelings for freedom and human nobility were ripe in his soul earlier than friendship for Carlos; this branch was grafted first thereafter upon that stronger trunk. Even in the moment, where his pride is overcome through the great sacrifice of his friend, he doth not lose sight of the Prince's son. "I will repay thee," he said, "when *thou* art the *King*." Is it possible, that in such a young heart with this living and ever-present feeling of the inequality of their conditions, *friendship* could generate itself, whose essential condition is nevertheless *equality*? Thus even then already it was less love than gratitude, less friendship than compassion, which won the *Marquis* to the Prince. The feelings, presentiments, dreams, resolutions, which crowded dark and confused in this boy's soul, had to be communicated, to be looked upon in another soul, and Carlos was the only one, who could share presentiments, dreams and who reciprocated them. A spirit like Posa's had to strive to enjoy his superiority at an early age, and the loving Carl pressed himself to him so submissively, so docilely! Posa saw himself in this beautiful mirror and rejoiced at his image. Thus arose this academical friendship.

But now they are divided from one another, and everything becomes different. Carlos comes to the court of his father, and Posa hurls himself into the world. The former, spoiled by his early attachment to the noblest and most fiery youth, finds nothing in the entire circle of a despot's court, that satisfied his heart. Everything around him is void and unfruitful. Alone amidst the crowd of so many courtiers, oppressed by the present, he refreshes himself on sweet reminiscences of the past. Thus with him these early impressions continue warm and living, and his heart, created for benevolence, to which a worthy subject is lacking, consumes itself in never satisfied dreams. Thus he sinks by degrees into a state of *idle schwärmerei, inactive contemplation.* In the continuing struggle with his situation his strength wears out, the unfriendly encounters of a father dissimilar to him spread a dark melancholy over his being—the gnawing worm of every blossom of the spirit, the death of inspiration. Compressed, without energy, lifeless, brooding within himself, exhausted by severe fruitless struggles, chased around between frightened extremes, no longer strong enough to recover on his own—thus *first love* finds him. In this condition he can set against it no further strength; all those earlier ideas, which alone could have counterbalanced it, are become alien to his soul; it rules him with despotic force; thus he sinks into a painfully-voluptuous condition of *suffering.* Upon a single subject are all of his powers now drawn together. A never-pacified longing holds his soul fettered within itself.—How should it have streamed forth into the universe? Incapable, to satisfy this wish, still more incapable, to subdue it through inner strength, he withers away half-living, half-dying in visible consumption; no diversion for the burning pain of his bosom, no sympathizing heart opening to him, to which he could pour it forth.

> For I have no one—no one—
> Upon this earth, so great and wide, I've no one.
> So far the scepter of my father reaches,
> So far as navigation sends our flags,
> There is no place—not one—not one—where I
> May shed the burden of my tears, but this.

Helplessness and poverty of the heart lead him back now to the very point, where fullness of heart had caused him to commence. More keenly he feels the need for sympathy, while he is *alone* and *unhappy.* Thus is he found by his returning friend.

Entirely otherwise hath it gone in the meantime with this one. With open senses, with all the powers of youth, all the urges of genius, all the warmth of heart cast into the wide universe, he sees man act in the great as in the small; he finds opportunity, to test the ideals brought along with him on the effective powers of the entire species. Everything, that he hears, that he sees, is devoured by him with living enthusiasm, everything is felt in *reference* to that ideal, thought and employed. Man appears to him in several varieties; he comes to know him in several climates, constitutions, degrees of culture and heights of happiness. Thus arises in him gradually a composed and exhalted idea of man in the *great* and the *whole*, as against which every constricting smaller proportion sinks into insignificance. He now steps out of himself, in the vastness of space his soul expands in scope.—Remarkable men, who cast themselves in his orbit, divert his attention, share in his esteem and love.—With him the entire species now takes the place of an individual; a passing youthful emotional state expands into an all-embracing unbounded philanthropy. From an idle enthusiast hath emerged an energetic, active man. Those former dreams and presentiments, which laid yet dark and undeveloped in his soul, have purified themselves into clear ideas, have put idle projects into action, a general indeterminate longing to be active is transformed into purposeful activity. The spirit of nations is studied by him, their strengths, their resources are weighed, their constitutions examined; in intercourse with related spirits his ideas have won manysidedness and form; proven men of the world, like William of Orange, Coligny and others take from them the romantic and tune them by degrees down to pragmatic usefulness.

Enriched with a thousand new fruitful ideas, full of striving powers, creative impulses, bold and far-embracing designs, with active mind, glowing heart, permeated by the great inspiring idea of universal human power and human nobility, and kindled with greater fire for the happiness of this great whole, that hath been present to him in so many individuals,* thus he now returns from the great harvest, burning with

---

*In his subsequent conversations with the King these favorite ideas come to light. "One pen-stroke from this hand of yours," he says to him, "and new the world will be created.

Give to us the liberty of thought.
                    As the strong,
With generosity, let human bliss
Stream from your horn of plenty.—Minds mature
Within your worldly structure!
                    Restore to all mankind
Its lost nobility. The citizen
Be once again, what he had been before.
The Crown's sole aim—no duty doth him bind
Except his brother's equal, sacred duty.
The farmer take his pride i' th' plow and grant

longing, to find a scene of action, upon which he could realize these ideals, could bring these assembled treasures into application. The condition of Flanders tenders itself to him. He finds everything here prepared for a revolution. Acquainted with the spirit, the powers and the resources of this people, which he takes into account against the power of its oppressor, he already regards the great undertaking as concluded. His ideal of republican freedom can find no more favorable moment and no more responsive soil.

> So many rich and blooming provinces!
> A people great and vigorous—and also
> A people good—*and father of this people!*
> That, thought I, that must be divine.

The more miserable he finds this people, the nearer this longing presses to his heart, the more he hastens, to bring it to fulfillment. Here, and *here* first, he is reminded vividly of his friend, whom he left with glowing feelings for human bliss in Alcala. He thinks of him now as savior of the oppressed nation, as the instrument of his higher design. Full of inexpressible love, because he thinks of him together with the favorite concern of his heart, he hastens towards Madrid into his arms, to find now in full seed that germ-nucleus of humanity and heroic virtue, which he once strewed in his soul, and to embrace in him the liberator of the Netherlands, the future creator of his *dreamt-of state*. More passionately than ever, with feverish vehemence, this one rushes to him.

> I press thee to my soul, I feel thine beat
> Almightily against mine own. O, now
> Is everything all well again. For now
> I lie upon *my* Rod'rick's neck!

The reception is the most fiery: but how doth Posa answer him? He, who left his friend in the full bloom of youth and now finds him once again like a walking corpse, dwells he upon this mournful change? Doth he inquire long and anxiously into its sources? Doth he descend to the smaller concerns of his friend? Dismayed and earnest he responds to this unwelcome reception.

> 'Twas not like this, I did expect to see
> Don Philip's son.—— That's not

The King, who is no farmer, his own crown.
In his own place of work the artist dream
To th' sculptor of a beauteous world. No bounds
Obstruct the soaring of the thinker more
Than the conditions of the finite world.

> The young man, bold as lions, unto whom
> A sore oppress'd heroic people sends me —
> For now I stand here not as Roderick,
> Not as the playmate of the boyish Carlos —
> As delegate of all mankind do I
> Embrace you—'tis the Flemish provinces,
> That weep upon your neck, etc.

Involuntarily his ruling idea escapes him immediately in the first moments of the so-longed-for reunion, where one usually hath so many more important small matters to discuss, and Carlos must present everything moving about his situation, must call forth the most distant scenes of childhood, in order to dislodge this favorite idea of his friend, to waken his sympathy and fasten it on his own sad situation. Posa sees himself terribly disappointed in the hopes, with which he hastened to his friend. An heroic character had he expected, who longed for deeds, whereto he wished to open up to him now the scene of action. He reckoned upon that reserve of sublime love of mankind, upon the vow, that he made him in those schwärmerisch days upon the broken-in-two Host, and finds passion for the wife of his father. —

> ——— He's no more the Carl,
> That in Alcala took his leave from thee.
> The Carl no more, who bravely trusts himself,
> To learn of paradise from the Creator
> And then at once as unrestricted Prince
> To plant it here in Spain. O, the conceit
> Was childish, but divinely beautiful!
> These dreams are now foreby! —

A hopeless passion, which consumes all his powers, which places his life itself in danger. How would a concerned friend of the Prince, who however had been entirely only *friend* alone and *not more*, have acted in this situation? and how hath Posa, the world citizen, acted? Posa, the Prince's friend and confidant, would have trembled far too much for the security of his Carlos, than that he should have dared, to assist a dangerous meeting with his Queen. It would have been the friend's duty, to think of the suffocation of this passion and in no way of its satisfaction. Posa, the agent of Flanders, acts entirely otherwise. To him is nothing more important, than this hopeless condition, in which the active powers of his friend disappear, to end as quickly as possible, even should it cost a small daring act. So long his friend languishes in unsatisfied desires, can he not feel the suffering of others; so long his powers are pressed down by melancholy, can he elevate himself to no heroic resolutions. Flanders hath nothing to hope from the unhappy Carlos, but perhaps from the happy. He hastens therefore, to satisfy his hottest wish, he himself leads him to the feet of his Queen; and thereby alone he doth not stop. He finds the motive no longer in the Prince's mind, which had at other times raised him to heroic resolutions: what can he otherwise do, than to kindle this extinguished heroic spirit on another fire and to use the only passion, which is present in the soul of the Prince? To this must he attach the new ideas, which he will now make ruling by her. A look into the Queen's heart convinces him, that he may expect everything from her cooperation. Only the first enthusiasm is it, which he wants to borrow from this passion. Hath it given assistance thereto, to give his friend this healing swing, then needs he it no more, and he can be certain, that it will be destroyed through its own action. Thus even this hindrance, that hurled itself against his great concern, even this unhappy love is converted now into an instrument for that more important purpose, and Flanders' destiny must speak through the mouth of love to the heart of his friend.

> ———— Within this hopeless flame
> I early glimps'd the golden beam of hope.
> To excellence I wanted to conduct him;
> The proudly regal fruit, which takes alone
> A lifetime to implant so slowly, should
> A swifter spring of wonder-working love
> Accelerate. To me his virtue should
> Mature within this robust view o' th' sun.

From the hands of the Queen Carlos now receives the letters, which Posa brought for him from Flanders. The Queen calls back his departed genius.

This subordination of friendship to the more important interests shows itself yet more visibly in the meeting at the cloister. A plan of the Prince upon the King is come to naught; this and a discovery, which he believes to have made to the advantage of his passion, plunge him back more vehemently into this, and Posa believes to observe, that sensuality is mixed with this passion. Nothing could be less compatible with his higher plan. All of the hopes, which he hath based upon Carlos' love of the Queen for the Netherlands, fall headlong, if this love descended from its highness. The displeasure, which he feels thereover, brings his convictions to light.

> ———— Oh, I feel,
> From what I must now wean myself. Yes, once,
> Once was't quite diff'rent. Then wert thou so rich,
> So warm, so rich! A planet had in thy
> Wide bosom, space enough to orbit. All

> Of that is past, devour'd by *one* desire,
> By one small-minded selfish interest.
> Thy heart is grown extinct. Not one tear for
> The monstrous fate of all the provinces,
> Not even one more tear!—O Carl, how poor,
> Since thou now lovest no one but *thyself*!

Afraid of a similar relapse, he believes he must risk a violent step. So long Carl remains in the proximity of the Queen, he is lost for the concern of Flanders. His presence in the Netherlands can give matters there an entirely different turn; therefore he doth not hesitate for a moment, to bring him thither in the most violent manner.

> ———   He should prove
> Himself defiant to the King, should make
> His way in secrecy to Brussels, where
> With open arms the Flemish wait for him.
> All Netherlands will break out in revolt,
> Upon his sole command. The worthy cause
> Will grow much stronger through the Monarch's son.

Would the *friend* of Carlos have been able to prevail upon himself, to play so daringly with the good name, yes even with the life of his friend? But Posa, to whom the liberation of an oppressed people was a far more urgent summons than the small concerns of his friend, Posa, the world citizen, had to act exactly so and not otherwise. Every step, which is undertaken in the course of the play, betrays a *daring boldness*, which an heroic purpose alone is able to imbue; friendship is oft faint-hearted and always apprehensive. Where is until now in the character of the Marquis even only a trace of this anxious care for an isolated creature, of this all-exclusive bent, wherein the peculiar character of passionate friendship alone exists? Where is with him the interest for the Prince not subordinated to the higher interest for humanity? Firm and persevering, the Marquis goes his great cosmopolitan way, and everything, that transpires around him, becomes important to him only through the connection, in which it stands to this higher subject.

Fourth Letter

This confession might cause him the loss of a large component of his admirers, but he will comfort himself with a small component of new reverers, which it bestows on him, and a character like that of his could never hope to achieve general acclaim universally. Lofty, effective benevolence towards the whole in no way excludes the tender interest in the joys and sufferings of a single being. That he loves the human species more than he loves Carl, doth his friendship for him no harm. Always would he him, even had destiny called him to no throne, have distinguished before all the rest through an especially tender concern; in his heart of hearts he would have borne him, as Hamlet his Horatio. One maintains, that benevolence grows thus weaker and more mild, the more its objects increase: but this case can not be applied to the Marquis. The object of his love demonstrates itself to him in the fullest light of inspiration; glorious and transfigured stands this image before his soul like the form of a beloved one. Since it is Carlos, who should realize this ideal of human happiness, so he confers it upon him, so he finally unites both inseparably in *one* feeling. In Carlos alone he now sees his ardently beloved humanity; his friend is the focal point, in which all his ideas of that compound whole are concentrated. It acts therefore still only in *one* object upon him, whom he embraces with all the enthusiasm and all the powers of his soul:

———   My heart, to but
A sole one consecrated, did embrace
The world entire!—Within my Carlos' soul
Did I create a paradise for millions.

Here is thus love for *one* being, without disregard for the universal— attentive care of friendship, without the inequity, the exclusiveness of this passion. Here universal, all-embracing philanthropy, concentrates in a single beam of fire.

And should even that have damaged the interest, which it had ennobled? This picture of friendship should lose in compassion and grace, what it won in extent? The friend of Carlos should have therefore less claim to our tears and our admiration, because he combines with the most restricted manifestation of benevolent emotion its widest extension and softens the divinity of universal love through its most human application?

With the ninth scene of the third act an entirely new sphere of action opens for this character.

Fifth Letter

Passion for the Queen hath finally led the Prince to the brink of ruin. Proofs of his guilt are in the hands of his father, and his imprudent ardor causes him to expose the most dangerous weaknesses to the lurking suspicion of his enemies; he hovers in self-evident danger, to become a victim of his insane love, of fatherly jealousy, of priestly hatred, of the vindictiveness of an offended enemy and of a rejected paramour. His external situation demands the most urgent help, still more however is it demanded by the inner state of his mind, which threatens to shatter all the expectations and designs of the Marquis. From this danger must the Prince be freed, he must be torn free from this spiritual condition, if those designs for Flanders' liberation should be brought to fulfillment; and the Marquis it is, from whom we expect both, who also even makes us hopeful thereof.

But on the same route, whence danger comes to the Prince, is also brought forth a spiritual condition in the King, which causes him to feel the necessity of communication for the first time. The pains of jealousy have restored him from the unnatural constraint of his station to the original station of man, have caused him to feel the emptiness and artificiality of his despotic greatness and wishes to arise in him, which neither power nor highness can satisfy.

> ———   A *King*! And only *King*,
> And *King* again!—No better answer than
> An empty, hollow echo? I do strike
> Upon this rock desiring water, water
> To quench my burning fever thirst—he gives
> Me gold that's glowing.

Exactly a course of events like the former, methinks, or none, could produce in a Monarch, like Philip II was, such a condition; and exactly such a condition must have been produced in him, in order to prepare the subsequent action and to be able to bring the Marquis near to him. Father and son have been led upon entirely different routes to the point, where the poet must have them; upon entirely different routes both were drawn thither to the Marquis of Posa, in whom alone is compressed at this stage the hitherto divided interest. Through Carlos' passion for the Queen and its ineluctable consequences with the King was the Marquis' entire course created: therefore was it necessary, that also the entire play was opened with that. In the face of it the Marquis himself had to be placed so long in the shadows and himself, until he could take possession of the entire action, had to content with a subordinate interest, because he could receive from it alone all the material of his future activity. The attention of the spectator might not thus be entirely prematurely drawn away therefrom, and for this reason was it necessary, that it was engaged up to here as the primary action, whereas the interest, that should subsequently become the ruling one, was made known only through hints from a distance. But so soon the edifice stands, falls the scaffolding. The history of Carlos' love, as the mere preparatory action, retreats, in order to make that place, for which alone it had worked.

Namely those hidden motives of the Marquis, which are not other than the liberation of Flanders and the future destiny of the nation, motives, which one had merely suspected under the cover of his friendship, step forth visibly now and begin, to possess all the attention. Carlos, as from the preceding becomes sufficiently evident, was regarded by him only as the *single indispensable instrument* to *that* fiery and steadfastly pursued aim and as such was embraced with the very same enthusiasm as the aim itself. From this more universal motive had to flow the same apprehensive interest in the weal and woe of his friend, the same tender solicitude for this instrument of his love, as always only the strongest *personal* sympathy would have been able to bring forth. Carl's friendship accords him the most complete enjoyment of his ideal. It is the point of union of all his wishes and activities. He knows yet no other and shorter way, to realize his high ideal of freedom and human happiness, than the one opened to him in Carlos. It never once occurred to him, to seek this in another way; least of all did it occur to him, *to take* this way directly through *the King*. As he is led thither to this one, he shows the highest indifference.

> He wants to see me? Me? I'm naught to him.
> I truly naught!—Me here within this room!
> How aimless and how without rhyme!—How can
> It mean much to him, if I am?—You see,
> It leads to naught.

But it is not long before he abandons this idle, this childish amazement. To a spirit, accustomed, as this one is, to perceive his profit in every circumstance, to fashion even the accident to the plan with the moulding hand, to consider every event in connection to his ruling favorite aim, remains the lofty practice not long concealed, which makes something of the present moment. Even the smallest element of time is to him a holy trust fund, wherewith a good return must be produced. As yet there is no clear, coherent plan, of which he thinks; merely a faint presentiment, and even this scarcely, merely fleeting, ascending idea is it, whether here perhaps something might opportunely be at work? He should step before that one, who hath the destiny of so many millions in his hands. One must make use of the moment, he says to himself, which comes only once. Were it even only a fire-spark of truth, cast into the soul of this man, who hath not yet heard the truth! Who knows, how importantly Providence can work on him with it?—He doth not think more thereby, than to make use of an accidental circumstance in the best manner, of which he is aware. In this state of mind he awaits the King.

Sixth Letter

I reserve for another occasion, in regard to the tone, in which Posa directly at the beginning addresses the King, how in general in regard to his whole behavior in this scene and the manner, how this is received by the King, to explain myself more precisely to you, if you desire, to hear me. Now I content myself merely, to stop at that, which stands in the most immediate connection to the character of the Marquis.

All, that the Marquis, according to his conception of the King, could hope from a rational point of view to bring forth from him—was an astonishment, connected with humiliation, that his great idea of himself and his low opinion of mankind might very well permit some exceptions; after that the natural, inevitable embarrassment of a small spirit before a great spirit. This effect could be beneficial, even if it merely served thereto, to shake the prejudices of this man for a moment; if it caused him to feel, that there were still effects beyond his drawn circle, which he would never have dreamt were possible. This single sound could still echo long in his life, and this impression must persist so much longer with him, the more it was without example.

But Posa had judged the King too shallowly, too superficially, or if he had even known him, so was he too little informed of the *then state of mind* of the same, to take it *along* into account. This state of mind was extremely favorable for him and prepared for his casual speech a reception, which he could have expected with no grounds of likelihood. This unexpected discovery gives him a more lively swing and to the play itself an entirely new turn. Emboldened by a success, which surpassed all his hopes, and through a few traces of *humanity*, which take him unawares in the King, placed in fire, he wanders astray, for a moment, to the extravagant idea, to knit his ruling ideal of Flanders' bliss, etc. directly to the person of the King, to bring it to fulfillment directly through this one. This assumption places him in a passion, which opens the entire foundation of his soul, brings to light all the offspring of his fantasy, all the results of his silent thoughts and discloses clearly, how fully these ideals rule him. Now, in this condition of passion, all the impulses become visible, which have put him until now into action, now he behaves like every schwärmer, who is overwhelmed by his ruling idea. He knows no limits more, in the fire of his inspiration *he ennobles the King*, who listens to him with astonishment, and forgets himself so far, to base hopes upon him, whereover he will blush in the very next peaceful moment. Carlos is now no longer remembered. What a long circuitous route, to wait first upon this one! The King offers him a far nearer and swifter satisfaction. Why postpone the happiness of mankind until his successor?

Would Carlos' bosomfriend have so far forgotten himself, would another passion than the ruling one have carried the Marquis *so* far away? Is the interest of friendship so motile, that one can transfer it with so little difficulty to another object? But everything is explained, so soon one *subordinates* friendship to that ruling passion. Then is it natural, that this in the very next occasion reclaims its rights and not long bethinks, to exchange its means and instruments.

The fire and candor, wherewith Posa his favorite feelings, which until now were secrets between Carlos and him, explains to the King; and the delusion, that this one understands them, even could bring them to fulfillment, was an obvious faithlessness, of which he made himself guilty towards his friend Carl. Posa, the world citizen, might so act, and it can be to him alone forgiven; on the part of his bosom friend Carl were it ever so condemnable, as it would be incomprehensible.

Longer than moments, of course, this blindness should not last. The first surprise, of passion, one forgives easily: but if he still continues even soberly, thereon to believe, so would he justly descend in our eyes to the dreamer. That it however actually found acceptance with him, is clear from a few passages, where he jests thereover or earnestly clears himself thereof. "Suppose," he says to the Queen, "I were to contemplate, to set my faith upon the throne?"

> QUEEN: No, Marquis.
> Not even once in jesting would I e'er
> Accuse you of such unripe fantasy.
> You are no dreamer, who would undertake,
> What can't be brought unto its end.
>   MARQUIS: That were
> Indeed the question, so I think.

Carlos himself hath seen deeply enough into the soul of his friend, in order to find such a resolution founded on his mode of conception, and that, what he himself says about it on this occasion, could alone be sufficient, to place the point of view of the author beyond doubt. "Thou thyself," says he to him, still always in the delusion, that the Marquis hath sacrificed him,

> Thou wilt thyself fulfill,
> What I should have and never could—*Thou* wilt
> Bestow the golden days upon the Spaniards,
> Which they have hop'd from me in vain. For me
> 'Tis over now—forever over. Thou
> Hast recogniz'd that—O this frightful love
> Hath snatch'd away beyond recall all of
> The early blossoms of my spirit. I
> Am dead to all thy noble hopes. The King
> Is led to thee by Providence or Chance—

My secret is the price, and he is *thine* —
Now thou art able to become his angel.
For me there is no rescue more—perhaps
For Spain!

And in another place he says to the Count of Lerma, in order to
excuse the supposed faithlessness of his friend:

He lov'd
Me, lov'd me much. I was as dear to him
As was his very soul. Oh, that I know —
A thousand tests have proven that to me.
Should not then millions, not his fatherland,
Be dearer to him far more than just *one*?
His bosom was too spacious for *one* friend,
And Carlos' luck too meager for his love.
He made me victim of his virtue.

Seventh Letter

Posa felt it full well, how much had been taken thereby from his
friend Carlos, that he had confided his favorite feelings to the King
and had made an attempt upon that one's heart. Just because he felt,
that these favorite feelings were the *true* bond of their friendship, so
he also knew nothing other, than that he had broken this in the very
moment, where he profaned them with the King. That knew Carlos
not, but Posa knew it full well, that this philosophy and these designs
for the future were the holy *palladium of their friendship* and the
important title, under which Carlos possessed his heart; just because
he knew that and presumed in his heart, that it also could not be
unknown to Carl—how could he dare, to admit to him, that he had
misappropriated this palladium? To confess to him, what had tran-
spired between him and the King, must in his thoughts be tantamount
to announcing to him, that there had been a time, where he was nothing
more to him. Had however, Carlos' future position on the throne, had
the King's son no part in this friendship, was it something subsisting
before itself and thoroughly *only* personal, so could it indeed have
been offended through that confidentiality towards the King, but not
betrayed, not severed; so could this accidental circumstance have noth-
ing against its essence. It was delicacy, it was compassion, that Posa,
the world citizen, concealed from the *future* Monarch the expectations,
which he had based upon the *present* one; but Posa, Carlos' friend,
could commit no more severe offense than through this reserve itself.

Indeed are the reasons for this reserve, the single source of all
subsequent confusions, which Posa attributes, as well to himself as

thereafter to his friend, of an entirely different nature. Act IV, Scene vi:

> The King did trust in the receptacle, to which
> He hath deliver'd his most sacred secret,
> And trust doth call for gratitude. What
> Were mere idle chatter, if my silence brings
> To thee no harm? Perhaps doth spare thee? Why
> Point out to the sleeping one the thundercloud,
> Which hangs above his crown?

And in the third scene of Act V:

> —But I, corrupted by false tenderness,
> Deceiv'd by proud delusion, to conclude
> This daring venture without thee, have kept
> Conceal'd my dang'rous secret from our friendship.

But to anyone, who hath cast only a few glances into the human heart, will it be clear, that the Marquis with these alleged reasons (which are in themselves by far too weak, to motivate such an important step) only seeks to deceive himself—because he dares not confess to himself the true causes. A far truer elucidation of his then-state-of-mind is provided by another passage, wherefrom it appears distinctly, that there must have been moments, in which he took counsel with himself, as to whether he should not sacrifice his friend directly? "It would have been within my power," he says to the Queen,

>   —to bring forth
> A new tomorrow over all this realm.
> The King had given me his heart. He call'd
> Me as his son—And I command his seal,
> And all his Albas are no more.

>   The King
> I do renounce. Upon this parched earth
> No rose of mine doth further bloom. That were
> But juggler's games of childish reasoning,
> Recanted shamefully by grown up men.
> The near approaching hopeful spring should I
> Extinguish, to affect a feeble glimpse
> Of sunshine in the North? To mitigate
> A worn out tyrant's final lash o' th' rods,
> Should risk the century's great liberty?
> Poor wretched fame! I like it not. The fate
> Of Europe ripens in my noble friend.
> To him I designated Spain. But woe!

> Woe be to me and him, should I repent!
> Perhaps I've chosen what is worse! If I
> Misread the hints so great of Providence,
> Which *me*, not *him*, upon this throne desired. —

Thus hath he nevertheless *chosen*, and in order to choose, he had to have thus considered the opposite as possible. From all of these cited cases one recognizes clearly, that the interest of friendship comes after a higher one, and that its direction is determined for it only through the latter. No one in the whole play hath judged this relation between both friends more correctly than Philip himself, from whom it was to be expected even from the first. In the mouth of this judge of men I set forth my apology and mine own judgment of the hero of the play, and with his words would like then also to conclude this inquiry:

> And this sacrifice was made
> For *whom*? The *boy*, my son? O nevermore.
> That I do not believe. A Posa doth
> Not perish for a boy. The scanty flame
> Of friendship doth not fill a Posa's heart.
> That beats for all mankind. *His bent was for*
> *The world with all its coming generations.*

Eighth Letter

But, will you say, whereto this entire inquiry? All the same, whether it hath been involuntary promptings of the heart, harmony of character, reciprocal personal necessity for one another, or from externally-added relations and free choice, which the bond of friendship hath knitted between these both—the effects remain the same, and in the course of the play itself nothing thereby is altered. Hence whereto this effort right from the beginning, to tear the reader from an error, which is perhaps more pleasing to him than the truth? How would it stand with the charm of most moral appearances, if every time one had to illuminate the innermost depths of the human heart and see them as it were *arise*? Enough for us, that everything, which Marquis Posa loves, is assembled in the Prince, is *represented* through him, or at least through him alone is maintained, that he finally inseparably combines this accidental, conditional interest, only borrowed for his friend, with the essence of the same, and that everything, which he feels for him, expresses itself in a personal preference. We enjoy then the pure beauty of this picture of friendship as a simple moral element, unconcerned, in how many parts the philosopher may as well still dissect it.

What however, if the correction of this difference were important for the entire play?—Is, namely, the final aim of Posa's aspirations extended *forth* beyond the Prince, is to him this one only so important as an instrument to a higher purpose, satisfies he through his friendship for him another impulse than *only* this friendship, so can a narrower limit indeed not be placed on the play itself—so must the final object of the play at least coincide with the aim of the Marquis. The great destiny of an entire state, the happiness of the human species for many generations to come, whereupon all the aspirations of the Marquis, as we have seen, are driving, can not indeed *be episodes in an action, which hath for its aim the issue of a love story*. Have we thus misunderstood one another in respect to Posa's friendship, so fear I, we have likewise in respect to the final aim of the whole tragedy. Let me show you it from this new standpoint, perhaps, that many incongruities, to which you hitherto took offense, disappear under this new view.

And what were thus the so-called unity of the play, if *love* it should not be and *friendship* never could be? From the former proceeds the three first acts, from the latter the two remaining, but none from both occupies the whole. Friendship sacrfices itself, and love is sacrificed; but neither the latter nor the former is it, which is made a sacrifice by the other. Thus must still some third be at hand, that is different from friendship and love, for which both have worked and to which both have been sacrificed—and if the play hath a unity, where else could it lie than in this third?

Recall, dear friend, a certain discussion, which about a favorite subject of our decade—about spreading of a purer, gentler humanity, about the highest possible freedom of the *individual* within the state's highest blossom, in short, about the most perfect condition of man, as it in his nature and his powers lies given as achievable—among us became lively and enchanted our fantasy in one of the loveliest dreams, in which the heart revels so pleasantly. We concluded at that time with the fanciful wish, that chance, which indeed hath already achieved greater wonders, might be pleased in the next Julian cycle, to awaken once again our sequence of thoughts, our dreams and convictions, fertilized with the same vitality and just so much good will, in the first born-son of a future ruler of ** or of ** in this or another hemisphere. What with an earnest discussion was mere play, might, as it appeared to me, with such a play, as the tragedy is, be raised to the dignity of earnestness and the truth. What is not possible to fantasy? What is not permitted to a poet? Our conversation had long been forgotten, as I in the meantime made the acquaintance of the Prince of Spain; and soon I took note of this inspirited youth, that he indeed might be that one, with whom we could bring our design to realization. Thought, done! Everything found I, as through a ministering spirit, thereby played into my hands; sense of freedom in struggle with despotism, the fetters of stupidity broken asunder, thousand-year long prejudices shaken, a nation, which reclaims its human rights, republican virtues brought into practice, brighter ideas into circulation, the minds in ferment, the hearts elevated by an inspired interest—and now, to complete the happy constellation, a beautifully organized young soul at the throne, come forth under oppression and suffering in solitary unhindered bloom. Unhappy—so we decided—must the king's son be, in whom we wanted to bring our ideal to fulfillment.

> Be you
> A man upon King Philip's throne! You too
> Have come to know affliction—

From the bosom of sensuality and fortune might he not have been taken; art might not yet have lain a hand on his character, the world at that time might not yet have impressed its stamp on him. But how should a regal Prince of the sixteenth century—Philip the Second's son—a pupil of monks, whose hardly awakening reason is watched by such severe and sharp-sighted guardians, acquire this liberal philosophy? Behold, this too was provided for. Destiny gave him a friend—a friend in the decisive years, where the blossoms of the spirit unfold, ideals are conceived and the moral sentiment is purified—a spiritually rich, sensitive youth, over whose education itself, what hinders me, to suppose this? a favorable star hath watched, unusually good fortune hath interposed and whom some hidden sage of his century hath educated for this beautiful enterprise. An offspring of friendship thus is this bright human philosophy, which the Prince will bring into practice upon the throne. It clothes itself in all the charms of youth, in all the grace of poetry; with light and warmth it is deposited in his heart, it is the first bloom of his being, it is his *first love*. To the Marquis it is a matter of extreme concern, to preserve in it this youthful vitality, to cause it to persist as an object of passion in him, because only passion can help him conquer the difficulties, which will encounter its exercise. "Tell you him," he charges the Queen:

> That he should hold in high esteem his dreams
> Of youth, if he will be a man one day,
> And that he should not open up the heart
> Of these most tender godly flowers to
> Reputed better reason's deadly insect—
> That he not stray, e'en if the voice of wisdom
> Speak out from muddy depths its calumny
> Against enthusiasm, heaven's daughter.
> I've told him this before—

Among both friends forms thus an *enthusiastic design, to bring forth the happiest condition, which is achievable to human society, and of this enthusiastic design, how it namely appears in conflict with the passion,* treats the present drama. The point was thus, to put forward a *Prince*, who should realize the highest possible ideal of civil bliss for his age—not to educate this Prince first to this aim; for this had to have been done long beforehand and could also indeed not be made into the subject of such a work of art; still less to let him apply his actual hand to this job, for how much would this have overstepped the narrow limits of a tragedy?—The point was, to only *show* this Prince, to make ruling in him the state of mind, which must be the basis of such an effect, and to raise its *subjective* possibility to a high degree of likelihood, unconcerned, whether fortune and chance will realize it.

Ninth Letter

I want to explain myself more precisely in respect to the preceding.

The youth, namely, of whom we should expect this extraordinary effect, had to have mastered the desires beforehand, which can become dangerous to such an undertaking; like that Roman must he hold his hand over flames, in order to convince us, that he be enough of a man, to conquer the pain; he had to pass through the fire of a fearful test and prove himself in this fire. Then only, if we have seen him wrestle successfully with an *internal* enemy, can we promise him victory over the external hindrances, which are thrown against him upon the bold reformer's path; then only, if we him in the years of sensuality, with the fervent blood of youth, have seen bid defiance to temptation, can we be entirely certain, that it will not be dangerous further to the mature man. And what passion could produce for me this effect in greater measure than the most powerful of all, *love*?

All passions, of which for the great aim, whereto I reserved him, could be feared, this one excepted, are banished from his heart or have never dwelt therein. In a depraved, immoral court he hath preserved the purity of first innocence; not his *love*, also not exertion through principles, entirely alone his moral instinct hath preserved him before this pollution.

The shaft of lust was broke upon this breast
Yet long before Elizabeth ruled here.

Toward the Princess of Eboli, who so often out of passion and plan forgot herself in his presence, he shows an innocence, which comes very near to *naivete*; how many, who read this scene, would have understood the Princess far more quickly? My intention was, to place in his nature a purity, against which no seduction can have any power.

The kiss, which he gives the Princess, was, as he himself says, the first kiss of his life, and this was yet certainly a very virtuous kiss! But also one should see him exalted above a *more subtle* seduction; hence the entire episode of the Princess of Eboli, whose wanton arts are frustrated by *better love*. With this love alone had he thus to do, and virtue will have him *entirely*, if he will succeed, also to conquer this love; and thereof the play now treats. You comprehend now also, why the Prince was depicted exactly *so* and not otherwise; why I have permitted, that the noble beauty of this character through so much vehemence, so much unsteady ardor, like a clear water through undulation, is muddied. A gentle, benevolent heart, enthusiasm for the great and the beautiful, delicacy, courage, steadfastness, unselfish generosity should he possess, beautiful and bright glimpses of the spirit should he show, but *wise* should he not be. The future great man should slumber in him, but a fiery blood should not yet now permit him, it truly to be. All, which makes the excellent regent, all, which can justify the expectations of his friend and the hopes of a world awaiting upon him, all, which must be united, to realize his principal ideal of a future state, should be found together in this character: but it should not yet be developed, not yet from passion separated, not yet refined to pure gold. Thereupon it first occurred in reality, to bring him nearer to this perfection, in which he is now still deficient; a more perfect character of the Prince had spared me the entire play. Likewise you comprehend at present, why it was necessary, to give the character of Philip and his spiritual kin a so great room to play—a not too excusable fault if these characters should have been nothing further than the machinery, to entangle and disentangle a love story—and why above all such a wide field was permitted to *spiritual*, *political* and *domestic* despotism. Since, however, my actual theme was, to cause the future *creator of human bliss* to *emerge* from the play, so was it very fitting, to present the *creator of misery* alongside him and through a complete, horrible picture of despotism to elevate ever more his charming opposite. We see the despot upon his sad throne, see him famish in the midst of his treasures, we experience from his mouth, that he in the midst of all his millions is *alone*, that the furies of suspicion fall on his sleep, that his creatures offer him molten gold in place of a refreshing drink; we follow him into his solitary chamber, see there the ruler of half the world for a—human being pray and him then, if fate hath granted him this wish, like a mad man, himself destroy the gift, of which he was no longer worthy. We see him unconsciously be a servant to the lowest passions of his slaves; are eyewitnesses, how they twist the cords, whereby they him, who imagines himself, to be the sole author of his deeds, guide like a boy. Him, before whom one trembles in distant parts of the world, we see before a domineering priest give a degrading account and atone for a mild transgression with an ignominious punishment. We see him struggle against nature and humanity, which he can not entirely conquer, too proud, to recognize its power, too powerless, to evade it; shunned by all its enjoyments, but pursued by its weaknesses and horrors; severed from his kind, in order as a cross between creature and creator—to excite our pity. We despise this greatness, but we mourn over his misunderstanding, because even out of this distortion we ourselves still perceive traits of humanity, which make him one of us, because he also is miserable merely through the remaining rest of humanity. The more however, this horrible picture repelled us, the stronger are we attracted by the image of gentler humanity, which is transfigured before our eyes in Carlos, in his friend's and in the Queen's character.

And now, dear friend, look over the play from this new standpoint once more. What you held for *overloading*, will now perhaps be less; in the *unity*, whereover we are now agreed, will be resolved all the individual components of the same. I could pursue yet further the initial thread, but it be enough for me, to have indicated to you through some hints, whereover in the play itself the best information is unfolded. It is possible, that, in order to discover the primary idea of the play, more peaceful reflection is required, than is compatible with the hastiness, wherewith one is accustomed, to peruse such writings; but the aim, whereon the artist hath worked, must indeed show itself fulfilled at the end of the work of art. Wherewith the tragedy is concluded, wherewith it must have occupied itself, and now one hears, how Carlos parts from us and his Queen.

> I've lain within a long and heavy dream.
> I was in love—And now I am awake.
> Forgotten be the past! At last I see,
> There is a higher good, more to be wish'd
> For than possessing thee—Here are your letters
> Return'd. Destroy those which are mine. You need
> Fear no more agitation from me. 'Tis
> Foreby. A purer fire hath purified
> My being.—I will build a monument
> To him, like hath become no Monarch yet —
> And over where his ashes rest will bloom
> A paradise!
>   So have I wanted you!
> That was the noble meaning of his death!

Tenth Letter

I am neither an illuminati nor a freemason, but if both brotherhoods have a moral aim common with one another, and if this aim is the most important for human society, so must it with that one, which Marquis

Posa proposed to himself, be at least very nearly related. What these seek to effect through a secret union of a few active members, scattered through the world, will the latter, more completely and concisely, carry out through a single subject: through a Prince namely, who hath the expectation, to mount the greatest throne of the world and is enabled through this exalted standpoint to effect such a work. In this single subject makes he the sequence of ideas and the mode of feeling ruling, wherefrom that beneficent effect must flow as a necessary consequence. To many this subject for the dramatic action might appear too abstract and too serious, and if they have prepared themselves for naught more than the picture of a passion, so had I to be sure disappointed their expectation; but it seemed to me not entirely unworthy of an attempt, "truths, which to anyone, who means well by his species, which must be the *holiest* and which until now were only the property of science, to transfer to the domain of the fine arts, to animate with light and warmth and, planted as living, acting motives in the heart of man, to exhibit in a powerful struggle with passion." Hath the genius of tragedy taken revenge on me for the violation of these limits, so are on that account a few not entirely unimportant ideas, which are put down here, for—the honest finder not lost, who it perhaps will not unpleasantly surprise, observations, of which he is reminded from his Montesquieu, to see applied and confirmed in a tragedy.

Eleventh Letter

Ere I take my final leave from our friend Posa, yet a few words about his puzzling conduct towards the Prince and about his death.

Many namely have reproached him, that he, who cherishes such high notions of freedom and continuously bears it in his mouth, yet arrogates to himself a despotic arbitrariness in respect to his friend, that he him *blindly*, like a minor, guides and him leads thus thereby to the brink of destruction. Wherewith, say you, can it be excused, that Marquis Posa, instead of revealing to the Prince at once the relation, wherein he now stands in respect to the King, instead of discussing with him in a rational manner the necessary measures and, whilst he makes him an accessory to his plan, at once to prevent all overhaste, whereto ignorance, mistrust, fear and imprudent ardor could otherwise transport the Prince and also subsequently have actually transported, that he, instead of taking this, so innocent, so natural course, runs rather the most extreme risk, awaits rather these so easy-to-avoid consequences and them thereafter, if they actually come to pass, seeks to remedy through a means, that can turn out just as unhappy, as it is brutal and unnatural, namely through the arrest of the Prince? He knew the pliant heart of his friend. Still recently the poet caused him to furnish proof of the power, with which he ruled the such. Two words had spared him this unfavorable expedient. Why doth he take refuge in *intrigue*, where he would have come to the goal through a *direct* method incomparably quicker and incomparably safer?

Since this violent and erroneous behavior of the Maltese hath led hereby to all the subsequent situations and above all to his self-sacrifice, so assumed one, a little hastily, in advance, that the poet hath been carried away by this insignificant advantage, to do violence to the inner truth of this character and to misdirect the natural course of the action. Since this was, to be sure, the most convenient and shortest path, to reconcile this strange behavior of the Maltese, so sought one no *more direct* explanation in the coherence of this character; for that were too much to demand of a critic, to withhold his verdict merely therefore, because the author fares badly thereby. But some claim I believed I had acquired yet to this equity, because in the play more than once the *brilliant situation* hath been considered less important than *the truth*.

Incontestibly! the character of the Marquis Posa had gained in beauty and purity, if he had acted completely *straightforward* and had ever remained exalted above the ignoble expedient of intrigue. Also I confess, this character affects me, but, what I hold for truth, affects me more. I hold for truth, "that *love* for some *actual object* and love for an ideal must be just as imcomparable in their effects, as they are different from one another in their essence—that the most unselfish, purest and noblest man is quite often launched from enthusiastic devotion to *his notion* of virtue and of the happiness he intends to bring forth, to dispose just as arbitrarily of individuals as only alwaysthe most self-serving despot, because the subject of both aspirations dwells *in* them, not *outside* them and because that one, who models his actions after an inner spiritual image, lies with the freedom of another well nigh as much in variance as this one, whose final goal is *his own ego.*" True greatness of the mind leads often not less to transgressions of the freedom of others than egoism and the desire to rule, because it acts for the sake of the action, not for the single subject. Just because it acts in steady regard to the whole, vanishes only all too easily the smaller interest of the individual in this vast prospect. Virtue acts largely for the sake of the law; schwärmerei for the sake of its ideals; love for the sake of its object. From the first class we would choose lawgivers, judges, kings, from the second *heroes*, but only from the third our friend. This first we *revere*, the second *admire*, the third *love*. Carlos hath found reasons, to repent, that he left this difference out of account and made a great man into his bosom friend.

What is the Queen to thee? And lovest *thou*
The Queen? Should thy strict virtue have to ask
The narrow-minded worries of my love?
——— Ah, here is nothing to condemn,
Naught, naught except my furious delusion,
Not to have realiz'd until this day,
That thou—art just as *great* as thou art *gentle*.

To act noiselessly, without assistants, in silent greatness, is the Marquis' schwärmerei. Silently, as Providence cares for a sleeping one, he desires to undo the fate of his friend, he would save him, as a God—and precisely thereby he destroys him. That he looked too much towards his ideal of virtue into the heights and too little down upon his friend, ruined both of them. Carlos comes to an unhappy end, because his friend did not content himself, to save him in a common manner.

And here, methinks, I encounter a not unremarkable experience in the moral world, which to no one, who hath to some extent taken time, in order to look around or to watch the course of his own feelings, can be entirely foreign. It is this: that the moral motives, which are derived from *a too-reaching ideal of excellence*, lie not naturally in the human heart and just therefore, because they are brought inside into the same first through art, act not always beneficently, but quite often, through a quite human devolution, are exposed to an injurious misuse. Through practical laws, not through artificial offspring of theoretical reason should man be guided in his moral actions. Indeed alone this, that every such moral ideal or edifice of art is yet no more than an idea, which, like all other ideas, participates in the restricted point of view of the individual, to whom it listens, and thus in its application can also not be capable of the universality, in which man cares to employ it, indeed this alone, I say, had to make it into the most extremely dangerous instrument in his hand: but yet it becomes far more dangerous through the alliance, into which it but all too rapidly steps with certain passions, which are found more or less in all human hearts; I mean lust for power, self-conceit and pride, which immediately seize it and become inseparably mingled with it. Name to me, dear friend—in order to select from countless examples only one—name to me the founder of an order or even the fraternal order itself, which itself—with the purest aims and with the noblest impulses—had always kept pure of arbitrariness in the application, of *violence* against the freedom of others, of the spirit of *secrecy* and *lust for power*? Who in the carrying out of one, from every impure admixture even still thus free moral aim, insofar as they imagine this aim as something subsisting for itself and desire to achieve it in purity, as it had appeared to their reason, had not been carried away unobserved, to violate the freedom of others, to set aside the respect toward other's rights, which were otherwise always the most holy to them, and to practice not seldom the most arbitrary despotism, without the aim itself exchanged, without having to suffer a corruption of their motives? I explain this phenomenon to myself from the need of restricted reason, to *shorten* its course, to simplify its business and to convert individualities, which distract and confuse it, into universalities. From the general inclination of our heart to the desire for power or the aspiration, to push everything away, which hinders the play of our powers. I selected on this account an entirely well-wishing character, entirely exalted over every self-serving desire, I gave him the highest respect for another's rights, I even gave him the creation of a universal *enjoyment of freedom* as his aim, and I believe myself to be in no contradiction with universal experience, if I cause him, even on the way thither, to stray into despotism. It lay in my plan, that he should ensnare himself in this trap, which besets everyone, who finds himself upon a similar path with him. How much had it cost me as well, to bring him foreby in good condition therefrom and to the reader, who grew fond of him, to give the unalloyed enjoyment of all the remaining beauties of his character, if I had not held it for an incomparably greater gain, to remain on the side of human nature and to confirm an experience, never enough taken heed of, through his example. This, mean I, that one distances oneself in moral things not without danger from the natural practical feeling, in order to elevate oneself to general abstractions, that man confides himself far more safely to the suggestions of his heart or to the already present and individual feelings of right and wrong than to the dangerous direction of universal ideas of reason, which he hath created artificially—for naught leads to the *Good*, which is not *natural*.

Twelfth Letter

It only remains still, to say a few words about his self-sacrifice.

One hath it namely criticized, that he plunges himself wantonly into a violent death, which he had been able to evade. All, one says, was indeed not yet lost. Why had he not been able to flee just as well as his friend? Was he more sharply watched than this one? Did not his friendship for Carlos make it a duty for him, to preserve himself for this one? and could he not serve him vastly more with his life than in all probability with his death, even if everything had come to pass in conformity with his plan? Could he not—indeed! What had the calm spectator not have been able to do, and how much more wisely and prudently would this one have managed his life! 'Tis a pity only, that the Marquis had neither the happy coldbloodedness nor the leisure to enjoy, which was necessary to such a rational estimate. But, will one say, the forced and even ingenious means, to which he takes his refuge, in order to die, could not possibly have presented itself to him voluntarily and in the first moment, wherefore had he the reflection and time, which it took him, not just as well been able to employ, to devise a rational plan of escape or rather to seize immediately the one, which lay so near to him, which springs forthwith to the eyes of even the most shortsighted reader? If he didn't intend to die, in order to be dead, or (as one of my reviewers expresses himself) if he did not *want to die for the purpose of martyrdom*, so is it scarcely comprehensible, how the so-affected means of destruction could have presented themselves earlier than the vastly more natural means of escape. There is seemingly much in this reproach, and so much the more is it worth the effort, to explain it.

The solution is this:

Firstly this objection grounds itself upon the false, and through the previously sufficiently refuted supposition, that the Marquis died *only* for his friend, which can indeed no more have been the case, after it had been shown, that *he lived not for him*, and that this friendship hath an entirely different peculiarity. He can thus not indeed die, in order to save the Prince; thereto might presumably even yet another, and less violent means of escape have presented itself to him other than death—"he dies, in order for his—in the Prince's soul deposited— ideal to do and to give, what a man can do and give for something, that is the most dear to him; in order to show him, in the most emphatic manner, which he hath in his power, how greatly he believes in the truth and beauty of this design and how important the fulfillment of the same be to him"; he dies therefor, why many great men died for a truth, which they wanted to have followed and taken to heart by many; in order to set forth through his example, how greatly it be worth it, that one suffer everything for it. As the lawgiver of Sparta saw his work completed and the Oracle at Delphi had made the pronouncement, the republic would blossom and endure, so long it respected Lycurgus' laws, he called the people of Sparta together and demanded an oath from them, to leave the new constitution unmolested so long at least, until he from a journey, which he just now planned, would be returned. As this was sworn to him through a solemn oath, Lycurgus left the territory of Sparta, ceased from this moment on, to take meals, and the republic awaited his return in vain. Before his death he explicitly ordered, even his ashes to be strewn in the sea, therewith might not even an atom of his being return to Sparta and his fellow citizens not even only plausibly be relieved of their oath. Could Lycurgus have believed in earnestness, to bind the Lacedaemonian people through this sophistry and to secure his state constitution through such a game? Is it even only thinkable, that such a wise man should have sacrificed his life for such a fanciful idea, that was so important to his fatherland? But it seems to me very thinkable and worthy of him, that he sacrificed it, in order to engrave through the greatness and extraordinariness of his death an indelible impression of his self in the heart of his Spartans and to shower a higher venerability over his work, in which he made the creator of the same into an object of feeling and admiration.

Secondly it is here, as one easily sees, not a matter of importance, how *necessary*, how *natural* and how *useful* this expedient was *in fact*, rather how it occurred to that one, who had to seize it, and how *easy* or *difficult* he fell thereupon. It is thus far less the condition of things than the mental constitution of him, upon whom these things act, which must come here into consideration. Are the ideas, which lead the Marquis to this heroic resolution, *familiar* to him, and do they occur to him easily and with liveliness, so is the resolution neither affected nor forced; are these ideas fully the advancing and ruling in his soul and stand the ones thereagainst in the shadows, which could lead him upon a milder path of escape, so is the resolution, which he seizes, *necessary*; have those sentiments, which would combat this resolution in any other, less power over him, so can even the execution of the same not cost him quite so much. And this is that, which we must now examine.

First: Under what circumstances doth he proceed to this resolution?—In the most intense situation wherein a man ever found himself, where terror, doubt, and displeasure with himself, pain and despair at once assail his soul. *Terror*: he sees his friend on the point, to that person, whom he knows as his most dreadful foe, of revealing a secret, whereon his life depends. *Doubt*: he knows not, whether this secret is out or not? Knows it the Princess, so must he act towards her as an accessory; knows she it not yet, so can a single syllable make him a traitor, the murderer of his friend. *Displeasure with himself*: he alone hath through his unhappy reserve carried the Prince along to this overhaste. *Pain and despair*: he sees his friend lost, he sees in his friend all hopes lost, which he hath grounded upon the same.

> Foresaken by the only one, thou throw'st
> Thyself i' th' arms of Princess Eboli—
> Unhappy man! into a devil's arms:
> For this one 'twas, who thee betray'd. I see
> Thee hasten off. A bad presentiment
> Flies through my heart. I follow thee. Too late
> Thou lie'st before her feet. Already the
> Confession flows across thy lips. For thee
> There is no rescue more—
>   Here turns it night before my senses!

Naught—naught—no remedy—no help—at all
In nature's whole circumference!—

In this moment now, where such different emotions assail his soul, should he on the spur of the moment devise a means of rescue for his friend. Which will it be? He hath lost the correct use of his powers of judgment and with this the thread of things, which only calm reason is able to pursue. He is no more master of his sequence of thoughts—he hath thus given in to the power of those ideas, which have attained the most light and the greatest familiarity with him.

And of what kind are these now? Who doth not discover in the entire coherence of his life, as he lives it before our eyes here in the play, that his whole fantasy is filled and penetrated by images of romantic greatness, that the heroes of Plutarch live in his soul and that of two expedients always the *heroic* must first and foremost occur to him? Did not his previous appearance with the King show us, what and how much this man for that, which he deems true, beautiful and excellent, be able to venture?—What is on the other hand more natural, than that the displeasure, which he feels with himself in this moment, causes him to seek at first between those means of rescue, which cost him something; that he believes it to be to some extent due to justice, to effect the rescue of his friend at *his own* expense, because it was his own imprudence, which plunged that one into this danger? Take into consideration thereby, that he can not hasten enough, to tear himself from this suffering state, to obtain once again the free enjoyment of his being and command of his feelings. A spirit like this one however, you will have to admit, seeks *in* itself, not *outside* itself, for help; and if the merely *prudent* man would have let his first be, the situation, in which he found himself, to test from all sides, until he got the better of it: so is it grounded in the opposite entirely in the character of the heroic schwärmer, to shorten the road, through some extraordinary deed, to regain his self-respect through an immediate elevation of his being. So were the resolution of the Marquis to a certain extent explainable as indeed an heroic palliative, whereby he, from an immediate feeling of *stupidity* and *despondency*, the most dreadful condition for such a spirit, seeks to escape. Add then to this yet, that indeed since his boyhood, since the very day, when Carlos voluntarily tendered himself in his place for a painful penalty, the desire, to repay him for this generous deed, disturbed his soul, tortured him like an unpaid debt, and the weight of the foregoing reasons must thus in this moment not be less strengthened. That he had this recollection actually in mind, is demonstrated by a passage, where it involuntarily escapes him. Carlos urges thereupon, that he should flee, ere the consequences of his bold deed come to pass. "Was I so scrupulous, Carlos," he answers him, "When thou had'st shed thy blood for me—a boy?" The Queen, carried away by her pain, even accuses him, that he hath carried this resolution around with himself quite a long time —

You plung'd yourself into this deed, which you
Deem lofty. But deny it not! I know
You, you have long been thirsting for it!

Finally I do not intend to thoroughly have absolved the Marquis of schwärmerei. Schwärmerei and enthusiasm touch one another so closely, their line of demarcation is so fine, that it can be overstepped in conditions of passionate excitement only all too easily. And the Marquis hath only a few moments for this choice! The same attitude of mind, wherein he resolves the deed, is also the same, wherein he took the irrevocable steps to its execution. He is not granted the privilege, to look at his resolution once more in another condition of the soul, ere he brings it to fulfillment—who knows, whether he had prepared it then not otherwise! Such an other condition of the soul for example is it, wherein he departs from the Queen. "O!" he exclaims, "yet life is beautiful!"—But this discovery he makes too late. He wraps himself up in the greatness of his deed, in order to feel no remorse thereover.

THEATER CONSIDERED AS A MORAL INSTITUTION

Theater Considered as a Moral Institution

Read at a public session of the Elector's German Society in Mannheim in the year 1784

TRANSLATED BY JOHN SIGERSON AND JOHN CHAMBLESS

Theater was born out of a universal, irresistible attraction to the new and extraordinary, a desire to feel oneself put into a state of passion, to use Sulzer's expression. Exhausted by higher mental exertions, worn down by the monotonous, often oppressive affairs of daily life, and bombarded by sensuality, man necessarily felt an inner emptiness which clashed with his eternal desire for activity. Our nature, equally incapable of remaining forever in a bestial condition or of continuously carrying on the intricate work of the Understanding, required an intermediate condition that would unite these two contradictory extremes, resolving their harsh tension into gentle harmony and facilitating the alternating passage from one state into the other. This service is performed by the Aesthetic Sense, or the Sense of the Beautiful. But since the wise legislator's chief object must be to select the superior of two possible courses of action, he will not acquiesce in merely neutralizing popular sentiments, but will, whenever possible, use those sentiments as means to accomplish higher ends, endeavoring to transform them into a source of general happiness. And that is why he chose theater above all else, since it opens up infinite horizons to the spirit thirsting for activity, providing nourishment to the soul's every power without overtaxing any single one, and uniting the acculturation of mind and heart with the noblest sort of entertainment.

Whoever first observed that *religion* is the mightiest pillar of the state, and that laws themselves lose their power once religion is removed, has perhaps given us—without knowing or intending it—our best defense of the theater on behalf of its noblest side. This inadequacy, this unstable character of political laws, which makes religion indispensable to the State, also conditions the moral influence exerted by the stage. Laws, he was trying to say, revolve around duties of denial; religion extends its demands to true action. Laws restrict only those activities which tend to weaken society's cohesion; religion ordains those which deepen it. Laws rule only over the outward expressions of the will, and deeds are their only subjects; religion extends its jurisdiction into the heart's most hidden recesses, and pursues thoughts to their most inward source. Laws are slippery and malleable, as changeable as mood and passion; religion forms strong and eternal bonds. Now, if we were to assume something which is not the case— if we conceded that religion possessed this tremendous power over every human heart, then will it, or can it completely develop our character? Religion (and here I am dealing solely with its divine, and not its political aspects) generally acts more upon the sensuous side of the population—indeed, it is probably because of this effect on the sensuous that its influence is so sure. Deprived of this, religion's power vanishes—and whence the influence of the stage? Religion ceases to exist for the greater part of humankind, the moment we destroy its symbols and mysteries, the moment we efface its renderings of Heaven and Hell. And yet, these are merely fantastic portraits, riddles without solution, terror-figures, and distant enticements. Consider now, how religion and law are strengthened as they enter into alliance with the theater, where virtue and vice, happiness and misery, wisdom and folly are accurately and palpably led out before man in a thousand images; where Providence solves its riddles, untangles its knots before his eyes; where the human heart confesses its subtlest stirrings while tortured on the rack of passion; where all masks fall away, the makeup is removed, and truth sits in judgment, incorruptible as Rhadamanthus.

The jurisdiction of the stage begins where the domain of secular law leaves off. Whenever justice is dazzled by gold and gloats in the pay of infamy; when the crimes of the mighty mock their own impotence, and mortal fear stays the ruler's arm—then theater takes up the sword and scales, and hauls infamy before the dreadful tribune of justice. The entire realm of fantasy and history, past and present, stand at its beck and call. Monstrous criminals, long rotted to dust, are summoned by poesy's omnipotent call, to relive their shameful lives for the grim edification of later generations. Unconsciously, like empty shadows, the horrors of their own age pass before our eyes while we, horrified yet fascinated, curse their memory. Someday, when morality is no longer taught, when religion is no longer met with mere faith, when laws become superfluous, we shall still tremble as Medea totters down the palace steps, fresh from the murder of her child. Mankind shall still be seized with healthy terror, and all will silently rejoice over their own clear conscience, as Lady Macbeth, the dreadful sleepwalker, washes her hands and summons all the perfumes of Arabia to extinguish the hateful odor of murder. As surely as visual representation is more compelling than the mute word or cold exposition, it is equally certain that the theater wields a more profound, more lasting influence than either morality or laws.

In doing so, it is merely *assisting* human justice; but yet another, broader field is open to it as well. The theater has the power to punish the thousand vices which justice must patiently tolerate; the thousand virtues which the latter must let pass without comment, on the stage are held up for general admiration. And here, at its side, are wisdom and religion. From their pure fountain it draws its lessons and examples, and clothes stern duty in charming and alluring robes. How it swells our soul with great emotions, resolves, passions—what a divine ideal it sets up for us to emulate! When good-hearted Augustus extends his hand to the traitor Cinna,[1] who could already read the death sentence on his lips, and Augustus, great as his gods, says: "Cinna, let us be friends"—who among the audience, at *that* moment, would not also like to be shaking the hand of his own mortal enemy, in imitation of this god-like Roman? When Franz von Sickingen,[2] on his way to punish a prince and wage war for others' rights, inadvertently turns his head and sees the smoke rising from his fortress, where his helpless wife and children have remained behind, and he—*moves onward* to keep his sacred word—how great does man become for me at that moment, how small and contemptible his dreaded, invincible fate!

In the theater's fearsome mirror, the vices are shown to be as loathsome as virtue is lovely. When, in night and tempest, old Lear[3] knocks in vain at his daughter's door; when, his white hair streaming in the wind, he tells the raging elements of his Regan's unnatural conduct; when his agony finally bursts from his lips with those awful words: "I have given you all!"—how despicable does ingratitude seem to us then! How solemnly we vow to practice filial love and respect!

But the stage extends its sphere of influence further still. Even in those regions where religion and law deem it beneath their dignity to accompany human sentiment, the theater is still at work for our cultural weal. Human folly can disturb social harmony just as easily as can crime and vice. A lesson as old as history itself teaches that in the fabric of human events, the greatest weights are often suspended by the most slender and delicate threads, and, if we follow actions back to their sources, we will have to laugh ten times before we draw back once in horror. With each day I grow older, my catalogue of villains grows shorter, and my index of fools longer and more complete. If the entire moral guilt of the one species of person stems from one and the same source; if all the monstrous extremes of vice which have ever branded him, are merely altered forms, higher grades of a quality which, in the end, we can all laugh about and love—why, then, would nature have taken some different route with the other species? I know of only *one*

Editor's Notes
1. Corneille, *Cinna*.
2. *Franz von Sickingen*, by an unknown playwright.
3. Shakespeare, *King Lear*, II, iii, iv.

secret for guarding man against depravity, and that is: to arm his heart against weaknesses.

We can expect a great share of this work to fall to the stage. The stage holds up a mirror to that most populous class, the fools, and exposes their thousand varieties to relief-bringing ridicule. What in the former case it effected through emotional turmoil and horror, here it accomplishes (and, perhaps, more speedily and infallibly) through humor and satire. If we were to evaluate tragedy and comedy according to the magnitude of achieved effect, then experience would probably decide in favor of the latter. Man's pride is more deeply wounded by ridicule and contempt, than his conscience is tormented by abhorrence. Our cowardice, when confronted with terror, crawls away in fear; but this very cowardice delivers us over to the sting of satire. Laws and conscience can protect us *most of the time* from crimes and vices; the ludicrous requires a more refined discernment, and nowhere can this be presented to greater effect than on the stage's forum. We might perhaps instruct a friend to assault our morals and our heart, but we can scarcely prevail upon ourselves to forgive him a single laugh. Our transgressions might abide a monitor and judge, but we can scarcely suffer witnesses to our private perversities. Only the stage is permitted to ridicule our weaknesses, since it spares our sensibilities, and knows no such thing as a guilty fool. Without reddening with embarrassment, in its mirror we can see our own mask fall away, and thank it secretly for this gentle reproach.

But its sphere of influence is greater still. The stage is, more than any other public institution, a school of practical wisdom, a guide to our daily lives, an infallible key to the most secret accesses of the human soul. I am the first to admit that its influence is not infrequently nullified by self-love and mental obduracy; that a thousand vices still impudently step before its glass; that a thousand fine emotions are pushed away by the cold-hearted audience. I will even venture to say that Molière's Harpagon[4] has probably never reformed a single usurer, that the suicide Beverly[5] has held few of his brothers back from the gambling table, that the robber Karl Moor's[6] tragic story will scarcely make the highways any less dangerous. But, even if we so qualify this great effect of the stage, even if we are so unfair as to deny it altogether—what a wealth of influence it still retains! Although it has neither eradicated nor diminished the sum of our vices, did it not first make us familiar with them?—We will always have to live with vicious and foolish people. We must either avoid or confront them; we either seek

---

4. Molière, *The Miser.*
5. Friedrich Schroder, *Beverley, or, the English Gambler.*
6. Friedrich Schiller, *The Robbers.*

to undermine them, or must become their victims. But no longer do they take us by surprise. Now we are prepared for their assaults. The theater has fathomed the secrets of how to root them out and render them harmless. It was the theater which drew the mask from the hypocrite's face, and revealed the traps which cabals and intrigues have laid for us. It has hauled falsehood and deception out from its twisted labyrinths, and exposed its awful face to the light of day. It may be that the dying Sara[7] does not deter a single debauchee; that all the world's depictions of the seducer punished will not quench his own fire; and that the coquettish actress herself does her best to allay this effect—is it not reward enough, that unsuspecting innocence can now recognize its snares; that the theater has taught it to mistrust its oaths and to shrink back from its attestations of love?

The theater sheds light not only on man and his character, but also on his destiny, and teaches us the great art of facing it bravely. In the fabric of our lives, *chance* and *design* play equally important roles; the latter is directed by *us*, while we must blindly submit to the former. We have already come a long way, if the inevitable does not catch us wholly unprepared, if our courage and resourcefulness have already been tested by similar events, and our heart has been hardened for its blow. The stage brings before us a rich array of human woes. It artfully involves us in the troubles of others, and rewards us for this momentary pain with tears of delight and a splendid increase in our courage and experience. In its company, we follow the forsaken Ariadne[8] through echoing Naxos; we descend into Ugolino's[9] tower of starvation; we ascend the frightful scaffold, and witness the solemn hour of death. What our soul only senses as distant premonition, here we can hear audibly and incontrovertibly affirmed by the startled voice of nature. Under the tower's vault, the deceived favorite is deprived of his queen's favor[10]; now that he must die, the intimidated Moor finally drops his treacherous sophistry. Eternity leaves its dead behind, so that they may reveal secrets which the living could never divine, and the cocksure villain is driven from his final ghastly lair, for even graves blurt out their secrets.

But, not satisfied with merely acquainting us with the fates of mankind, the stage also teaches us to be more just toward the victim of misfortune, and to judge him more leniently. For, only once we can plumb the depths of his tormented soul, are we entitled to pass judgment on him. No crime is more heinous than that of the thief; but do

7. Lessing, *Miss Sara Sampson*—a very popular play in colonial America.
8. Johann Christina Brandes, *Ariadne at Naxos*.
9. Gerstenberg, *Ugolino*.
10. Corneille, *Count Essex*.

we not all soften our verdict with a tear of compassion, when we imagine
ourselves in the same horrible predicament which compels Eduard[11]
to commit the deed?—Suicide is generally detested as sacrilege; but
when Marianne,[12] assailed by an enraged father's threatenings, assailed
by love and by the thought of a dreadful convent's prisons walls, drinks
from her poisoned cup—who among us will be the first to condemn
this pitable victim of an infamous social practice?—Humaneness and
toleration are becoming the pedominant spirit of our times; their rays
have penetrated into the courtrooms, and further still, into the hearts
of our rulers. What share of this divine labor falls to our theaters? Is
it not *these* which have acquainted man with his fellow man, and have
explored the hidden mechanism of his actions?

One noteworthy class of men has special grounds for giving par-
ticular thanks to the stage. Only here do the world's mighty men hear
what they never or rarely hear elsewhere: Truth. And here they see
what they never or rarely see: Man.

Thus is the great and varied service done to our moral culture by
the better-developed stage; the full enlightenment of our intellect is
no less indebted to it. Here, in this lofty sphere, the great mind, the
fiery patriot first discovers how he can fully wield its powers.

Such a person lets all previous generations pass in review, weighing
nation against nation, century against century, and finds how slavishly
the great majority of the people are ever languishing in the chains of
prejudice and opinion, which eternally foil their strivings for happiness;
he finds that the pure radiance of truth illumines only a few isolated
minds, who probably had to purchase that small gain at the cost of a
lifetime's labors. By what means, then, can the wise legislator induce
the entire nation to share in its benefits?

The theater is the common channel through which the light of
wisdom streams down from the thoughtful, better part of society,
spreading thence in mild beams throughout the entire state. More
correct notions, more refined precepts, purer emotions flow from here
into the veins of the population; the clouds of barbarism and gloomy
superstition disperse; night yields to triumphant light. From among
the myriad and magnificent fruits of the better-developed stage, I will
select only two. Who could not notice the universal spread of toleration
toward religious sects in recent years? Long before Nathan the Jew
and Saladin the Saracen[13] filled us with shame and preached to us that
the divine doctrine of submission to God's Will is not irrevocably tied
to whatever we might imagine His nature to be, and long before Joseph

---

11. Iffland, *Ruined by Ambition*.
12. F.W. Gotter, *Marianne*.
13. Lessing, *Nathan the Wise*.

II[14] combated the fearsome hydra of pious hatred, the theater had already emplanted humanity and gentleness into our hearts. The revolting spectacle of the priests' pagan fanaticism taught us to eschew religious hatred; within the frame of this dreadful mirror, Christianity washed out its shameful stains. From the stage's forum, we might also combat errors in *education* with equal success; we are still awaiting the piece which deals with this noteworthy theme. For, judging from its consequences, no subject has greater importance for the future of the republic, than education; and yet, no area has been more neglected, and none so completely abandoned to the individual citizen's illusions and caprice. The stage alone would be able to confront him with touching, soul-stirring scenes depicting the unfortunate victims of neglected education; here our fathers could learn to forego their foolish maxims, and our mothers to temper their love with rationality. False notions can lead even the finest heart astray; and what a disaster, when these begin to boast a *method*, and systematically spoil the tender stripling within the walls of philanthropic institutes and academic hot-houses.

No less readily—if only the chiefs and guardians of the state learned to do this—the stage could be utilized to correct the nation's opinions concerning the government and those it governs. Here, legislative power might speak to the subject through unfamiliar symbols, could respond to his complaints even before these were uttered, and could quash his doubts without seeming to do so. Even industry and inventiveness could and would be imbued with fiery emotion on the stage's forum, if our poets ever deemed it worth their while to be patriots, and if the state would ever condescend to listen to them.

I cannot possibly neglect to mention the great influence that a fine standing theater would have upon the spirit of our nation. I define a people's national spirit as the similarity and agreement of its opinions and inclinations concerning matters in which another nation thinks and feels differently. Only the stage is capable of eliciting a high degree of such agreement, because it ranges throughout the entire domain of human knowledge, exhausts all the situations of life, and pokes its rays into the heart's every cranny; because within it, it unites all classes and social strata, and can boast the most well-beaten pathway to our heart and our understanding. If *one* principle feature could characterize all our plays; if our poets could agree amongst themselves to establish a firm alliance to this end; if their works could be guided by a rigorous selection process, and they applied their brush only to subjects of

14. Joseph II, Emperor of Austria (1741-1790), a participant in Benjamin Franklin's international republican conspiracy which created the United States of America, who also played a key role in Pope Clement XIV's banning of the evil Jesuit order in 1773.

national import—in short, if we could witness the birth of our own national theater, then we would truly become a nation. What bound the Greeks so firmly together? What was it that drew its people so irresistibly to its stage? Nothing other than the patriotic content of their pieces; it was the Grecian spirit, the great, overwhelming interest of the republic, and of a better humanity which lived and breathed within them.

The stage posses another merit, one which I am all the more willing to claim, since I suspect that its legal contest with the prosecution has already been won. What we have heretofore undertaken to demonstrate—that the stage wields critical, determining influence over morality and enlightened thought—was a dubious quest. But even the theater's worst enemies concede that of all contrivances of luxury, and of all the institutions of public entertainment, it reigns supreme. But what it accomplishes in this repect, is more important than we are wont to imagine.

Human nature cannot bear the uninterrupted and eternal rack of daily business; and sensual excitement simply dies with its own gratification. Man, overwrought by animal enjoyments, fatigued from protracted labors, tormented by his eternal compulsion to remain active, thirsts for better and more select amusement—either this, or he will blindly plunge into wild revelry, accelerating his own demise and disrupting the peace of society. Bacchanalian debauchery, ruinous gambling, a thousand follies hatched from idleness—these are the inevitable consequences of the legislator's inability to rechannel these tendencies within the population. The businessman is in danger of developing stomach ulcers as his atonement for a life of selfless dedication to the state; the scholar is in danger of degenerating into a dull pedant; the common man, into a beast. The stage is the institution where instruction and pleasure, exertion and repose, culture and amusement are wed; where no one power of the soul need strain against the others, and no pleasure is enjoyed at the expense of the whole. When grief gnaws at our heart, when melancholy poisons our solitary hours; when we are revolted by the world and its affairs; when a thousand troubles weigh upon our souls, and our sensibilities are about to be snuffed out underneath our professional burdens—then the theater takes us in, and within its imaginary world we dream the real one away; we are given back to ourselves; our sensibilities are reawakened; salutary emotions agitate our slumbering nature, and set our hearts pulsating with greater vigor. Here the unfortunate, seeing another's grief, can cry out his own; the jolly will be sobered, and the secure will grow concerned. The delicate weakling becomes hardened into manhood, and here the first tender emotions are awakened within the barbarian's breast. And then, at last—O Nature! what a triumph for you!—Nature, so frequently trodden to the ground, so frequently risen from its ashes!—when man at last, in all districts and regions and classes, with all his chains of fad and fashion cast away, and every bond of destiny rent asunder—when man becomes his brother's brother with a *single* all-embracing sympathy, resolved once again into a *single* species, forgetting himself and the world, and reapproaching his own heavenly origin. Each takes joy in others' delights, which then, magnified in beauty and strength, are reflected back to him from a hundred eyes, and now his bosom has room for a *single* sentiment, and this is: to be truly *human*.

NUN KOMMT DIE SCHILLERZEIT

"Patriots and world citizens."
Schiller Institute trip to Valley
Forge, Pa.

A young contestant in the
international poetry recitation
for children sponsored by the
Schiller Institute.

Contest winner Sascha Nixberg recites "The Glove" at the Fourth International Schiller Conference.

Celebrating Schiller's 225th birthday, these children re-enact the characters of William Tell in a New York City parade.

WILLIAM TELL

*"No, there is a limit
to the tyrant's power!"*

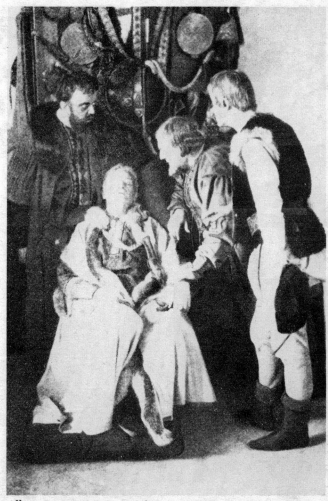

Albert Basserman as Attinghausen in William Tell. *Schiller
Theater, Berlin, 1951.*

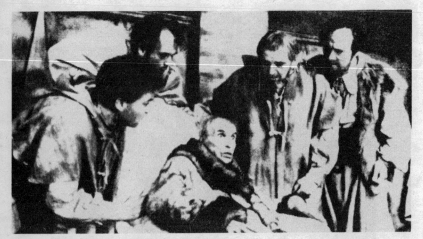

Bernhard Baumeritz as Attinghausen, 1904.

INTRIGUE
AND LOVE

*Three scenes from
Intrigue and Love,
Neues Theater, 1904. In
this play Schiller first
expressed his sympathy
for the American
Revolution.*

CELEBRATIONS OF SCHILLER'S 100th BIRTHDAY

In Bavaria in 1859.

In Leipzig in 1859.

DON CARLOS

1909. Harry Walden in the title role.

1956. Hilde Mikulicz as Elizabeth.

1963. Ernst Deutsch as King Philip.

SCHILLER CELEBRATIONS IN AMERICA

Statues of Schiller and Goethe in the German Cultural Center, Cleveland, Ohio.

Schiller statue in St. Louis.

IN MEMORIAM.

Schiller Gedächtniss-Feier

zum hundertjährigen Todestag

FRIEDRICH VON SCHILLER

in der Carnegie Musik-Halle.

AM SONNTAG, DEN 7. MAI 1905

unter den Auspicien der

Vereinigten Sänger von New York.

SOUVENIR-PROGRAMM.

Program in memory of Schiller under the auspices of United Singers of New York, 1905.

Erinnerungsblätter

zur

Schiller - Gedächtnisfeier

gehalten in

San Franzisko, 1905.

unter den Auspizien

des deutsch-amerikanischen Verbands von Kalifornien

im Golden Gate Park

Sonntag Vormittag, den 7ten Mai

und

im Alhambra Theater

Dienstag Abend, den 9ten Mai.

Program in memory of Schiller under the auspices of German-American Union of California, San Francisco 1905.

Schiller celebration in Chicago, 1984.

SCHILLER
AND HIS CIRCLE

Schiller statue in Marbach.

The house where Schiller was born, in Marbach.

Charlotte Schiller, the poet's wife.

The Schiller linden tree in Blasewitz, near Dresden.

Statue of the Maid of Orleans, Joan of Arc.

Schiller in discussion with members of his republican circle.

Schiller on a donkey, painted by Reinhart.

OVER THE AESTHETICAL EDUCATION OF MAN

In A Series
Of Letters

Over the Aesthetical Education of Man

In a Series of Letters

TRANSLATED BY WILLIAM F. WERTZ, JR.

First Letter

You wish thus to permit me, to place before you the results of my inquiries *into the beautiful* and *art* in a series of letters.

Livelily feel I the weight, but also the charm and the dignity of this undertaking. I shall speak of a subject, which stands with the best part of our happiness in an immediate, and with the moral nobility of human nature, in no very distant connection. I shall lead the cause of beauty before a heart, which feels and practices her whole might and which with an inquiry, where one is just as oft compelled, to appeal to feelings as to principles, will take upon itself the most difficult part of my business.

What I wanted to request of you as a favor, you make in a generous manner into a duty for me and leave me then the appearance of a merit, where I merely yield to my inclination. The freedom of action, which you prescribe to me, is no constraint, rather a need for me. Little practiced in the use of forms suited to schools, I shall scarcely be in danger, through misuse of the same, of sinning against good taste. My ideas, created more from uniform intercourse with my self than a rich experience of the world or acquired through lectures, will not deny their origin, will make themselves guilty of any other error rather than sectarianism and rather fall from their own weakness, than maintain themselves through authority and alien strength.

Indeed I will not conceal from you, that it is in greatest part Kantian principles, upon which the subsequent assertions will rest; but ascribe it to my inability, not to those principles, if you should be reminded in the course of these inquiries of any particular philosophical school. No, the freedom of your mind should be inviolable to me. Your own feeling will furnish me the facts upon which I build, your own free power of thought will dictate the laws, upon which I should proceed.

With regard to those ideas, which in the practical part of the Kantian system are the dominant, only the philosophers are divided in two, but men, I trust myself to prove, at all times have been at one. One liberates them from their technical form, and they become as the inveterate claims of common reason and appear as facts of the moral instincts, which wise nature appointed as guardian of man, until clear insight makes him of age. But even this technical form, which the truth manifests to the understanding, she again conceals from the feelings; for unfortunately the understanding must first destroy the object of the inner sense, if it will make it *itself* into its own. Like the chemist, so the philosopher as well finds the connection only through analysis and the work of voluntary nature only through the agony of art. In order to catch the fleeting appearance, he must put it in the fetters of rule, its beautiful body rend to pieces in conceptions and in a miserable skeleton of words preserve its living spirit. Is it a wonder, if the natural feeling doth not find itself once more in such an image and the truth appears in the report of the analyst as a paradox?

Permit me therefore as well some forbearance, if the following inquiries should remove their object from the sense, while they seek to draw it nearer to the understanding. What is true there of moral experience, must be true in a still higher degree of the appearance of beauty. The entire magic of the same is based upon its mystery, and with the necessary bond of its elements its being is also dissolved.

Second Letter

But should I of the freedom, which is granted me by you, not perhaps be able to make a better use, than to engage your attention upon the theater of beautiful art? Is it not at least beyond the time, to look around for a book of laws for the aesthetical world, since the concerns of the moral offer a so much nearer interest and the philosophical spirit of inquiry is invited so forcibly by the circumstances of the time, to engage itself with the most perfect of all works of art, with the construction of a true political freedom?

I would not like to live in another century and to have worked for another. One is just as good a citizen of the age, as one is citizen of the state; and if it unseemly, yea unpermitted is found, oneself from the customs and practices of the circle, in which one lives, to exclude, why should it be less a duty, in the choice of one's activity to accord a voice to the wants and the taste of the century?

This voice seems however in no way to precipitate the benefit of art; at least not that, upon which alone my inquiries will be directed.

The course of events hath given to the genius of the time a direction, which threatens to remove it yet more and more from the art of the ideal. This must leave reality and elevate itself with suitable boldness above want; for art is the daughter of freedom and from the necessity of the spirit, not from the pressing need of matter will she receive her prescriptions. Now however, want rules and sunken humanity bends under its tyrannical yoke. *Utility* is the great idol of the time, for which all powers slave and all talents should pay homage. Upon this coarse balance hath the spiritual merit of art no weight, and, robbed of all encouragement, it vanishes from the noisy mart of the century. Even the philosophical spirit of inquiry tears away from conceptual power one province after the other, and the limits of art narrow themselves, the more science enlarges her boundaries.

Full of expectation the eyes of the philosopher as of the man of the world are fastened upon the political theater of action, where now, as one believes, the great destiny of humanity is treated. Betrays it not a blameworthy indifference towards the welfare of society, not to share this universal discussion? So closely as this great action, because of its contents and its consequences, everyone, who calls himself a man, concerns, so much must it, because of its mode of discussion, especially interest every self-thinker. A question, which would otherwise only be answered through the blind right of the stronger, is now, as it seems, made pending before the tribunal of pure reason, and only he who is always able, to place himself in the center of the whole and to raise his individuality to that of the species, may regard himself as a member of that tribunal of reason, at the same time as he as man and world citizen is party and sees himself more nearly or distantly involved in the outcome. It is therefore not merely his own cause, which comes to a decision in this great action, it should also be declared according to laws, which he himself as a rational spirit is capable and entitled to dictate.

How attractive must it be for me, to take under investigation such a subject with one who is just as gifted a thinker as he is a liberal citizen of the world and to rely upon a heart, that devotes itself with beautiful enthusiasm to the welfare of humanity, for the decision. How pleasantly surprising, with a yet so great difference of position and with the wide distance, which the circumstances in the real world make necessary, to concur with your unprejudiced mind in the same result on the field of ideas! That I resist this alluring temptation and cause beauty to walk in front of freedom, I believe not merely to be able to excuse with my inclination, but to justify through principles. I hope, to convince you, that this matter is far less foreign to the wants than to the taste of the age, yea that one, in order to solve the political problem in experience, must take the path through the aesthetical, because it is beauty, through which one proceeds to freedom. But this proof can not be offered, unless I bring to your remembrance the principles, through which reason chiefly guides itself in a political legislation.

Third Letter

Nature commences with man not any better than with her remaining works: she acts for him, where he is not yet able to act as a free intelligence for himself. But even that which makes him a man, that he doth not stand still at that, which bare nature made of him, rather possesses the capability, the steps, which she anticipated with him, to retrace through reason, in order to transform the work of necessity into his free choice and to elevate physical necessity to a moral.

He comes to himself out of his sensual slumber, recognizes himself as a man, looks around himself and finds himself—in the state. The force of necessity threw him into it, before he could choose this condition in his freedom; necessity established the same according to mere laws of nature, before *he* could according to laws of reason. But with this state of necessity, which had only arisen from his natural determination and also had only been calculated upon this, could and can he not be satisfied as a moral person—and bad for him if he could! He therefore abandons, with the same right, wherewith he is a man, the rule of a blind necessity, as he parts from it in so many other respects through his freedom, as he, in order to give just *one* example, extinguishes through morality and ennobles through beauty the common character, which need impressed upon sexual love. So he later makes up, in an artificial manner, for his childhood in his majority, forms for himself a *natural condition* in the idea, which is given him indeed through no experience, but is established necessarily through the determination of his reason, lends to himself a purpose in this ideal state, of which he was not conscious in his real natural condition, and a choice, of which he was not then capable, and now proceeds not otherwise, than if he commenced anew and exchanged the condition of independence out of clear insight and free determination for a condition of compacts. However artfully and firmly blind caprice may have founded its work, however arrogantly it may maintain it and with whatever appearance of veneration may surround it—he may, with this operation, consider it as fully undone, for the work of blind power possesses no authority, before which freedom need bow, and all must accomodate itself to the highest purpose, which reason erects in his personality. In this way the attempt of a people come of age, to transform its natural state into a moral, arises and justifies itself.

This natural state (as any political body can be called, which derives its establishment originally from forces, not from laws) indeed now contradicts the moral man, whom mere legality should serve as law, but it is nevertheless sufficient for the physical man, who for this reason only gives himself laws, to accomodate himself to force. Now however the physical man is *real*, and the moral only *problematical*. Thus reason lifts the natural state, as she necessarily must, when she wants to place that of her own in its stead, thus she weighs the physical and real man against the problematical moral, thus she weighs the existence of society against a merely possible (although morally necessary) ideal of society. She takes from man something, that he really possesses, and without which he possesses naught, and assigns him something therefor, that he could and should possess; and had she reckoned too much on him, so would she for a humanity, which he is still wanting and can be wanting without detriment to his existence, have deprived him of even the means of animal existence, which however is the condition of his humanity. Before he had had time, to adhere to the law with his will, she would have pulled the ladder of nature out from under his feet.

The great deliberation is therefore, that the physical society may not cease *in time* for a moment, whilst the moral forms itself *in the idea*, that his existence may not fall into danger for the sake of the dignity of man. If the artist hath to repair a clockwork, so he lets the wheels run down; but the living clockwork of the state must be repaired, whilst it strikes, and here it means, to exchange the rolling wheel during its revolution. One must therefore search for a support for the continuance of society, which makes it independent of the natural state, which one wants to dissolve.

This support doth not find itself in the natural character of man, which, selfishly and violently, aims much more towards the destruction than towards the preservation of society; it finds itself just as little in his moral character, which, according to the hypothesis, should first be formed, and which, because it is free and *because it never appears*, could never be worked and never with certainty be reckoned upon by the lawgiver. It would therefore depend thereon, to separate the caprice of the physical character and the freedom of the moral—it would depend thereon, to make the former harmonious with law, the latter dependent upon impressions—it would depend thereon, to distance the former somewhat further from matter, to bring the latter somewhat nearer to it—in order to produce a third character, which, related with these both, prepared a transition from the rule of naked force to the rule of law, without hindering the moral character in its development, but served rather as a sensual pledge of invisible morality.

Fourth Letter

Thus much is certain: only the predominance of such a character in a people can make a state transformation according to moral principles uninjurious, and also only such a character can guarantee its duration. In the establishment of such a moral state the moral law is reckoned upon as an active power, and free will is drawn into the realm of causes, where all things hang together mutually with stringent necessity and constancy. We know however, that the determination of human will remains always accidental and that only in the Absolute Being doth the physical necessity coincide with the moral. Thus if the moral conduct of man should be relied upon as upon *natural* results, so it must *be* nature, and he must surely be led through his instincts to such a proceeding, as only a moral character can always bring about. The will of man stands perfectly free between duty and inclination, and no physical necessity can and may seize the majestic right of his person. Should he therefore retain this power of choice and notwithstanding be a dependable link in the causal chain of forces, so can this only be effected thereby, that the effects of both those instinctive springs sally forth perfectly equally in the realm of appearances and, with every difference of form, the matter of his volition remains the same; that therefore his instincts are sufficiently harmonious with his reason, in order to be of use as universal legislation.

Every individual man, one can say, carries by predisposition and destiny, a purely ideal man within himself, to agree with whose immutable unity in all his alterations is the great task of his existence.* This pure man, who gives himself to be recognized more or less distinctly in every subject, is represented through the *state*; the objective and as it were canonical form, in which the multiplicity of the subjects strives to unite itself. Now however let two different ways be considered, how the man in time can coincide with the man in the idea, hence just as many, how the state can maintain itself in the individual; either thereby, that the pure man suppresses the empirical, that the state abolishes the individual; or thereby, that the individual *becomes* the state, that the man of time *ennobles* himself to the man in the idea.

Indeed, in the one-sided valuation this difference falls away; for reason is satisfied, if her law alone is valued unconditionally: but in the complete anthropological valuation, where with the form also the content is considered and the living feeling likewise hath a voice, the same will come so much the more into consideration. Unity demands indeed reason, nature however multiplicity, and man is claimed by

---

* I refer here to a recently published work: "Lectures on the Destiny of the Savant," by my friend Fichte, where a very lucid and never before in this manner attempted derivation of this proposition is found.

both legislations. The law of the former is imprinted upon him through an incorruptible consciousness, the law of the other through an indelible feeling. Hence it will everytime bespeak of a still deficient education, if the moral character can maintain itself only with the self-sacrifice of the natural; and a state constitution will still be very imperfect, which is only capable of effecting unity through the suppression of multiplicity. The state should not merely respect the objective and general, it should also respect the subjective and specific character in the individual and, whilst it spreads the invisible realm of the moral, should not depopulate the realm of appearance.

When the mechanical artist places his hand on the formless mass, in order to give it the form of his purpose, so he hath no hesitation, to do it violence; for the nature, upon which he works, deserves no respect for itself, and he is not interested in the whole for the sake of its parts, rather in the parts for the sake of the whole. When the artist of beauty lays his hand on the same mass, so he hath even less hesitation, to do it violence, he only avoids, to show it. The stuff, upon which he works he doth not respect in the least more than the mechanical artist; but the eyes, which take the freedom of this stuff under protection, he will seek to deceive through an apparent forebearance towards the same. It is entirely different with the pedagogical and political artist, who immediately makes man into his material and into his task. Here the purpose returns to the stuff, and only because the whole serves the parts, the parts may accomodate themselves to the whole. With an entirely different respect, than is that, which the artist of beauty shows his material, must the artist of the state approach that of his, and he must not merely subjectively and for an illusory effect on the senses, but rather objectively and for the inner essence spare its peculiarity and personality.

But for just this reason, because the state should be an organization which forms itself through itself and for itself, so can it also only in so far become real, as the parts have raised themselves to the idea of the whole. Because the state serves as representative of pure and objective humanity in the breast of its citizens, so will it have to observe the same relationship towards its citizens, in which they stand to themselves, and also only be able to respect their subjective humanity to *the* degree, that it is ennobled to the objective. Is the inner man one with himself, so will he even in the highest universalization of his conduct save his peculiarity, and the state will be merely the interpreter of his beautiful instincts, the more distinct formula of his inner legislation. On the contrary, offers the subjective man in the character of a people still such contradictory resistance to the objective, that only the suppression of the former can create victory for the latter, so the state will also take up the severe earnestness of the law, and, in order not to be its victim, will have to crush under its feet a so hostile individuality without respect.

Man can, however, be opposed to himself in a twofold manner: either as a savage, if his feelings rule over his principles; or as a barbarian, if his principles destroy his feelings. The savage despises art and recognizes nature as his unrestricted master; the barbarian derides and disrepects nature but, more contemptible than the savage, he frequently enough continues, to be the slave of his slaves. The educated man makes nature into his friend and honors its freedom, while he merely bridles its caprice.

When reason therefore brings her moral unity into physical society, so she may not damage the multiplicity of nature. When nature strives to maintain her multiplicity in the moral structure of society, so may occur thereby no breach in the moral unity; equally far from uniformity and confusion rests the victorious form. *Totality* of character must therefore be found in the people, which should be capable and worthy, to exchange the state of necessity for the state of freedom.

Fifth Letter

Is it this character, which the present age, which the current events manifest to us? I direct my attention at once to the most prominent object in this vast picture.

True is it, the repute of opinion is fallen, caprice is unmasked, and, although still armed with power, yet it obtains no more dignity; man is aroused from his long indolence and self-deception, and with an emphatic majority he demands the restoration of his inalienable rights. But he doth not merely demand them, on that side and this side he rises up, to take by force, what in his opinion is wrongfully denied him. The edifice of the natural state rocks, its worn out foundations give way, and a *physical* possibility seems given, to place the law upon the throne, to honor man finally as an end in himself and to make true freedom the basis of political union. Vain hope! The *moral* possibility is wanting; and the generous moment finds an unresponsive people.

In his deeds man paints himself, and what form is it, which is reflected in the drama of the present time! Here return to a savage state, there a state of enervation: The two greatest extremes of human degeneration, and both united in *one* space of time.

In the lower and more numerous classes brutal lawless instincts present themselves to us, which unleash themselves after the dissolved bond of the civil order and hasten with unruly fury to their animal satisfaction. It may therefore be, that the objective humanity had had cause, to complain of the state; the subjective must honor its institu-

tions. May one blame him, that he placed the dignity of human nature
out of sight, so long it still mattered, to defend its existence? That he
hastened, to separate through force of gravity and to bind through the
force of cohesion, where he was no longer to think of the educating?
Its dissolution contains its justification. The unfastened society, instead
of hastening upward into organic life, falls back into the elemental
realm.

On the other side, the civilized classes give us the still adverse
sight of slackness and of a depravity of character, which revolts so much
the more, because culture itself is its source. I no longer remember,
which ancient or modern philosopher made the observation, that the
more noble would be in its destruction the more horrible, but one will
find it true as well in the moral. From the son of nature emerges,
when he indulges in excess, a raving madman; from the pupil of art a
worthless villain. The enlightenment of the understanding, on which
the refined classes not entirely with injustice pride themselves, shows
in the whole so little an ennobling influence on the inner convictions,
that it rather strengthens the corruption through maxims. We deny
nature on her legitimate field, in order to experience her tyranny on
the moral, and while we resist her impressions, we receive our prin-
ciples from her. The affected decency of our manners refuses her the
pardonable *first* voice, in order to yield to her, in our materialistic
ethics, the decisive *last*. In the very bosom of the most refined social
life egoism hath founded its system, and without producing a social
heart, we experience all contagions and all tribulations of society. Our
free judgment we subject to its despotic opinion, our feeling to its
bizarre customs, our will to its seductions, only our caprice do we
maintain against her holy rights. Proud self-sufficiency contracts the
heart of the man of the world, that still frequently beats sympathetically
in the brutal man of nature, and as from a burning city everyone seeks
only to rescue his miserable property from the devastation. Only in
a complete renunciation of sentimentality doth one think to find shelter
from its aberrations, and mockery, which often wholesomely chastises
the schwaermer, slanders with equally little forbearance the noblest
feeling. Culture, far removed, to place us in freedom, develops with
every power, which it forms in us, only a new want, the bonds of the
physical always tie themselves up more anxiously, so that the fear, to
lose, stifles even the fiery instinct towards improvement and the maxims
of suffering obedience are considered the highest wisdom of life. Thus
one sees the spirit of the time waver between perversity and brutality,
between the unnatural and mere nature, between superstition and
moral unbelief, and it is merely the equal weight of evils, which at
times still places limits upon him.

Sixth Letter

Should I with this description of the age indeed have done too much? I do not expect this reproach, but rather another: that I have proven too much thereby. This picture, you will say to me, indeed resembles the present humanity, but it resembles primarily all peoples, who are engaged in culture, because all must indiscriminately fall away from nature through sophistry, before they can return to her through reason.

But with some attention to the character of the times, the contrast must put us in astonishment, which is encountered between the present form of humanity and between the previous, especially the Greek. The glory of education and refinement, which we with justice put forward as against every other *mere* nature, cannot stand us in good stead in comparison to the Greek, which was married to all the charms of art and to all the dignity of wisdom, but without, like ours, being the sacrifice of the same. The Greeks shame us not merely through a simplicity, which is foreign to our age; they are at the same time our rivals, yea frequently our models in the same good qualities, with which we are wont to comfort ourselves over the natural unpleasantness of our manners. At once full of form and full of abundance, at once philosophizing and creating, at once tender and energetic, we see them unite the youth of phantasy with the manliness of reason in a glorious humanity.

At that time, with that beautiful awakening of the powers of the mind, the senses and the mind still had no rigidly separated peculiarity; for no conflict had yet provoked them, to hostilely part from one another and to determine their border. Poetry had not yet had illicit intercourse with wit and speculation had not yet violated itself through sophistry. Both could in case of need exchange their functions, because each, only in his own way, honored truth. As high as reason also climbed, so it yet always drew matter lovingly after it, and as purely and sharply as it also separated, so it yet never mutilated. It indeed dissected human nature and presented it magnified in its glorious circle of gods but not thereby, that it tore it to pieces, rather thereby, that it mixed it repeatedly, for the whole of humanity was missing in no individual god. How entirely different with us moderns! Likewise with us is the image of the species presented magnified in individuals—but in fragments, not in altered mixtures, such that one must ask around from individual to individual, in order to gather together the totality of the species. Among us, one would almost attempt to assert, the mental powers express themselves in experience as well as separated, as the psychologist separates them in the representation, and we do not see merely the individual subject, but rather entire classes of men unfold only a part of their natural gifts, while the rest, as with stunted plants, scarcely are suggested with a faint trace.

I am not unaware of the good qualities, which the present age, regarded as unity and upon the balance of the understanding, may maintain before the best in former ages; but in closed ranks must it begin the contest and the whole must measure itself as against the whole. Which individual modern steps forth, to contend man against man with the individual Athenian for the prize of humanity?

Whence indeed this disadvantageous relation of individuals with every advantage of the species? Why did the individual Greek qualify himself to represent his time, and why may the individual modern not dare this? Because to the former the all-uniting nature, to the latter the all-dividing understanding imparted his forms.

It was culture itself, which inflicted these wounds upon modern humanity. So soon on the one side the enlarged experience and the more determinate thinking made necessary a sharper separation of the sciences, on the other side the more complicated clockwork of the state a stricter division of ranks and occupations, so likewise the inner bond of human nature ruptured, and a destructive struggle divided her harmonious powers. The intuitive and speculative understanding dispersed themselves now hostilely-minded upon their different fields, whose boundaries now began to be guarded with mistrust and jealousy, and with the sphere, upon which one confined its effectiveness, one hath given also unto oneself a lord, who not seldom is wont to end with the suppression of the remaining abilities. Whilst here the luxuriant conceptual power devastates the laborious plantings of the understanding, there the spirit of abstraction extinguishes the fire, in which the heart had been warmed and phantasy should be kindled.

This disruption, which art and learning began in the inner man, made the new spirit of government complete and universal. It was of course not to be expected, that the simple organization of the first republic survived the simplicity of the first customs and relations, but instead of climbing to a higher animal life, it sank down to a common coarse mechanism. The polyp-nature of the Greek state, where each individual enjoyed an independent life and, if it were necessary, could become the whole, now made place for an elaborate clockwork, where from the disintegration into the infinitely many, but inanimate parts, a mechanical life is formed in the whole. Torn asunder now were the state and the church, the laws and the customs; enjoyment was separated from the work, the means from the end, the effort from the reward. Eternally chained to only a single fragment of the whole, man only develops himself as a fragment, eternally only the monotonous noise of the wheel, that he revolves, in the ear, he never develops the harmony of his being, and instead of impressing humanity upon his nature, he becomes merely an imprint of his business, of his science. But even the scanty fragmentary part, which still knits the individual member to the whole, doth not depend upon forms, which they automatically give themselves (for how might one confide such an artificial and light-shunning clockwork to their freedom?), but rather is prescribed to them with scrupulous severity through a formula, in which one holds their free insight bound. The dead letter replaces the living understanding, and a practiced memory guides more safely than genius and feeling.

If the common being makes the office the measure of the man, if it honors in one of its citizens only the memory, in another the tabular understanding, in a third only mechanical facility, if it here, indifferent to character, insists only on knowledge, there on the other hand allows the greatest darkness of the understanding to the benefit of the spirit of order and a lawful behavior—if it at the same time wants to see these individual facilities driven to a just as great intensity, as it permits the subject to forego in extension—may we then wonder, that the remaining abilities of the mind are neglected, in order to the one, which honors and rewards, to devote all care? Indeed we know, that the powerful genius doth not make the limits of his business into the limits of his activity, but the mediocre talent consumes in the business, that falls to his lot, the whole scanty sum of his energy, and it must no doubt be no common head, in order, without detriment to his profession, to reserve the remainder for favorite pursuits. Moreover it is seldom a good recommendation with the state, if one's powers exceed one's commission, or if the higher spiritual needs of the man of genius provide a rival to his office. So jealous is the state of the exclusive possession of its servants, that it is easier to be decided thereon (and who can find it unjustified), to share its man with a Venus Cytherea than with a Venus Urania?

And so the individual concrete life is then gradually extirpated, therewith the abstract of the whole may devour his scanty existence, and eternally the state remains foreign to its citizens, because feeling doth not find it anywhere. Compelled to relieve itself of the multiplicity of its citizens through classification and to receive humanity never otherwise than through second hand representation, the governing part at last loses sight of it altogether, whilst it confuses it with a mere concoction of the understanding; and the governed can receive not otherwise than with coldness the laws, which are so little directed to himself. Finally weary of entertaining a bond, the which is lightened so little by the state, the positive society falls to pieces (which is long since the fate of most European states) in a moral natural condition, where the public power is only one party *more*, hated and deceived by those, who make it necessary, and only by those, who can do without it, respected.

Could humanity with this double power, which presses upon it from within and without, indeed take another direction than it actually took? Whilst the speculative mind strove in the realm of ideas after inalienable possessions, it had to become a stranger in the sensual world and lose the matter on account of the form. The spirit of business encompassed in a uniform circle of objects and in this restricted still more by formulas, had to see the free whole removed from its sight and at the same time impoverished within its sphere. Just as the former is tempted, to model the actual after the thinkable and to elevate the subjective conditions of his power of imagination to constitute laws for the existence of things, so the latter rushed to the opposite extreme, to value all experience on the whole based upon a particular fragment of experience and to wish the rules of his business to adapt to every business without distinction. The one had to become prey to an empty subtlety, the other to a pedantic narrow-mindedness, because the former stood too high for the individual, the latter too low for the whole. But the disadvantage of this direction of mind did not confine itself merely to knowledge and bringing forth; it extended itself no less to feeling and action. We know, that the sensibility of the mind depends, for its degree upon the liveliness, for its extent upon the richness of the conceptual power. But now the predominance of the analytical capability must necessarily rob phantasy of its power and its fire and a more restricted sphere of objects diminish its richness. The abstract thinker hath for this reason very often a *cold* heart, because he analyzes impressions, which yet only move the soul as a totality; the businessman hath very often a *narrow* heart, because his conceptual power, confined in the uniform circle of his profession, can not expand itself to a foreign mode of conception.

It lay in my path, to uncover the disadvantageous direction of the character of the time and its sources, not to show the advantages, whereby nature makes it good. Gladly will I admit to you, that, as little as individuals can enjoy the dismemberment of their being, yet the species had been able to make progress in no other mode. The appearance of Grecian humanity was incontestably a maximum, that could on these steps neither continue nor climb higher. Not continue; for the understanding through the supply, which it already had, had to be compelled inevitably, to separate itself from the feeling and intuition and to strive towards clarity of knowledge: also not climb higher; because only a determinate degree of clearness can exist together with a determinate fullness and warmth. The Greeks had achieved this degree, and if they wanted to progress to a higher de-

velopment, so must they, as we, give up the totality of their being and
pursue the truth on separate roads.

To develop the manifold abilities in man, there was no other means,
than to place them in opposition to one another. This antagonism of
forces is the great instrument of culture, but also only the instrument;
for so long as the same lasts, one is only on the road to this one.
Thereby alone, that individual forces are isolated in man and take upon
themselves an exclusive legislation, they come into conflict with the
truth of things and compel the common sense, which otherwise rests
with lazy contentedness upon the external appearance, to penetrate
into the depths of objects. Whilst the pure understanding usurps an
authority in the sensual world and the empirical is engaged, to subject
it to the conditions of experience, both talents develop themselves to
the highest possible ripeness and exhaust the whole extent of their
sphere. Whilst here the conceptual power dares through its caprice
to extinguish the world order, there it compels reason, to climb to the
supreme sources of knowledge and to invoke against it the law of
necessity for help.

One-sidedness in the exercise of its powers leads the individual
inevitably to error, but the species to truth. Thereby alone, that we
assemble the whole energy of our mind in *one* focal point and con-
centrate our whole being in a single power, we add wings to this single
power as it were and lead it thence artificially far beyond the bounds,
which nature seems to have imposed on it. So certain is it, that all
human individuals, taken together, with the power of sight, which
nature grants them, never would have come thither, to spy out a satellite
of Jupiter, which the telescope of the astronomer discovers; just as
completely certain is it, that the human mental power never would
have produced an analysis of infinity or a critique of the pure reason,
if the reason had not separated itself into particular- thereto-destined
subjects, had as it were unwound itself from all matter and had armed
its view into the unconditioned through the most unremitting abstrac-
tion. But will indeed such a mind, as it were, dissolved in pure
understanding and pure intuition, be capable thereof, to exchange the
severe fetters of logic for the free action of the power of poetry and to
seize the individuality of things with faithful and chaste sense? Here
nature even imposes a limit on the universal genius, which it can not
overstep, and the truth will make martyrs so long, as philosophy must
still make it her principal business, to make preparations against error.

However much may therefore be won for the whole of the world
through this divided cultivation of human powers, so it is not to be
denied, that the individuals, who encounter it, suffer under the curse
of this world aim. Through gymnastic exercises athletic bodies are
developed, but only through the free and uniform play of the limbs is

beauty. Just so, the harnessing of individual powers of mind can indeed produce extraordinary, but only the uniform temperature of the same, happy and perfect men. And in which relationship stand we to past and coming ages, if the education of human nature made such a sacrifice necessary? We had been the servants of mankind, we had engaged in slave labor for it for a few thousand years and impressed upon our mutilated nature the shameful traces of this servitude—therewith the later generation could await in a happy idleness their moral health and develop the free growth of its humanity!

However can man indeed be certain thereof, to neglect himself for some other end? Should nature be able to rob us through her own ends of a perfection, which reason prescribes to us through hers? It must therefore be false, that the cultivation of individual powers makes the sacrifice of their totality necessary; or if even the law of nature yet strove so much thither, so must it stand with us, to reestablish this totality in our nature, which art hath destroyed, through a higher art.

Seventh Letter

Should this effect perhaps be expected from the state? That is not possible, for the state, as it is now constituted, hath occasioned evil, and the state, as reason conceives it in the idea, instead of being able to found this better humanity, had to be grounded thereupon. And thus had the previous inquiries led me back once again to the point, from which they took me away for some time. The present age, far removed, from showing us this form of humanity, which is become recognized as a necessary condition of a moral improvement of the state, on the contrary shows us the direct opposite therefrom. Are therefore the principles, advanced by me, correct, experience confirms my picture of the present age, so must one declare every attempt of such an alteration of state as untimely and every thereupon-grounded hope as chimerical, until the division in the inner man is once again dissolved and his nature is sufficiently fully developed, in order itself to be the artist and to guarantee the reality of the political creation of reason.

Nature shows us the way in her physical creation, which one hath to travel in the moral. Not earlier, than until the struggle of elementary forces in the lower organizations is pacified doth she elevate herself to the noble form of the physical man. Even so must the elementary strife in the ethical man, the conflict of blind instincts, be at first becalmed, and the coarse antagonism must have ceased in himself, before one may dare, to favor multiplicity. On the other side, the independence of his character must be secured and the subservience to foreign despotic forms have made place for a decent freedom, before one may subordinate the multiplicity in him to the unity of the ideal. Where the natural man still abuses his caprice so lawlessly, there one may scarcely show him his freedom; where the artificial man still employs his freedom so little, there one may not take his caprice from him. The gift of liberal principles becomes treason to the whole, when it associates itself with a still fermenting force and transmits strength to an already too powerful nature; the law of conformity becomes tyranny against the individual, when it knits itself to an already ruling weakness and physical restriction and so extinguishes the last glimmering spark of self-activity and particularity.

The character of the time must therefore raise itself up first from its deep degradation, there escape the blind power of nature and here return to its simplicity, truth and fullness; a task for more than *one* century. Meanwhile, I gladly admit, some attempt in the particular can succeed, but nothing will be improved on the whole thereby, and the contradiction of conduct will always be proof against the unity of maxims. One will in another part of the world honor humanity in the negro and in Europe revile it in the thinker. The old principles will remain, but they will wear the clothes of the century, and to an oppression, which the church at other times authorized, philosophy will lend its name. Alarmed by freedom, which in its first attempts always announces itself as an enemy, one will there throw oneself into the arms of a comfortable servitude and here, brought to despair by a pedantic tutelage, escape into the wild license of the natural condition. The usurpation will plead the weakness of human nature, insurrection the dignity of the same, until finally the great ruler of all human things, blind force, steps in between and decides the ostensible contest of principles like a common boxing-match.

Eighth Letter

Should philosophy therefore, dejectedly and without hope, retreat from this domain? Whilst the dominion of forms extends itself in every other direction, should this most important of all goods be abandoned to formless chance? Should The conflict of blind forces continue eternally in the political world and the social law never triumph over hostile egoism?

Not in the least! Reason herself will indeed, with this raw might, which resists her arms, not directly attempt combat and as little, as the son of Saturn in the Iliad, acting on her own, descend to the dark field of action. However from the midst of the combatants she selects the worthiest, beclothes him, as Zeus his grandson, with godly arms and through his triumphing force brings about the great decision.

Reason hath performed, what she can perform, when she finds and promulgates the law; it must be executed by the courageous will and the living feeling. If truth should obtain victory in struggle with force, so must she herself first become *force* and advance an *instinct* to plead her cause in the realm of phenomena; for instincts are the only moving forces in the sensible world. Hath she until now her triumphing force yet so little demonstrated, so this is not due to the understanding, which she did not know to unveil, but rather to the heart, which remained closed to her, and to the instinct, which did not act on her behalf.

For whence this still so universal dominion of prejudices and this darkness of the head in the midst of all the light, that philosophy and experience turned on? The age is enlightened, that is, the knowledge is discovered and publicly revealed, which would suffice, to rectify at least our practical principles. The spirit of free inquiry dispelled the delusions, which for a long time barred access to the truth, and undermined the grounds, upon which fanaticism and fraud erected their throne. Reason hath purified herself from the deceptions of the senses and from a fraudulent sophistry, and philosophy herself, which at first made us faithless to her, calls us loudly and urgently back into the bosom of nature—whereon is it, that we are still always barbarians?

There must therefore, since it doth not lie in things, be something present in the minds of men, which stands in the way of the reception of truth, even if she radiated yet so brightly, and the acceptance of the same, even if she persuaded yet so livelily. An ancient wise man hath perceived it and it lies concealed in the many-meaning expression: sapere aude.

Embolden thyself, to be wise. Energy of courage is needed therefor, to combat the hindrances with which the inertia of nature as well as the cowardice of the heart oppose instruction. Not without meaning the ancient mythos caused the goddess of wisdom to emerge in full armament from Jupiter's head; for her first action is already warlike. Already at birth hath she a hard battle to endure with the senses, which do not want to be torn from their sweet repose. The more numerous part of mankind is far too much exhausted and enervated by the battle with necessity, to rally itself to a new and harder battle with error. Satisfied, if it itself avoids the hard labor of thinking, it gladly abandons the guardianship of its conceptions to others, and if it happens, that higher needs are aroused in it, so it grasps with thirsting faith the formula, which the state and the priesthood hold in readiness for this case. If these unhappy men deserve our compassion, so our just contempt befalls the others, whom a better lot sets free from the yoke of want, but their own choice bends thereunder. These prefer the twilight of obscure conceptions, where one feels more livelily and phantasy fashions comfortable forms at its own pleasure, to the beams of truth, which chase away the pleasant deceptions of their dreams. Upon these very delusions, which the hostile light of knowledge should dispel, have they founded the entire edifice of their happiness, and should they purchase a truth so dearly, which commences therewith, to take everything from them, which possesses worth for them? They had to already be wise, in order to love wisdom: a truth, which that one already felt, who gave philosophy its name.

Not enough therefore, that all enlightenment of the understanding only deserves respect insofar, as it flows back upon the character; it proceeds also to a certain extent from the character, since the way to the head must be opened through the heart. Development of the capacity of feeling is therefore the more pressing need of the time, not merely because it is a means, to make the improved insight into life effective, but rather even therefore, because it awakens to improvement of insight.

Ninth Letter

However is this not perhaps a circle? Theoretical culture should bring about the practical and the practical be yet the condition of the theoretical? All improvement in the political should proceed from the ennoblement of the character—but how can the character ennoble itself under the influence of a barbarous state constitution? One had thus to search for an instrument to achieve this end, which the state doth not provide, to open up springs thereto, which preserve themselves pure and clear in the midst of every political corruption.

Now I have reached the point, to which all my previous considerations have striven. This instrument is beautiful art, these springs open up in its immortal models.

From everything, that is positive and that human conventions established, art like science is released, and both enjoy an absolute *immunity* from the caprice of man. The political lawgiver can cordon off her domain, but he can not rule therein. He can banish the friend of truth, but the truth subsists; he can degrade the artist, but he can not falsify art. Indeed there is nothing more common, than that both, science and art pay homage to the spirit of the age and the creative taste receives the law from the critical. Where the character grows rigid and hardens itself, there we see science guard her boundaries strictly and art proceed in the heavy fetters of rules; where the character relaxes and loosens up, there will science strive to please and art to gratify. For entire centuries philosophers like artists have shown themselves engaged, to plunge truth and beauty down into the depths of vulgar humanity; the former go under therein, but with their own indestructible vital power the latter struggle upwards victoriously.

The artist is indeed the son of his time, but bad for him, if he is at the same time its pupil or even yet its favorite. A beneficent deity snatches the suckling betimes from his mother's breast, nourishes him with the milk of a better age and lets him mature under distant Grecian skies to full age. If he is then become a man, he thus returns, a strange form, to his century; but not, in order to please it with his appearance, but rather, frightful as Agamemnon's son, in order to purify it. The matter will he indeed take from the present, but the form derive from a nobler time, yea beyond all time, from the absolute immutable unity of his essence. Here from the pure ether of his daemonic nature flows forth the spring of beauty, uncontaminated by the corruption of the generations and ages, which roll deep beneath it in turbid eddies. Its matter whim can dishonor, as it hath ennobled it, but the chaste form is removed from its alteration. The Roman of the first century had long ago already bent his knee to his emperor, when the statues still stood upright, the temples remained holy to the eye, when the gods long ago were fit for laughter, and the disgraceful crimes of a Nero and of a Commodus were put to shame by the noble style of the building, which gave its cover thereto. Humanity hath lost its dignity, but art hath saved it and preserved it in meaningful stone; the truth lives on in illusion, and from the copy the original will be restored. So as noble art *survived* noble nature, so too she strode ahead of the same in inspiration, forming and awakening. Yet before truth sends her triumphing light into the depths of the heart, the power of poetry intercepts her beams, and the summits of humanity will glisten, when a damp night still lies in the valleys.

But how doth the artist preserve himself before the corruptions of his time, which surround him from every side? If he despises its judgment. He glances upwards towards his dignity and the law, not downwards towards fortune and need. Equally free from vain activity, which would gladly impress its trace on the fleeting moment, and from the impatient schwaermer spirit, which employs the measure of the unconditioned to the miserable offspring of time, let him abandon to the understanding, which here is at home, the sphere of the actual; let him strive however, to produce the ideal from the bond of the possible with the necessary. Let him stamp this on illusion and truth, stamp it on the play of his creative power and on the earnestness of his deeds, stamp it on all sensuous and spiritual forms and hurl it silently into infinite time.

But not on everyone, in whom this ideal glows in the soul, was the creative repose and the great patient sense bestowed, to impress it upon the silent stone or to pour it forth in the sober word and to entrust it to the faithful hands of time. Much too stormy, to proceed by these peaceful means, the godly instinct of form often plunges immediately into the present and into active life and undertakes, to remold the formless matter of the moral world. Urgently the unhappiness of his species speaks to the feeling man, more urgently its degradation; enthusiasm is inflamed, and the glowing desire strives in powerful souls impatiently to the deed. But did he also ask himself, if these disorders in the moral world offend his reason or not rather cause pain to his self-love? Knows he it not yet, so will he recognize it by the eagerness, wherewith he presses for definite and expedited effects. The pure moral instinct is directed at the unconditioned, there is no time for it, and the future becomes the present to it, so soon it must necessarily develop out of the present. Before a reason without limits is the direction at once the completion, and the way is traversed so soon it is taken.

Give thus, I shall give as answer to the young friend of truth and beauty, who would know from me, how he may satisfy the noble instinct in his breast, in the face of all the opposition of the century, give the world, upon which thou actest, the *direction* towards the good, so will the calm rhythm of time bring the development. This direction thou hast given it, when thou, teaching, elevatest its thoughts to the necessary and eternal, when thou acting or forming, transformest the necessary and eternal into an object of its instinct. The structure of delusion will fall and of arbitrariness, it must fall, it hath already fallen, so soon thou art certain that it inclines; but in the inner, not merely in the outer man must it incline. In the modest stillness of thy heart educate the victorious truth, set it forth from within thyself in beauty, that not merely the thoughts pay homage to it, but rather also the sense lovingly seizes its appearance. And therewith lest it befall thee, to receive the model from the actual, that thou shouldst give it, so venture not sooner into its doubtful society, until thou art assured of an ideal following in thy heart. Live with thy century, but be not its creature; give to thy contemporaries, but what they need, not what they praise. Without having shared their guilt, share with noble resignation their punishments and bend with freedom beneath the yoke, that they equally badly dispense with and bear. Through the steadfast courage, with which thou despisest their fortune, wilt thou prove, that thy cowardice doth not submit to their sufferings. Imagine them to thee, as they should be, if thou hast to act upon them, but imagine them to thee, as they are, if thou wilt attempt to act for them. Seek their applause through their dignity, but upon their unworthiness reckon their happiness, so there will thine own nobility awaken that of theirs and here their unworthiness not destroy thy purpose. The earnestness of thy principles will frighten them away from thee, but in play they bear them still; their taste is more chaste than their heart, and here must thou seize the shy fugitive. Their maxims wilt thou storm in vain, their deeds condemn in vain, but thou canst try thy forming hand upon their idleness. Chase away the caprice, the frivolity, the roughness from their pleasures, so wilt thou banish them imperceptibly too from their actions, finally from their character. Where thou findest them, surround them with noble, with great, with ingenious forms, enclose them all around with symbols of excellence, until appearance overcomes reality and art, nature.

Tenth Letter

You are thus at one with me thereon and convinced by the content of my former letters, that man can deviate from his destiny upon two opposing roads, that our age is actually proceeding upon both false roads and here is become the prey of roughness, there of enervation and perversity. From this twofold aberration it should be led back through beauty. But how can beautiful culture encounter both opposing defects at once and unite in itself two contradictory qualities? Can it put nature in the savage in fetters and place the same in the barbarian in freedom? Can it at once tighten and loosen—and if it doth not really do both, how can such a great effect, as is the education of mankind, be reasonably expected from it?

Indeed hath one already had to hear to the point of satiety the assertion, that the developed feeling for beauty refines the manners, so that it appears to need no new proof further hereto. One relies upon the everyday experience, which almost universally shows an educated taste united with clarity of the understanding, agility of feeling, liberality and even dignity of conduct, with an uncultivated one usually the opposite. One cites, confidently enough, the example of the most cultured of all the nations of antiquity, with which the feeling of beauty achieved its highest development, and the opposite example of those partially savage, partially barbarous peoples, who expiate their insensibility to the beautiful with a rough or yet austere character. Nonetheless, it occurs occasionally to thinking heads, either to deny the facts, or yet to doubt the legitimacy of the conclusions derived therefrom. They think not quite so badly of that savagery, of which one reproaches uncultivated peoples, and not quite so favorably of this refinement, which one praises in the cultivated. Already in antiquity there were men, who held beautiful culture for anything but a benefit and on this account were very inclined, to deny entrance into their republic to the arts of imaginative power.

Not of those do I speak, who merely for that reason inveigh against the Graces, because they never experienced their favor. They, who know no other measure of worth than the effort of acquisition and palpable gain—how should they be able, to value the quiet work of taste in the outer and inner man, and not lose sight of its essential advantages on account of the accidental disadvantages of beautiful culture? The man without form despises all grace in diction as corruption, all refinement in social intercourse as dissimulation, all delicacy and greatness in conduct as overstraining and affectation. He cannot forgive the favorite of the Graces, that he as companion brightens every circle, as businessman guides all heads towards his purpose, as author impresses his spirit perhaps upon his whole century, whilst that *he*, the victim of diligence, with all his learning can exact no attention, move no stone from its place. Since he is never able to learn, the genial secret, to be pleasant, from that one, so nothing else remains left to him, than to bemoan the perversity of human nature, which pays more homage to appearance than to substance.

But there are voices worthy of respect, which declare themselves against the effects of beauty and are armed by experience with frightful grounds thereagainst. "It is undeniable," they say, "the charms of the beautiful can in good hands effect laudable ends, but it doth not contradict their essence, in bad hands to do just the opposite and to employ its soul-fettering power for error and injustice. Exactly for this reason, because taste pays attention only to the form and never to content, so it finally gives the disposition the dangerous direction, to neglect all reality in general and to sacrifice truth and morality to a charming investiture. All essential distinction among things disappears and it is merely the appearance, which determines their value. How many men of talent," they continue, "are not drawn away by the seductive power of the beautiful from an earnest and strenuous effectiveness, or at least induced, to treat it superficially! How many weak minds are merely for that reason at odds with the civic organization, because it pleased the phantasy of poets, to erect a world, wherein everything occurs quite differently, where no convenience binds opinion, no art suppresses nature. What dangerous dialectic have the passions not learned, since they are resplendent with the most glistening colors in the pictures of the poets and commonly maintain the field in combat with laws and duties? What hath society indeed won thereby, that beauty now gives laws to social intercourse, over which truth formerly ruled, and that the external impression decides the respect, which should only be confined to merit. It is true, one now sees all virtues blossom, which produce a pleasing effect in appearance and bestow a value in society, therefor however all excesses prevail as well and all vices are in vogue, which are compatible with a beautiful exterior. It must indeed excite reflection, that in well-nigh every epoch of history, where the arts blossom and taste rules, mankind is found sunken and also not a single example can be produced, that a higher degree and a great universality of aesthetical culture among a people had gone hand in hand with political freedom and civil virtue, beautiful manners with good morals and polish of conduct with truth of the same.

So long as Athens and Sparta maintained their independence, and respect for the law served as the foundation of their constitution, taste was still not mature, art still in its childhood, and it was still very much lacking, that beauty governed dispositions. Indeed poetry had already taken an exalted flight, but only with the swings of genius, of which we know, that it borders nearest to savagery and is a light, that gladly shimmers from the darkness; which testifies therefore rather against the taste of its age than for the same. When under Pericles and Alexander the golden age of art came hither, and the reign of taste was spread more universally, one no longer finds Greece's strength and freedom, eloquence falsified the truth, wisdom gave offense in the mouth of a Socrates, and virtue in the life of a Phocion. The Romans, we know, first had to exhaust their strength in civil wars and, unmanned by oriental opulence, bend beneath the yoke of a fortunate dynast, before we see the Grecian art triumph over the rigidity of their character. Also the dawn of culture did not arise among the Arabs sooner, than until the energy of their warlike spirit was relaxed beneath the scepter of the Abbasidae. In modern Italy beautiful art did not manifest itself sooner, than after the glorious alliance of the Lombards was torn asunder, Florence had submitted to the Medici and the spirit of independence in all those courageous cities had made place for an inglorious surrender. It is well-nigh superfluous, to still recall to mind the example of modern nations, whose refinement increased in the same proportion, as their independence ceased. Whither we always direct our eyes in the bygone world, there do we find, that taste and freedom flee from one another and that beauty only grounds her dominion upon the ruin of heroic virtues.

And yet exactly this energy of character, with which aesthetical culture is usually purchased, is the most effective spring of all greatness and excellence in man, the lack of which no other advantage, however great can replace. Keeps one therefore solely to that, which previous experiences teach about the influence of beauty, so can one indeed not be very encouraged, to develop feelings, which are so dangerous to the true culture of man; and one will prefer, at the risk of roughness and harshness, to dispense with the melting power of beauty, rather than see ourselves, with all the advantages of refinement surrendered to her enervating effects. But perhaps *experience* is not the tribunal, before which to decide a question such as this, and before one accorded weight to her evidence, it had to be placed first beyond doubt, that it is the same beauty, of which we speak and against which those examples bear witness. However this appears to presuppose a concept of beauty, which hath another source than experience, since through the same should be discerned, whether that, which is called beautiful in experience, bears this name with justice.

This pure *rational conception* of beauty, if such may be exhibited, must therefore—since it can be created from no actual case, rather first rectifies and guides our judgment in respect to every actual case—be sought upon the path of abstraction and be able to be inferred already from the possibility of sensuous-rational nature: with one word: beauty had to exhibit itself as a necessary conditon of mankind. To the pure conception of humanity must we therefore elevate ourselves henceforth, and since experience shows us only particular circumstances of individual men, but never humanity, so must we discover the Absolute and the Enduring from these their individual and changeable modes of appearance, and through the casting away of all accidental limitations, seek to secure ourselves the necessary conditions of their existence. Indeed this transcendental course will for a time remove us from the intimate circle of phenomena and from the living presence of things and dwell upon the naked fields of abstract ideas, but we strive yea towards a firm ground of knowledge, which nothing ever should shake, and who doth not venture out beyond reality, he will never conquer the truth.

Eleventh Letter

When abstraction ascends as high, as it ever can, so it arrives at two ultimate conceptions, at which it must stand still and recognize its limits. It distinguishes in man something, that endures and something that changes incessantly. The enduring it names his *person*, the changing his *condition*.

Person and condition—the self and its determinations—which we imagine to ourselves in the Necessary Being as one and the same, are eternally two in the finite. In spite of all persistence of the person the condition changes, in spite of all change of condition the person persists. We go from rest to activity, from emotional state to indifference, from agreement to contradiction, but *we* are yet always, and what immediately ensues from *us*, endures. In the absolute subject alone persist *with* the personality also all its determinations, because they flow *from* the personality. Everything, that divinity is, it is for that reason, *because* it is; it is consequently everything for eternity, because it is eternal.

Since in man, as finite being, person and condition are distinct, so can neither the condition be grounded upon the person, nor the person upon the condition. Were the latter, so the person would have to change; were the former, so the condition would have to persist; therefore in every case either the personality or the finiteness would have to cease. Not because we think, will, feel, are we; not because we are, think, will, do we feel. We are, because we are; we feel, think and will, because outside of us there is still something other.

The person must thus be its own ground, for the Enduring can not flow from the changeable; and so we had then first of all the idea of the absolute, in-itself-grounded Being, i.e. *freedom*. Condition must have a ground; since it is not through the person, and is therefore not absolute, it must *result*; and so we had secondly the condition of all dependent being or becoming, time. Time is the condition of all becoming: is an identical thesis, for it says nothing other than: the result is the condition, that something results.

The person, which manifests itself in the eternally persistent I and only in this, can not become, not commence in time, because time must on the contrary commence in it, because something persevering must lay the basis for change. Something must be altered, if alteration should exist; this something can therefore not itself be alteration. Whilst we say, the flower blooms and fades, we make the flower into the enduring in this transformation and lend it as it were a person, in which both those conditions are manifested. That man first becomes, there is no objection, for man is not merely person in general, but rather person, which finds itself in a determinate condition. Every condition however, every determinate existence arises in time, and so must man therefore, as phenomenon, have a beginning, although the pure intelligence in him is eternal. Without time, that is, without becoming it, he would never be a determinate being; his personality would indeed exist in capacity, but not in fact. Only through the succession of its notions doth the persevering I itself become a phenomenon.

Thus the matter of activity or the reality, which the highest Intelligence creates out of itself, man must first *receive*, and indeed he receives the same as something outside of him existing in space and as something in him changing in time upon the path of perception. This in-him-changing matter is accompanied by his never-changing I— and in all change to remain constantly *he* himself, to make all perceptions into experience, i.e., into unity of knowledge and each of its modes of appearance in time into law for all time, is the prescription, which is given him by his rational nature. Only whilst he changes, doth he *exist*; only whilst he remains unchangeable, doth *he* exist. Man, conceived in his perfection, were accordingly the persistent unity, which in the flood of alteration remains eternally the same. Now although an infinite being, a deity, cannot *become*, so must one yet name a tendency divine, which hath the most essential characteristic of divinity, absolute announcement of capacity (reality of everything possible) and absolute unity of appearance (necessity of everything real) as its infinite task. Incontrovertibly man carries the predisposition for divinity in his personality within himself; the way to divinity, if one can name a way, that which never leads to the goal, is open to him in the *senses*.

His personality, considered for itself alone and independent of all sensuous matter, is merely the predisposition to a possible infinite expression; so long he doth not intuit and doth not feel, he is still nothing further than form and empty capacity. His sensuousness, regarded for itself alone and separately from all self-activity of the mind, can do nothing further, than that it makes him, who without sensuousness is mere form, into matter, but in no way, that it unites matter with him. So long he merely feels, merely desires and acts from mere appetite, he is still nothing further than *world*, if we understand by this term merely the formless content of time. His sensuousness it is alone, indeed, which makes his capacity effective power, but it is only his personality, which makes his action his own. Therefore in order not to be merely world, he must impart form to matter; in order not to be mere form, he must give the predisposition, which he bears within himself, reality. He realizes the form, if he creates time and opposes change to the persevering, the manifoldness of the world to the eternal unity of his I; he forms matter, if he annuls time again, maintains perseverance in change and makes the manifoldness of the world subordinate to the unity of his I.

Hence flow now two opposite demands upon man, the two fundamental laws of senuous-rational nature. The first insists upon absolute *reality*; he should make everything into world, which is mere form, and bring all his predispositions into appearance: the second insists upon absolute *formality*: he should extirpate everything in himself, which is mere world, and bring about harmony in all his alterations; in other words: he should externalize everything internal and give form to everything external. Both tasks, considered in their highest fulfillment, lead back to the conception of divinity, from which I have proceeded.

Twelfth Letter

To the fulfillment of this double task, to bring the necessary *in us* into reality and to subject the real *outside of us* to the law of necessity, we are urged by two opposite forces, which one, because they impel us, to realize their object, entirely appropriately calls instincts. The first of these instincts, which I will call the sensuous, proceeds from the physical existence of man or from his sensuous nature, and is concerned, to place him in the limits of time and to make him into matter: not to give matter to him, because a free activity of the person already belongs thereto, which matter receives and distinguishes from itself, the persistent. However matter is here nothing but alteration or reality, which fills time; consequently this instinct demands, that alteration be, that time have a content. This condition of merely filled time is called sensation, and it is it alone, through which physical existence announces itself.

Since everything, that is in time, is *successive*, so thereby, that something is, everything else is excluded. Whilst one touches a note upon an instrument, among all notes, which it can possibly sound, only this single one is real; whilst man perceives the present the entire infinite possiblity of his determinations is limited to this single mode of existence. Where therefore this instinct works exclusively, there is necessarily the highest boundary at hand; man is in this condition nothing but a unity of magnitude, a filled moment of time—or on the contrary *he* is nothing, for his personality is annulled so long as sensation rules him and time carries him forth.*

So far man is finite, the domain of this instinct extends; and since every form appears only in matter, everything absolute only through the medium of limits, so is it of course the sensuous instinct, in which ultimately the entire appearance of mankind is fostered. But although it alone awakens and unfolds the predispositions of mankind, so is it yet it alone, which makes their perfection impossible. With indestructible bonds it fetters the higher striving spirit to the world of sense, and it calls back abstraction to the boundaries of the present from its freest wandering into the infinite. The thought may indeed escape it for a moment, and a firm will victoriously resists its demands; but soon suppressed nature steps back again into her rights, to press for reality of existence, for a content to our knowledge and for a purpose to our actions.

The second of these instincts, which one can call the *formal instinct*, proceeds from the absolute existence of man or from his rational nature and strives, to set him free, to bring harmony to the diversity of his

---

* Language hath the very appropriate expression for this condition of loss of self under the domination of sensation; *to be beside oneself*, that is, to be outside one's I. Although this phrase only occurs there, where the sensation becomes an emotional state and this condition more noticeable by its longer duration, so is yet everyone beside himself, so long as he only perceives. To return to self-possession from this condition, one just as correctly calls: *to go into oneself*, that is, return to one's I, restore one's person. Of one, who lies in a swoon, one doth not say: he is beside himself, rather he is *passed out*, i.e., he hath been robbed of his I, since he is simply not in the same. Hence he, who returned from a swoon, is only *come to*, which can exist quite well with being beside oneself.

appearance and to maintain his person despite all changes of condition. Now that the latter as absolute and indivisible unity can never be in contradiction with itself, *since we are we to all eternity*, so that instinct, which insists upon the maintenance of the personality, can never demand something other, than what it must demand to all eternity; it therefore decides for ever, as it decides for now, and commands for now, what it commands for ever. Hence it encompasses the whole succession of time, that is as much as: it annuls time, it annuls alteration, it wishes, that the real be necessary and eternal, and that the eternal and necessary be real: in other words: it insists upon truth and upon justice.

If the first only produces cases, so the other gives *laws*; laws for every judgment, if it concerns knowledge, laws for every will, if it concerns action. Be it now, that we recognize an object, that we attribute objective validity to a condition of our subject, or that we act from knowledge, that we make the objective the determining ground of our condition—in both cases we tear this condition from the jurisdiction of time and grant to it reality for all men and all time, i.e., universality and necessity. Feeling can merely say: that is true *for this* subject and *in this moment*, and another moment, another subject can come, that takes back the statement of the present sensation. But if the thought once pronounces: *that is*, so it decides for ever and eternally, and the validity of the pronouncement is vouched for by the personality itself, which defies all change. Inclination can merely say: that is good for *thy individuality* and *for thy present need*; but thy individuality and thy present need will be carried away by alteration and, what thou now ardently desirest, one day will be made into the object of thine abhorrence. If however the moral feeling says: *that should be*, so it decides for ever and eternally—if thou confessest truth, because it is truth, and practicest justice, because it is justice, so hast thou made a single case into the law for all cases, treated one moment in thy life as eternity.

Where therefore the formal instinct exerts dominion and the pure object acts in us, there is the highest enlargement of being, there disappear all limits, there from the unity of magnitude, in which the needy sense confined him, hath man arisen to a unity of ideas, which contains the entire realm of phenomena under itself. We are with this operation no more in time, rather time is in us with its entire never-ending succession. We are no more individuals, rather species; the judgment of all spirits is expressed by that of our own, the choice of all hearts is represented by our deed.

Thirteenth Letter

At first sight nothing appears to be more opposed to one another than the tendencies of both of these instincts, in that the one insists upon alteration, the other upon immutability. And yet it is both of these instincts, which exhaust the conception of mankind, and a third fundamental instinct, which could mediate both, is an absolutely unthinkable conception. How shall we therefore restore the unity of human nature, which seems fully annulled by this original and radical opposition?

True is it, their *tendencies* contradict themselves, however, what is well to observe, not in *the same objects*, and what doth not encounter another, can not collide with another. The sensuous instinct indeed demands alteration, but it doth not demand, that it also be extended to the person and its domain: that there be a change of principles. The formal instinct insists upon unity and perseverance—but he doth not wish, that the condition also be fixed with the person, that there be identity of sensation. They are therefore not opposed to one another by nature, and if notwithstanding this they so appear, so they have first become through a free transgression of nature, in that they misunderstand themselves and confuse their spheres.*

In a transcendental philosophy, where everything depends thereon, to liberate the form from the content and to preserve the necessary

---

* So soon as one maintains an original, hence necessary antagonism of both instincts, so there is indeed no other means, to preserve the unity in man, than that one unconditionally subordinates the sensuous instinct to the rational. However, therefrom mere uniformity, but no harmony can arise and man still remains divided for ever. The subordination must by all means be, but reciprocal; for although the limits can never establish the absolute, thus freedom can never be dependent upon time, so is it just as certain, that the absolute through itself can never establish the limits, that the condition in time can not be dependent upon freedom. Both principles are therefore at once subordinated to one another and coordinated, i.e., they stand in reciprocity; without form no matter, without matter no form. (This concept of reciprocity and the entire importance of the same one finds excellently set forth in Fichte's "Foundation of the Whole Theory of Science," Leipzig 1794.) How it stands with the person in the realm of ideas, we of course do not know; but that it, without receiving matter, can not manifest itself in the realm of time, we know for certain; in this realm therefore matter will have to determine something not merely *under* the form, but rather also *alongside* the form and independent of the same. As necessary as it is therefore, that feeling decide nothing in the domain of reason, equally necessary is it, that reason presume to determine nothing in the domain of feeling. Already in that one awards a domain to each of both, one excludes the other therefrom and places a boundary on each, which can not be passed over except to the disadvantage of both.

pure of everything accidental, one is easily accustomed, to think of the matter itself merely as hindrance and to represent sensuousness, because it stands directly in the way in *this* business, as in a necessary contradiction with reason. Such a mode of representation lies indeed in no way in the *spirit* of the Kantian system, but it could very well lie in the *letter* of the same.

To watch over these and to secure for each one of both of these instincts its boundary, is the task of *culture*, which therefore owes both an equal justice and hath not merely to maintain the rational instinct against the sensuous, rather also the latter against the former. Its business is therefore twofold: *firstly*: to secure sensuousness against the encroachments of freedom: *secondly*: to secure the personality against the power of sensations. The former it achieves through the education of the capacity of feeling, the latter through the education of the capacity of reason.

Since the world is something prolonged in time, alteration, so will the perfection of that capacity, which places man in relation with the world, have to be the greatest possible mutability and extensiveness. Since the person is the subsisting in alteration, so will the perfection of that capacity, which should be opposed to change, have to be the greatest possible self-reliance and intensity. The more many-sided the receptivity is developed, the more motile the same is, and the more surfaces it offers to phenomena, so much the more world doth man *apprehend*, so much the more potentialities doth he develop in himself; the more strength and depth the personality, the more freedom the reason wins, so much the more world doth man *comprehend*, so much the more form he creates outside himself. His culture will therefore subsist therein: *firstly*: to provide to the receiving capacity the most manifold contacts with the world and upon the side of the feeling to drive passivity to its highest: *secondly*: to acquire for the determining capacity the highest independence from the receiving and upon the side of reason to drive activity to its highest. Where both qualities are united, there will man combine with the highest fullness of existence the highest self-reliance and freedom and, instead of losing himself in the world, he will rather draw this into himself with the entire infinity of its phenomena and subject it to the unity of his reason.

This relation man can now *invert* and thereby fail to achieve his destiny in a twofold manner. He can place the intensity, which the active power requires, upon the passive, forestall the formal instinct by means of the instinct of matter and make the receiving capacity into the determining. He can assign the extensiveness which is proper to the passive power, to the active, forestall the instinct of matter by means of the formal instinct and substitute the determining for the receiving capacity. In the first case he will never be *he himself*, in the second he will never be *something else*; hence precisely for that reason in both cases he will be *neither one*, consequently—nought.*

Becomes in fact the sensuous instinct determining, is sense the lawgiver, and the world oppresses the person, so it ceases in the same proportion, to be object, as it grows in power. So soon as man is only

---

* The bad influence of a preponderant sensuality upon our thinking and action easily catches the eye of everyone; not so easily, although it occurs just as frequently and is just as important, the disadvantageous influence of a preponderant rationality upon our knowledge and our conduct. Permit me therefore, to recall only two out of the great number of relevant cases, which can bring to light the damage of an encroaching mental and will power to intuition and sensation.

One of the most eminent causes, why our natural sciences make such slow strides, is evidently the universal and scarcely conquerable propensity towards teleological judgments, by which, so soon as they are used constitutively, the determining capacity is substituted for the receiving. Nature may touch our organs ever so energetically and ever so variously—all her manifoldness is lost for us, because we seek nothing in her, but what we have put in her because we do not permit her, to move *inward towards us*, but on the contrary strive with impatiently anticipating reason *from within towards her*. Comes after that in centuries one, who nears her with calm, chaste and open senses and for this reason encounters a number of phenomena, which we by our prevention have overlooked, so we are highly astonished thereover, that so many eyes should have observed nothing on such a bright day. This premature striving towards harmony, before one hath gathered together the individual tones, which should constitute it, this violent usurpation of the mental power in an area, where it doth not govern unconditionally, is the grounds of fruitlessness of so many thinking heads for the best of science, and it is difficult to say, whether the sensuousness, which assumes no form, or the reason, which awaits no content, hath done more damage to the enlargement of our knowledge.

Just as difficult may it be to determine, whether our practical philanthropy is more disturbed and chilled by the vehemence of our desires or by the rigidity of our principles, more by the egoism of our senses or by the egoism of our reason. In order to make us into cooperating, helpful, active men, feeling and character must be united, just as in order to furnish us experience, openness of the senses must be combined with energy of the understanding. How can we, with ever so praiseworthy maxims, be just, good and human towards others, if the capacity fails us, to include foreign nature faithfully and truly in ourselves, to appropriate foreign situations to ourselves, to make foreign feelings our own? This capacity however is suppressed as well in the education, which we receive, as in that, which we give ourselves, in the same measure, as one seeks to break the power of desires and to strengthen the character by means of principles. Because it is difficult, to remain faithful to his principles amid all the activity of the feelings, so one seizes the more comfortable means, to make the character more secure by blunting the feelings; for no doubt it is infinitely easier, to be calm before an unarmed opponent, than to master a courageous

the content of time, so is he not, and he hath consequently also no content. With his personality his condition is also annulled, because both are conceptions of change—because alteration demands a persevering and the limited reality an infinite. Is the formal instinct received, that is, doth the power of thought anticipate sensation and is the person substituted for the world, so it ceases in the same proportion, to be self-supporting power and subject, as it thrusts itself into the place of the object, because the persevering demands alteration, and the absolute reality limits to its manifestation. So soon as man *is* only form, so *hath* he no form; and the person is consequently also annulled with the condition. In one word: only in so far as he is self-supporting, is reality outside him, is he receptive; only in so far as he is receptive, is reality in him, is he a thinking power.

Both instincts therefore have limitation and, in so far as they are thought of as energies, necessary relaxation; the former, that it may not invade the domain of legislation, the latter, that it not enter into the domain of sensation. This relaxation of the sensuous instinct may however by no means be the effect of a physical incapacity and of a bluntness of sensation, which overall only deserves contempt. It must be an act of freedom, an activity of the person, which by its moral intensity moderates the sensuous and by mastering the impressions takes from them in depth, in order to give to them in surface. The character must determine for the temperament its limits, for the sense may lose *only to the mind*. That relaxation of the formal instinct may be just as little the effect of a spiritual incapacity and of a flaccidity of thought or will powers, which would degrade mankind. Fullness of sensations must be its glorious source; sensuousness itself must maintain

---

and robust enemy. In this operation then consists also for the most part, what one calls *to form a man*; and indeed in the best sense of the word, where it means cultivation of the inner, not merely the outer man. A man so formed will indeed be secured therefrom, to be raw nature and to appear as such; he will however at once be armoured against all sensations of nature by means of principles, and humanity *from without* will be as little able to reach him as humanity *from within*.

It is a very pernicious misuse, which is made of the ideal of perfection, if one in the judgment of other men and in the cases, where one should act for them, sets it up in all its severity as the ground. The former will lead to schwaermerei, the latter to harshness and to coldness. One makes his social duties uncommonly easy to be sure, if one for the *actual* man, who demands our help, substitutes in thought the *ideal man*, who could probably help himself. Severity with oneself, combined with softness towards others, constitutes the truly excellent character. But mostly he who will be soft towards other men will also be thus towards himself, and he who will be severe towards himself will also be thus toward others; soft towards oneself and severe towards others is the most contemptible character.

its domain with victorious power and resist the violence, which by its encroaching activity the mind would fain inflict upon it. In one word: the material instinct must be held by the personality, and the formal instinct by the receptivity or nature in its proper limits.

Fourteenth Letter

We have now been led to the conception of such a reciprocal action between both of the instincts, where the effectiveness of the one establishes and limits at the same time the effectiveness of the other, and where each one thereby reaches for itself its highest manifestation precisely in that the other is active.

This reciprocal relation of both instincts is indeed merely the task of reason, which man is capable of fully achieving only in the completion of his being. It is in the truest sense of the word the *idea of his humanity*, hence an infinite, to which he can approach ever more closely in the course of time, but without ever reaching it. "He should not strive for form at the cost of his reality, and not for reality, at the cost of form; on the contrary he should seek the Absolute Being through a determinate and the determinate being through an infinite. He should place opposite himself a world, because he is person, and should be person, because a world stands opposite him. He should feel, because he is conscious of himself, and should be conscious of himself, because he feels."—That he truly in conformity with this idea, hence, in the full meaning of the word, is man, can he never bring into experience, so long as he only satisfies one of both instincts exclusively or only one after the other; for so long as he only feels, his person or his absolute existence remains to him, and, so long as he only thinks, his existence in time or his condition remains to him a mystery. Were there however cases, where he made this double experience *at the same time*, where he were at once conscious of his freedom and felt his existence, where he at once felt himself as matter and came to know himself as spirit, so had he in these cases, and positively only in these, a complete intuition of his humanity, and the object, which provided him this intuition, would serve him as a symbol of his *realized destiny*, consequently (because this is to be achieved only in the totality of time) as a representation of the infinite.

Supposing, that cases of this kind can occur in experience, so would they awaken a new instinct in him, which just therefore, because both of the others work together in it, would be opposed, to each one of the same, considered alone and with justice would be regarded as a new instinct. The sensuous instinct desires, that there be alteration, that time have a content; the formal instinct desires, that time be annulled, that there be no alteration. That instinct therefore, in which both act in combination (it be me for the time being, until I shall have justified this appellation, permitted, to call it *play instinct*), the play instinct therefore would be directed thither, to annul the time in time, to reconcile Becoming with Absolute Being, alteration with identity.

The sensuous instinct wants to *become* determinate, it wants to receive its object; the formal instinct wants to determine *itself*, it wants to bring forth its object: the play instinct will therefore be exerted so to receive, as it would have brought itself forth, and so to bring forth, as the sense aspires to receive.

The sensuous instinct excludes from its subject all self-activity and freedom, the formal instinct excludes from its, all dependency, all passivity. Exclusion of freedom is however physical, exclusion of passivity is moral necessity. Both instincts therefore compel the mind, the former through natural laws, the latter through laws of reason. The play instinct therefore, as in which both act in combination, will compel the mind at once morally and physically; it will therefore, because it annuls all contingency, annul all compulsion also and set man free not only physically but also morally. If we embrace someone with passion, who is worthy of our contempt, so feel we painfully the *compulsion of nature*. If we are disposed hostilely towards another, who compels our respect, so feel we painfully the *compulsion of reason*. But so soon as he at once interests our inclination and hath gained our respect, so disappears not only the constraint of feeling but also the constraint of reason, and we begin, to love him, i.e., at once to play with our inclination and with our respect.

Whilst moreover the sensuous instinct compels us physically and the formal instinct morally, so the former leaves our formal, the latter our material constitution contingent; i.e., it is contingent, whether our happiness is in agreement with our perfection, or the latter with the former. The play instinct therefore, in which both act in union, will make at the same time our formal and our material constitution, at once our perfection and our happiness contingent; it will therefore, just because it makes *both* contingent, and because the contingency also disappears with the necessity, annul the contingency again in both, hence bring form into the material and reality into the form. In the same measure as it takes from the feelings and emotional states their dynamic influence, it will bring them into agreement with ideas of reason, and in the same measure, as it takes away from the laws of reason their moral compulsion, it will reconcile them with the interest of the senses.

Fifteenth Letter

I am coming ever nearer to the goal, towards which I am leading you upon a not very cheerful path. May it please you, to follow me yet a few steps further, so a freer horizon will disclose itself and a brighter prospect perhaps reward the labors of the way.

The object of the sensuous instinct, expressed in a universal concept, is *life* in its broadest meaning; a concept, which means all material being and everything immediately present in the senses. The object of the formal instinct, expressed in a universal concept, is *form*, not only in the figurative but also in the literal meaning; a concept, which includes within itself all formal qualities of things and all relations of the same to the thinking powers. The object of the play instinct, represented in a universal scheme, will therefore be able to be called *living form*; a concept, which serves to designate all aesthetical qualities of phenomena and, in a word, what one calls *beauty* in the broadest meaning.

By means of this explanation, if it were one, is beauty neither extended to the entire domain of the living, nor merely confined in this domain. A block of marble, although it is and remains lifeless, can therefore nonetheless become a living form through the architect and sculptor; a man, although he lives and hath form, is therefore still not by any means living form. That requires, that his form be life and his life form. So long as we merely think about his form, it is lifeless, mere abstraction; so long as we merely feel his life, it is formless, mere impression. Only in that his form lives in our feeling and his life forms itself in our understanding, is he living form, and this will be primarily the case, where we judge him to be beautiful.

Thereby however, that we know to indicate the component parts, which in their fusion bring forth beauty, the genesis of the same is still in no manner explained; for it would be required, that one conceive *that fusion itself*, which to us, as in general all reciprocal action between the finite and infinite, remains inscrutable. Reason sets up the demand out of transcendental grounds: there shall be a communion between the formal instinct and material instinct, i.e., a play instinct, because only the unity of reality with form, of contingency with necessity, of passivity with freedom completes the conception of humanity. It must set up this demand, because it is reason—because it insists in accord with its essence upon completeness and upon removal of all limitations, but every exclusive activity of one or the other instinct leaves human nature incomplete and establishes a limit in the same. So soon therefore as it makes the decision: there shall exist a humanity, so hath it thereby established the law: there shall be a beauty. Experience can answer us, *whether* there is a beauty, and we shall know it, so soon as it hath taught us, whether there is a humanity. But *how* a beauty can be, and how a humanity is possible, neither reason nor experience can teach us.

Man, we know, is neither exclusively matter, nor is he exclusively spirit. Beauty, as consummation of his humanity, can therefore be neither exclusively mere life, as by ingenious observers, who adhered too precisely to the evidence of experience, hath been maintained, and whereto the taste of the times would fain pull it down; nor can it be exclusively mere form, as hath been judged by speculative philosophers, who removed themselves too far from experience, and by philosophizing artists, who let themselves be guided in explanation of the same all too much by the needs of art:*

It is the common object of both instincts, that is, of the play instinct. This name is completely justified by the usage of language, which is accustomed to denote everything, which is neither subjectively nor objectively contingent and yet compels neither outwardly nor inwardly, with the word play. Since the mind finds itself in the intuition of beauty in a happy mean between law and need, so precisely therefore, because it is divided between both, is it withdrawn not only from the constraint of the one but also of the other. The material instinct like the formal instinct is *earnest* in its demands, because the one relates, in its cognition, to the reality, the other to the necessity of things; because, in action, the first is directed to the maintenance of life, the second to the preservation of dignity, both therefore to truth and perfection. However life becomes more indifferent as dignity is intermixed, and duty compels no more, so soon as inclination attracts: just as the mind takes up the reality of things, the material truth, more freely and calmly, so soon as such encounters the formal truth, the law of necessity, and feels itself no longer strained by abstraction, so soon as the immediate intuition can accompany it. In a word: whilst it comes into communion with ideas, everything real loses its earnestness, because it becomes *small*, and whilst it encounters sensation, necessity puts aside its own, because it becomes *easy*.

Is, however, you would long have been tempted to object to me, is not the beautiful degraded thereby, that one makes it into mere play, and places it on an equal level with frivolous objects, which were all along in possession of this name? Doth it not contradict the rational conception and the dignity of beauty, which are yet regarded as an

---

* In his "Philosophical Inquiry into the Origin of Our Conception of the Sublime and the Beautiful," Burke makes beauty mere life. As far as I am aware, it is made into mere form, by every follower of the dogmatic system, who hath ever made his confession on this subject: among artists Raphael Mengs in his "Thoughts on Taste in Painting"; not to mention others. So as in all, also in this piece hath *critical* philosophy opened the way, to lead empiricism back to principles and speculation back to experience.

instrument of culture, to limit it to a *mere play*, and doth it not contradict the concept of play from experience, which can exist together with exclusion of all taste, to limit it merely to beauty?

But what then is a *mere* play, when we know, that in all conditions of man it is precisely play and only play, which makes him complete and unfolds at once his twofold nature? What you, according to your representation of the matter, call *limitation*, that I call, according to mine, which I have justified through proofs, *enlargement*. I would therefore rather say precisely the reverse: with the agreeable, with the good, with the perfect man is *only* earnest, but with beauty he plays. Of course we do not permit ourselves to mention here the plays, which are in process in real life and which are commonly only directed to very material objects; but in the actual life we would also seek in vain for the beauty, of which we are here speaking. The actually present beauty is worthy of the actually present play instinct; but by the ideal of beauty, which reason establishes, an ideal of the play instinct is also presented, which man should have before his eyes in all his plays.

One will never err, if one seeks a man's ideal of beauty upon the same path, upon which he satisfies his play instinct. If the Grecian peoples delight themselves in the athletic sports at Olympia in the bloodless contests of strength, of speed, of agility and in the nobler conflict of talents, and if the Roman enjoy themselves in the death struggle of a slain gladiator or of his Libyan opponent, so becomes it comprehensible to us from this single trait, why we must seek for the ideal form of a Venus, a Juno, an Apollo not in Rome, but rather in Greece.*

But now reason speaks: the beautiful should not be merely life and not merely form, but rather living form, that is, beauty; in that it dictates to man the two-fold law of the absolute formality and the absolute reality. Hence it also makes the decision: man shall with beauty only *play*, and he shall *only with beauty play*.

For, in order to finally say it at once, man plays only, where he in the full meaning of the word is man, and *he is only there fully man, where he plays*. This thesis, which in this moment perhaps appears paradoxical, will receive a great and deep meaning, if we have first

---

* If one (in order to remain in the modern world), contrasts the horse races in London, the bull fights in Madrid, the spectacles of former times in Paris, the gondola races in Venice, the animal hunts in Vienna and the happy, beautiful life of the Corso in Rome, so can it not be difficult to determine the shades of taste of these different people. However, far less uniformity is displayed among the popular games in these different lands than among the games of the fashionable society in just these lands, which is easy to explain.

come thither, to apply it to the twofold earnestness of duty and of
destiny; it will, I promise you, bear the whole structure of aesthetical
art and the yet more difficult art of life. But this thesis is also only in
science unexpected; it long since lived and acted in the art and in the
feeling of the Greeks, its most distinguished master; only that they
transferred to Olympus, what should have been realized upon the earth.
Guided by the truth of the same, they caused not only the earnestness
and the work, which furrow the cheeks of mortals, but also the futile
pleasure, which smooths the empty visage, to vanish from the brows
of the blissful gods, freed the eternally satisfied from the fetters of
every aim, every duty, every concern and made *idleness* and *indiffer-
ence* the envied lot of the godly state; a merely more human name for
the freest and most sublime Being. Not only the material constraint
of natural laws but also the spiritual constraint of moral laws lost itself,
in its higher conception of necessity, which embraced both worlds at
once, and from the unity of these two necessities issued forth to them
true freedom for the first time. Inspired by this spirit, they extin-
guished from the features of their ideal at once together with *inclination*
also all traces of the *will*, or better, they made both unrecognizable,
because they knew to knit both into the most intimate alliance. It is
neither grace, nor is it dignity, which speaks to us from the glorious
countenance of a Juno Ludovici; it is not one of both, because it is at
once both. Whilst the womanly god demands our worship, the godlike
woman enkindles our love; but whilst we allow ourselves to dissolve
in the heavenly loveliness, the heavenly self-sufficiency frightens us
back. In itself rests and dwells the whole form, a completely closed
creation, and as if it were beyond space, without yielding, without
resistance; there is no force, which struggled with forces, no weak
point, where temporal power could break in. Irresistibly seized and
attracted by that one, by this one held at a distance, we find ourselves
at once in the condition of highest rest and of highest motion, and there
results that wonderful emotion, for which the understanding hath no
conception and language no name.

Sixteenth Letter

From the reciprocal action of two opposite instincts and from the
combination of two opposite principles we have seen the beautiful arise,
whose highest ideal is therefore to be sought in the most perfect possible
union and *equilibrium* of reality and form. This equilibrium remains
however always only an idea, which can never be fully achieved by
reality. In reality there will always remain a preponderance of the *one*
element over the other, and the highest, that experience achieves, will
consist of an *oscillation* between both principles, where now reality,

now the form is predominant. Beauty in the idea is therefore eternally but indivisibly single, because there can only be one single equilibrium; beauty in experience on the contrary will eternally be double, because in oscillation the equilibrium can be overstepped, in a twofold manner, namely on this side and that side.

I have observed in one of the foregoing letters, also it follows with rigorous necessity from the coherence of the previous, that a dissolving and a tensing effect be expected simultaneously from the beautiful: a *dissolving*, in order to keep not only the sensuous instinct but also the formal instinct within their bounds; a *tensing*, in order to preserve both in their strength. Both of these modes of action of beauty should however, in idea, be absolutely only a single one. She should dissolve, thereby that she makes both natures uniformly tense, and should become tense, thereby that she dissolve both natures uniformly. This follows already from the conception of a reciprocal action, in virtue of which both parts necessarily condition one another at once and are conditioned through one another, and beauty is the purest product thereof. However, experience offers us no example of such a perfect reciprocal action, rather, here everytime, more or less, the excess weight will establish a deficiency and the deficiency an excess weight. What therefore is distinguished in the ideally beautiful only in the conception, that is distinct in the beautiful in the experience of existence. The ideally beautiful, although indivisible and simple, shows in different conditions not only a melting but also energetic quality; in experience there *is* a melting and energetic beauty. So is it, and so will it be in all cases, where the Absolute is placed within the limits of time and the ideas of reason should be realized in humanity. So the reflecting man conceives of virtue, truth, happiness; but the acting man will merely practice *virtues*, merely seize *truths*, merely enjoy *happy* days. To lead these latter back to the former—to put in the place of morals morality, in the place of information knowledge, in the place of blisses happiness, is the business of physical and moral education; to make beauty from beauties, is the task of the aesthetical.

Energetic beauty can preserve man just as little before a certain residue of savagery and harshness, as the melting protect him before a certain degree of softness and enervation. For since the effect of the first is, to make the disposition tense, not only in the physical but also moral, and to augment his elasticity, so it happens only too easily, that the resistence of temperament and character diminishes receptiveness to impressions, that also the gentler humanity experiences an oppression, which should have only befallen his raw nature, and that his raw nature participates in a gain of strength, which should only have applied to his free person; therefore one finds in the ages of strength and abundance true greatness of conception together with the gigantic and adventurous, and the sublimity of conviction paired with the most horrible outbursts of passion; therefore in the ages of rules and form one will find nature just as often oppressed as mastered, just as often offended as surpassed. And because the effect of melting beauty is, to dissolve the disposition in the moral as in the physical, it occurs just as easily, that with the violence of desire energy of feeling is also stifled and that the character also shares a loss of strength, which should only affect passion: therefore one will see in the so-called refined ages softness degenerate not seldomly into effeminacy, plainness into insipidity, correctness into emptiness, liberality into arbitrariness, lightness into frivolity, calm into apathy and the most contemptible caricature border upon the most glorious humanity. For the man under the constraint either of matter or of form, melting beauty is therefore a need, for he is long moved by greatness and strength, ere he begins to become sensitive to harmony and grace. For the man under the indulgence of taste the energetic beauty is a need, for only all too gladly he frivolously forfeits in a state of refinement a strength, which he brought over from a state of savagery.

And henceforth, I believe, every contradiction will be explained and answered, which one usually encounters in the judgments of men about the influence of the beautiful and in the valuation of aesthetical culture. It is explained, this contradiction, so soon as one recalls, that in experience there is a twofold beauty and that both parties assert of the whole species, what each is only able to prove of a particular kind of the same. It is lifted, this contradiction, so soon as one distinguishes the double need of humanity, to which that double beauty corresponds. Both parties will therefore probably be found right, if they are only first agreed with one another, which kind of beauty and which form of humanity they have in mind.

I shall therefore, in the continuation of my inquiries make the path, which nature follows with man in respect to aesthetics, also my own, and elevate myself from the kinds of beauty to the species conception of the same. I shall examine the effects of the melting beauty in the relaxed man upon the effects of the energetic in the tense, in order to dissolve at last both of the opposite kinds of beauty in the unity of the ideally beautiful, just as those two opposite forms of humanity perish in the unity of the ideally human.

Seventeenth Letter

So long as it was merely a matter, of deriving the universal idea of beauty from the conception of human nature in general, we could call to mind no other limits to the latter, than which are directly established in the being of the same and are inseparable from the conception of finiteness. Unconcerned about the accidental limitations, which it might suffer in the real phenomenon, we created the conception of the same directly from reason, as the source of all necessity, and with the ideal of humanity was at once also given the ideal of beauty.

Now however we climb down from the region of ideas into the scene of reality, in order to meet man *in a determinate* condition, hence under limitations, which do not flow originally from his conception, but rather from external circumstances and from an accidental use of his freedom. But in however manifold ways the idea of humanity may also be limited in him, so the mere content of the same already teaches us, that in the whole only *two* opposite deviations from the same can occur. Lies, that is to say, his perfection in the harmonious energy of his sensuous and spiritual powers, so can he fail to achieve this perfection only either through a deficiency of harmony or through a deficiency of energy. Therefore before we have even heard the testimony of experience thereon, we are already certain in advance through mere reason, that we shall find the actual, consequently limited man either in a condition of tension or in a condition of relaxation, according as either the one-sided activity of single forces disturbs the harmony of his being or the unity of his nature is grounded upon the uniform slackening of his sensuous and spiritual powers. Both opposite limits are, as now should be demonstrated, lifted by beauty, which restores in the tense man harmony, in the relaxed, energy and in this way, in conformity with her nature, leads the limited condition back to an absolute and makes man into a whole, complete in himself.

Therefore in reality she in no way belies the conception, which we conceived of her in speculation; except that she hath here an incomparably less free hand than there, where we were able to apply her to the pure conception of humanity. In man, as experience establishes him, she finds an already rotten and resisting matter, which robs her just as much of her ideal perfection, as it mixes in of his *individual* nature. She will therefore in reality appear everywhere only as a particular and limited species, never as pure genus, she will in tense dispositions lay aside her freedom and manifoldness, she will in relaxed, her enlivening force; however, we who have by now become more familiar with her true character, shall not be led astray by this contradictory appearance. Far from determining with the great crowd of critics their conceptions from isolated experiences and making *her* responsible for the deficiencies, which man shows under her influence, we know on the contary, that it is man, who transfers to her the imperfections of his individuality, who through his subjective limitation stands incessantly in the way of her perfection and reduces her absolute ideal to two limited forms of phenomenon.

The melting beauty, it was asserted, be for a tense disposition, and for a relaxed the energetic. But I call the man tense not only, if he finds himself under the constraint of conceptions. Every exclusive domination of one of his two fundamental instincts is a condition of constraint for him and of violence; and freedom lies only in the co-operation of both his natures. The man ruled one-sidedly by feelings or sensuously tense is thus dissolved and set free by form; the man ruled one-sidedly by laws or spiritually tense is dissolved and set free by matter. The melting beauty, in order to satisfy this double task, will therefore reveal herself under two different forms. She will *firstly* as a calm form soften the savage life and pave the way for a transition from sensations to thoughts; she will *secondly* as living image equip the abstract form with sensuous force, lead the conception back to intuition and the law to feeling. The first service she renders to the natural man, the second to the artificial man. But because she in both cases doth not rule with complete freedom over her matter, but rather depends upon that, which either formless nature or unnatural art offers her, so she will in both cases bear yet traces of her origin and lose herself there more in the material life, here more in the mere abstract form.

In order to be able to form for ourselves a conception thereof, how beauty can become a means, to remove that double tension, we must seek to explore the origin of the same in the human disposition. Make up your mind therefore to yet one short sojourn in the domain of speculation, in order to leave it thereupon for ever and with more secure steps to stride forth upon the field of experience.

Eighteenth Letter

Through beauty is the sensuous man led to form and to thought; through beauty is the spiritual man led back to matter and restored to the world of sense.

From this it appears to follow, that between matter and form, between passivity and activity there must be a *middle condition*, and that beauty transfers us into this middle condition. This conception of beauty is also actually formed by the greatest part of man, so soon as he hath begun, to reflect upon her effects, and all experiences point thereto. On the other side, however, nothing is more absurd and contradictory than such a conception, since the distance between matter and form, between passivity and activity, between sensation and thought is *infinite* and can become mediated absolutely through nothing. How do we now remove this contradiction? Beauty combines the two opposite conditions of feeling and of thinking, and yet there is absolutely no middle between both. The former is certain through experience, the latter is immediately through reason. This is the essential point, to which the whole question of beauty finally leads, and if we succeed, to solve this problem satisfactorily, so we have at the same time found the thread, which leads us through the whole labyrinth of aesthetics.

It hereby concerns however two utterly different operations, which must necessarily support one another in this inquiry. Beauty, it is said, knits together two conditions, *which are opposed to one another* and never can become one. From this opposition must we proceed: we must apprehend and recognize it in its whole purity and strictness, so that both conditions are separated in the most definite way; otherwise we mix, but do not unite. Secondly, it is said: beauty *combines* those two opposite conditions and therefore cancels the opposition. However because both conditions remain eternally opposed to one another, so are they not otherwise to be combined, than in that they are cancelled. Our second business is therefore, to make this combination perfect, to realize it so purely and completely, that both conditions disappear entirely in a third and no trace of the division remains behind in the whole; otherwise we isolate, but do not unite. All disputes, which have ever prevailed in the philosophical world about the conception of beauty and in part still prevail to this day, have no other origin, than that one either began the inquiry not with the requisite rigorous distinction, or did not carry it through to a completely pure union. Those among the philosophers, who in reflection on this subject blindly trust in the guidance of their *feelings*, can achieve no *conception* of beauty, because they distinguish nothing individual in the totality of sensuous impressions. The others, who take the understanding exclusively as a guide, can never achieve a conception of *beauty*, because they never see in the totality of the same anything other than the parts, and spirit and matter remain divided eternally to them even in their most perfect unity. The first fear, to cancel beauty *dynamically*, i.e. as acting power, if they should separate, what is yet combined in feeling; the others fear, to cancel beauty *logically*, i.e. as conception, if they should unite, what is yet separated in the understanding. The former want to think of beauty, just as she acts; the latter want to cause her to act, just as she is thought. Both must therefore miss the truth, the former because they attempt to imitate infinite nature with their limited capacity of thought; the latter, because they want to limit infinite nature according to their laws of thought. The first fear, to rob beauty of its freedom through a too-strict dissection; the others fear, to destroy the definiteness of its conception through a too-bold union. The former do not reflect however, that the freedom, in which they with all justice place the essence of beauty, is not lawlessness, but rather harmony of laws, not arbitrariness, but rather the highest inner necessity; the latter do not reflect, that the definiteness, which they with equal justice demand from beauty, consists not in the *exclusion of certain realities*, but rather in the *absolute inclusion of them all*, that she therefore is not restriction, but rather infinity. We shall avoid the rocks, on which both are run aground, if we begin from the two elements, in which beauty is divided before the understanding, but thereupon also elevate ourselves to the pure aesthetical unity, through which she acts on sensation and in which both those conditions completely vanish.*

Nineteenth Letter

There can be distinguished generally in man two different conditions of passive and active determinability and just as many conditions of passive and active determination. The explanation of this thesis leads us most quickly to the goal.

The condition of the human spirit before all determination, which is given him through impressions of the senses, is a determinability without bounds. The endlessness of space and of time is given to his conceptual power for free use, and because, according to hypothesis, nothing in this wide realm of the possible is fixed, consequently also nothing is yet excluded, so one can call this condition of indeterminability an *empty infinity*, which is by no means to be mistaken for an infinite emptiness.

Now should his senses be moved, and from the infinite number of possible determinations a single reality should obtain. A conception should arise in him. What in the foregoing condition of mere determinability was nothing but an empty capacity, that now becomes an acting power, that receives a content; but at the same time it receives, as acting power, a limit, since it, as mere capacity was unlimited.

---

* To the attentive reader the observation will have presented itself in the comparison drawn here, that the sensual aestheticians, who value the testimony of sensation more than that of reason, are *in respect to reality* far less distant from the truth than their opponents, although *in respect to insight* they cannot match them; and this relationship one finds everywhere between nature and science. Nature (sense) everywhere unites, the understanding everywhere separates, but reason unites again; hence man is, before he begins to philosophize, nearer to truth than the philosopher, who hath not yet ended his inquiry. One can on this account declare without all further examination a philosophical statement to be erroneous, so soon as the same, *in respect to result*, hath common feeling against it; with the same justice however one can hold it as suspect, if it in respect to form and method, hath the common feeling on its side. With the latter every writer may be consoled, who cannot expound a philosophical deduction, as many readers seem to expect, like a fireside chat. With the former one may reduce everyone to silence, who wants to found new systems at the expense of human understanding.

Reality is therefore there, but the infinity is lost. In order to describe
a form in space, we must *limit* the endless space; in order to conceive
to ourselves an alteration in time, we must *divide* the totality of time.
We arrive thus at reality only through limits, only through *negation*
or exclusion at *position* or at actual affirmation, only through annulment
of our free determinability at determination.

But from a mere exclusion no reality would arise in eternity, and
from a mere sense perception no conception would arise in eternity,
if there were not something present, *from which* it was excluded, if
through an absolute action of the mind the negation were not related
to something positive and from non-affirmation, antithesis did not arise;
this activity of the mind is called judging or thinking, and the result
of the same, *thought*.

Before we determine a place in space, there is really no space for
us; but without absolute space we would never again determine a place.
Likewise with time. Before we have the moment, there is really no
time for us; but without eternal time we would never have a conception
of the moment. We thus arrive, to be sure, only through the part at
the whole, only through the limit at the unlimited; but we also arrive
only through the whole at the part, only through the unlimited at the
limit.

If therefore it is now asserted of the beautiful, that it paves the
way for man to a transition from feeling to thought, so is this by no
means so to be understood, as if by beauty the gap could be filled,
which divides feeling from thought, passivity from activity; this gap
is infinite, and without the intervention of a new and independent
capacity nothing universal in eternity can arise from the individual,
nothing necessary can arise from the contingent. Thought is the im-
mediate action of this absolute capacity, which must indeed be called
forth through the senses, to express itself, but in its expression itself
so little depends on sensuousness, that it manifests itself on the contary
only through opposition to the same. The independence, with which
it acts, excludes every foreign influence, and not insofar as she helps
in thinking (which contains an obvious contradiction), merely insofar
as she secures for the mental powers the freedom, to express themselves
according to their own laws, can beauty become a means, to lead man
from matter to form, from sensations to laws, from the limited to an
absolute existence.

But this presupposes, that the freedom of the mental powers could
be checked, which appears to conflict with the conception of an in-
dependent capacity. A capacity namely, which receives from outside
nothing but the material of its work, can be hindered only through
withdrawal of the material, thus only negatively in its work, and one
misconstrues the nature of spirit, if one attributes to the sensuous

passions a power, to be able to positively suppress the freedom of the mind. Indeed, experience provides examples in number, where the powers of reason appear suppressed in the same proportion, as the sensuous powers act more passionately, but instead of deriving this weakness of mind from the strength of the emotional state, one must on the contrary explain this predominant strength of the emotional state through this weakness of the mind; for the senses can not otherwise represent a power over man, than insofar as the mind hath freely neglected, to demonstrate itself as such.

But whilst I seek through this explanation to meet an objection, I have, as it seems, involved myself in another and have only saved the independence of the mind at the expense of its unity. For how can the mind take *from itself* at the same time the grounds of inactivity and activity, if it is not itself divided, if it is not opposed to itself?

Here we must now recall, that we have the finite, not the infinite mind before us. The finite mind is that, which becomes active not otherwise than through passivity, only achieves the absolute through limits, only, in so far as it receives matter, acts and forms. Such a mind will therefore combine with the instinct towards form or towards the absolute an instinct towards matter or towards limits, as which are the conditions, without which he could neither have nor satisfy the first instinct. In how far in the same being two so opposite tendencies could subsist together, is a task, which can indeed place the metaphysician, but not the transcendental philosopher in embarrassment. The latter by no means claims, to explain the possibility of things, but rather satisfies himself, to establish the knowledge, from which the possibility of experience is apprehended. And since experience were just as little possible without that opposition in the mind as without the absolute unity of the same, so he sets up both conceptions with perfect right as equally necessary conditions of experience, without troubling himself further about their reconcilability. This indwelling of two fundamental instincts moreover in no way contradicts the absolute unity of the mind, so soon as one merely distinguishes *the mind itself* from both instincts. Both instincts exist and act indeed *in it*, but it itself is neither matter nor form, neither sensuousness nor reason, which those seem not always to have considered, who only allow the human mind itself to act there, where its proceedings agree with reason, and where this contradicts reason, declare it merely passive.

Each of these two fundamental instincts strives, so soon as it hath achieved development, according to its nature and necessarily towards satisfaction, but just for that reason, because both strive necessarily and both yet towards opposite objectives, so this double necessity mutually cancels itself, and the will preserves complete freedom between both. It is therefore the will, which acts towards both instincts as a *power* (as ground of reality), but neither one can act for itself as a power towards the other. Through the most positive impulse to justice, whereof he by no means lacks, the violent man is not deterred from injustice, and through the most lively temptation to enjoyment the strong-minded man is not brought to a breech of his principles. There is no other power in man than his will, and only that which annuls the man, death and the theft of consciousness, can annul his inner freedom.

A necessity *outside us* determines our condition, our existence in time by means of sense perception. This is entirely involuntary and so, as it acts upon us, must we suffer. In the same manner, a necessity *in us* reveals our personality, at the instigation of that sense perception and through opposition to the same; for self-consciousness can not depend on the will, which presupposes it. This original announcement of the personality is not our merit, and the lack of the same not our defect. Only from him, who is conscious of himself, is reason, i.e. absolute consequence and universality of consciousness demanded; beforehand he is no man, and no act of humanity can be expected from him. So little as the *metaphysician* can explain the limits, which the free and independent mind suffers through the sensation, so little as the *physical scientist* comprehends the infinity, which is revealed at the instance of these limits in the personality. Neither abstraction nor experience guides us back to the source, from which our conceptions of universality and necessity flow; its early appearance in time shields it from the observer and its super-sensuous origin, from the metaphysical inquirer. But enough, that self-consciousness is there, and at once with the inalterable unity of the same the law of unity for all, that is *for* man, and for everything, that *through* him should become, is established for his cognition and action. Inescapable, incorruptible, incomprehensible the conception of truth and justice present themselves even in the age of sensuousness, and without one knowing to say, whence and how it arose, one observes the eternal in time and the necessary in the train of the contingent. So arise sensation and self-consciousness completely without assistance from the subject, and the origin of both lies just as much beyond our will, as it lies beyond the sphere of our knowledge.

Are both however real, and hath man, by means of sensation, the experience of a definite existence, hath he through self-consciousness had the experience of his absolute existence, so will both his fundamental instincts arise with their objects. The sensuous instinct awakens with the experience of life (with the commencement of the individual), the rational, with the experience of the law (with the commencement of the personality), and only now, after both are come into existence, is his humanity erected. Until this hath occurred, everything in him ensues according to the law of necessity; but now the hand of *nature* abandons him, and it is his concern, to assert the humanity, which she established and revealed in him. So soon, that is to say, as two opposite fundamental instincts are active in him, so both lose their compulsion and the antithesis of two necessities produces the origin of freedom.*

Twentieth Letter

That freedom could not be acted upon, ensues from its very conception; but that *freedom itself* be an effect of nature (this word taken in its widest sense), not a work of man, that it therefore also could be promoted and hampered by natural means, follows equally necessarily from the preceding. It takes its start first, when man is *complete* and *both* his fundamental instincts have developed; it must therefore be lacking, so long as he is incomplete and one of both instincts is excluded, and must by all that, that gives him back his completeness, be able to be restored.

Now a moment may indeed be exhibited, not only in the entire species but also in the individual man, in which man is not yet complete and one of both instincts is exclusively active in him. We know, that he commences with mere life, in order to end with form; that he is an individual earlier than a person, that he proceeds from limitations to infinity. The sensuous instinct comes into effect earlier than the rational, because sensation precedes consciousness, and in this *priority* of the sensuous instinct we find the key to the entire history of human freedom.

For there is now a moment, where the life instinct, because the formal instinct doth not yet counteract it, acts as nature and as necessity; where sensuousness is a power because man hath not yet begun; for in man himself there can be no other power than the will. But in the state of thinking, to which man should now pass over, reason should precisely on the contrary be a power, and a logical and moral necessity should replace the physical. The power of sensation must therefore be annihilated, ere the law can be elevated thereto. It is therefore not enough, that something begin, which did not yet exist; something

---

* In order to prevent all misinterpretation, I observe, that, so often as freedom is here discussed, that kind is not meant, which necessarily befits man, regarded as intelligence, and can neither be given to him nor taken from him, but rather that kind, which is grounded upon his mixed nature. Thereby, that on the whole man acts only rationally, he demonstrates a freedom of the former kind, thereby, that he acts rationally within the limits of matter and materially under the laws of reason, he demonstrates a freedom of the second kind. One could explain the latter simply by means of a natural possibility of the former.

must first cease, which was. Man can not immediately pass over from sensation to thought; he must *take a step backward*, because only, in that one determination is again annulled, can the contrary take place. He must therefore, in order to exchange passivity for self-activity, a passive determination for an active, *be free of all determination* momentarily and pass through a condition of mere determinability. Hence must he return in a certain manner to that negative condition of mere indeterminability, in which he found himself, ere anything made an impression upon his sense. That condition however was completely empty of content, and it is now a matter thereof, to unite an equal indeterminability and an equal unlimited determinability with the greatest possible contents, because something positive should follow immediately from this condition. The determination, which he receives through sensation, must therefore be held fast, because he may not lose the reality; at the same time however, insofar as it is limitation, it must be annulled, because an unlimited determinability should take place. The task is therefore, to annihilate and at the same time to preserve the determination of the condition, which is only possible in the single fashion, that one *opposes another* to it. The scales of the balance stand level, if they are empty; however they also stand level, if they contain equal weights.

The mind therefore passes over from sensation to thought by means of a middle state of mind, in which sensuousness and reason are *simultaneously* active, however, just for this reason, mutually annul their determining power and effect a negation through an opposition. This middle state of mind, in which the mind is compelled neither physically nor morally and yet is active in both manners, deserves pre-eminently to be called a free state of mind, and if one names the condition of sensuous determination the physical, but the condition of rational determination the logical and moral, so must one call this condition of real and active determinability the *aesthetical*.*

---

* For readers, to whom the pure meaning of this word—through ignorance so often misused—is not entirely familiar, may the following serve as an explanation. All things, which can come forth anywhere in the phenomenon, may be thought of under four different connections. One thing can be connected to our sensuous condition (our existence and well-being); that is its physical nature. Or it can be connected to the understanding and supply us knowledge; that is its *logical* nature. Or it can be connected to our will and be regarded as an object of choice for a rational being; that is its *moral* nature. Or finally, it can be connected to the entirety of our different powers, without being a specific object for a single one of the same; that is its *aesthetical* nature. A man can be agreeable to us through his readiness to serve; he can cause us to think through his conversation; he can instill respect through his character; finally however, independent of all these, and without our taking

Twenty-first Letter

There is, as I observed at the beginning of the preceding letter, a double condition of determinability and a double condition of determination. Now I can make this thesis clear.

The mind is determinable, merely insofar as it is not determined at all; it is however determinable, insofar as it is not exclusively determined, i.e., is not limited by its determination. The former is mere indeterminacy (it is without limits, because it is without reality); this is the aesthetical determinability (it hath no limits, because it unites all reality).

The mind is determined, only insofar as it is limited at all; it is however also determined, insofar as it limits itself out of its own absolute capacity. In the first case it finds itself, when it perceives, in the second, when it thinks. Therefore what the thinking is in regard to determination, that the aesthetical composition is in regard to determinability; the former is limitation from inner infinite power, the latter is a negation from inner infinite fullness. Just as sensation and thinking touch one another in the single point, that in both conditions the mind determines, that man is exclusively something—either individual or person—but otherwise are removed from one another into the infinite; precisely thus the aesthetical determinability agrees with the mere indeterminacy in one single point, that both of them exclude every determined existence, whilst they in all remaining points like nothing and something, are consequently infinitely different. If therefore the latter, indeterminacy from deficiency, were conceived as an *empty infinity*, so must the aesthetical freedom of determination, which is the real counterpart of the same, be regarded as a *fulfilled infinity*; a

---

into consideration either any law, or any purpose in our judgment of him, he can also please us in mere contemplation and through his mere mode of appearance. In this quality we judge him aesthetically. Thus there is an education for health, an education for insight, an education for morality, an education for taste and for beauty. This last hath for its purpose, to cultivate the whole of our sensuous and spiritual powers in the greatest possible harmony. Because one is in the meanwhile led astray by a false taste and through a false reasoning fortified still more in this error, takes the conception of arbitrariness gladly along into the conception of the aesthetic, so I here observe superfluously (although these letters about aesthetic education are concerned with almost nothing other, than to refute that error), that the mind in the aesthetical condition indeed acts free and in the highest degree free from all constraint, but in no way free from the law, and that this aesthetical freedom is only distinguished thereby from the logical necessity in thought, and from the moral necessity in willing, that the laws, according to which the mind operates, *are not conceived* and, because they find no resistance, do not appear as compulsion.

conception, which with that, which the foregoing inquiries teach, coincides most exactly.

In the aesthetical condition man is therefore *naught*, insofar as one pays attention to a single result, not to the whole capacity and takes into consideration the lack of any particular determination in him. Thus one must recognize as completely right those, who declare the beautiful and the state of mind, into which it transports our mind, in regard to *knowledge* and *inner conviction*, to be fully indifferent and unfruitful. They are completely right, for beauty gives absolutely no individual result either for the understanding or for the will, she realizes no individual, either intellectual or moral purpose, she finds no single truth, helps us fulfill no single duty, in a word, equally inept, to establish the character and to enlighten the head. Thus the personal worth of a man or his dignity, insofar as these can depend only upon himself, still remains fully undetermined by aesthetical culture, and nothing further is achieved, than that it is now made possible for him *on account of nature*, to make of himself, what he will—that to him the freedom, to be, what he should be, is completely restored.

But precisely thereby is something infinite achieved. For so soon as we recall, that precisely this freedom was taken from him by the one-sided compulsion of nature in sensing, and by the excluding legislation of reason in thinking, so must we regard the capacity, which is given back to him in the aesthetical state of mind, as the highest of all gifts, as the gift of humanity. Certainly he already possesses this humanity as disposition before any determinate condition, into which he can come, but in reality he loses it, with any determinate condition, into which he comes, and it must, if he should be able to pass over to an opposite, be given back to him anew every time by the aesthetical life.*

Thus it is not merely allowed poetically, but also philosophically correct, when one calls beauty our second creator. For although she merely makes humanity possible for us, and in the rest leaves it to our

---

* Indeed the celerity, with which certain characters pass over from sensations to thoughts and to resolutions, allows the aesthetical state of mind, which they most necessarily pass through in this time, to become scarcely or not at all observable. Such dispositions can not long endure the condition of indeterminacy and press impatiently for a result, which they do not find in the condition of aesthetical boundlessness. On the other hand, with others, who locate their enjoyment more in the feeling of the *whole capacity* than of a *single* action of the same, the aesthetical condition spreads itself *out* over a far *greater surface*. So much as the first are frightened before emptiness, so little can the latter endure limitation. I scarcely need to mention, that the first are born for detail and subordinate occupations, the latter, provided, that they unite reality at the same time with this capacity, for the whole and to great roles.

free will, to what extent we want to make it real, so hath she this with our original creator, nature, in common, which gives us likewise nothing further than the capacity for humanity, but leaves the use of the same to our own willful determination.

Twenty-second Letter

If therefore the aesthetical disposition of the mind in *one* regard must be considered as *naught*, so soon, that is, as one directs his attention to individual and determinate effects, so is it in another regard to be looked upon again as a condition of *the highest* reality, insofar as one thereby considers the absence of all limits and the sum of powers, which are jointly active in the same. One can therefore just as little consider those wrong, who declare the aesthetical condition to be the most fruitful in regard to knowledge and morality. They are perfectly right; for a disposition of the mind, which contains in itself the whole of humanity, must necessarily also every individual expression of the same, according to its capacity, include in itself; a disposition of mind, which removes all limits from the whole of human nature, must necessarily remove them also from every individual expression of the same. Just for that reason, because it takes no individual function of humanity exclusively under protection, so is it favorable to everyone without distinction, and it favors no single one pre-eminently, only because it is the ground of the possibility of all. All other exercises give to the mind some particular fate, but place upon it therefor also a particular limit; the aesthetical alone leads to the unlimited. Every other condition, in which we can come, sends us back to a previous, and requires for its solution a following; only the aesthetical is a whole in itself, since it unites in itself all conditions of its origin and of its continuance. Here alone do we feel ourselves as if swept out of time; and our humanity expresses itself with a purity and *integrity*, as if it had not yet experienced injury from the influence of external forces.

What flatters our senses in immediate sensation, that opens our soft and pliant disposition to every impression, but makes us also in the same degree less fit for exertion. What strains our thinking powers and invites to abstract conceptions, that strengthens our mind for every kind of resistance; but hardens it also in the same proportion and robs us just as much of receptiveness, as it helps us towards a greater self-activity. Just for this reason, the one also finally leads like the other necessarily to exhaustion, because matter cannot long do without the formative power, because the power cannot long do without the plastic matter. Have we on the contrary given ourselves up to the enjoyment of genuine beauty, so are we in such a moment master in the same degree of our passive and active powers, and we shall turn with equal ease to earnestness and to play, to rest and to movement, to compliance and to resistance, to abstract thinking and to intuition.

This lofty equanimity and freedom of mind, combined with strength and vigor, is the state of mind, in which a genuine work of art should set us free, and there is no more certain touchstone of true aesthetical goodness. Find we ourselves after an enjoyment of this kind pre-eminently disposed to some particular mode of feeling or mode of action, to another, on the other hand, awkward and annoyed, so this serves as an unerring proof, that we have experienced no *pure aesthetical* effect; be it now, that it be owing to the object or to our mode of feeling or (as almost always is the case) to both at once.

Since in reality no pure aesthetical effect is to be met (for man can never step outside the dependence of forces), so can the excellence of his art work merely consist in his greater approximation to that ideal of aesthetical purity, and with all freedom, to which one may enhance it, we shall always leave it in a particular state of mind and with a specific direction. The more universal the state of mind and the less limited the direction is, which is given to our disposition by a definite kind of art and by a definite product of the same, the nobler is that kind and the more excellent such a product. One can attempt this with works from different arts and with different works of the self-same art. We leave beautiful music with aroused feeling, a beautiful poem with enlivened conceptual power, a beautiful picture and building with awakened understanding; but whoever wanted to invite us immediately after a high musical enjoyment to abstract thinking, immediately after a high poetical enjoyment employ us in a ceremonious affair of common life, immediately after contemplation of beautiful paintings and sculptures inflame our conceptual powers and surprise our feelings, he would not choose his time well. The reason is, beause even the most spiritually rich music stands *through its material* in a still greater affinity to the senses, than true aesthetical freedom allows, because even the happiest poem shares still more of the arbitrary and accidental play of the imagination, *as its medium*, than the inner necessity of true beauty permits, because even the most excellent picture, and this perhaps most of all, borders on earnest science *through the definiteness of its conception*. However, these particular affinities are lost with every higher degree, which a work from among these three kinds of art achieves, and it is a necessary and natural consequence of their perfection, that, without displacing their objective borders, the different arts *in their effect upon the mind* always become more similar to one another. Music in its highest ennobling must become form and work upon us with the serene power of the antique; graphic art in its highest perfection must become music and move us through its immediate sensuous presence; poetry in its most perfect cultivation must, like musical art, seize us powerfully, but at the same time, like the plastic, surround us with serene clarity. Therein is revealed the perfect style in any art, that it knows to remove the specific limitations of the same, without however annulling its specific advantages, and through a wise utilization of its peculiarity, imparts to it a more universal character.

And not merely the limitations, which the specific character of the type of art brings along with it, but also those which adhere to the particular matter, which he works, the artist must overcome through the treatment. In a truly beautiful work of art the content should do nothing, but the form everything; for through the form alone is an effect produced upon the whole of man, through the content, on the contrary, only upon individual powers. The content, however exalted and comprehensive it be, always acts therefore, restrictively upon the spirit, and only from the form is true aesthetical freedom to be expected. Therein therefore consists the real artistic secret of the master, *that he destroys the material through the form*; and the more imposing, arrogant, seductive the material is in itself, the more arbitrarily the same thrusts itself forward with *its* operation, or the more inclined the observer is, to involve himself with the material, the more triumphant is the art, which forces the former back and asserts its dominion over the latter. The disposition of the viewer and hearer must remain completely free and unimpaired, it must go forth from the magic circle of the artist pure and perfect as from the hands of the Creator. The most frivolous subject must be so handled, that we remain disposed, to pass over directly from the same to the most severe earnestness. The most earnest material must be so handled, that we retain the capability, to exchange it immediately for the lightest play. Arts of the emotions, such as tragedy is, are no exception; for *firstly* they are not entirely free arts, since they stand under the servitude of a particular aim (the pathetic), and then no true connoisseur of the arts will indeed deny, that works, even from this class, are all the more perfect, the more they care for the freedom of the mind even in the highest storm of the emotions. There is a beautiful art of passion, but a beautiful passionate art is a contradiction, for the unfailing effect of the beautiful is freedom from passion. No less contradictory is the conception of a beautiful instructing (didactic) or improving (moral) art, for nothing disagrees more with the conception of beauty, than to give to the disposition a definite tendency.

Nonetheless it doth not always prove formlessness in the work, if it merely makes an effect through its content; it can just as often evidence a deficiency of form in the critic. Is this one either too tense or too slack, is he accustomed, either merely to absorb with the understanding or merely with the senses, so will he hold to the parts even with the happiest whole and only to the matter with the most beautiful form. Only responsive to the raw *element*, he must first destroy the aesthetical organization of a work, before he finds an enjoyment therein, and carefully disinter the particular, that the master with infinite art made disappear in the harmony of the whole. His interest therein is simply either moral or physical, only precisely, what it should be, aesthetical, is it not. Such readers enjoy a serious and pathetic poem like a sermon and a naive or painful, like an intoxicating drink; and were they tasteless enough, from a tragedy and epic, even if it were a Messiah, to demand *edification*, so shall they without fail be scandalized by a song after the fashion of Anacreon or Catullus.

Twenty-third Letter

I take up once again the thread of my inquiry, which I have only broken off for this reason, in order to make application of the theses laid down to the practising art and to the judgment of its works.

The transition from the passive condition of feeling to the active of thinking and willing occurs therefore not other than through a middle condition of aesthetical freedom, and although this condition in itself decides something neither for our insights nor convictions, hence leaves our intellectual and moral worth entirely problematical, so is it yet the necessary condition, under which alone we can attain an insight and a conviction. In one word: there is no other way, to make the sensuous man rational, than that one makes the same aesthetical first.

But, would you object to me, ought this mediation to be thoroughly indispensable? Ought not truth and duty to be able to find for themselves alone and through themselves entry to the sensuous man? Hereupon I must reply: they not only can, they absolutely ought to be indebted for their determining power merely to themselves, and nothing would be more contradictory to my previous assertions, than if they had the appearance, to defend the opposite opinion. It hath been expressly proven, that beauty gives no result either for the understanding or the will, that she mingles in no affair either of thinking or of resolution, that she imparts to both merely the capacity, but determines absolutely nothing in respect to the actual use of this capacity. With this, all foreign help falls away, and the pure logical form, the conception, must speak directly to the understanding, the pure moral form, the law, directly to the will.

But that she is really only capable of this—that there is really only one pure form for the sensuous man, this, I maintain, must be made possible first through the aesthetical disposition of the mind. Truth is nothing, which can be received from outside like the reality or the sensuous existence of things; it is something, that the power of thought produces self-actively and in its freedom, and it is just this self-activity, this freedom, which we miss in the sensuous man. The sensuous man is already (physically) determined and hath consequently no free determinability any longer: this lost determinability he must necessarily first recover, before he can exchange the passive determination for an active. He cannot however recover it otherwise, than either in that he loses the passive determination, which he had, or *in that he contains already in himself the active*, to which he should pass over. Lost he merely the passive determination, so would he lose at the same time with the same, also the possibility of an active one, because thought needs a body and the form can only be realized by way of matter. He will therefore already contain the latter in himself, he will be determined at the same time passively and actively, that is, he will have to become aesthetical.

Through the aesthetical disposition of mind is the self-activity of reason thus already revealed in the field of sensuousness, the power of sensation already broken within its own borders and the physical man so far ennobled, that the intellectual now merely needs to develop himself out of the same according to the laws of freedom. The step from the aesthetical condition to the logical and moral (from beauty to truth and to duty) is thence infinitely easier, than the step from the physical condition to the aesthetical (from the mere blind life to form) was. The former step man can accomplish through his mere freedom, since he needs merely to take, and not to give himself, merely to individualize, not to expand his nature; the aesthetically-inclined man will judge universally, and act universally, so soon as he will wish it. The step from raw matter to beauty, where an entirely new activity should be revealed in him, nature must facilitate for him, and his will can command nothing in respect to a state of mind, which itself first gives existence to the will. In order to lead the aesthetical man to insight and great convictions, one may give him nothing further than weighty reasons; in order to achieve even that from the sensuous man, one must first alter his nature. With the former it often needs nothing but the challenge of a sublime situation (which most directly operates upon the capacity of the will), in order to make him into a hero and into a sage; one must first transplant the latter under another sky.

It therefore appertains to the most important task of culture, to subject man even in his mere physical life to form and, so far as the realm of beauty can ever extend, to make him aesthetical, because only from the aesthetical, but not from the physical condition can the moral be developed. Should man in each individual case possess the capacity, to make his judgment and his will the judgment of the species, should he find from every limited existence the passage through to an infinite one, from every dependent condition to be able to take the upward swing to self-dependence and freedom, so must he take care therefor, that he be in no moment mere individual and merely serve the law of nature. Should he be able and ready, to elevate himself out of the narrow circle of natural ends to rational ends, so must he already within the former have practiced for the latter and have already realized his physical determination with a certain freedom of mind, i.e., according to laws of beauty.

And indeed he is capable of this, without thereby contradicting in the least his physical aim. The demands of nature upon him are directed at that, *which he works*, *at the contents* of his action, about the way, *in which* he works, about the form of the same, nothing is determined by natural ends. The demands of reason on the other hand are directed strictly to the form of his activity. So necessary as it is therefore for his moral determination, that he be purely moral, that he show an absolute self-activity, so indifferent is it for his physical determination, whether he is purely physical, whether he conducts himself absolutely passively. In regard to this latter it is therefore placed entirely at his discretion, whether he wants to act upon it merely as being of sense and as natural force (namely as a force, which only acts, according as it suffers), or whether at the same time as absolute force, as being of reason, and there may indeed be no question, which of both corresponds more to his dignity. On the contrary, so much as it degrades and dishonors him, to do from sensuous impulse that, which he ought to have determined from pure motives of duty, so much as it honors and ennobles him, to strive for legality, for harmony, for boundlessness even there, where the common man only satisfies his legitimate longing.* In one word: in the domain of truth and morality sensation may

---

* This intellectually-rich and aesthetically-free treatment of common reality is, where one encounters it, the characteristic of a *noble* soul. In general a disposition is to be called noble, which possesses the gift, to transform even the most limited business and the most trivial object through the mode of treatment into an infinite one. Noble is every form called, which impresses the stamp of self-dependence, upon that, which according to its nature merely serves (is merely a means). A noble spirit is not satisfied thereby, to be free himself, he must set free all else around him, even the lifeless. But beauty is the only possible expression of freedom in the phenomenon. The predominant expression of the *understanding* in a face, a work of art and the like, can therefore never turn out noble, just as it is then also never beautiful, because it lays stress on the dependence (which is not separate from appropriateness), instead of concealing it.

The moral philosopher indeed teaches us, that one could never do *more* than his duty, and he is perfectly right, if he merely means the relation, which actions have to the moral law. But in respect to actions, which merely relate to a purpose, to pass *beyond this purpose* into the supersensuous (which can here be called nothing other than to perform the physical aesthetically), is

have nothing to determine; but in the province of happiness form may exist and the play instinct may govern.

Therefore even here, upon the indifferent field of physical life, man must commence to be moral; yet in his passivity he must begin his self-activity, yet within his sensuous limits, his rational freedom. Already must he impose the law of his will upon his inclinations; he must, if you will permit me the expression, play the war against matter within its own boundaries, thereby he be spared, from fighting upon the holy soil of freedom against this frightful foe; he must learn to desire *more nobly*, thereby he need not, *to will sublimely*. This is accomplished through aesthetical culture, which subjects to the laws of beauty all that, in which neither laws of nature nor laws of reason bind human caprice, and in the form, which it gives to the outer life, already reveals the inner.

Twenty-fourth Letter

There are therefore three different moments or stages of development to be distinguished, which not only the individual man but also the entire species must necessarily and in a definite order pass through, if they should realize the entire circle of their determination. Through accidental causes, which lie either in the influence of external things or in the free choice of man, the individual periods can indeed

---

tantamount to passing *beyond duty*, in that the latter can only direct, that the *will* be holy, not that *nature* too have already been hallowed. There is therefore indeed no moral, but there is an aesthetical surpassing of duty, and such a conduct is called noble. However just for this reason, because an excess is always observed in the noble, in that that also possesses a free formal worth, which needed to have merely a material, or unites with the inner worth, which it should have, yet an outer, which may be lacking to it, so many have confused aesthetical excess with a moral and, seduced by the appearance of the noble, have introduced into morality itself an arbitrariness and contingency, whereby it would be entirely annulled.

From a noble conduct is a sublime to be distinguished. The first goes beyond moral obligation, but not so the last, although we esteem it far higher than the other. But we esteem it not for this reason, because it surpasses the rational conception of its object (the moral law), but rather because it surpasses the empirical conception of its subject (our knowledge of human goodness of will and strength of will), because it oversteps the nature of the subject, out of which it must on the contrary flow forth completely unconstrained, but rather because it steps beyond the nature of its object (the physical aim) into the spiritual realm. There, one might say, we are astounded at the victory, which the object wins over man; here we admire the swing, which man gives to the object.

be now lengthened, now shortened, but none can be entirely leapt over, and even the order, in which they follow one another, can be reversed either through nature or through the will. Man in his *physical* condition merely suffers the power of nature; he frees himself from this power in the *aesthetical* condition, and he rules over it in the *moral*.

What is man, before beauty lures from him his free enjoyment and peaceful form calms the savage life? Eternally uniform in his aims, eternally changing in his judgments, self-serving, without being himself, unrestrained, without being free, a slave, without serving any rule. In this epoch the world is to him mere destiny, not yet object; everything hath existence for him, only insofar as it provides existence to him, what neither gives to him nor takes from him, is not existent to him at all. Isolated and cut off, as he finds himself in the series of beings, every phenomenon stands there before him. Everything, that is, is through the moment's word of command, every alteration is to him an entirely fresh creation, because with the necessary *in him* the necessity *outside him* is lacking, which binds together the changing forms into a world-all and, whilst the individual flees, holds fast the law upon the field of action. In vain doth nature let her rich multiplicity pass before his senses; he sees in her glorious fullness nothing but his prey, in her power and greatness, nothing but his foe. Either he rushes into objects and wishes to pull them to himself, in desire; or the objects press destructively upon him, and he pushes them from himself, in abhorrence. In both cases his relation to the world of sense is immediate *touch*, and eternally anxious from its pressure, restlessly tormented from the imperious need, he finds rest nowhere but in enervation and limits nowhere but in exhausted desire.

> Indeed the mighty bosom and the Titans'
> Most pow'rful heart is his . . . . . .
> Assured heritage; and yet the god
> Did forge a brazen band around his brow,
> Advice, restraint, sagacity and patience
> He hid before his timid, gloomy look.
> In him each craving grows unto a rage,
> And limitless his rage doth rush around.
> —*Iphigenia in Tauris*

Unaware of his own human dignity, he is far removed, from honoring it in others, and conscious of his own savage greed, he fears it in every creature, which looks similar to him. Never doth he perceive others in himself, only himself in others, and society, instead of expanding him to the species, confines him only more narrowly in his individuality. In this dull limitation he wanders through the night-filled life, until a favorable nature rolls away the burden of material from his darkened senses, reflection separates *himself* from things and the objects finally show themselves in the reflection of consciousness.

This condition of raw nature, as it is here described, cannot indeed be shown in any definite people and age; it is mere idea, but an idea, with which experience agrees in individual features most exactly. Man, one can say, was never entirely in this animal condition, but he hath never entirely escaped it. Even in the roughest subjects one finds unmistakeable traces of rational freedom, just as in the most cultivated moments are not lacking, which recall that gloomy natural state. It is peculiar to man, to unite the highest and the lowest in his nature, and if his *dignity* is founded upon a strict distinction of one from the other, so his *happiness* is founded upon a skillful removal of this difference. Culture, which should bring his dignity into agreement with his happiness, will have to provide for the highest purity of both these principles in their most intimate mixture.

The first appearance of reason in man is therefore not yet the beginning of his humanity. The latter is first determined by his freedom, and reason commences at first thereby, to make his sensuous dependence limitless; a phenomenon, that seems to me not yet sufficiently developed for its importance and universality. Reason, we know, makes itself known in man through the demand for the absolute (the upon-itself founded and necessary), which, as it can be satisfied in no single condition of his physical life, compels him to leave the physical entirely and ascend from a limited reality to ideas. But, although the true sense of that demand is, to tear him away from the limitations of time and to lead him aloft from the sensuous world to an ideal world, so it can yet through a (in this epoch of prevailing sensuousness scarcely to be avoided) misinterpretation, be directed to physical life and, instead of making him independent, plunge man into the most fearful servitude.

And thus it stands also in reality. On the wings of conceptual power man leaves the narrow limits of the present, in which mere animality is enclosed, in order to strive forwards toward an unlimited future; but whilst the infinite rises before his reeling imagination, his heart hath not yet ceased, to live in the individual and to serve the moment. In the midst of his animality the instinct to the absolute surprises him—and as in this dull condition all his strivings are directed only at the material and temporal and are confined merely to his individuality, so he is merely induced by that demand, to extend his individuality, instead of abstracting from the same, into the endless, to strive for an inexhaustible matter instead of for form, for an everlasting alteration and for an absolute affirmation of his temporal existence instead of for the immutable. The same instinct, which, applied to his thinking and action, should lead him to truth and morality, now brings forth, relative to his passion and feeling, nothing but an unlimited desire, but an absolute want. The first fruits, which he harvests in the realm of spirits, are therefore *care* and *fear*; both of them the effects of reason, not of sensuousness, but of a reason, which mistakes its object and applies its imperative immediately upon matter. All unconditional systems of happiness are fruits of this tree, may they have the present day or the whole life or, what makes them no more venerable, the whole eternity for their object. An unlimited duration of existence and well-being, merely for the sake of existence and well-being, is merely an ideal of the desires, hence a demand, which can only be thrown up by an animality striving towards the absolute. Without therefore winning something for his humanity by a rational expression of this kind, he loses thereby merely the happy limitation of the animal, before which he now merely possesses the unenviable privilege, to lose possession of the present over striving towards the distant, yet without seeking in the whole limitless distance anything other than the present.

But even if reason doth not mistake its object and err in the question, so sensuousness will yet for a long time falsify the answer. So soon as man hath begun, to employ his understanding and to knit together the phenomena around him according to cause and effect, so reason presses, according to its conception, for an absolute knitting together and for an unconditioned cause. In order to be able to merely put forward such a demand, man must have already stepped beyond sensuousness; but it makes use of this demand, in order to fetch back the fugitive. Here were in fact the point, where he had to leave the world of sense entirely and swing up into the pure realm of ideas; for the understanding remains eternally within the conditioned and questions eternally, without coming to a last one. But as the man, who is here discusssed, is not yet capable of such an abstraction, what he doth not find in his sensuous *sphere of knowledge* and not yet seek above the same in pure reason, so will he seek beneath it in his *sphere of feeling*, and apparently find. Sensuousness indeed shows him nothing, which were its own cause and gave itself law; but it shows him something, which knows of no cause and respects no law. As he therefore can bring the questioning understanding to rest through no final and inner cause, so, he brings it silence at least through the conception of the *causeless* and remains within the blind compulsion of matter, since he is not yet capable of comprehending the sublime necessity of reason. Because sensuousness knows no other *aim* than its advantage and feels itself driven by no other *cause* than blind chance, so he makes the former the determiner of his actions and the latter the ruler of the world.

Even the holy in man, the moral law, cannot with its first appearance in sensuousness escape this falsification. As it speaks only forbiddingly and against the interest of his sensuous self-love, so must it appear to him as something foreign so long, as he hath not yet come, to consider that self-love as the foreign and the voice of reason as his true self. He therefore feels only the fetters, which the latter imposes on him, not the infinite liberation, which it procures for him. Without suspecting in himself the dignity of the lawgiver, he feels merely the constraint and the impotent resistance of the subject. Because the sensuous instinct *precedes* the moral in his experience, so he gives to the law of necessity a beginning in time, a *positive origin*, and through the most unhappy of all errors he turns the immutable and eternal in himself into an accident of the ephemeral. He persuades himself, to consider the conceptions of right and wrong as statutes, which are established by a will, not which are valid in themselves and in all eternity. As he passes beyond *nature* in explanation of particular natural phenomena and seeks outside the same, that which can be found only in its inner lawfulness, just as he steps beyond *reason* in explanation of the moral and forfeits his humanity, whilst he seeks a divinity upon this road. No wonder, if a religion, which was purchased with the casting away of his humanity, shows itself worthy of such an origin, if he holds laws, which have not been binding *from* eternity, also not to be unconditional and binding *to* all eternity. He hath to do thus not with a holy, merely with a powerful Being. The spirit of worship of God is therefore fear, which degrades him, not reverence, which elevates him in his own estimation.

Although these manifold aberrations of man from the ideal of his determination can not all take place in the self-same epoch, whilst the same hath to wander through several stages from thoughtlessness to error, from lack of will power to depravity of will, so yet all these belong to the consequences of his physical condition, because in all the instinct of life plays master over the formal instinct. Be it now, that reason may not yet have spoken in man at all and the physical still may rule over him with blind necessity; or that reason may have not yet purified itself enough from the senses and the moral still may serve the physical, so in both cases the sole principle authoritative in him is a material one, and man, at least in his ultimate tendency, a sensuous being; with the single difference, that he is in the first case a reasonless, in the second a rational animal. But he should be neither, he should be man; nature should not rule him exclusively and reason should not rule him conditionally. Both legislations should exist completely independent of one another and yet be completely at one.

Twenty-fifth Letter

So long as man, in his first physical condition, receives the world of sense merely passively into himself, merely perceives, he is also still fully one with the same, and just because he himself is mere world, so is there no world yet for him. Not until he sets it outside himself or *contemplates* it in his aesthetical condition, is his personality differentiated from it, and a world appears to him, because he hath ceased, to be constituted as one with the same.*

The contemplation (reflection) is the first liberal relation of man to the world-all, that surrounds him. If desire directly seizes its object, so contemplation moves its, into the distance, turns it thereby into its true and inalienable property, such that it secures it from passion. The necessity of nature, which governed him in the condition of mere sensation with undivided power, abandons him in reflection, in the senses an instantaneous peace ensues, time itself, the eternally changing, stands still, whilst dispersed beams of consciousness are gathered, and an after-image of the infinite, *the form*, is reflected upon the ephemeral ground. So soon as it becomes light in man, it is also no longer night outside him, so soon as it becomes still within him, the storm in the world-all also subsides, and the contending forces of nature find calm between remaining boundaries. Hence no wonder, if the ancient poems speak of the great occurrence in the inner man as of a revolution in the outer world and make sensuous the thought, which triumphs over the laws of time, in the image of Zeus, who terminates the reign of Saturn.

From a slave of nature, so long as he merely perceives her, man becomes her lawgiver, so soon as he thinks her. She who governed him formerly only as *might*, stands now as *object* before his judging view. What is object to him, hath no power over him, for in order to be object, it must experience that of his. So far as he gives form to

---

* I recall once more, that both these periods are indeed in idea to be necessarily separated from one another, but in experience are more or less mingled. One must also not think, as if there had been a time, where man found himself only in this physical state, and a time, where he had freed himself entirely from the same. So soon as man *sees an object*, so is he already no more in a merely physical condition, and so long as he will continue, to see an object, he will also not run from that physical state, because he can only see, insofar as he perceives. Those three moments, which I noted at the beginning of the twenty-fourth letter, are therefore indeed, regarded in full, three different epochs for the development of humanity as a whole and for the whole development of an individual man, but they may also be distinguished in every single perception of an object and are in a word the necessary conditions of every cognition, which we receive through the senses.

matter, and so long as he gives it, he is invulnerable to her effects; for nothing can injure a spirit, but what robs him of his freedom, and he proves that of his, in that he gives form to the formless. Only where the mass rules heavily and shapelessly and the dim outlines waver between uncertain boundaries, hath fear its residence; to every terror of nature man is superior, so soon as he knows to give it form and to transform it into his object. Just as he begins, to assert his self-dependence towards nature as phenomenon, so he asserts also his dignity towards nature as power, and with noble freedom he rises up against his gods. They throw off the ghostly masks, wherewith they had frightened his childhood, and surprise him with his own image, in that they become his conception. The godly monster of the Orient, that administers the world with the blind strength of the beast of prey, contracts in the Grecian phantasy into the friendly contour of humanity, the realm of the Titans falls, and the infinite force is restrained by the infinite form.

But whilst I merely sought an exit from the material world and a passage into the world of mind, the free run of my conceptual power hath already led me into the midst of the latter. The beauty, which we seek, lies already behind us, and we have sprung over her, in that we passed directly from the mere life to the pure form and to the pure object. Such a spring is not in human nature, and in order to keep even pace with the latter, we shall have to return to the world of sense.

Beauty is certainly the work of the free contemplation, and we tread with her into the world of ideas—but it must be observed, without thereby leaving the sensuous world, as occurs with cognition of truth. The latter is the pure product of abstraction from everything that is material and contingent, pure object, in which no barrier of the subject may remain behind, pure self-activity without admixture of a passion. Indeed there is a way back to sensuousness from the highest abstraction, for thought moves the inner sensation, and the conception of logical and moral unity passes over into a feeling of sensuous agreement. But when we take delight in cognition, so we distinguish very exactly our conception of our sensation and look upon this latter as something accidental, which could very well be omitted, without that on this account the cognition cease and truth were not truth. But it would be an entirely futile undertaking, to want to sever this relation to the capacity of sensation from the conception of *beauty*; hence it is not sufficient for us, to think of the one as the effect of the other, but rather we must look upon both conjointly and reciprocally as effect and as cause. In our pleasure in cognition we distinguish without effort the *passage* from activity to passivity and observe distinctly, that the first is over, when the last commences. In our liking of beauty, on the contrary, no such succession, between activity and passivity, may be distinguished, and here reflection dissolves so completely with feeling, that we believe we perceive the form immediately. Beauty is therefore indeed an *object* for us, because reflection is the condition, under which we have a sensation of it; but it is at the same time a *state of our subject*, because the feeling is the condition, under which we have a conception of her. It is therefore indeed form, because we contemplate her, but she is at the same time life, because we feel her. In one word: she is at the same time our state and our deed.

And just because she is at the same time both of these, so she serves us thus as a triumphant proof, that passivity in no way excludes activity, nor matter form, nor limitation infinity—that consequently man's moral freedom is in no way annulled by his necessary physical dependence. She proves this, and, I must add, she *alone* can prove it to us. For since in the enjoyment of truth or of logical unity feeling is not necessarily at one with thought, rather accidentally follows the same, so the same can merely prove to us, that a sensuous nature can follow a rational and conversely, not, that both subsist together, not, that they act upon one another reciprocally, not, that they are to be absolutely and necessarily united. Rather, on the contrary, from this exclusion of feeling, so long as there is thought, and of thought, so long as there is feeling, an *incompatibility* of both natures must be concluded, in consequence of which analysts do not really know to adduce any better proof of the practicability of pure reason in mankind than, that it is imperative. But since in the enjoyment of beauty or *aesthetical unity* a real union and interchange of matter with form and of passivity with activity takes place, so is proven thereby the *compatibility* of both natures, the practicability of the infinite in finiteness, hence the possibility of the most sublime humanity.

We may therefore be no longer at a loss, to find a passage from sensuous dependence to moral freedom, according as the case is given by beauty, that the latter can exist together perfectly with the first, and that man in order to show himself as mind, need not escape from matter. Is he however already free in association with sensuousness, as the fact of beauty teaches, and is freedom something absolute and supersensuous, as its conception necessarily implies, so the question can longer be, how he succeed thereto, to elevate himself from the limited to the absolute, to oppose sensuousness in his thinking and will, since this hath already occurred in beauty. It can, in one word, no longer be the question, how he passes from beauty to truth, which in its capacity already lies in the former, rather how he makes his way from a common reality to an aesthetical, from mere feelings of life to feelings of beauty.

Twenty-sixth Letter

Since the aesthetical disposition of mind, as I have developed in the foregoing letters, first gives rise to freedom, so is it easy to realize, that it cannot arise from the same and consequently can have no moral origin. A gift of nature must it be; the favor of chance alone can loosen the fetters of the physical state and lead the savage to beauty.

The germ of the latter will develop itself equally little, where a scanty nature robs man of every refreshment, and where a prodigal one frees him of every effort of his own—where blunt sensuousness feels no need, and where vehement desire finds no satiation. Not there, where man hides himself like a *troglodyte* in caves, is eternally individual and never finds humanity *outside himself*, also not there, where he moves *nomadically* in great multitudes, is eternally only number and never finds humanity in himself—there alone, where he speaks in his own hut quietly with himself and so soon he emerges, with the entire race, will her lovely bud unfold. There where a light ether opens the senses to every gentle touch and an energetic warmth animates the abundant matter—where the realm of blind mass is over- thrown even in the inamimate creation and the triumphing form en- nobles even the basest natures—there in the joyous relations and in the blessed zone, where only activity leads to enjoyment and only enjoyment to activity, where from life itself the holy order wells up and from the law of order life alone develops—where conceptual power eternally escapes from reality and yet never goes astray from the sim- plicity of nature—here alone will sense and mind, receiving and form- ing power develop in the happy equilibrium, which is the soul of beauty and the condition of humanity.

And what kind of phenomenon is it, through which the entrance to humanity of the savage is announced? So far as we also examine history, it is the same in all races, who have escaped the slavery of the animal state: the joy in *appearance*, the inclination for *adornment* and for *play*.

The highest stupidity and the highest understanding have therein a certain affinity with one another, that both seek only the *real* and are entirely insensible to mere appearance. Only through the im- mediate presence of an object in the senses is the former torn from its rest, and only through reduction of conceptions to the data of experience is the latter brought to rest; in one word, dumbness cannot be elevated above reality and the understanding not remain below. Insofar there- fore as the need of reality and adherence to the real are mere conse- quences of deficiency, the indifference to reality and the interest in appearance are a true enlargement of humanity and a decisive step towards culture. In the first place it is evidence of an external freedom, for so long as necessity commands and need impels, conceptual power is bound with strong fetters to the real; only when the need is satisfied, doth it develop its unbounded capacity. But it is evidence also of an inner freedom, because it lets us see a force, which independent of an external material sets itself in motion through itself, and possesses enough energy, to keep back from itself the pressing matter. The reality of things is their (the things') work; the appearance of things is the work of man, and a disposition, which feasts itself on appearance, delights itself no longer in that, which it receives, but rather in that, which it makes.

It is well understood, that only aesthetical appearance is being discussed here, which one distinguishes from reality and truth, not the logical, which one confounds with the same—which one consequently loves, because it is appearance, and not, because one holds it to be something better. Only the first is play, since the last is mere deception. To value appearance of the first kind, can never do harm to the truth, because one never runs the danger, of substituting it for the same, which is after all the only way, in which the truth can be injured; to despise it, is to despise all beautiful art in general, whose essence is appearance. However, it sometimes occurs to the understanding, to drive its zeal for reality to such an intolerance and over the entire art of beautiful appearance, because it is mere appearance, to utter a disparaging judgment; but this occurs to the understanding only then, when it recalls the above-mentioned affinity. Of the necessary limits of beautiful appearance I shall take occasion to speak in particular once again.

It is nature herself, which lifts man aloft from reality to appearance, whilst she endowed him with two senses, which lead him merely through appearance to cognition of the real. In the eye and the ear the pressing matter is already rolled away from the senses, and the object removes itself from us, which we directly touch in the animal senses. What we *see* through the eyes is different from that, which we *feel*; for the understanding springs forth beyond the light to the objects. The object of tact is a force, which we endure; the object of the eyes and the ears is a form, which we create. So long as man is still a savage, he enjoys merely with the senses of feeling, which the senses of appearance merely serve in this period. He elevates himself to seeing either not at all, or he is certainly not satisfied with the same. So soon as he begins, to enjoy with the eye, and seeing acquires a self-dependent value for him, so is he also already aesthetically free, and the play instinct hath unfolded.

Immediately, just as the play instinct is aroused, which finds pleasure in appearance, the imitative formative instinct will also follow, which treats appearance as something self-dependent. So soon as man is once come so far, to distinguish appearance from reality, form from body, so is he also able, to separate the one from the other; for he hath already done that, in that he distinguishes them. The capacity for imitative art is therefore generally given with the capacity for form; the urge to the same rests upon another predisposition, of which I need not treat here. How early or how late the aesthetical instinct of art should develop, will depend merely upon the degree of love, with which man is able, to dwell on mere appearance.

Since every real existence derives from nature, as a foreign power, but all appearance originally comes from man, as conceiving subject, so he merely makes use of his absolute proprietary right, when he takes the appearance back from the essence and deals with the same according to his own laws. With unbounded freedom he can, what nature divided, join together, so soon as he can merely think of it together, and divide, what nature knitted together, so soon as he can but separate it in his understanding. Nothing need be holy to him here but his own law, so soon as he merely observes the boundary, which separates *his* province from the existence of things or the province of nature.

This human right to rule he practices in the *art of appearance*, and the more strictly he here distinguishes the mine and thine from one another, the more carefully he divides the form from the being, and the more self-dependence he knows to give the same, the more he will not merely enlarge the realm of beauty, but rather preserve even the boundaries of truth; for he cannot purify appearance of reality, without at the same time setting reality free from appearance.

But he possesses this sovereign right absolutely only in the *world of appearance*, in the unsubstantial realm of conceptual power, and only, so long as he conscientiously abstains in theory, from affirming the existence thereof, and so long as he in practice renounces, imparting existence thereby. You see herefrom, that the poet in a like manner steps outside his boundaries, when he attributes existence to his ideal, and when he aims at a definite existence thereby. For he cannot otherwise realize both, than in that he either steps beyond his poetic right, encroaches through the ideal upon the province of experience and presumes to determine real existence through the mere possibility, or in that he gives up his poetic right, lets experience encroach upon the province of the ideal and confines possibility to the conditions of reality.

Only insofar as he is *upright* (expressly renounces all claim to reality), and only insofar as he is *self-dependent* (dispenses with all assistance), is the appearance aesthetical. So soon as it is false and simulates reality, and so soon as it is impure and in need of reality for its effect, it is nothing but a degraded instrument for material ends and can prove nothing for the freedom of the mind. Moreover, it is not at all necessary, that the object, in which we find the beautiful appearance, be without reality, if only our judgment thereover pays no regard to this reality; for insofar as it pays regard to this, it is not aesthetical. A living womanly beauty will please us no doubt just as well and yet a little better than an equally beautiful, merely painted one; but insofar as she pleases us better than the last, she pleases no longer as self-dependent appearance, she pleases no longer the pure aesthetical feeling, even the living may please this latter only as appearance, even the real only as idea; but certainly it requires a still far higher degree of beautiful culture, to perceive in the living itself only the pure appearance, than to do without life in the appearance.

In whichever individual men of entire people one finds the upright and self-dependent appearance, there one may infer intellect and taste and every thereto-related excellence—there will one see the ideal, that governs real life, honor triumph over possession, thought over pleasure, the dream of immortality over existence. There the public voice will be the only terrible one, and an olive wreath will be honored more highly than a purple robe. Only impotence and perversity have recourse to false and needy appearance, and individual men as well as entire peoples, who either "lend reality assistance by means of appearance or the (aesthetical) appearance by means of reality"—both are often combined—show at the same time their moral unworthiness and their aesthetical incapacity.

To the question, "how far may appearance exist in the moral world?" the answer is therefore so short and concise as this: insofar as it is aesthetical appearance, i.e., appearance, which neither wants to replace reality nor needs to be replaced by the same. The aesthetical appearance can never become dangerous to the truth of morals, and where one finds it otherwise, there it may be shown with difficulty, that the appearance was not aesthetical. Only a stranger in fashionable society, for example, will consider assurances of politeness, which is a universal form, as signs of personal affection and, when he is disappointed, complain about dissimulation. But also only a bungler in fashionable society will, in order to be polite, call falsehood to his aid and flatter, in order to be pleasing. The first still lacks the sense for self-dependent appearance, hence he can give meaning to the same only by means of truth; the second lacks reality, and he would fain compensate for it by means of appearance.

Nothing is more common, than to hear from certain trivial critics of the age the complaint, that all solidity be lost from the world and that being be neglected for appearance. Although I by no means feel called upon, to justify the age against this reproach, so it follows sufficiently even from the wide extent, which these stern moralizers give their accusation, that they reproach the age not merely for the false, but also for upright appearance; and even the exceptions, which they make by chance in favor of beauty, concern more the needy than the self-dependent appearance. They do not merely attack the deceptive cosmetic, which conceals the truth, which presumes to substitute itself for reality; they also become overzealous against the beneficent appearance, which fills up the emptiness and cloaks the misery, also against the ideal, which ennobles a vulgar reality. The falsity of manners rightly offends their strict sense of truth; but too bad, that they class even politeness also with this falsity. It displeases them, that external empty glitter so often obscures true merit; but it grieves them no less, that one also demands appearance from merit and doth not exempt the inner content from pleasing form. They miss the hearty, robust and solid of former times, but they would also like to see reestablished the awkward and coarse of early manners, the ponderous of ancient forms and the former Gothic superabundance. They show through judgments of this kind a respect for *matter in itself*, which is not worthy of humanity, which ought on the contrary to treasure matter only insofar, as it is able to receive form and to enlarge the realm of ideas. The taste of the century need not therefore listen much to such voices, if only it stands steadfast otherwise before a better court. Not that we place a value upon aesthetical appearance (we do this for a long time not sufficiently), but rather that we have not yet brought it to pure appearance, that we have not yet sufficiently separated existence from phenomenon and thereby secured the boundaries of both forever, it is this, for which a rigorous judge of beauty can reproach us. This reproach we shall deserve so long as we cannot enjoy the beautiful of living nature, without coveting it, can not admire the beautiful of imitative art, without asking for an end—so long as we still do not concede to conceptual power its own absolute legislation and show it its dignity, through the respect, which we show its works.

Twenty-seventh Letter

You need fear nothing for reality and truth, if the high conception, which I advanced in the previous letter of the aesthetical appearance, should become universal. It will not become universal, so long as man is still uneducated enough, to be able to make a misuse thereof; and became it universal, so this could only be effected through a culture, which at once made every misuse impossible. To strive after self-dependent appearance, demands greater capacity for abstraction, more freedom of the heart, more energy of the will, than man needs, in order to confine himself to reality, and must have this latter already behind himself, if he wishes to arrive at the former. How badly is he therefore advised, if he wished to enter upon the road to the ideal, in order to spare himself the road to reality! From appearance, as it is here understood, we should therefore not have much to fear for reality; but so much the more might there be to fear from reality for appearance. Chained to the material, man hath for a long time allowed this latter merely to serve his aims, ere he conceded to it its own personality in the art of the ideal. For the last, it requires a total revolution in his whole mode of feeling, without which he would not find himself even once *upon the road* to the ideal. Where we therefore discover traces of a disinterested free estimation of pure appearance, there can we infer such an upheaval of his nature and the real beginning of humanity in him. But traces of this kind are actually found already in the first raw attempts, which he makes towards *beautification* of his existence, makes even at the risk, that he should spoil it thereby according to its sensuous content. So as he but commences at all, to prefer form to matter and to risk reality for appearance (which he must however recognize therefor), so is his animal sphere opened, and he finds himself upon a course, which doth not end.

Not content with that alone, which satisfies nature and which need requires, he demands superfluity; in the beginning, indeed, merely a superfluity *of matter*, in order to conceal from desire its boundaries, in order to secure enjoyment beyond the present need; but soon a superfluity *in the matter*, an aesthetical supplement, in order to satisfy the formal instinct too, in order to expand the enjoyment beyond every need. Whilst he merely gathers provisions for a future use and enjoys the same in advance in the imagination, so he indeed steps beyond the present moment, but without stepping altogether beyond time; he enjoys *more*, but he doth not enjoy *differently*. But whilst he at the same time draws the form into his enjoyment and attends to the forms of the objects, which satisfy his desires, he hath not merely enhanced his enjoyment in extent and degree, but also ennobled it in kind.

No doubt nature hath also given even the reasonless more than the necessaries and strewn into the dark animal life a shimmer of freedom. When no hunger gnaws the lion and no beast of prey challenges to battle, so idle strength creates for itself an object; with courageous roaring he fills the resounding desert; in purposeless display his exuberant power enjoys itself. With joyous life the insect swarms in the sunbeam; also it is surely not the cry of desire, which we hear in the melodious song of the singing bird. Undeniably there is freedom in these movements, but not freedom from need in general, merely from a definite, from an external need. The animal *labors*, when a deficiency is the motive of its activity, and it *plays*, when the richness of its power is this motive, when the superfluous life stimulates itself to activity. Even in inanimate nature such a luxury of powers and a laxity of determination are shown, which in that material sense one could very well call play. The tree sprouts innumerable buds, which perish undeveloped, and spreads out far more roots, branches and leaves for nourishment, than are used for the preservation of its individual and its species. What it gives back from its lavish fullness, unused and unenjoyed, to the elements, the living may feast upon in joyous movement. Thus nature gives us even in her material realm a prelude of the unlimited, and even here removes *in part* the fetters, which she casts away entirely in the realm of form. From the constraint of need or *physical earnestness*, she passes through the constraint of the superfluous, or the *physical play*, to aesthetical play, and before she elevates herself to the high freedom of the beautiful above the fetters of every end, she already approaches this independence, at least from a distance, in the *free movement*, which is itself end and means.

Like the bodily organs, so conceptual power also hath in man its free movement and its material play, in which it, without any reference to form, merely enjoys its arbitrary power and lack of fetters. Insofar as nothing of form is yet mixed at all in these plays of phantasy and an unconstrained succession of images makes up the entire charm of the same, they belong, although they can belong to man alone, merely to his animal life, and merely prove his liberation from every external sensuous constraint, without allowing the inference as yet of a self-dependent forming power in him.*

From this play of *the free succession of ideas*, which is still wholly of a material kind, and accounts for itself by mere laws of nature, conceptual power finally makes the spring to aesthetical play in the attempt at *a free form*. One must call it a spring, because an entirely new force leaps into action here; for here, for the first time, the law-giving mind is mixed with the actions of a blind instinct, subjects the arbitrary process of the power of conception to its immutable eternal

---

* The majority of games, which are in vogue in common life, rest either entirely upon this feeling of a free succession of ideas, or at any rate, borrow their greatest charm from the same. But so little as it proves in itself a higher nature, and as willingly as the most flaccid souls are wont to yield to this free steam of images, yet this very independence of fantasy from external impressions is at least the negative condition of its creative capacity. Only in that it tears itself free from reality, doth the forming power elevate itself to the ideal, and before the imagination can act in its productive quality according to its own law, it must have already made itself free from foreign laws in its reproductive process. Of course there is still a very large step to make, from mere lawlessness to a self-dependent inner legislation, and an entirely new power, the capacity for ideas, must be blended here into the play—but this power can now be developed also with greater ease, since the senses do not counteract it and the indeterminate borders, at least negatively, on the infinite.

unity, imposes its self-dependence on the changeable and its infinity on the sensuous. But so long as raw nature is still too powerful, which knows no other law, than to hasten forth restlessly from alteration to alteration, she will strive against that necessity by her unsteady caprice, that steadiness by her unrest, that self-dependence by her need, that sublime simplicity by her insatiability. The aesthetical play instinct will therefore still be scarcely recognizable in its first attempts, since the sensuous intervenes incessantly with its capricious temper and its savage desires. Hence we see the raw taste first seize the new and surprising, the many-colored, adventurous and bizarre, the vehement and savage, and fly before nothing so much as before simplicity and calm. He fashions grotesque forms, loves rash transitions, exuberant forms, dazzling contrasts, glaring lights, a pathetic song. In this epoch beautiful is to him merely, what excites him, what gives him material— but excites to self-acting resistance, but gives material *for a possible forming*, for otherwise it would not be the beautiful even for him. With the form of his judgment, therefore, a remarkable alteration hath taken place; he seeks these objects not, because they give him something to endure, but rather because they give him something to treat; they please him not, because they meet a need, but rather because they satisfy a law, which, although still softly, speaks in his breast.

Soon he is no longer content therewith, that things please him; he wishes to please himself, at first indeed only through that, which is *his*, finally through that, which is *he*. What he possesses, what he produces, may no longer bear upon it merely the traces of servitude, the anxious form of its purpose; besides the service, for which it is there, it must at the same time reflect the gifted understanding, which thought it, the loving hand, which realized it, the serene and free mind, which selected and established it. Now the ancient German searches for more brilliant animal pelts, more magnificent antlers, more elegant drinking horns, and the Caledonian selects the nicest shells for his festivals. Even weapons may now no longer be mere objects of terror, but rather also of pleasure, and the artistic baldrick will not be less observed than the deadly edge of the sword. Not content, to bring an aesthetical superfluity into the necessary, the freer play instinct finally tears itself entirely free of the fetters of necessity, and the beautiful becomes for itself alone an object of its striving. He *adorns* himself. Free delight is numbered among his needs, and the unnecessary is soon the best part of his joys.

Just as the form gradually approaches him from outside, in his dwelling, his household utensils, his clothing, so it finally begins, to take possession of him himself and in the beginning to transform merely the outer, finally, also the inner man. The lawless spring of joy turns to dance, the formless gesture to a graceful, harmonious miming, the confused tones of sensation unfold themselves, begin, to obey measure and bend themselves to song. When the Trojan army with piercing cries storms like a flock of cranes across the battle field, so the Greek approaches the same calmly and with noble strides. There we see merely the arrogance of blind force, here the victory of form and the simple majesty of the law.

A more beautiful necessity now links the sexes together, and the sympathy of the heart helps to preserve the union, that desire only pievishly and changeably knits. Released from its gloomy fetters, the calmer eye apprehends the form, the soul looks into the soul, and out of a self-seeking exchange of pleasure grows a generous interchange of affection. Desire extends and elevates itself to love, just as humanity unfolds in its object, and the base advantage over sense is distained, in order to gain by fighting a nobler victory over the will. The need to please subjects the mighty to the delicate tribunal of taste; he can steal pleasure, but love must be a gift. For this higher prize he can only contend through form, not through matter. He must cease, to touch upon feeling as force, and to confront the understanding as a phenomenon. He must allow freedom, because he wishes to please freedom. Just as beauty resolves the conflict of natures in its simplest and purest example, in the eternal opposition of the sexes, so she resolves it—or at least aims thither, to resolve it also in the complicated totality of society and after the model of a free union, which she knits there between manly force and womanly mildness, to reconcile everything gentle and violent in the moral world. Now weakness becomes holy, and untamed strength dishonors; the injustice of nature is corrected through the generosity of chivalrous practices. He whom no force may frighten, the gracious blush of shame disarms, and tears stifle a revenge, which no blood could quench. Even hatred pays heed to the tender voice of honor, the sword of the conqueror spares the disarmed enemy, and a hospitable hearth smokes for the stranger on the dreaded coast, where only murder formerly received him.

In the midst of the terrible realm of force and in the midst of the holy realm of law, the aesthetical forming instinct builds unobserved, a third, joyous realm of play and of appearance, wherein it takes away from man the fetters of all circumstances and sets him free from everything, which is called constraint, not only in the physical but also in the moral.

If in the *dynamic* state of rights man encounters man as force and restricts his actions—if he opposes him in the *ethical* state of duty with the majesty of law and fetters his will, so he may appear to him in the sphere of beautiful society, in the *aesthetical* state, only as form, confront him only as object of free play. *To give freedom through freedom* is the fundamental law of this realm.

The dynamic state can merely make society possible, in that it tames nature through nature; the ethical state can merely make it (morally) necessary, in that it subjects the individual will to the universal; the aesthetical state alone can make it real, because it fulfills the will of the whole through the nature of the individual. If need compels man into society and reason implants social principles in him, so can beauty alone impart to him a *social character*. Taste alone brings harmony into society, because it establishes harmony in the individual. All other forms of conception divide man, because they are exclusively based either upon the sensuous or the intellectual part of his being; only the beautiful conceptioin makes a whole of him, because both his natures must accord thereto. All other forms of communication divide society, because they relate exclusively either to the private receptiveness or to the private skill of individual members, therefore to the distinctive, between man and man; only beautiful communication unites society, because it relates to what is held in common by all. We enjoy the joys of the senses merely as individuals, without the species, which dwells in us, taking part therein; therefore we cannot extend our sensuous joys into universal, because we cannot make our individuality universal. The joys of cognition we enjoy merely as species, and in that we carefully remove every trace of individuality from our judgment; we cannot therefore make our rational joys universal, because we cannot exclude the traces of individuality from the judgment of others as from that of our own. We enjoy alone the beautiful as individual and at the same time as species, i.e., as *representatives* of the species. Sensuous good can make only *one* happy, since it is based upon appropriation, which always implies an exclusion; it can also make this *one* only one-sidedly happy, because the personality doth not participate therein. The absolute good can only secure happiness under conditions, which are not to be universally assumed; for truth is the only reward of renunciation and only a pure heart believes in pure will. Beauty alone makes all the world happy, and every being forgets its limitations, so long as it experiences her magic.

No superiority, no absolute power is tolerated, as far as taste rules and the realm of beautiful appearance is spread. This realm stretches upwards, to where reason governs with unconditioned necessity and all matter ceases; it stretches downwards, to where the natural instinct rules with blind coercion and form doth not yet begin; indeed, even upon these outermost boundaries, where the lawgiving power is taken from it, taste still doth not allow its executing power to be torn away. Unsocial desire must renounce its selfishness and the pleasurable, which otherwise only entices the senses, cast the net of grace also over minds. The stern voice of necessity, duty, must change its reproaching formula, which only resistance justifies, and honor willing nature through a nobler confidence. Out of the mysteries of science taste leads knowledge under the open sky of common sense and transforms the property of the schools into a common good of the entire human society. In its province even the most powerful genius must give up its highness and descend familiarly to the comprehension of a child. Force must let itself be bound by the Graces, and the defiant lion obey the rein of love. Therefor it spreads out its softening veil over physical need, which in its naked form offends the dignity of free spirits, and conceals from us the dishonoring relationship with matter in a lovely delusion of freedom. Bewinged by it, even fawning mercenary art swings up from the dust, and the fetters of bondage fall, touched by its wand, from the lifeless as from the living. In the aesthetical state everything—even the subservient tool is a free citizen, who hath equal rights with the noblest, and the understanding, which bends the suffering mass violently to its ends, must here ask it for its assent. Here, therefore, in the realm of aesthetical appearance, the ideal of equality is fulfilled, which the schwaermer so gladly would see realized in reality also; and if it is true, that the beautiful tone matures earliest and most completely near the throne, so must one also recognize here the good dispensation, which often only seems to restrict man in reality, in order to impel him into an ideal world.

But doth such a state of beautiful appearance even exist, and where is it to be found? As a need, it exists in every finely-tuned soul, as a reality, one might indeed only find it, like the pure church and the pure republic, in a few select circles, where not the mindless imitation of foreign manners, but rather one's own beautiful nature guides conduct, where man passes through the most complicated circumstances with bold simplicity and calm innocence and needs neither, to impair others freedom, in order to maintain his own, nor to cast away his dignity, in order to display grace.

POEMS

POEMS
TABLE OF CONTENTS

ALL POEMS TRANSLATED BY WILLIAM F. WERTZ, JR. UNLESS
OTHERWISE SPECIFIED

THE GREATNESS OF THE WORLD

Through the hovering world which the creating Might,
Out of chaos once form'd flew I in windy flight,
    To the seaside
    Of its billows do I glide,
Anchor cast, where no breeze blows more
At creation's far bound'ry shore.

Stars observ'd I as they youthfully did arise,
Spinning thousands of years round through the starry skies,
    Saw them playing
    After goals so enchanting;
Wand'ring search'd all around my gaze,
Saw the spaces — devoid of blaze.

To the region of naught fir'd into further flight,
Steer I valiantly forth, take I the flight of light,
    Mistlike dreary
    Heaven passing beside me,
Worldwide systems, floods in the beck
After the solar wanderer trek.

See, a Pilgrim doth walk down the lonely way
Rashly towards me — "Hold on! Palmer, what seekst thou pray?"
    "To the coastline
    Of its world my own path line!
Sail I hence, where no breeze blows more
At creation's far bound'ry shore." —

"Stay! thou sailest for naught — 'fore thee Infinity!"
"Stay! thou sailest for naught — Pilgrim, behind me too! —
    Sink down nether,
    Eagle-idea, thy wing's feather!
Daring sailoress, Fantasy,
Cast an anchor dejectedly!"

THE BAD MONARCHS

To your praise my lyre is now climbing —
Earthly gods — it was but mildly chiming
    On sweet Anadyomenes' day;
Softly round the pompous sounding loudness,
Shyly round the purple flaming of your greatness
    Trembles now my lay.

Answer! should I golden strings be playing,
When, transported high by jubilating,
      O'er the battlefield your chariots range?
When ye, tir'd of iron hard embraces,
Heavy armor for the tender rose embraces
      Of your Phryne change?

Should perhaps i' th' golden circle's gleaming
Gods, the daring hymn you now be seizing,
      Where, in mystic darkness overcome,
With the thunderbolt your spleen is playing,
And with *crime* a *human nature* is arraying,
      Till — the grave be dumb?

I'm 'neath diadems to *peace* now singing?
Should I, Princes, glorify your *dreaming*?
      When the worm the Monarch's heart doth tear,
Golden slumber round the Moor doth flutter,
Who upon the palace gates doth guard the treasure,
      And — it covets ne'er.

Show, o Muse, just how with galley labor
Kings upon a *single* pillow slumber,
      Lightning bolts act friendly when *suppress'd*,
Where their tempers are now never tort'ring,
Ne'er the Minotaurs o' th' theater are blust'ring
      And — the lions rest.

Upwards! With thy magic seal deliver,
Hecate, the bars o' th' burial chamber!
      Hark! the doors do thunder quickly clear!
Where the mouldy breath of death doth murmur,
Dreadful air doth rigid tresses upward pucker,
      Sing I — *Princes' cheer.* — —

Here the seashore? — Here within this harbor
Do your wishes' haughty navies founder?
      Here — wherein your grandeur's tide abates?
Never once with glory to grow warmer,
Forgeth here the night with blacken'd arms of terror
      Hardy potentates.

On the chest of death doth sadly glisten
Your own crown, the pearl encircl'd burden,
      Your own scepter's splendor thank'd no more.
How so beautif'lly the mould is gilded!
Yet but worms are with the body compensated,
      Which — the world watch'd o'er.

Haughty plants in such a lowly bedding!
See yet! — how with majesty that's fading
      Death unblushing doth obscenely taunt!
Who through north and east and west did proffer —
The disgusting smut of fiends they're made to suffer,
      And — no Sultans daunt?

Spring up yet, ye obstinate dumbfounded,
Shake away the sleep that's thousand-pounded,
      Vict'ry drums are beating from the fight!
Hearken yet, how clear the trumps are blaring!
How you're worshipp'd by the people's boist'rous *cheering*!
      Kings, regain your sight!

Seven sleepers! — o thus hear the shining
Clarions ringing and the large dogs baying!
      Fire from out a thousand barrels roars;
Cheerful steeds are for the forest neighing,
Bloody is the boar upon his bristles rolling,
      And — the triumph's yours!

What is that? Are even princes silent?
Ninefold through the howling arched basement
      Doth a mocking echo at me boom —
Hear yet but the chamber squire half-sleeping:
"The Madonna you with secret keys is gracing
      To — her sleeping room."

Not an answer — Earnest is the quiet —
E'en on Monarchs then doth fall the blanket,
      Which the eyes of flatt'rers doth encase? —
And ye ask for worship in the embers,
That the blinded harlot *fate* within your coffers
      May — a world emplace?

And ye clatter, God's gigantic puppets,
Lofty thence in proudly childish grouplets,
      Like the juggler on the opera floor? —
Vulgar devils do applaud the jingling,
But his angels sad with weeping are now hissing
      The exalted boor.

To the area of gentler notions'
Dignity — o'ercame they limitations —
      'Round snake charmers do your brokers turn;
Learn yet, that, so yours may be unfurling,
Glances, which e'en Pharisaic masks are rending,
      From the heav'n discern.

Coin ye — Scorn their counterfeited tinkle! —
Your own image on the lying metal,
            Filthy copper ye exalt to gold —
Your own Jews do with the coinage barter, —
Yet like others doth it ring beyond that border,
            Where the weight is told!

Cover your seraglio then and tower,
When the heaven's terrifying printer
            Presses for the int'rest on great pounds?
Ye repay the bankruptcy o' th' stripling
With sworn statements, and with *virtue so amusing*,
            Which — the jester founds.

Hide forever the sublime dishonor
In *majestic right's* nocturnal vesture!
            Scamper from the ambush of the crown!
Tremble though before the ballad's parlance,
Boldly through the purple strikes the shaft of vengeance
            Princes' bosoms down.

THE WIRTEMBERGER

The name of Wirtemberg
Is drawn from Wirt am Berg —
A Wirtemberger *without wine*
Is this the Wirtemberger line?

TO JOY

Joy, thou beauteous godly lightning,
Daughter of Elysium,
Fire drunken we are ent'ring
Heavenly, thy holy home!
Thy enchantments bind together,
What did custom's sword divide,
Beggars are a prince's brother,
Where thy gentle wings abide.

Chorus.

Be embrac'd, ye millions yonder!
Take this kiss throughout the world!
Brothers — o'er the stars unfurl'd
Must reside a loving father.

Who the noble prize achieveth,
Good friend of a friend to be;
Who a lovely wife attaineth,
Join us in his jubilee!
Yes — he too who but *one* being
On this earth can call *his* own!
He who ne'er was able, weeping
Stealeth from this league alone!

Chorus.

He who in the great ring dwelleth,
Homage pays to sympathy!
To the stars above leads she,
Where on high the *Unknown* reigneth.

Joy is drunk by every being
From kind nature's flowing breasts,
Every evil, every good thing
For her rosy footprint quests.
Gave she *us* both *vines* and kisses,
In the face of death, a friend,
To the worm were given blisses
And the Cherubs God attend.

Chorus.

Fall before him, all ye millions?
Know'st thou the Creator, world?
Seek above the stars unfurl'd,
Yonder dwells he in the heavens.

Joy commands the hardy mainspring
Of the universe eterne.
Joy, oh joy the wheel is driving
Which the worlds' great clock doth turn.
Flowers from the buds she coaxes,
Suns from out the hyaline,
Spheres she rotates through expanses,
Which the seer can't divine.

Chorus.

As the suns are flying, happy
Through the heaven's glorious plane,
Travel, brothers, down your lane,
Joyful as in hero's vict'ry.

From the truth's own fiery mirror
On the searcher doth *she* smile.
Up the steep incline of honor
Guideth *she* the suff'rer's mile.
High upon faith's sunlit mountains
One can see *her* banner flies,
Through the breach of open'd coffins
She in angel's choir doth rise.

Chorus.

Suffer on courageous millions!
Suffer for a better world!
O'er the tent of stars unfurl'd
God rewards you from the heavens.

Gods can never be requited,
Beauteous 'tis, their like to be.
Grief and want shall be reported,
So to cheer with gaiety.
Hate and vengeance be forgotten,
Pardon'd be our mortal foe,
Not a teardrop shall him dampen,
No repentance bring him low.

Chorus.

Let our book of debts be cancell'd!
Reconcile the total world!
Brothers — o'er the stars unfurl'd
God doth judge, as we have settl'd.

Joy doth bubble from this rummer,
From the golden blood of grape
Cannibals imbibe good temper,
Weak of heart their courage take —
Brothers, fly up from thy places,
When the brimming cup doth pass,
Let the foam shoot up in spaces:
To the goodly Soul this glass!

Chorus.

Whom the crown of stars doth honor,
Whom the hymns of Seraphs bless,
To the goodly Soul this glass
O'er the tent of stars up yonder!

Courage firm in grievous trial,
Help, where innocence doth scream,
Oaths which sworn to are eternal,
Truth to friend and foe the same,
Manly pride 'fore kingly power —
Brothers, cost it life and blood, —
Honor to whom merits honor,
Ruin to the lying brood!

Chorus.

Closer draw the holy circle,
Swear it by this golden wine,
Faithful to the vow divine,
Swear it by the Judge celestial!

Rescue from the tyrant's fetters,
Mercy to the villain e'en,
Hope within the dying hours,
Pardon at the guillotine!
E'en the dead shall live in heaven!
Brothers, drink and all agree,
Every sin shall be forgiven,
Hell forever cease to be.

Chorus.

A serene departing hour!
Pleasant sleep beneath the pall!
Brothers — gentle words for all
Doth the Judge of mortals utter!

Note: A later version of Schiller's
first stanza reads as follows:

Joy, thou beauteous godly lightning,
Daughter of Elysium,
Fire drunken we are ent'ring,
Heavenly, thy holy home!
Thy enchantments bind together,
What did custom stern divide,
Every man becomes a brother,
Where thy gentle wings abide.

THE POWER OF SONG

A streaming rain from boulders cracking,
It comes with thund'ring vehemence,
A mountain-wreck attends its gushing,
And oaks beneath it tumble hence;
Amaz'd, with blissful awe inspiring,
The wand'rer hears it, turns and harks,
He hears the flood from boulders storming,
Yet knows not, whence its rush embarks:
Thus surges forth a wave of singing
From fountains ne'er before known springing.

In union with the dreadful beings,
That threads of life do calmly twist,
Who can unloose the singer's charmings,
Who his resounding tones resist?
Like heaven's messenger with piping
The heart bestirr'd his powers ply:
He steeps it in the realm of dying,
He lifts it towards the wondrous sky
And rocks it 'twixt the grave and playful
Upon the scale of feelings supple.

As if at once into the orbit
Of joyfulness, with giant stride,
With air mysterious born of spirit
A monstrous destiny doth glide —
Then bows down every mighty earthling
Before the stranger heaven born,
The hollow din of celebrating
Grows dumb, and each one's mask is torn,
And fore the truth all mighty winning
Each work of falsehood comes to nothing.

Thus freed from every idle burden,
Whene'er the call of song resounds,
To noble spirit man is driven
And enters unto holy grounds;
With gods on high fraternal is he,
To him comes nothing earthly nigh,
And every other might stands mutely,
And no misfortunes at him fly;
The wrinkles of each care grow smoother,
So long the charms of song have power.

And just as after hopeless yearning,
And pain from being long apart
A child with tears repentant burning
Embraces his dear mother's heart,
So to his early childhood shelter,
To purest joys of innocence,
From distant lands with foreign manner
The singing leads the exile thence,
Unto the faithful arms of nature
From chilling precepts to be warmer.

THE EVENING
(After a picture)

Sink thou, radiant god — the fields are thirsting
For restorative dew, the man is pining,
Fainter pull on thy chargers —
Sink thou thy chariot below.

See thou, who from the sea's crystalline billows
With sweet smiles to thee waves! Doth know thy heart her?
Rasher fly on thy chargers,
Tethys, the godlike one, waves.

Swift from chariot into her embraces
Springs the driver, the reins are seiz'd by Cupid,
Calmly halt now thy chargers,
Drink from the cooling deluge.

Unto heaven above with gentle paces
Comes the sweet smelling night; delightful love doth
Follow. Rest ye and love ye!
Phoebus, the loving one, rests.

THE DIVISION OF THE WORLD

"Take thence the world!" call'd Zeus from his high summit
To all mankind. "Take, that which yours should be.
As heritage eterne to you I grant it —
Divide it ye, yet brotherly!"

Then did all hands to preparations scurry,
Both young and old industrious became.
The farmer seiz'd the produce from the country,
The Junker through the woods stalk'd game.

The merchant in his stores had riches hoarded,
The abbot chose the noble vintage wine,
The king had all the roads and bridges boarded
And claim'd: "the tithe of all is mine."

Quite late, just as division was accomplish'd,
The poet near'd, he came from far away —
Ah! nothing more remain'd to be distinguish'd,
A lord o'er everything had sway!

"Ah! Woe is me! for why should I then solely
Forgotten be, I, thy most faithful son?"
Thus did he make his accusation loudly
And threw himself fore Jove's high throne.

"If thou to dwell in dreamland have decided,"
Replied the god, "then quarrel not with me.
Where wert thou then, when I the world divided?"
"I was," the poet said, "by thee."

"Mine eyes did hang on thy expression,
Upon thy heaven's harmony my ear —
Forgive the spirit, which, by thy reflection
Enrapt, did lose the earthly sphere."

"What can be done?" said Zeus, "for all is given;
The crops, the hunt, the marts are no more free.
Wouldst thou abide with me within my heaven —
Whene'er thou com'st, 'twill open be to thee."

ARCHIMEDES AND THE STUDENT

To Archimedes came a youth desirous of knowledge.
"Tutor me," spake he to him, "in the most godly of arts,
Which such glorious fruit to the land of our father hath yielded
And the walls of the town from the Sambuca preserv'd!"
"Godly nam'st thou the art? She is't," responded the wise one;
"But she was that, my dear son, ere she the state ever serv'd.
Wouldst thou but fruits from her, these too can the mortal
     engender;
Who the Goddess doth woo, seek not the woman in her."

HUMAN KNOWLEDGE

While thou readest in her, what thyself thou in her hast written,
While thou in groups for the eye dost her phenomena range,
Thine own cords hast extended upon her unending expanses,
Thinkst thou, thy spirit doth grasp knowingly Nature's extent.
The astronomer doth so describe the heaven with figures,
That i' th' eternal expanse lighter the view is discern'd,
Knits remote solar bodies, through Sirius-distances parted,
To another i' th' swan and in the horns of the bull.
But understands he therefore the mystic dances o' th' orbits,
While him the vault of the stars showeth its global design?

EPIGRAMS

TO PROSELYTIZERS

"But a little o' th' planet be granted me outside the planet,"
So the godlike man spake, "and I do move it with ease."
For a moment alone permit me, outside my very
Self to betake me, and swift will I become one of yours.

THE CHILD IN THE CRADLE

Fortunate suckling! To thee is an infinite space yet the cradle,
Grow to a man, and to thee small grows the infinite world.

THE IMMUTABLE

"Irresistibly hastens time hence." — It seeks the unchanging.
Be thou true, and thou lay'st fetters eternal on it.

DIGNITIES

How the column of light on the waves o' th' rivulet sparkle —
Brightly as from its own glow flameth the gold-tinted edge,
But doth the stream run off with the wave, through the radiant
    channel
Presseth another one then, swift as the first one to flee —
So doth dignity's shine give light to man who is mortal;
Not he himself, but the place, through which he wander'd, doth
    shine.

GERMANY AND ITS PRINCES

Great are the monarchs thou hast produc'd and art of them worthy,
The obedient alone maketh the governing great.
Yet attempt it, O Germany, and make it to thine own rulers
Harder, as kings to be great, easier but to be men!

THE TWO PATHWAYS TO VIRTUE

Two are the pathways, on which mankind to virtue strives upward;
Closeth the one unto thee, opens the other to thee.
Acting attains the fortunate her, the suff'rer enduring.
Blest is he, whom his fate loving on both hath convey'd!

THE SOWER

See, full of hope thou entrustest to th' earth the seed which is
    golden
And expectest in spring joyous the blossoming crop.
But in the furrows of time bethink'st thou thy actions to scatter,
Which, by thy wisdom sown, still for eternity bloom?

THE MERCHANT

Whither saileth the ship? It bears Sidonian seamen,
Who from the freezing cold North carry the amber, the tin.
Bear it graciously, Neptune, and rock it softly, ye breezes,
In a sheltering cove rush him a drinkable spring.
To you, ye Gods, doth belong the merchant. Goods to seek after,
Goes he, yet to his ship goodness is knitted thereto.

THE BEST STATE

"Whereon discern I the best of states?" Whereon thou the best of
Wives ken'st! thereon, my friend, that one of neither doth speak.

COLUMBUS

Steer, courageous sailor! Although the wag may deride thee,
And the skipper at th' helm lower his indolent hand —
Ever, ever to th' West! There *must* the coastline be present,
Lies it yet clearly and lies shimm'ring before thine own ken.
Trust in the pilot God and follow the silent ocean!
Were it still not, 'twould climb now from the torrents aloft.
Genius stands with Nature in everlasting union:
What doth promise the one, surely the other fulfils.

WISDOM AND PRUDENCE

Wouldst thou, friend, the sublimest degree of wisdom ascend to,
Dare to take every risk, for which thee prudence derides.
The short-sighted one sees but the bank, that from thee recedeth,
Not the one, where one day landeth thy spirited flight.

THE HIGHEST

Seek'st thou the highest, the greatest? The plant is't able to teach
thee:
What it unwillfully is, be thou that willf'lly — that's it!

IMMORTALITY

'Fore the grave dost fear thou? Thou wishest, to live on immortal?
Live i' th' whole! And when thou long art foreby, it endures.

THEOPHANIA

Come forth the happy to me, I forget then the gods of the heavens,
Yet do they stand ere me, when I the suffering see.

SCRUPLE

What 'fore virtuous ears thee aloud to say be permitted?
What a virtuous heart softly permits thee to do!

ZENITH AND NADIR

Where thou e'er wand'rest in space, so knit thy zenith and nadir
Thee to th' heaven thereto, thee to th' axis o' th' world.
How thou e'er actest in thee, so thy purpose affecteth the heaven,
Through the axis o' th' world moves the direction o' th' deed.

IDEAL FREEDOM

From this life to depart are two pathways before thee open'd:
To th' ideal doth lead one, and the other to death.
See, that thou in time while still free on the first one escapest,
Ere the fates using force thee on the other abduct.

POLITICAL LESSON

All, that thou doest, be right, yet thereby let rest the matter,
Friend, and content thyself yea, all, that is right, to effect.
'Tis enough to true zeal, that the existent *perfected*
Be; the false e'er desires that the perfected *exist*

THE BEST STATE CONSTITUTION

That can I only as such distinguish, which each doth enable,
Good to think, and yet ne'er, that he so thinketh, requires.

TO LAW GIVERS

Always assume in advance, that men in general for justice
Wish, i'th' particular though reckon I never thereon.

THE DIGNITY OF MAN

Naught more thereof, I beg you. To nourish give him, to shelter,
Have ye the naked bedeck'd, dignity comes on its own.

MAJESTAS POPULI

Majesty of the nature of man! Thee should I in numbers
Seek? With the few alone hast thou at all times remain'd.
Only a few ever count, the remaining ones all are but empty
Blanks, and their vacuous throng shrouds but the prizes within.

THE VENERABLE

Honor ye always the whole, I can prize individuals only,
In individuals alone have I the whole e'er beheld.

THE PRESENT GENERATION

Was it always as now? This age I'm not able to fathom:
Only what's old is young, ah! and what's youthful is old.

THE FALSE IMPULSE TO STUDY

O how many new foes of the truth! My spirit is bleeding,
See I the species of owls, that to the light is impell'd.

THE FOUNTAIN OF REJUVENATION

Trust me, it is no fable, the fountain of youth, it is running
Truly and always. Ye ask, where? In poetical art.

THE OBSERVER

Sternly as mine own conscience observ'st thou, where I've offended,
Therefore have I thee e'er as — mine own conscience belov'd.

THE CIRCLE OF NATURE

All, thou serene one, is circl'd within thy kingdom; so turneth
E'en the greybeard to th' child, childish and childlike once more.

THE EPIC HEXAMETER

Reeling bears it thee forth on restless pulsating billows,
After thee see'st thou, thou see'st fore thee but heaven and sea.

THE DISTICH

In hexameter climbs the fountain's affluent column,
In pentameter then falls it melodically down.

THE EIGHT-LINE STANZA

Stanza, th'art form'd by love, the tender languishing — threefold
Fleest thou chastely and turn'st threefold desiringly back.

HOMER'S HEAD AS A SEAL

Trusty ancient Homer! Thee confide I the delicate secret,
Of affectionate bliss knoweth the singer alone.

THE GENIUS WITH THE INVERTED TORCH

Lovely surely doth he appear with his torch now extinguish'd,
But, ye gentlemen, death is so aesthetical not.

THE MIGHT OF WOMAN

Mighty are ye, ye are through your presence's peaceful
    enchantment,
What the still doth not work, worketh the thundering ne'er.
Strength expect I from man, the commandment's dignity keep he,
But through her grace alone reigneth and reign womankind.
Many for certain have reign'd through the might of spirit and action,
But at that time have they thee, highest of crowns, done without.
Queen in truth is alone the woman's womanly beauty,
Where she appear, she doth reign, reigns merely for she appears.

THE VIRTUE OF WOMAN

Virtues requireth the man, he plungeth himself in life boldly,
Treadeth with fortune more strong into the hazardous strife.
Just one virtue sufficeth the woman: 'tis there, it appeareth
Loving to th' heart, to the eye loving it always appears!

WOMANLY VERDICT

Men pass judgment for reasons, the woman's verdict is her own
Love, where loveth she not, woman already hath judg'd.

THE FORUM OF WOMAN

Women, never pass judgment on man's individual actions,
Rather over the man utter the judging decree.

THE WOMANLY IDEAL
To Amanda

Everywhere yieldeth the wife to th' man; but in what is highest
To the most womanly wife yields e'er the manliest man.
What be highest to me? The peaceful clearness of triumph,
As from thy brow on me, gracious Amanda, it shines.
Swims e'en the clouds of great grief 'round the disk that brightly is
    glist'ning,
Fairer the picture but paints in the aroma of gold.
Fancies the man he's free! *Thou art* so; for ever essential
Know'st thou no other choice, nor a necessity more.
What thou e'er giv'st, thou always giv'st fully, but one art thou ever,
E'en thy tendermost sound is thine harmonious self.
Here is youth everlasting with never exhaustible fullness,
And with the flowers at once pluck'st thou the golden ripe fruit.

THE MOST BEAUTIFUL APPEARANCE

Sawest thou ne'er the beautiful in a moment of suff'ring,
       Never hast thou the beautiful seen.
Saw'st thou the joyful not e'er in a beautiful visage,
       Never hast thou the joyful then seen!

TO ASTRONOMERS

Prate to me not so much of suns and nebulous objects,
Nature is only great, while she doth give you to count?
Though your object may be the sublimest that space hath within it,
Yet, my friends, within space dwells the Sublime not at all.

INSIDE AND OUTSIDE

"God but seeth the heart." — Precisely, since God but the heart
    sees,
Mind you, that *we* as well something that's bearable see.

FRIEND AND FOE

Dear is the friend to me, yet too from the foe can I profit.
Shows me the friend, what I can, tells me the foe, what I should.

EXPECTATION AND FULFILLMENT

Into the ocean doth sail with a thousand masts the stripling,
Still, in a boat that's been sav'd drifteth the old man to port.

THE COMMON FATE

See, how we hate, how we quarrel, opinion and bias divide us,
Meanwhile however thy locks whiten just like those of mine.

HUMAN PERFORMANCE

At the entrance to th' road doth lie eternity open,
Yet with the narrowest curve halteth the wisest of men.

THE FATHER

Work, as much as thou wilt, thou standest alone there forever,
Till by Nature, the strong, th'art to the universe knit.

LOVE AND DESIRE

Truly said, locksmith! One *loves*, what one hath, one *desires*, what
    one hath not,
For but the bountiful mind loves, but the needy desires.

GOODNESS AND GREATNESS

But two virtues there are, o were they forever united,
Ever the good also great, ever the great also good!

THE OBELISK

On a pedestal lofty hath me the master erected.
Stand thou! spake he; and I stand for him strong and with joy.

THE TRIUMPHAL ARCH

Fear thou not, stated the master, the arch o' th' heaven; I set thee
Infinite just like it into infinity forth.

PETER'S CHURCH

Seek'st thou to find the measureless here? thou hast made an error.
Mine own greatness is it, greater to make thee thyself.

THE THREE AGES OF NATURE

Life receiv'd she from fable, the schools have render'd her soulless,
Life that's creative anew reason doth give back to her.

MUSICAL ART

Life is breath'd by the formative art, bards ask I for spirit,
Yet the soul doth give but Polyhymnia voice.

THE GIRDLE

In the girdle preserves Aphrodite her charms' hidden secret,
That which lends magic to her, is, what she bindeth, her shame.

XENIA

THE MORAL POET

Yes, the man is a miserable wight, I know — yet that wish'd I
Just to forget and then came, ah how I rue it, to thee!

THE ARTIFICE

Wish ye to please at once both the children o' th' world and the
    pious?
Paint ye delight, except — paint ye the devil thereto!

THE SUBLIME SUBJECT

'Tis thy Muse doth extol, how God on all mankind takes pity;
And yet can *that* be a poem, that He them pitiful found?

THE MOMENT

A momentous epoch hath the cent'ry engender'd,
Yet the moment so great findeth a people so small.

KANT AND HIS COMMENTATORS

How but a singular rich man so many beggars provides with
Work! When the sovereigns build, carters have something to do.

KNOWLEDGE

She is to one the high, the celestial goddess, to th' other
Just a capable cow, which him with butter provides.

CERTAIN MELODIES

This is music for thinking! So long one it hears, stays one frozen,
Four, five hours thereof makes its effect even more.

THE ASTRONOMICAL HEAVEN

So exalted, so great is, so vastly distant the heaven!
Yet did smallness of mind find e'en to yonder its way.

NATURALIST AND TRANSCENDENTAL PHILOSOPHERS

Enmity be betwixt you! yet comes the union too early,
If ye i' th' search do divide, will first the truth be disclos'd.

EXCEPTION

Wherefore blamest thou many not openly? While he a friend is.
Like my very own heart blame I in silence the friend.

RAYNARD THE FOX

Many centuries ere would a poet this have been singing?
How can that be? For the stuff yea is from olden and now.

THE HIGHEST AIM OF ART

Pity the beautiful gift of the glorious artist! O had he
Out o' th' marble block yet us a crucifix made!

THE TWO FEVERS

Scarce hath the chilly fever of Gallomania departed,
Breaks out in Greekomania one that's more fiery still.

GREEKISM

Greekism, what was't? Understanding, Measure, Clearness! Thus
    thought I:
Rather some patience, ye Lords, ere ye of Greekism speak!

WARNING

For an excellent cause are ye fighting — but with understanding,
Beg I, that it to scorn and to derision not lead.

THE HIGHEST HARMONY

Oedipus tears out both of his eyes, Jocasta herself hangs,
Both are guiltless; the play hath been harmoniously solv'd.

RESOLVED RIDDLE

It is finally out, why Hamlet thus doth attract us,
While he, mark ye it well, drives us in full to despair.

DANGEROUS CONSEQUENCES

Friends, consider ye well, the truth which is deeper, and bolder
Loudly to utter: at once falleth the world on your head.

URN AND SKELETON

Into the grave implanted the humanly Greeks the immortal,
And thou foolheaded age plac'st midst the living the dead.

UNNAMED TYRANTS

Even a soul that is knavish is able to hate a tyrant,
Only who tyranny hateth, is noble and great.

WHEN PROFITS MY POEM

Tell me, when profits my poem, o Muses? When it the noble
Wakes in the moment of time, when he himself doth forget.

VOTIVE TABLETS

THE DEDICATION

That which God hath me taught, that which through life hath me
   aided,
Hang I, thankful and meek, here in the sacred most place.

DIFFERENT VOCATION

Millions concern themselves therefor, that the species continue,
Yet through but only a few propagates mankind itself.
Thousands of seeds are bestrewn by the fall, yet yield scarce a single
Fruit, to the element then most of them do harken back.
Yet if unfoldeth even but *one* — that one doth alone strew
Forth an inspirited world full of creations eterne.

THE ENLIVENING

Only in life's high summit, the flower, kindles what's novel
In the organic domain, or in the sensible world.

TWO KINDS OF ACTION

Work the good, and humanity's godlike plant dost thou *nourish*,
Form the beauteous, thou strew'st *seeds* of the godlike abroad.

DIFFERENCE OF STATION

E'en in the ethical world there's nobility; common place natures
Reckon by that, which they *do*, beauteous by that, which they *are*.

WORTH AND THE WORTHY

Hast thou something, so give it here and I purchase, what's proper,
Art thou something, o then do we our spirits exchange.

THE MORAL FORCE

Canst thou not beauty feel, thee remains yet to will with thy reason,
And as a spirit to do, that which as man thou canst not.

THE MESSAGE

From the wickedest hand can truth still act with power,
By the beauteous alone formeth the vessel the soul.

TO THE MUSE

What I were without thee, I know't not; however I shudder,
See I, without thee what hundreds and thousands now are.

THE ERUDITE WORKER

Ne'er delights him the fruit o' the' tree, which he tiresomely raises,
Only his taste enjoys, what erudition doth plant.

THE FAVOR OF THE MUSES

With the Philistine dies e'en his fame. Thou, Muse of the Heavens,
Bear'st, those who love thee, whom thou lov'st, in Mnemosyne's
    womb.

DUTY FOR ALL

Ever strive for the whole, and canst thou thyself no whole then
Be, as subordinate limb join thee thyself to a whole.

THE AGREEMENT

Truth we both of us search for, thou outside in life, and I inside
In the heart, and this way findeth it each one indeed.
Is the eye in good health, so it outside doth meet the creator;
Is't the heart, then indeed mirrors it inside the world.

THE KEY

Wouldst thou thyself recognize, so behold, how the others are
    acting;
Wouldst thou the others know well, look thou within thine own
    heart.

THE SUBJECT

Weighty truly is art and hard, itself to look after,
Yet more difficult is this: from thyself to escape.

THE INQUIRERS

Everything mankind now seeks from the inside, from outside to
    fathom.
Truth, where escap'st thou thyself thence ere the raging pursuit?

THE ATTEMPTS

Thee to capture do they set out with nets and with pokers,
But with a spirit's tread stridest thou thence through their midst.

THE PHILOSOPHIES

Which from all the philosophies truly endureth? I know not,
But philosophy shall, hope I, forever exist.

MY BELIEF

Which religion do I acknowledge? None from the many,
Thou to me namest! — And why none? — On religious grounds.

MY ANTIPATHY

Heartfelt is vice repugnant to me, and 'tis twofold repugnant
To me, while there's so much chatter of virtue takes place.
"What, thou hatest then virtue?" I would, that we all did it
    practice,
And so spake, please it God, further no man more thereof.

THE IMPULSES

Always terror impels the slave with its staff made of iron,
Pleasure, leadest thou me always to roseate bonds.

TO MYSTICS

That's precisely the truest of secrets, which 'fore each one's vision
Lies, surrounds you eterne, yet hath by no one been seen.

LIGHT AND COLOR

Dwell, thou eternally one, there beside the One that's eternal,
Color, thou varying, come friendly to mankind below.

TRUTH

One is it only for all, and yet seeth it everyone diff'rent;
That it one still remains, maketh the different true.

BEAUTY

Beauty is ever but one, and yet multiply changeth the beauteous,
That it changeth, makes but beautiful even the one.

TASK

No one be like the other, though like be each to the highest!
How to achieve that? Each one be in his person complete.

CONDITION

Ever striv'st thou in vain, thee to make resemble the godly,
Hast thou the godly at first not thine own character made.

THINE OWN IDEAL

Everyone shares, what thou think'st, thine own is alone, what thou
    feelest,
Should he thy very own be, feel thou the God, whom thou think'st.

BEAUTIFUL INDIVIDUALITY

One indeed shouldst thou be, not *one* with the whole however,
Thou through the reason art one, one with the whole through the
    heart.
Voice of the whole is thy reason, thine own heart thou thyself art,
Good for thee, if fore'er reason abides in thy heart.

MULTIPLICITY

Many are good and sagacious, yet all for the one only reckon,
For by conception they're rul'd, ah! by the loving heart not.
Sadly conception doth reign, from thousandfold frolicking figures
Bringeth it empty and poor always but one to the fore.
But with life doth it rush and delight, where lovingly beauty
Reigns, the eternally one changeth she thousandfold new.

THE GODLY

Had she been never fading, the Beautiful, naught could be like her,
Naught, where the godly doth bloom, know I to th' godly the like.
An infinity knoweth, a highest createth the reason,
In the beautiful form lives it to th' heart, to the view.

PHANTASY

She can indeed create stuff, yet the wild can not ever form it;
From the harmonic alone all that's harmonic doth spring.

GENIUS

Understanding indeed can repeat, what here once existed,
That which nature hath built, builds it by choice after her.
In excess of nature builds reason, yet only i' th' vacuum —
Thou alone, Genius, dost nature in nature enlarge.

THE IMITATOR

Goodness from goodness, that can each sensible being conceive of,
But the genius doth goodness from evil call forth.
What's conceiv'd alone may'st thou gain, imitator, through
    practice —
Self-conceiv'd is the stuff only o' th' mind that conceives.

GENIUS

Whereby doth Genius make itself known? Whereby the Creator
Makes Himself known in the world, in the infinite whole.
Clear is the ether and yet of depth that can ne'er be fathom'd,
Open to th' eye, to the sense stays it yet secret eterne.

THE DIFFICULT UNION

Wherefore are good taste and genius so seldom united?
That one feareth strength, this one despiseth the rein.

CORRECTNESS

Free from censure to be, is the lowliest state and the highest,
For but the feeble leads or but the lofty thereto.

SAFETY

But the fiery steed, the spirited, falls on the racetrack,
With deliberate pace strideth the donkey therefrom.

THE LAW OF NATURE

So 'twas always, my friend, and so 'twill remain forever.
Weakness hath rules for itself, but hath the potent success.

CHOICE

Canst thou to all give no pleasure through thine own deed and thine
    artwork,
Give it well to the few; many 'tis bad to please.

LANGUAGE

Why can the living spirit not ever appear to the spirit!
Speaks the soul, and so speaks ah! then the *soul* never more.

TO THE POET

Let thy speech be to thee, what the body's to th' loving one; *he* but
'Tis, who the creatures parts and who the creatures unites.

THE MASTER

Every other master discerns one in that, which he utters,
What he wisely conceals, shows me the master of style.

THE DILETTANTE

While a verse thou achieveth in a poetical language,
Which for thee authors and thinks, dream'st thou a poet to be.

THE BABBLER OF ART

Good in the arts do ye ask for? Be ye o' th' good then full worthy,
That but continuous war 'gainst you yourself doth create?

GERMAN GENIUS

Struggle, Germans, for Roman-like strength, for Grecian-like
    beauty!
Both thou attaineth, yet ne'er prosper'd the gallic-like leap.

WORDS OF FAITH

I'll name you three content-laden words;
      From mouth to mouth they are chasing,
But not from outside of us do they emerge—
      'Tis words from the heart we are facing.
Mankind is of all his value bereft
If in these three words no faith is left.

Man was created free—*is* free
      E'en though he were born in shackles.
Do not be deceived by the rabble's bray
      Or idiots' abusive cackles.
Before the slave, from his chains uncaught,
Before man set free, O tremble not!

And virtue—this is no meaningless sound—
      Can be practiced each day if we trouble;
And much as we tend to go stumbling around,
      Toward paradise, too, can we struggle.
And what no logician's logic can see
The child-like mind sees obviously.

And one God there is, a Will divine,
      However man's own will may waver;
Supremely above all space and all time
      The living Idea moves forever.
And though all's e'er-changing in form and in scene,
Within that change rests a spirit serene.

Keep these three content-laden words;
      From mouth to mouth implant them.
And if from without they do not emerge,
      Then your innermost soul must grant them.
Mankind is never of value bereft
As long as his faith in these three words is left.

                  John Sigerson

LIGHT AND WARMTH

The better man treads in the world
With happiness confiding,
He thinks what in his soul has swelled,
He'll find outside abiding,
He swears with noble ardor warm,
To Truth, his ever faithful arm.

Yet everything's so small, so bleak!
When this he's first detected,
Then he in worldly throng doth seek
Alone to be protected.
His heart in colder, proud repose,
At last itself to love doth close.

Alas, it gives not always fire,
This truth in bright arrayment.
Be glad, if knowledge you acquire
Without the heart as payment.
So join, for your most fair success,
The dreamer's zeal with worldliness.
                              Marianna Wertz

BREADTH AND DEPTH

There glitter many in the world,
Who all things respond to so witting,
And where what's charming, and where pleasure-filled,
One ascertains answers quite fitting;
You'd think, had you heard them 'loud confide,
That they had actually conquered the bride.

Yet go they from the world quite still,
Their lives were wasted sadly;
Who any excellence gaineth will,
Who'd bring forth greatness so gladly,
Must concentrate so still and tight
In tiniest point the highest might.

The trunk doth rise into the air
With uppish branches in splendor,
The glitt'ring leaves breathe a scent so fair,
Yet they can the fruit not engender;
The seed alone i'th' space so wee
Conceals the pride o'th' forest, the tree.
                              Marianna Wertz

THE CRANES OF IBYCUS

Unto the songs and chariot fighting,
Which all the strains of Greece are joining,
On Corinth's isthmus festive gay,
Made Ibycus, gods' friend, his way.
The gift of song Apollo offer'd,
To him the sweeten'd voice of song;
Thus on a light staff forth he wander'd,
From Rhegium, with god along.

Now beckons high on mountain ridges
High Corinth to the wand'rer's glances,
And then doth he, with pious dread,
Into Poseidon's spruce grove tread.
Naught stirs about him, just a swarming
Of cranes which join him on his way,
Which towards the distant southern warming
Are flying forth in squadrons grey.

"Receive my greetings, squads befriended,
Which o'er the sea have me escorted!
I take you as a goodly sign,
Your lot, it doth resemble mine:
From distant lands we are arriving
And pray for a warm dwelling place.
Be the hospitable good willing,
Who wards the stranger from disgrace!"

And merrily he strides on further
And finds himself i'th' forest's center —
Abruptly, on the narrow way,
Two murderers upon him prey.
He must himself for battle ready,
Yet soon his wearied hand sinks low,
It had the lyre's strings drawn so gently,
Yet ne'er the power of the bow.

He calls on men, and on the godly,
No savior answers his entreaty,
However wide his voice he sends,
No living thing him here attends.
"So must I here foresaken perish,
On foreign soil, unwept-for be,
Through evil scoundrels' hands thus vanish,
Where no avenger do I see!"

And gravely struck he sinketh under,
The feathers of the cranes then thunder,
He hears, though he can see no more,
Their nearing voices dreadful roar.
"From you, ye cranes that are up yonder,
If not another voice doth rise,
Be rais'd indictments for my murder!"
He calls it out, and then he dies.

The naked body is discover'd,
And soon, though 'tis from wounds disfigur'd,
The host in Corinth doth discern
Those traits, which are his dear concern.
"And must I thee so rediscover
And I had hop'd with wreath of pine
To crown the temples of the singer,
Which from his glow of fame do shine!"

And all the guests hear it lamenting,
While at Poseidon's fest assembling,
The whole of Greece with pain doth toss,
Each heart doth suffer from his loss;
The people crowd to the Prytanis
Astorm, his rage they supplicate
To vengeance of the slain man's tresses,
With murd'rers' blood to expiate.

Yet where's the clue, that from the crowding,
Of people streaming forth and thronging,
Enchanted by the pomp of sport,
The blacken'd culprit doth report?
Is't robbers, who him slew unbravely?
Was't envy of a secret foe?
That Helios can answer only,
Who on each earthly thing doth glow.

Perhaps with bold steps doth he saunter
Just now across the Grecian center,
While vengeance trails him in pursuit,
He savors his transgression's fruit;
Upon their very temple's op'ning
He spites perhaps the gods, and blends
Thus boldly in each human swelling,
Which towards the theater ascends.

For crowded bench to bench they're sitting,
The stage's pillars are near breaking,
Assembl'd from afar and near,
The folk of Greece are waiting here;
Just like the ocean waves' dull roaring,
With humans teeming, swells the place
In arched curves forever wid'ning
Unto the heaven's bluish space.

Who names the names, who counts the people
Who gather'd here together cordial?
From Theseus' town, from Aulis' strand
From Phocis, from the Spartan's land,
And from the distant Asian region,
From every island did they hie
And from the stage they pay attention
To th' *chorus's* dread melody,

Which, stern and grave, i'th' custom aged,
With footsteps lingering and gauged
Comes forward from the hinterground,
The theater thus strolling round.
Thus strideth forth no earthly woman,
They are no mortal progeny!
The giant size of each one's person
Transcends by far what's humanly.

Their loins a mantle black is striking,
Within their fleshless hands they're swinging
The torch's gloomy reddish glow,
Within their cheeks no blood doth flow;
And where the locks do lovely flutter,
And friendly wave o'er human brow,
There sees one snakes and here the adder
Whose bellies swell with poison now.

And in the circle ghastly twisted
The melody o'th' hymn they sounded,
Which through the heart so rending drives,
The fetters round the villain ties.
Reflection robbing, heart deluding
The song of Erinnyes doth sound,
It sounds, the hearer's marrow eating,
And suffers not the lyre to sound.

"He's blest, who free from guilt and failing
The child's pure spirit is preserving!
We may not near him vengingly,
He wanders on life's pathway free.
Yet woeful, woeful him, who hidden
Hath done the deed of murder base!
Upon his very soles we fasten,
The black of night's most dreadful race.

And hopes he to escape by fleeing,
On wings we're there, our nets ensnaring
Around his flying feet we throw,
That he is to the ground brought low.
So tiring never, him we follow,
Repentance ne'er can us appease,
Him on and on unto the Shadow
And give him even there no ease."

So singing are they roundly dancing,
And silence like the hush of dying
Lies o'er the whole house heavily,
As if had near'd the deity.
And solemnly, i'th' custom aged,
The theater thus strolling round,
With footsteps lingering and gauged
They vanish in the hinterground.

And 'twixt deceit and truth still hovers
Each hesitating breast, and quivers
And homage pays to that dread might,
That judging watches hid from sight,
Inscrutably, and fathomlessly,
The darksome coil of fate entwines,
Proclaims what's in the heart so deeply,
Yet runs from where the sunlight shines.

Then hears one from the highest footing
A voice which suddenly is crying:
"See there! See there, Timotheus,
Behold the cranes of Ibycus!" —
And suddenly the sky is dark'ning,
And o'er the theater away,
One sees, within a blackish swarming,
A host of cranes pass on its way.

"Of Ibycus!" — That name beloved
Each breast with new grief hath affected,
As waves on waves in oceans rise,
From mouth to mouth it quickly flies:
"Of Ibycus, whom we are mourning,
Whom by a murd'rer's hand was slain!
What is't with him? What is his meaning?
And what is't with this flock of crane?"

And louder still the question's growing,
With lightning strikes it flies foreboding
Through every heart: "'Tis clear as light,
'Tis the Eumenides' great might!
The poet's vengeance is now granted,
The murderer hath self-confess'd!
Be him, who spoke the word, arrested,
And him, to whom it was address'd!"

But scarce the word had him departed,
Fain had he in his breast it guarded;
In vain! The mouth with horror white
Brings consciousness of guilt to light.
And 'fore the judge they're apprehended,
The scene becomes the justice hall,
And guilty have the villains pleaded,
Struck by the vengeance beam they fall.

HOPE

All people discuss it and dream on end
Of better days that are coming,
After a golden and prosperous end
They are seen chasing and running;
The world grows old and grows young in turn,
Yet doth man for betterment hope eterne.

'Tis hope delivers him into life,
Round the frolicsome boy doth it flutter,
The youth is lur'd by its magic rife,
It won't be interr'd with the elder;
Though he ends in the coffin his weary lope,
Yet upon that coffin he plants — his hope.

It is no empty, fawning deceit,
Begot in the brain of a jester,
Proclaim'd aloud in the heart is it:
We are born for that which is better!
And what the innermost voice conveys,
The hoping spirit ne'er that betrays.

THE TROOPER SONG

Cheer up, my brave comrades, to mount, to mount!
To th' field and to freedom let's hasten!
I'th' field, there the man is still of account,
There still the heart's weight is taken.
There's no one else from whom help is shown,
For himself he standeth there all alone.

From the world hath liberty disappear'd,
But lords and servants one traces,
Deceit and falsehood have domineer'd,
O'er the timid humanly races.
He who death i'th' face is able to see,
The soldier alone is a man who's free.

The cares of living, he casts aside,
Hath no more to fear, nor to sorrow,
Along to his fate he doth boldly ride,
Be't not today, then be it tomorrow.
And be't tomorrow, then let us today
Yet slurp up the close of the excellent day.

From the heav'n to him falls his lot of mirth,
It needs no toil to discover,
The slave, he doth seek in the bowels o'th' earth,
There thinks he his wealth to uncover.
He digs and shovels, his life doth slave,
And digs, until fin'lly he digs his grave.

The trooper and steed with rapid stride,
Are guests who all have affrighted,
The lamps are now flick'ring i'th' house o'th' bride,
To the feast he comes uninvited.
He woos not long, nor doth gold display,
By storm he seizes on love's full pay.

Why weepeth the wench and near death grieves she?
Let's hasten away, let's hasten!
On earth no permanent quarters hath he,
Can faithful love give no haven.
Impet'ous fate, doth him drive away,
His repose in no place behind doth stay.

Afresh, my brave comrades, now bridle your steed,
In battle the breast's elevated!
The youth doth thunder, and life doth seeth,
Fresh up! ere the mood's dissipated!
And if you dare not your life to stake,
That life you then never your own will make.

NAENIA

E'en the beaut'ous must perish! What men and the gods doth
   o'erpower,
Ne'er the bronze-plated breast moves of the Stygian Zeus.
Only once did love ever soften the Lord of the Shadows,
And at the threshold did he, sternly, his gift then recall.
Nor heals Aphrodite the wound o'th' beauteous stripling,
Which in his delicate side cruelly the boar did inflict.
Nor delivers the mother immortal the hero so godlike,
When he, at Scaean gate falling, his fate did fulfill.
But she ascends from the sea with all the Daughters of Nereus,
And the wailing begins over her glorified son.
See ye! There gods are lamenting, there goddesses all are
   lamenting,
That the beauteous fades, and that the perfect doth die.
E'en a woe-song to be i'th' mouth of the loved one, is glor'ous,
Since what is vulgar falls soundless to Orcus below.

WORDS OF DELUSION

Three words doth man hear, with meaning full
     In good and in best mouths extolling;
They sound off but idly, their ring is null,
     They can not give any consoling.
And mankind doth forfeit this life's own fruit,
As long as mere shadows are his pursuit.

As long he trusts in the Goldenest Age,
      Where the righteous, the good conquer evil —
The righteous, the good in battle e'er rage,
      N'er will he vanquish the Devil,
And thou strangle him not in the air that's blue,
E'er grows in him strength from the earth anew.

As long he trusts, that a coquettish chance
      Is with nobleness bound up in spirit —
The evil she trails with loving glance,
      Not the earth will the good men inherit.
He is a stranger, he goes to roam
And seeks an everlasting home.

As long he trusts, that mere logic can grasp
      The truth that is ever shining,
Then her veil lifts not any mere mortal clasp,
      We're left but supposing, divining.
Thou'd 'prison the soul in an empty sound,
But it wanders off in the storm unbound.

So, noble soul, from delusion tear thee,
      And to heavenly trust be most faithful!
What no ear doth hear, what the eyes do not see,
      It is this that's the beaut'ous, the truthful!
It is not outside, there fools do implore,
It is *in* you, you bring it forth evermore.
                Marianna Wertz

THE COMMENCEMENT OF THE NEW CENTURY

Noble friend! Where is to peace imparted,
Where to liberty a refuge place?
In a storm the century is departed,
And the new with murder shows its face.

And the bond uniting lands is lifting,
And the old traditions do decline,
Not the ocean hinders war from raging
Not the Nile-god nor the ancient Rhine.

Two prodigious nations now do wrestle
Over sole possession of the world,
Every country's liberty to cancel,
Are the bolt and trident by them whirl'd.

Gold must every region to them render,
And, like Brennus in the savage day,
Doth the Frank his heavy iron saber
On the balance scale of justice lay.

Spreads the Briton wide his merchant navy
Greedily like polyparms to roam,
And the kingdom of free Amphitrite
He embraces like his very home.

To the Southpole's unseen starry skyline
His unhinder'd restless course doth race,
Every island, every distant coastline
Finds he — but of Paradise no trace.

Ah in vain on maps of every kingdom
Dost thou for the blessed region scout,
Where the garden ever green of freedom,
Where the beauteous youth of man doth sprout.

Fore thy glances doth the world lie endless,
And the shipping can it scarce embrace,
Yet upon its back so vast and boundless
Is there for ten happy men no space.

To the heart's divinely peaceful dwelling
Must thou fly from life's oppressive throng:
Freedom is but in the realm of dreaming
And the beauteous blossoms but in song.

THE MAID OF ORLEANS

The noble image of mankind to sully,
Contempt doth roll thee in the deepest dust;
Wit wageth war eternally on Beauty,
In angel and in God he holds no trust;
To rob the heart her treasures he intendeth,
Illusion he besets and faith offendeth.

Yet, like thyself, from childlike generation,
A shepherdess like thou of piety,
To thee doth poetry extend her godly sanction,
To the eternal stars she swings with thee;
Within a halo she doth thee encircle—
The heart form'd thee! Thou wilt live on immortal.

The world doth love, the radiant to dirty
And the sublime to drag i'th' dust below;
Yet have no fear! There still are hearts of beauty,
Which for the high, the glorious do glow.
The noisy market Momus may make mirthful,
A nobler mind loves forms which are more noble.

Sheila Jones

THE FOUR AGES OF THE WORLD

The glass is a-shimmer with purple-red wine,
  The callers' eyes sparkle and glisten;
The Singer appears, to the good and the fine
  He brings forth the best—do you listen?
For missing the lyre in the heavenly place,
At the nectar-meal even, the merriment's base.

To him the gods gave a pure innocent mind,
  That mirrors the world, the unending,
He saw all that ever on earth was combined,
  Or hides in the future's portending.
He sat in the primeval gods' council-board,
And the secretmost seed of all things, overheard.

And lusty and shining this life many-fold,
  He joyfully spreads out before us,
Adorns as a temple the earthly household,
  His gift from the Muses' sweet chorus;
No roof is too lowly, no hut is too small,
A sky-full of deities comes at his call.

As Zeus's son, wielding his fanciful powers,
  On the face of the shield newly-brazen,
The earth and the sea and the circle of stars
  With cunning divine did emblazon,
So prints he the form of the ever-unbound
In the vanishing instant's fast-onrushing sound.

He comes from the first age of innocent men,
  The epoch of youth and of laughter;
The happiest wand'rer, he mingled again
  With all folk and all times ever after.
Four ages of man did he witness from nigh
And watches the fifth as it passes him by.

First Saturn was sovereign, strict and straight,
  Today was the same as tomorrow;
The shepherds who lived then, a race free of hate,
  Felt never a want nor a sorrow;
They loved and they toiled not a whit in the field,
The earth gave them all from her bountiful yield.

Thereafter came work, and the struggle began
  With dragons and monsters and giants,
And heros came forward, to rule over man,
  And the weak sought the mighty's alliance.
On fields of scamander the strife was long hurled,
Yet beauty was ever the god of the world.

Then triumph marched out of the battle and fire,
  From force blossomed mildness perfected,
The Muses there sang in celestial choir,
  And statues of gods were erected—
The age of divine and fantastical lore
Has vanished, it cannot return any more.

From heavenly thrones sank the gods of the morn,
  Down tumbled the glorious palace,
And lo, to a Virgin the Son was born,
  To heal the frail earth from its malice;
Delight of the senses was banned and suppressed,
And thoughtful, man groped in his inmost breast.

And the idle, voluptuous charm disappeared,
  Which the happy young world had begilted,
The monk and the nun took the lash and endured,
  The iron knight joisted and tilted.
But though life was ever so gloomy and wild,
Yet love remained evermore lovely and mild.

And the Muses an altar both holy and chaste
  Preserved for their silent thanksgiving;
And what had been noble and decent, embraced
  In woman's shy bosom, kept living;
The flame of sweet song kindled upward anew,
When the troubadors chanted of love-so-true.

Now women and singers must plait a sweet bankd,
　　They work it and weave it forever,
Encircling the fair and the just, hand in hand,
　　A tie that no mortal can sever.
For singing and love, wed in beauty and truth,
Keep life ever bright with the sparkle of youth.
　　　　　　　　　　　　Nora Hamerman

THE FAVOR OF THE MOMENT

And again in merry meeting
We assemble all around,
New and green, the singer's fleeting
Wreath of laurel shall be wound!

But to which Immortal bring we
First an offering of song?
First before all others, sing we
Him who send us Joy along!

What if Ceres merely nourish
Us with life-sustaining bread,
Or if Bacchus' vineyard flourish
And the wine run purple-red?

But if Heaven's spark appear, it
Strikes a flame of lightning-dart,
For the fire-drunken spirit,
And the overflowing heart.

From the gods, like summer showers,
Blessing falls from cloudless sky,
And the greatest of all powers
Is — the twinkling of any eye.

From the first of all endeavor,
When the universe was wrought,
The Divine on earth has ever
Been a lightning-flash of thought.

Stone by stone the work arises;
Slow the hours pass on earth.
Swift the work's *design* surprises;
Swift the spirit gave it birth.

As the sunlight's sparking glances
Weave a tapestry of hue
When immortal Iris dances
In a raincloud passing through,

So the Beautiful must vanish
Like a sudden bolt of light,
Which the stormy vapors banish
To the darkling grave of night.

D. P. Goldman

THE PILGRIM

Still i'th' springtime of my living
Was I, and I went to roam,
And the youthful joyous dancing
Left I in my father's home.

All my 'heritage, my having
Threw I trustingly behind,
And on pilgrim's staff alighting
Went I forth with childlike mind.

For a mighty hoping drove me
And a darksome word of faith:
Wander forth, the way runs freely,
Always on the rising path.

Till unto a golden portal
Thou dost come, then enter thee,
For the earthly things will there all
Heavenly and deathless be.

Ev'ning came becoming morning,
Never, never stood I still,
But it's always kept in hiding,
What I seek for, what I will.

Mountains lay before my pathway,
Torrents hemm'd my every stride,
Over gulfs I built a gangway,
Bridges o'er the rapid tide.

And unto a stream's embankments
Came I, which flows toward the East,
Gladly trusting to its currents,
Cast myself upon its breast.

Hence to an unbounded ocean
Playful billows 'neath me roll,
Fore me lies a vain expansion,
Nearer I'm not to the goal.

Ah no pathway will lead yonder,
Ah o'er me the heaven's sphere
Will the earthly never border,
And the There is never here!

THE ARCHER'S SONG
(from *Wilhelm Tell*)

With the shaft, the crossbow
Over mounts and streams
Doth the archer follow
Soon as morning beams.

As in realms of breezes
Kites soar regally,
Over mounts and gorges
Rules the archer free.

He commands the yonder,
That his shaft achieves,
That is his own plunder,
What there creeps and flees.

THE
GHOST
SEER

The Ghost Seer

TRANSLATED BY GEORGE GREGORY

BOOK ONE

I shall relate an affair that will appear incredible to many, and of which I was, for the most part, an eyewitness. For those informed about a certain political matter, it will provide some welcome information—if these pages find them still among the living; and, for others who lack this key, it will perhaps be an important contribution to the history of deception and aberration of the human spirit. One will be astounded at the boldness of the ends which evil is capable of designing and pursuing. One will be amazed at the peculiarity of the means it is capable of summoning to assure itself of these ends. Pure, strict truth shall guide my pen, for when these pages enter the world, I will no longer be, and will have neither anything to lose, nor to gain on account of the report I make.

It was on my journey back to Kurland in the year 17**, around Carneval time, that I visited the prince of *** in Venice. We had come to know each other when we were in the military service of ***, and now renewed a friendship interrupted by peace. As I wanted to see the sights of the city in any case, and the prince was only waiting for money to return to ***, he easily convinced me to provide him company, and to postpone my departure for the time being. We agreed not to part for as long as our sojourns in Venice lasted, and the prince was kind enough to offer me his own apartment in The Moor hotel.

The prince lived strictly *incognito* because he wanted to come and go as he pleased, and because his meager allowance would not have permitted him to live as high as would befit his state. Two knights, whose silence he could entirely count upon, and a few loyal servants were all that attended him. He avoided pomp, more out of temperament than frugality. He kept distance from diversions; at the age of 35, he had resisted all of the enticements of this city of temptations. He had been totally indifferent to the fair sex up to now. A deep seriousness and eccentric melancholy shaped his disposition. His inclinations were gentle, but he was stubborn to the extreme. Slow and diffident in choosing acquaintances, he was warm and eternal in his fidelity. Amidst a clamorous crowd, he found his way alone; shut off in the world of his imagination, he was often a stranger in the real one. There was never one more born to be ruled than he, although he was not weak. He was, nonetheless, intrepid and reliable, as soon as he had been won over, and was equally disposed to do battle against an acknowledged prejudice, or to die for another one.

Being the third prince of his house, there was hardly any prospect that he would rule one day. His ambitions had never been awakened, and so his passions had taken other directions. Content not to be dependent upon a will other than his own, he felt no temptation to rule over others: the quiet freedom of private life, and enjoyment of a lively intellectual company were the utmost of his desires. He read a good deal, but without being selective; an education neglected, and early military service had not permitted his mind to mature. All of the knowledge he accumulated later only increased the confusion of his conceptions, because they had not been built on firm foundations.

He was Protestant by birth, as was his entire family, albeit his convictions were not the result of inquiries; these he had never made, though at one point in his life he had been a religious fanatic. As far as I know, he never became a Freemason.

One evening, while we were walking over St. Mark's Square, well disguised and secretively as usual—it had become late and the crowds were dispersed—the prince remarked that a person in disguise was following us wherever we went. This disguised person was an Armenian, and he was alone. We accelerated our steps and tried to confuse him, changing our course often—but to no avail; our pursuer remained close by. "Surely, you have not been involved in any intrigues here?" the prince finally said. "The husbands of Venice are dangerous."—"I have absolutely no relations with a lady," I answered him.—"Let us sit down here and speak in German," he continued. "I have a notion that we are mistaken for someone else." We sat down on a stone bench and expected the disguised person to pass us by. He walked directly toward us and took his seat right beside the prince. The prince pulled out his watch and, addressing me loudly and in French, standing up at the same time, said, "It is past nine o'clock. Come. We are forgetting that we are expected at the Louvre." He only said this to throw our pursuer off the track. "Nine o'clock," repeated the other. "Good luck Prince ***," said he, calling the prince by his true name. "He died at nine o'clock." Therewith he stood up and left us.

We glanced at each other, perplexed. "Who died?" the prince finally asked, after a long silence. "Let us follow him," I suggested, "and demand an explanation." We wound our way around every corner of St. Mark's Square—our pursuer was nowhere to be found. Disappointed, we returned to our rooms. The prince said nothing at all along the way, but walked apart and alone, apparently engaged in a fierce struggle, as he later confessed to me he in fact was.

"It is ridiculous," he said at last, "that a fool should be able to shatter a man's serenity with but two words." We wished each other good-night, and as soon as I was in my rooms I wrote the day and hour of the incident on my writing pad. It was Thursday.

"Shall we not take a stroll over the square and look for our mysterious Armenian?" the prince suggested the following evening. "I am interested in getting to the bottom of this comedy." I approved the suggestion. We stayed on the square until eleven o'clock. The Armenian was nowhere to be seen. We repeated the same procedure the following four evenings, and with no better success.

As we left our hotel on the sixth evening, it occurred to me—whether by chance or design, I no longer remember—to leave notice with the servants where we could be found should we be asked for. The prince took note of my prescience, and praised it with a smiling mien. There was an immense crowd on St. Mark's Square when we arrived. We had hardly taken thirty steps when I recognized the Armenian, working his way quickly through the throng, apparently looking for someone. We were just about to catch up with him when Baron von *** came up to us, breathless, bearing a letter to the prince. "It is sealed in black," he added. "We suspected it would be urgent." That fell upon me like a blow. The prince had gone to a lantern and began to read. "My cousin has died," he called over to us. "When?" I interrupted. He looked at the letter again—"Last Thursday. In the evening at nine o'clock."

We had no time to recover from our astonishment when the Armenian appeared in our midst. "You have been recognized here, most gracious lord," he said to the prince. "Hurry back to The Moor. There you will find deputies from the Senate. Do not hesitate to accept the honor they desire to bestow upon you. And, I am to tell you that your money has arrived." At this, he lost himself in the crowd.

We hurried back to our hotel. Everything was as the Armenian had said. Three *nobili* of the Republic stood ready to welcome the prince and, with pomp, to accompany him to the assembly, where the high nobility of the city awaited him. The prince hardly had time to indicate to me that I should wait up for him.

He returned in the night, at eleven o'clock. Serious and deep in thought he entered the room, and, after dismissing the servants, took my hand. "Count," he said, in the words of Hamlet, "there are more things in heaven and on earth than we dream of in our philosophies."

"Most gracious Prince," I replied, "you seem to forget that you go to bed the richer of a great hope." (The deceased had been crown prince, the only son of the governing ***, who was old and sick, now without hope that his son would succeed him. An uncle of our Prince, also without progeny or prospects of obtaining any, was all that stood between the prince and the throne. I mention this because of the discussion of it in what follows.)

"Do not remind me," said the prince. "And even if a crown were now mine to be won, I should now have more to do than think about this trivial matter . . . if it were really that this Armenian did not merely guess that. . . ."

"How is that possible?" I interrupted.

"I would exchange all my princely hopes with you for a monk's cowl."

The following evening we went to St. Mark's Square earlier than usual. A sudden cascade of rain drove us to a coffee house where there was gambling. The prince positioned himself behind the chair of a Spaniard and observed the play. I made my way into an adjoining room where I read newspapers. After a while I heard a commotion. Prior to the prince's arrival, the Spaniard had been losing consistently, but now he was winning on every card. The entire play was notably changed, and the bank was in danger of being challenged by the adversary who had made this change of affairs the more audacious. The Venetian who was playing told the prince in an insulting tone that he was spoiling the luck of the play, and ought to leave the table. The prince looked at him coldly, and remained; he maintained this attitude as the Venetian repeated his insult in French. The latter thought the prince had understood neither of the two languages, and turned disparagingly to the others with a snicker: "Tell me, gentlemen, how am I to make myself understood to this boor?" At this he stood up and moved to take the prince by the arm; here the prince lost his patience, grabbed the Venetian and threw him roughly to the floor. The entire house was in an uproar. Upon hearing the commotion, I rushed into the room and without a thought called to the prince by name. "Take care, Prince," I added imprudently, "we are in Venice." At the name of the prince everyone fell silent, and this soon gave way to a murmuring that seemed dangerous to me. All the Italians present gathered together and stepped aside. They left the room one after the other until, at last, we found ourselves alone with the Spaniard and a few Frenchmen. "You are lost, most gracious Prince," said the latter, "if you do not leave the city immediately. The Venetian you have so roughly treated is wealthy and enjoys a considerable reputation. It would only cost him 50 zechin to have you killed." The Spaniard offered to provide for the security of the Prince, and to accompany us home himself. The Frenchmen wanted to do the same. We were still standing there considering what we ought to do when the doors opened and a number of servants of the State Inquisition entered. They showed us an Order of the Government, wherein we were both directed to follow them without further ado. We were led to the canal by a numerous escort. Here a gondola was waiting for us, and we were forced to enter it. Our eyes were bound before we disembarked. We were led up a large stone staircase, and then through a long, winding cavern, as I concluded from the echoes resounding under our feet. We finally reached another staircase which led us down twenty-six steps into the depths. At the end, we stepped into a room where the blindfolds were taken from our eyes. We found ourselves in a circle of venerable old men, all clothed in black, the entire room hung with black tapestries and dimly lit, deathly stillness in the entire gathering, which made a horrible impression. One of the venerables, presumably the Supreme State Inquisitor, approached and asked the prince in a solemn tone, as the Venetian was being led forward, "Do you recognize this man here as the same who insulted you in the coffee house?"

"Yes," answered the prince.

Thereupon the Inquisitor turned to the prisoner. "Is this the person you intended to have killed this evening?"

"Yes," replied the prisoner.

All at once the circle opened, and with horror we saw the head of the Venetian parted from his torso. "Is this sufficient satisfaction for you?" the State Inquisitor inquired. But the prince lay unconscious in the arms of his attendants.

"Go now," commanded the Inquisitor in a horrible voice, and turning to me, said, "and in the future, do not be so precipitous in your judgment of justice in Venice."

We could not guess who the clandestine friend was, who had rescued us from certain death by the swift arm of justice. We returned to our apartment, benumbed with terror. It was after midnight. The officer of the chambers, von Z***, awaited us impatiently on the steps. "How good it was that you sent word," he remarked to the prince as he lit our way.—"The news that the Baron von F*** brought us from St. Mark's Square had made us deathly anxious on your account."

"I sent word? When? I know nothing of it."

"It was this evening, after eight o'clock," von Z*** insisted. "You said we should not be concerned if you came somewhat later in the night."

At this the prince glanced at me. "Have you taken this caution, perhaps, without my knowledge?"

I knew nothing of it.

"It must be so, Your Highness," said the officer of chambers, "for here is your watch that you sent along to identify yourself." The prince felt his pocket. The watch was indeed gone, and he acknowledged that the one shown him was his. "Who brought it?" he asked perturbed.

"Someone unknown, wearing a mask, an Armenian who absented himself at once."

We stood there and looked at each other.—"What do you think?" asked the prince after a long silence. "I seem to have a secret guardian here in Venice."

The terrible events this night had made the prince feverous, so that he had to confine himself to his rooms for eight days. In this time, our hotel teemed with natives and foreigners who had hit upon the identity of the prince. They outdid each other offering their services, each one in his own way making tribute. The affair in the State Inquisition was never mentioned again. As the court of *** wished that the prince postpone his departure for a time, a number of money changers received instructions to pay him considerable sums of money. He was thus put in a position, against his will, to extend his stay in Venice, and I too resolved to postpone my departure at his request.

As soon as he was sufficiently recovered to be able to leave his rooms, the physician convinced him to take a tour on the Brenta for a change of air. The weather was magnificent, and the proposal was accepted. As we were about to board the gondola, the prince noticed that he was missing the key to a small privy purse that contained very important papers. We returned at once to look for it. He precisely remembered having locked up the privy purse the previous day, and had not left the room since that time. But all of our searching was in vain, and we had to give it up, not to lose time. The prince, whose soul was above harboring suspicions, declared the key for lost and asked not to speak of it again.

The trip was most pleasant. A painter's landscape that seemed to outdo itself in wealth and beauty with each bend of the river, the most gorgeous skies making a day in May out of one in mid-February, enticing gardens and tasteful land-houses adorning both banks of the Brenta; behind us the majestic Venice, with hundreds of towers and masts leaping upon the water. All of this provided us with the most wonderful theater in the world. We surrendered ourselves entirely to the magic of this beautiful nature; our mood was the most excited, the prince himself lost his serious mien, and competed with us in frivolous jokes. Joyous music greeted us as we went on land a few Italian miles from the city. It came from a small village, where the annual market was being held; there teemed scores of people of every sort. A troop of young girls and boys, all theatrically dressed, welcomed us with a pantomime dance. It was a new invention, agility and grace besouling every movement. Before the dance was over, the leader, who represented a queen, suddenly seemed as if she were held aright by invisible arms. She stood lifeless. The music fell silent. Not a breath was to be heard; there she stood, fixing her gaze upon the earth; all motion was frozen. Suddenly she reached into the sky with the rage of rapture, tearing her crown from her head, and laid it . . . at the feet of the prince!

Everyone turned his eyes toward the prince—they had been held in uncertainty for a long time as to whether there was any meaning in this ritual play, so thoroughly deceptive had been the affected earnestness of the player. A general applause finally broke the silence. My eyes sought the prince. I noticed that he was quite moved, and was making every effort to avoid the searching gaze of the audience. He threw money among the children and hurried to escape the throng.

We had taken only a few steps when a venerable, barefooted man worked his way through the crowd and stepped in the way of the prince. "Lord," said the monk, "give the Madonna something of your wealth; you shall require her prayers." He stated this in a voice that startled us. Then the crowd swept him away.

Our company had grown in the meantime. An English lord, who had seen the prince before in Nice, some merchants from Livorno, a German prebendary, a French abbot with some ladies, and a Russian officer were now part of our entourage. The physiognomy of the latter had something unusual about it, which drew our attention to him. Never in my life have I seen so many *lines*, and so little *character*, so much alluring beneficence, with so much repulsive frigidity, domiciled all together in one single human face. Every passion seemed to have gnawed its way into it, only to have left once again. Nothing remained but the still, penetrating gaze of a perfected judge of men, who would frighten away the gaze of anyone who met him. This curious personage had been following us a long way, but seemed to be taking merely passing interest in what was happening.

We came to a stall where lots were being drawn. The ladies made their bets, and we others followed their example. The prince, too. He won a snuff-box. When he opened it, I saw him recoil, fainting—the *key* was within!

"What is this?" the prince asked me, when we were alone for a moment. "A higher power is pursuing me. Omniscience hovers over me. An invisible being whom I cannot escape watches my every step. I must find the Armenian, and he will shed light on this."

The sun was setting as we came to the cottage where dinner was served. The name of the prince had enlarged our company by now to sixteen persons. In addition to those named above, there was also a virtuoso from Rome, some Swiss, and an adventurer from Palermo*

Translator's note: This reference is to the well-known figure of "Count" Cagliostro of the time, who had the reputation of being able to summon spirits. Schiller began *Der Geisterseher* in the Fall of 1786, playing on the battles for

who wore a uniform and pretended to be a captain. It was decided that we would spend the entire evening here, and ride home by torch-light. Discussion during dinner was very lively, and the prince could not resist telling the story of the key, which resulted in general amaze-ment. The matter was hotly debated. Most of our company pertly asserted that all of these secret arts were mere frauds; the abbot, who already had a good deal of wine in him, challenged the entire kingdom of spirits to emerge from the closets; the Englishman uttered only blasphemies; the musician made the sign of the cross to ward off the devil. A few, the prince among them, held that one would have to reserve judgment on such things; in the meantime, the Russian officer held conversation with the ladies, and seemed to pay no attention to all the talk. In the heat of the debate, no one had noticed, that the Sicilian had left us. After passage of a short half-hour, he reappeared, encapsuled in a cloak, and positioned himself behind the chair of the Frenchman. "Up to now you have been audacious enough to say you would tangle with all spirits—would you like to try one?"

"Gods!" exclaimed the abbot, "if you want to take it upon yourself to summon me one."

"That is what I want to do," replied the Sicilian, "once these ladies and gentlemen have left us."

"Why that?" cried the Englishman, "a stout-hearted spirit shall not fear a small and merry company."

"I will not be held responsible for the outcome," answered the Sicilian.

"For Heaven's sake, no!" cried the ladies, rising from their chairs.

"Let your spirit come," said the abbot stubbornly, "but warn him beforehand that there are some very pointed blades here," and there-with asked one of the guests for his dagger.

"You may attempt what you will," replied the Sicilian, "if you still care to, afterwards." Here he turned to the prince. "Most gracious Lord," he began, "you claim that your key has been in the hands of a stranger—do you have any suspicion in whose hands it has been?"

"No."

---

the succession to the throne in Württemberg, where there was suspicion that the Jesuits were trying to undermine the Protestant succession. Prince Fried-rich Eugen of Württemberg had written an essay in the *Berlinisches Monatsheft* in July 1788 attesting, on religious grounds, the veracity of conjuring spirits. He was known to be susceptible to being converted to Catholicism. Elise von der Recke had written a book, *Nachricht von des berhümten Cagliostro Au-fenthalt in Mitau*, exposing the conjurer as a fraud, and then another essay, *Noch etwas ber geheime Gesellschaften im Protestantischen Deutschland*, which Schiller is likely to have drawn on for *Der Geisterseher*.

"Have you made no attempt to guess?"

"I obviously do have an idea. . . ."

"Would you recognize the person if you saw him in front of you?"

"Without the slightest doubt."

At this, the Sicilian threw back his cloak, and drew out a mirror which he held in front of the eyes of the prince.

"Is this he?"

The prince leaped back in terror.

"What did you see?" I asked.

"The Armenian."

The Sicilian buried the mirror under his cloak once more. "Was this the same person you meant?" the whole company inquired of the prince.

"The same."

At this everyone's face changed; the laughter ceased. All eyes were fixed in curiosity upon the Sicilian.

"Monsieur Abbot, the matter is becoming serious," said the Englishman. "I advise you to consider the retreat."

"This fellow has the devil in him," screamed the Frenchman, and ran out of the house; the ladies rushed out of the room, the virtuoso following them; the German snored in his chair; the Russian remained seated, indifferent.

"Perhaps you only wanted a swaggerer to have fun with," the prince started up, after the others had left—"or do you really mean to keep your word?"

"It is true," said the Sicilian. "With the abbot, I was not really serious. I only made him the offer because I knew the coward would not hold me to my word.—The affair itself is actually far too earnest to merely jest with."

"You allow, then, that it is in your power?"

The magician fell silent for a long time, and seemed to be examining the prince meticulously with his eyes.

"Yes," he answered finally.

The prince's curiosity was already piqued to the highest pitch. To be in contact with the world of spirits had previously been his most ardent desire, and, after that initial appearance of the Armenian, all of the ideas began to whirl in him once more, the which his more mature reason has shunned for so long. He took the Sicilian to one side, and I heard him negotiating with him intensely.

"You have here before you," he went on, "one who is burning with impatience to bring this important matter to a conviction. I would embrace him who could dispel my doubts and draw the shades from my eyes as my benefactor, first among my friends—do you mean to vie for this great reward?"

"What do you demand of me?" asked the magician, with considerable hesitation.

"For now, just an example of your art. Let me see an apparition."

"What purpose would that serve?"

"Then, from closer acquaintance with me, you may judge whether I am worthy of higher instruction."

"I esteem you above all others, most gracious Lord. A secret power in your visage, that you yet know not, bound me to you from the first moment. You are more powerful than you yourself know. All of my powers I place at your disposal, but. . . ."

"So, let me see an apparition."

"But first, I must be convinced that you do not demand this of me out of light curiosity. Although my will does, to a certain degree, command invisible forces, this is so only under the sacred condition that I do not profane the sacred secrets, in short that I do not abuse my powers."

"My intentions are the purest. I want the truth."

Here they stepped aside, and went over to a distant window where I could no longer hear them. The Englishman, who had also overheard this discussion, drew me to his side."

"Your Prince is a noble man. I deplore his permitting himself to be drawn in by a fraud."

"It will depend," said I, "upon how he pulls himself out of the business."

"Do you know something?" said the Englishman. "Now the poor devil is making himself valuable. He will not reveal his arts until he hears money jingle. There are nine of us. Let us take a collection, and lead him into temptation by the high price. That will trip him up and open the eyes of your Prince."

"Of that plan I approve," I responded.

The Englishman threw six guineas on a plate, and took up a collection. Each gave a few louis; our proposal seemed to exceedingly interest especially the Russian, and he laid a banknote of one hundred zechin on the plate—an extravagance that astounded the Englishman. We brought the collection to the prince. "Be so kind," said the Englishman, "to appeal to this good gentleman on our behalf, that he permit us to see an example of his art, and accept this small proof of our acknowledgment." The prince laid a precious ring on the plate too, and offered it to the Sicilian. The latter pondered for some seconds.—
"My lords and patrons," he began, "this magnanimity shames me. You seem to mistake me, but I will bow to your demands. Your wishes shall be fulfilled," whereupon he pulled out a bell. "As for this money, to which I myself have no right, you will permit me to deposit it with

the nearest Benedictine cloister as a small donation. The ring I shall keep as a treasured memento of the most worthy Prince."

In an instant there appeared the innkeeper, to whom the Sicilian delivered the money. "He is a scoundrel nonetheless," the Englishman whispered into my ear. "He refuses the money only because he is more after the prince."

"Or the innkeeper understands his job well," suggested another.

"Whom do you require that I summon?" the magician solemnly asked of the prince.

The prince considered for a moment. "First of all, he should be a great man," proposed the Englishman. "Demand the Pope Ganganelli. It will cost the Lord little."

The Sicilian bit his lips.—"I am not permitted to call forth those who have taken vows."

"Oh, what a pity," said the Englishman. "We might otherwise have found out from him of what illness it was that he died."*

"The Marquis of Lanoy," the prince prompted finally, "was a French brigadier in the previous war, and my most loyal friend. In the battle near Hastinbeck he was fatally wounded; he was carried into my tent, where he soon after died. As he was in the throes of death, he called to me. 'Prince,' he began, 'I will never see my fatherland again, and thus I wish that you learn a secret to which no one but I has the key. In a cloister, on the border to Flanders, there lives a . . .' And, at that very moment, he died. The hand of death tore the thread of his speech. I should like to see him here to hear the rest of his tale."

"You demand a great deal, by God!" exclaimed the Englishman. "I will vouch you are a second Solomon if you can solve this puzzle."

We were amazed at the prince's ingenious choice, and gave it our unanimous applause. Meanwhile, the magician was pacing in great strides back and forth, apparently struggling with himself, undecided.

"Was that all that the deceased left behind?"

"There was nothing else."

"Did you not inquire further about this in his fatherland?"

"In vain."

"The Marquis of Lanoy lived blamelessly?—I am not permitted to call upon the dead indiscriminately."

"He died in repentance of youthful excesses."

"Do you bear any memento of him?"

Translator's note: The reference is to Pope Clement XIV, who outlawed the Jesuits in 1773—only three years before the American Declaration of Independence. It was commonly known that "Pope Ganganelli" had been poisoned by the Jesuit order.

"Yes." In fact, the prince had a snuff-box, one emblazoned with a miniature portrait of the marquis; this was the one he had with him when he was having dinner.

"I do not need to know of it—leave me alone. You shall see the deceased," said the Sicilian.

We were asked to remove ourselves to another pavilion until such time as we should be called. The Sicilian also had all of the furniture removed from the rooms, all of the windows were unhung, and the shutters tightly closed. He ordered the innkeeper, with whom he appeared to be in confidence, to bring a vessel with glowing coals, and to carefully extinguish all fire in the house. Before we went away, he demanded the word of honor of each of us that we would never speak of that which we would observe, see, and hear. All of the rooms adjoining the pavilion were locked behind us.

It was after eleven o'clock, and a deep stillness reigned over the entire house. As he was about to go out, the Russian asked me if we had loaded pistols about us. "What for?" I asked.—"Just in case," he responded. "But just wait a moment, and I will look for some." He took his leave. Baron von F*** and I opened a window just across from the other pavilion, and it seemed to us as though we heard two men whispering to each other, and we thought we heard a sound as if someone were putting up a ladder. That was mere conjecture, however, and I would not have gone so far as to say that it was actually so. The Russian returned with a couple of pistols, having been away for half an hour. We saw him loading them. It was nearly two o'clock when the magician reappeared and announced that the time had come. Before we went in, we were ordered to take off our shoes, and to appear only in shirts, stockings and undergarments. Behind us, as before, the doors were locked.

As we entered, we found ourselves within a large circle drawn with coal, large enough for all of us to fit within it. The wallboards had all been removed from the four walls, so that we were standing as if on an island. In the middle of the circle, covered with a black tapestry, was an altar, a silver crucifix attached to it. Instead of candles, alcohol was burning in a silver capsule. A thick incense smoke darkened the room, nearly obscuring the light; the magician was dressed like we were, but barefoot; around his neck he wore an amulet on a chain of human hair, and he had wound a white skirt around his loins, decorated with enigmatic ciphers and symbolic figures. We were told to take each other's hands, and observe strict silence. He especially recommended that we pose no questions to the apparition. He had the Englishman and I (with respect to the two of us he seemed most mistrustful) raise two unsheathed daggers into a cross a certain distance over his head, and we were told to hold them there for as long as the session would last. We were standing in a crescent around him, the Russian officer pressing near to the Englishman, at first even standing on the altar. With his face to the east, the magician took his place on the carpet and sprinkled incense water in all directions of the Zodiac, bowing three times to the Bible. The conjuring, of which we understood nothing, lasted half a quarter of an hour; at the end, he gave those immediately behind him a sign they were to grab him firmly by the hair. He called to the deceased three times, twitching wildly, and the third time reached his hand toward the crucifix.

At once we all felt a shock, as if by lightning, and our hands flew apart; a sudden crash of thunder shook the house, the cover of the capsule on the altar fell shut, the light extinguished, and, on the opposite wall over the fireplace a human figure appeared in a bloody shirt, pale and with the face of one about to die.

"Who calls me?" queried the hollow, hardly audible voice.

"Your friend," the magician answered, "who honors your memory and prays for your soul," and then naming the prince.

The answers then followed, each after the other, with a considerable pause between them.

"What does he want?" the voice continued.

"He wants to hear your confession to its end, that which you began in this world but did not finish."

"In a cloister on the border to Flanders . . ."

The house shook anew, the doors slammed closed under a heavy bolt of thunder, their latches jangling, a streak of lightning lit the room, and another bodily form, bloody and pale like the first, appeared on the threshold. The alcohol on the altar began to burn of its own accord, and the room became as bright as before.

"Who is among us?" called the magician, terrified, as he threw a glance of horror over the assembly. "You I did not call upon."

The form walked with majestically light steps toward the altar and stood on the carpet facing us. He grasped the crucifix. The first figure was gone.

"Who calls me?" asked the second apparition.

The magician began to shiver terribly. Horror and amazement affixed us to our places. I reached for a pistol, but the magician tore it out of my hand and fired it at the form. The ball rolled slowly out on the altar, and the figure stepped unchanged from the smoke. Now the magician fell unconscious to the floor. "What is going to happen?" the Englishman cried as he began to take a stab at the form with his dagger. The form touched his arm and the blade fell to the floor. My brow was wet with the sweat of terror. Baron von *** confessed to us later that he had prayed. The prince stood fearless and calm the entire time, his eyes firmly fixed upon the apparition.

"Yes, I know you!" he exclaimed with great emotion. "You are Lanoy, you are my friend—where do you come from?"

"Eternity is mute. Ask me about the life past."

"Who lives in the cloister you told me of?"

"My daughter."

"What! You were a father?"

"Oh, that it was too little."

"Are you not happy, Lanoy?"

"God has judged."

"Is there any service I may still render you in this world?"

"None, other than to think of yourself."

"How must I do that?"

"This you will learn in Rome."

Then followed another crack of thunder. A black cloud of smoke filled the room; when it had dissipated the apparition was gone. I threw the shutters open. Nothing was there.

The magician now came out of his daze. "Where are we?" he called out as he saw the light of day. The Russian officer was standing near behind him, looking over his shoulder. "Trickster," he growled, with a terrifying gaze at the magician, "*you shall call no more spirits.*"

The Sicilian turned around, looked the Russian officer straight in the face, and then wailing a loud scream, fell at the Russian's feet.

At this we all looked at the supposed Russian. The prince recognized in him with no trouble our Armenian, and the word he had been about to stutter died in his mouth. Terror and surprise had turned us all to stone. Without a sound, immobile, we stared at this secretive being that looked through us with a gaze of silent power and magnitude. The silence lasted a minute, and then another. There was not a breath to be heard in the entire assembly.

A powerful pounding at the door finally brought all of us to ourselves once again. The door fell open, splintered, into the room, and deputies of the court with an entourage of guards pushed into the room. "Here we find you all together!" called the leader, and turned to his attendants. "In the name of the Government!" he addressed us, "I arrest you." We had no time to collect our thoughts; in a moment we were surrounded. The Russian officer, whom I now name our Armenian again, drew the leader of the officers to one side, and I noticed—as much as I could in my dazed state of mind—that he whispered a number of words to him and showed him something written. At once the officer left him silently, bowing in diffidence, and then turned to us and took off his hat. "Forgive me, my lords," he said, "that I should have confused you with this fraud here. I shall not ask who you are, but this gentleman here assures me that I have men of honor before me." He signaled to his attendants to release us. "This scoundrel is overripe," he added. "We have been watching for him for months."

This poor person was now truly an object of pity. The double horror of the second apparition and the unexpected intrusion had obviously overwhelmed his powers. He permitted himself to be bound like a child; his eyes were wide open, and stared in a death-like expression; his lips moved in silent tremors, without issuing a sound. We expected him to break down in convulsions at any moment. The prince felt compassion for his condition and undertook to effect his release with the servant of the court, to whom he introduced himself.

"Most gracious lord," said the officer, "do you know who this person is, on whose behalf you so magnanimously do suppliance? The deception he intended to play upon you is the least of his crimes. We have his accomplices. They testify horrible things of him. He may count himself fortunate if he comes out of this a galley slave."

Meanwhile, we saw the innkeeper and his house servants being led across the courtyard, their hands tied with a rope. "He too?" asked the prince. "What has he done to be guilty of?"—"He was an accessory to the crime, and the receiver of stolen goods," answered the officer, "who aided and abetted his tricks of deception and thievery, and shared the booty with him. Of that you shall have opportunity to convince yourself, most gracious lord," said he, turning to his attendants. "Search the entire house and bring me news at once of what has been found."

Now the prince looked around for the Armenian—but he was no longer there; in the general confusion accompanying the intrusion of the guards, he had found means to remove himself unnoticed. The prince was inconsolable; he wanted to send all of his people after him at once; he wanted to get away and look for him himself. I hurried to the window; the entire house was surrounded by curiosity seekers who had been drawn by rumors of the affair. It was impossible to penetrate the crowd. This I propounded to the prince. "If the Armenian is serious about hiding himself from us, he knows the artifices far better than we, and all of our researches shall be in vain. Let us, rather, stay here, most gracious Prince. Perhaps this officer of the court may tell us more of him, since unless I am mistaken the Armenian did reveal himself to him."

We now remembered that we were still undressed, and we hurried to our room to throw ourselves into our clothes. When we returned the search of the house had been completed.

After having cleared away the altar and breaking open the wallboards of the room, a generously sized recess had been discovered, one in which a man could sit rather comfortably. The recess had a door, which led down a narrow staircase into the cellar. In the recess were found an electric machine, a watch, and a small silver bell, which latter along with the electric machine, was in communication with the altar and the crucifix attached to it. A window shutter directly across from the fireplace had been broken through and equipped with a gliding bolt, in order—as we later learned—to guide a magic lantern into its opening, from which the apparition was projected onto the wall over the fireplace. Various drums were collected from the attic and the cellar, and large leaden spheres had been attached to them with strings, most likely to produce the noise of thunder we had heard. As the clothing of the Sicilian was searched, a small case of various powders was found, mercury in vials and cartridges, phosophorus in a glass bottle, a ring which we immediately recognized to be magnetized because it remained hanging on an iron door knob; in his pockets there was a set of rosary beads, some Old Man's Beard, a derringer, and a dagger. "Let us see if it is loaded," said one of the officers, taking the derringer and firing it into the fireplace. "Jesus Maria!" screamed a hollow voice, in fact just the one which had belonged to the first apparition—and in the same instant we saw a bleeding body fall out of the chimney. "Still not laid to rest, poor spirit?" said the Englishman, as we drew back in fear. "Go home to your grave. You have appeared to be what you were not; now you shall be what you appear to be."

"Jesus Maria! I have been wounded," repeated the one in the fireplace. The bullet had shattered his right leg. His wound was taken care of immediately.

"But who are you, and what evil demon was necessary to bring you here?"

"Poor and barefoot am I," answered the wounded one. "A strange gentleman offered me a zechin to. . ."

"Repeat a certain formula? And why did you not run away at once?"

"He wanted to give me a zechin if I would stay to the end; but there was no zechin, and when I wanted to climb out, the ladder had been taken away."

"And what was the formula he taught you?"

At this the man fainted, and nothing more was to be gotten out of him. As we looked at him more closely, we recognized that he was the same as the monk who had stepped in the way of the prince and so solemnly addressed him.

In the meantime, the prince had turned to the leader of the officers of the court. "You," he said, pressing a number of gold pieces into the officer's hand, "you have saved us from the hands of a scoundrel, and have given us justice without knowing us. Please make our obligation to you now complete, and disclose to us the identity of the stranger whom it cost only a few words to obtain our freedom."

"Whom do you mean?" asked the officer in a manner that clearly showed how unnecessary the question had been.

"I mean the gentleman in Russian uniform who took you to the side before, and showed you something written, and whispered a few words in your ear, whereupon you let us free at once."

"So, you do not know this gentleman?" asked the officer. "He was not of your company?"

"No," said the prince. "And for very important reasons, I want to become better acquainted with him."

"I know him no better myself," answered the officer. "I do not even know his name, and today I saw him for the first time in my life."

"What? In such a short time, with a few words, he was able to command so much of you that you declared him and all of us innocent?"

"Of course. By reason of one word."

"And what word was that?—I admit I would like to know it."

"This stranger, most gracious lord . . . ," said he—weighing the zechins in his hand—"You have been far too generous for me to keep it secret from you any longer—This stranger was . . . an officer of the State Inquisition."

"The State Inquisition! He! . . ."

"None other, most gracious lord—the papers he showed me convinced me of that."

"This person, you say? It is not possible!"

"I will tell you even more, most gracious lord. He it was, upon whose information I was sent here to arrest the conjurer of spirits."

We looked at each other in even greater amazement.

"That," said the Englishman, "would explain why the poor devil of a magician was so terrified when he looked him in the eyes. He recognized him for a spy, and therefore screamed and fell at his feet."

"Not at all," said the prince. "This person is everything he wants to be, and everything the moment dictates he ought to be. No mortal has yet learned what he actually is. Did you see how the Sicilian crumpled when he screamed the words into his ear, 'You shall never summon spirits again!'? There is more behind it. No one can convince me that someone can be so terrified of something human."

"On that account," said the English lord, "the magician himself may perhaps set us straight, if this gentleman," turning to the officer of the court, "could provide us the opportunity of speaking with his prisoner."

The officer promised us he would do so, and we arranged with the Englishman to look him up the very next morning. Then we returned to Venice.

Lord Seymour (for that was the name of the Englishman) was there at sunrise, and soon afterward there appeared a confidant of the officer of the court, sent to lead us to the prison.

I have forgotten to say that the prince had missed one of his corporals for some days, a man born in Bremen, and one who had served him honorably for many years, and enjoyed his full confidence. No one knew whether he had had an accident, been kidnapped, or had simply run away. There was no probable reason for the latter possibility, for he had always been an orderly and quiet person who had never given cause for criticism. All that his comrades could remember was that he had been quite melancholic of late, and whenever he could steal a moment, he had visited a certain Minorite cloister in the Giudecca, where he often held discussions with some of the brothers. This gave rise to our suspicion that he may have fallen into the hands of the monks and converted to Catholicism; and, as the prince was then still rather indifferent to the matter, he let it be, after having let a few inquiries be made. But the loss of this person, who had always been at his side during military campaigns, did bereave him; he had always been loyal, and was not so easily replaced in a foreign country. Now, as we were just about to leave, the prince's banker, who had been contracted to care for the prince's servants, announced himself. The banker introduced the prince to a well-educated, well-dressed person in his mid-years, one who had been in the service of the procurator for many years as a secretary, and spoke French and some German, and bore the best of references. He was physically attractive, and as he declared that his salary would depend upon the prince's satisfaction with his service, he was taken on without further ado.

We found the Sicilian in a private cell to which he had been temporarily brought, as the officer of the court said, to please the prince, before being put under the leaden roofs where he would no longer be accessible. These leaden roofs are the most horrible prisons in Venice, under the roof of St. Mark's Palace, where unfortunate criminals are often driven insane by the sun's withering heat collected by the lead sheathing. The Sicilian had recovered from the affair of the previous day and stood up respectfully when he saw the prince. One hand and one leg were bound, but otherwise he could move freely about the room. The guard at the door left as we entered.

"I have come," said the prince after we had taken our seats, "to demand an explanation of you concerning two points. The one you owe me, and it will not be to your detriment to satisfy me on the other as well."

"My role is played out," declared the Sicilian. "My fate is in your hands."

"Your sincerity alone," said the prince, "may ameliorate your fate."

"Ask, most gracious lord. I am prepared to answer, for I have nothing more to lose."

"You permitted me to see the face of the Armenian in your mirror. By what means did you effect this?"

"What you saw was not a mirror. It was merely a pastel drawing behind glass which represented a man in Armenian clothing; it was this that deceived you. My quickness, the thunder, and your surprise supported this deception. The picture will be found among the other articles taken into the possession of the court at the inn."

"But how were you able to know my thoughts so well, and guess that it was the Armenian?"

"That was not at all difficult, most gracious lord. Without a doubt, you have often spoken during meals in the presence of your servants about that which transpired between yourself and the Armenian. One of my people made a chance acquaintance in the Guidecca with a corporal in your service; after a time, he was able to draw out all that I required to know."

"Where is this corporal?" asked the prince. "I miss him, and you, most certainly, know of his absence."

"I swear I know nothing at all about that, most gracious lord. I myself have never seen him, and have never had any other intentions on his account than those I have just reported."

"Continue," said the prince.

"This was how I first received news of your presence in Venice, and I decided at once to take the opportunities offered. You see, most gracious lord, that I am sincere. I knew of your plan to take a ride on the Brenta; I made preparations, and a key which you accidentally lost first gave me the opportunity to try my arts on you."

"What? You mean I was mistaken? That little affair with the key was your work, and not that of the Armenian? You saw I lost the key?"

"When you pulled out your purse—and I took advantage of the moment, as no one was observing me, to cover it quickly with my foot. The person with whom you drew lots was in my confidence. She had you draw from a vessel where there were no blank lots, and the key was in the snuff-box long before you had won it."

"Now I am beginning to understand. And the barefoot monk who threw himself in my way and spoke to me?"

"He was the one who, as I hear, was pulled out of the fireplace wounded. He is one of my associates who has served me very well in this guise."

"And to what end did you design all of this?"

"In order to make you reflective—in order to prepare an emotional condition in you that would make you the more receptive for the wonders that I had in store for you."

"But the pantomime dance that took such a surprisingly curious turn—at least this, perhaps, was not of your invention?"

"The girl who played the role of the queen was instructed by me, and her entire role was my work. I suspected that it would astonish Your Highness not a little to be known in this place; and, forgive me, most gracious lord, the adventure with the Armenian permitted me to hope that you would already be inclined to dismiss natural explanations, and to look for traces of higher sources of the extraordinary."

"Indeed," remarked the prince in a manner at once chagrined and amazed, as he gave me an especially meaningful glance. "Indeed," said he, "I had not expected that."

"But," he continued, "how did you summon the apparition that appeared on the wall above the fireplace?"

"By means of the lantern affixed to the opposite window shutter, where you will also have noticed the opening constructed for that purpose."

"But how did it happen that no one among us noticed it?" asked Lord Seymour.

"You will recall, gracious sir, that a thick smoke clouded the entire room when you returned to it. I had also taken the precaution of having the wallboards which had been lifted away, leaned up against the window where the lantern was; I thereby prevented you from immediately seeing the shutters of the window. As for the rest, the lantern remained hidden by a sliding mechanism until you had all taken your places, and then I had no reason to fear that you would examine the room more thoroughly."

"It seemed to me," I interjected, "as if I heard a ladder being erected in the proximity of the room when I looked out of the window in the other pavilion. Was it really so?"

"Quite right. It was upon this ladder that my assistant climbed up to the said window shutter in order to direct the lantern."

"The form," the prince continued, "did seem to vaguely resemble my deceased friend; it was particularly appropriate that it was quite blond. Was this merely accidental, or how did you manage that?"

"Your Highness will recall that you had a small case lying next to you at dinner, upon which the portrait of an officer in the uniform of *** was emblazoned. I asked you whether you had any memento of your friend, to which you answered in the affirmative. I concluded that it might well be the small case. I had examined the portrait closely over the table, and as I am rather well practiced at drawing, it was easy for me to give my portrait the vague similarity which you indeed recognized; all the more so, for the facial lines of the Marquis are quite remarkable."

"But the form did seem to move. . . ."

"So it seemed—but it was not the form, but rather the smoke which moved, lit up by the glow of the image."

"And the person who fell out of the chimney, he was responsible for the voice of the apparition?"

"So it was."

"But he could not possibly have heard the questions clearly."

"He had no need to. You will recall, most gracious Prince, that I strictly forbade any of you from posing questions to the spirit yourselves. We had arranged beforehand what I would ask him, and what he would answer; and in order to avoid any mistakes, I allowed for pauses which he was to count off by the beats of the clock."

"You ordered the innkeeper to carefully extinguish all fires in the house; this was doubtless . . ."

"In order not to put my man in the chimney in danger of being asphyxiated, because all of the chimneys in the house are connected with one another, and I was not at all sure of your suite."

"But how did it happen," asked Lord Seymour, "that your spirit was there neither earlier nor later than you required?"

"My spirit was in the room a good while before I summoned him; but as long as the alcohol was burning, he was invisible. When I had finished my conjuring formulas, I let the vessel in which the alcohol was burning fall shut; the room was totally darkened, and only then did the figure on the wall become visible, although it had been reflected there for a long time."

"But at the very moment that the spirit appeared, we all felt an electric shock. How did you effect that?"

"You discovered the machine under the altar. You also saw that I stood upon a silken carpet. I had you stand around me in a crescent, and hold each other's hands; when the time came, I had one of you take my by the hair. The crucifix was the conductor, and you felt the shock when I touched it with my hand."

"You ordered us, the Count of *** and myself," said Lord Seymour, "to hold two daggers in a cross over your head for as long as the conjuring should last. To what purpose?"

"To no other purpose than to keep you two, whom I trusted the least, busy throughout the entire act. You will recall that I told you to keep them a certain distance above my head; since you had to concentrate upon keeping this distance, you were prevented from looking in any direction I did not want to have you look. At that point I had not yet seen my worst enemy."

"I confess," said Lord Seymour, "that everything was carefully arranged—but why did we have to be undressed?"

"Merely to make the action more exciting, and to tense your imaginations with the extraordinary."

"The second apparition did not let your spirit speak," the prince noted. "What were we to have learned from him?"

"Nearly the same that you later heard. It was not without design that I asked Your Highness whether you had told me everything that the deceased had said, and whether you had not made further inquiry on this account in his fatherland; this I found necessary in order not to run counter to facts which the testimony of my spirit might have contradicted. I inquired on account of youthful sins, whether the deceased had lived blamelessly, and I based my invention upon the answer."

"You have," the prince began, after a lengthy pause, "shed light upon all these matters to my satisfaction. But one point remains, upon which I demand clarification from you."

"If it is within my powers, and . . ."

"No conditions! The justice in whose hands you now find yourself will not ask so modestly. Who was the stranger before whom you fell to your kness? What do you know of him? And what is his connection to the second apparition?"

"Most gracious Prince . . ."

"When you looked him in the eyes, you screamed and fell at his feet. Why? What did that signify?"

"This stranger, most gracious Prince . . ." He held his breath, became visibly restless, and totally at a loss, looked at each of us in succession.—"Yes, by God, most gracious Prince, this stranger is a horrible being."

"What do you know of him? What is his relationship to you?—Do not hope to hide the truth from us." —

"I would be wary of even trying to do that, for . . . who can swear to me that he is not among us at this very moment?"

"Where? Who?" we all exclaimed in unison, as we glanced around us, half in laughter, half terrified.—"It cannot be possible!"

"Oh, to this human being—or, whatever he may be—things are possible that are far less comprehensible."

"But who is he then? Where does he come from? Is he Armenian or Russian? What part of what he pretends to be, is the truth?"

"Nothing of what he appears to be. There are few government assemblies, persons, or nations of which he has not worn the mask. Who might he be? Where did he come from? Where is he going?— No one knows. I wish neither to affirm nor to deny that he was in Egypt for a long time, as many claim, and there received his secret wisdom from a pyramid. Among us, one knows him only by the name of The Unfathomable. For instance, how old would you guess him to be?"

"To judge by external appearance, he could hardly have passed his fortieth year."

"And how old do you think I am?"

"Not far from thirty."

"Quite right—and if I tell you that I was a boy of seventeen when my grandfather told me of this man of wonders, and that my grandfather had seen him when he was approximately the same age as I now am, in Famagusta—and he seemed then as old as he seems today?"

"That is absurd, inconceivable, exaggerated."

"Not a bit. Did these chains not bind me, I would introduce you to venerable persons whose honorable reputation would leave you no further doubts. There are persons, those who can be believed, who remember having seen him in different parts of the world at the same time. There is no dagger's blade that can scratch him, no poison that has any effect upon him, no fire that singes him, no ship that sinks with him on board. Time itself seems to have lost its powers over him, the years have not sapped his strength, and age has proven incapable of bleaching his hair. No one has ever seen him eat, there was never a woman who touched him, sleep never visits his eyes. Of all the hours of the day, there is but one known over which he is not master, and at this hour he has never been seen, nor carried out any earthly business."

"So?" said the prince. "And which hour is that?"

"The twelfth in the night. As soon as the clock strikes midnight, he is no longer among the living. Wherever he is at that moment, he must depart; whatever he is doing at that moment, he must break it off. This horrible stroke of the clock tears him from the arms of friendship, drags him even from the altar, and would summon him from a battle to the death. No one knows where he goes then, nor what he does there. No one dares ask him, far less to follow him, for the lines of his face draw together into such an ominous and frightful earnestness once the feared hour strikes, that one is bereft of the courage either to look him in the eye or to address him. A deep, deathly stillness suddenly brings the liveliest of discussions to an end, and everyone around him awaits his reappearance in diffident horror without so much as daring to move from the spot, or to open the door through which he has gone."

"But," one of us asked, "does one notice nothing out of the ordinary about him when he returns?"

"Nothing, except that he looks pale and fatigued, more or less like a person who has just withstood a painful operation, or has received some very terrible news. Some claim to have seen drops of blood on his shirt, but I shall offer no opinion on that subject."

"And has no one ever at least attempted to keep the hour secret from him, or to divert his attention so that he would have to overlook it?"

"It is said that he did overstep the hour but once. He was in a numerous company, it had grown quite late, and all of the clocks had been incorrectly set; the flames of the debate tore him along. As the said hour arrived, suddenly he fell utterly mute and became rigid; all his limbs became stiff in the position they had chanced to assume; his eyes froze open and still; his pulse beat no longer, and all devices applied failed to awaken him; he remained in this condition until the hour had passed. Then he revived, opened his eyes, and commenced speaking again at the very syllable where he had been interrupted. The general amazement betrayed to him what had occurred, whereupon he declared that one ought to count himself fortunate to have come off with a mere fright. But that evening he left forever the city where this happened. It is commonly believed that during this secret hour he holds communion with his genius. Some even think he is a corpse, to whom it is permitted to wander among the living twenty-three hours of the day; in the last hour, it is thought, his soul must return to the underworld, there to stand judgment. Many think he is the famed Appolonius of Tyana, others than he is John the Disciple, of whom it is said he would remain on earth until the Day of Judgment."

"Clearly," said the prince, "there can be no dearth of adventurous conjectures about such an extraordinary man. Everything you have told about him up to now is mere hearsay; and yet his behavior toward you, and yours toward him, seem to suggest a closer acquaintance. Is there not a special story behind all this, one in which you were yourself participant? Keep nothing from us."

The Sicilian looked at us perplexed, and remained silent.

"If this concerns a matter," the prince continued, "that you do not want commonly known, I assure you, on behalf of these two gentlemen, of our complete silence. But speak out honestly and candidly."

"If I dare hope," the man began after some time, "that you do not intend to use it in testimony against me, I shall tell you of a remarkable experience with this Armenian, one to which I was eyewitness, and which will leave you no further doubts concerning the hidden powers of this person. Yet, you must allow me to leave certain names unspoken."

"Can this condition not be dispensed with?"

"No, most gracious lord. There is a family involved which I have reason to protect."

"Let us hear the story," said the prince.

"It is now perhaps five years ago," the Sicilian began, "when I was in Naples, working my arts with rather good fortune, that I made the acquaintance of a certain Lorenzo de M**nte, a knight of the Order of St. Stephan, a young and wealthy knight from one of the first houses of the realm, who overwhelmed me with favors and seemed to have great respect for my secrets. He disclosed to me that the Marchese de M**nte, his father, was a zealous worshipper of the Kabbala, and would count himself fortunate to have one such, world-wise (as he liked to call me) under his roof. The venerable man lived in nearly complete seclusion from humanity on one of his estates on the sea, approximately seven miles from Naples, where he mourned the memory of his dear son who had been torn from him by a terrible fate. The knight let it be known that he and his family might well require one such as I in this very serious matter, indeed, in order to possibly obtain some insight by means of my secret sciences, whereas all natural devices had been exhaustively and fruitlessly attempted. He especially, he added significantly, might one day have reason to consider me the cause of his respite and his entire earthly fortunes. I could not dare to make closer inquiry, and that was all the explanation that I was given for the moment. The matter itself unfolded as I now relate.

"This Lorenzo was the younger son of the marchese, for which reason it was determined that he was to enter an order; the earthly possessions of the house were to be beqeathed to the older brother. Jeronymo, for this was how the older brother was called, had spent many years in travels abroad, and returned home, some seven years before the events I relate, to marry the only daughter of the neighboring barony of C***tti, a marriage upon which the two families had agreed since the birth of the children in order to unify the considerable wealth of their estates. Although the union was purely a work of parental convenience, and no one had asked after the hearts of the betrothed in the selection, they had given it their own silent approval. Jeronymo del M**nte and Antonie C***tti had been raised together, and the little coercion exerted upon the two children, such as was custom at that time, to consider themselves a pair, had let a tender rapport arise between the two from their younger years. This was made the more firm by the harmony of their characters, and matured into love in later years. A four-year absence had done more to increase the flames of love than cool them, and Jeronymo returned as true and affire into the arms of his bride as though he had never torn himself from them.

"The delights of reunion had not yet passed, and preparations for the wedding were underway at a lively pace, when the bridegroom . . . disappeared. He often spent entire evenings at a land house with a view out over the sea, and often went sailing there. It happened following one such evening, that he stayed out at sea an uncommonly long time. Messengers were sent for him, boats were sent out to him on the sea; no one claimed to have seen him. None of his servants were missed, so that it was not possible that any of them had accompanied him. Night drew on, and he did not appear. It became morning, midday, and evening again, and still no Jeronymo. There were already the most horrible conjectures when news arrived that an Algerian corsair had landed on the coast the previous day, and various inhabitants had been taken away prisoner. Two galleys were manned at once, lying at bay ready to sail; the old marchese boarded one of them himself, determined to save his son at the risk of his own life. On the third morning, they sighted the corsair and were sailing on the lee with advantage of the wind; they soon made up the distance and came so near that Lorenzo, who had boarded the first galley, believed to have seen a sign of his brother on the enemy's foredeck when, suddenly, a storm separated them once more. The damaged ships held out the storm with considerable effort, but the prize was gone, and they were forced to land on Malta. The anguish of the family was without bounds; inconsolable, the old marchese tore out his grey hairs, and there was concern for the life of the young baroness.

"Searches were carried on in vain for five years. Inquiries were made along the entirety of the barbarian coasts; immense sums were offered for the freedom of the young marchese; but no one appeared to claim them. The most likely conjecture was, finally, that the storm that had separated the ships had sunk that of the pirates, and that its entire crew and its passengers had drowned in the waves.

"As probable as this conjecture was, much was lacking for certainty, and there was nothing to justify giving up all hope that the lost one might not reappear. But, in the case that he did not return, the entire family expired with him, or the second brother would have to give up the ordination and step into the rights of the first-born. As daring as this step were, and as unjust, to cast the possibly still living brother from his rights, it was thought that one ought not risk the fate of an old and glorious family, which otherwise would surely die out, but for this distant possibility. Grief and age were bearing the old marchese closer to the grave; hopes sank with each new, thwarted attempt to find the lost brother; the old marchese saw the fall of his house, the which was only to be prevented by a small injustice, were he only to decide in favor of the younger brother at the expense of the older. In order to consummate his union with the barony of C***tti, merely one name needed to be altered; the purpose of the two families were then fulfilled, whether Baroness Antonie became wife to Lorenzo or Jeronymo. The mere possibility of the reappearance of the latter could not be weighed in consideration against a certain and pressing evil, the complete extinction of the family; the old marchese, who felt the approach of death the stronger with each day that passed, impatiently wished to die, free at least of this anxiety.

"The only one who delayed this decision, and who resisted it most stubbornly, was he who stood the gain the most—Lorenzo. Unmoved by the enticements of immeasurable wealth, insensitive even toward possession of the love of the worthy creature who would be delivered into his arms, he refused with the most magnanimous conscientiousness to take from a brother who might live still, and who could demand the return of his properties. 'Is not the fate of my dear Jeronymo,' he asserted, 'not terrible enough for being held prisoner for so long, that I should make it even more bitter by commiting an act of thievery? With what heart would I implore heaven for his return if his wife lies in my arms? How should I rush to greet him if, finally, a miracle brings him back to us? And, supposing that he has been taken from us forever, how could we better honor his memory than to leave the breach, which his death has torn in our circle, unfilled for eternity? How else, than if we all sacrifice all of our hopes upon his grave, and that, that was his, leave untouched like a thing sacred?'

"But the arguments invented by brotherly delicacy were incapable of reconciling the old marchese to the extinction of his family, which had flourished for centuries. All that Lorenzo obtained, was a two-year respite before he was to lead the bride of his brother to the altar. During this time, new searches were pursued intensively. Lorenzo himself undertook various journeys at sea, and underwent numerous perils; no effort, no cost was spared to find the lost brother again. But these two years, too, passed without result, just as had the previous ones."

"And the Baroness Antonie?" asked the prince. "You have told us nothing of her condition. Did she resign herself to her fate so calmly?"

"Antonie's condition was a most embittered struggle between duty and passion, between aversion and admiration. The selfless magnanimity of brotherly love moved her; she felt herself torn to honor the man whom she would never be able to love; torn by opposing feelings, her heart bled. But, her antipathy toward the knight seemed to grow in just that degree that his claims upon her respect increased. He suffered, knowing the anguish that deformed her youth. A tender compassion stepped, unnoticed, into the place of that indifference with which he had previously looked upon her; but this treasonous sensibility betrayed him, and a furious passion began to make the exercise of virtue, the which had permitted him to rise above every temptation, laborious for him. But even at the cost of his heart, he continued to obey the inclinations of his magnanimity: it was this alone that protected the unfortunate victim against the caprice of the family. But all of his efforts went amiss; each victory he carried over his passion showed him only to be the more worthy of her, and the magnanimity with which he rejected her served only to deprive her of any apology.

"This is how matters stood, when the knight convinced me to visit him on his estate. The warm recommendations of my patron had prepared me a reception beyond all my wishes. I must not forget to add here, that I had succeeded in making my name famous among the lodges there by means of a few remarkable operations, and this may have contributed to the confidence of the old marchese being the greater, increasing, thus, his expectations of me. Permit me not to tell you how far I went with him, and what ways I went; you may draw your conclusions as to the rest from the confessions I have already made. By using the mystical books in the very considerable library of the old marchese, I was soon able to speak to him in his own language, and to bring my system of the invisible world into agreement with his own opinions. In a short while, he believed everything I wanted him to believe, and would have sworn with as much confidence upon the copulation of philosophers with salamanders and sylphs as upon a book of the Bible. As he was highly religious, and his capacity for faith and been highly developed in this school, my own stories found access all the easier, so that in the end I had so bound and knitted him up with mysticisms, that he would credit nothing natural any longer. In short, I was the revered apostle of the house. The usual content of my lectures was the exaltation of human nature, and discourse with higher beings, my authority rested in the infallible Count of Gabalis. The young Baroness, who, since the loss of her beloved, lived more in the world of spirits than in the real one, being drawn with passionate interest toward matters of this sort by the fantastic flight of her fantasies, caught up my suggestions with astonishing ease; even the servants of the house looked for something to do in the room I happened to be speaking, in order to be able to catch a word or two, fractions of which they then strung together in their own ways.

"I had spent perhaps two months on the estate in this way when, one morning, the knight came into my room. Deep anguish in his face, his disposition devastated, he threw himself into a chair with all the signs of desperation.

"'Captain,' said he, 'it is over for me. I must go away. I cannot hold out here any longer.'

"'What is wrong with you, knight? What is it?'

"'Oh, this terrible passion!' whereupon he lifted himself from the chair and threw himself into my arms.—'I have fought her like a man—now I can no longer.'

"'But whose decision must it be, dearest friend, if not yours? Is not everything in your power? Father, family . . .'

"'Father! Family! What does that mean to me?—Do I want to take the hand of one coerced, or of one of free inclination?—Do I not have a rival, indeed?—Oh! And such a one? A rival who is perhaps among the dead? Oh, let me go, let me go. Were it to take me to the end of the world, I must find my brother.'

"'But how? After so many frustrated attempts, can you still hope . . . ?'

"'Hope! In *my* heart, hope has long been dead. But in *hers?*— what does it matter whether I hope?—Can I be happy as long as a shimmer of this hope still glows in the heart of Antonie?—Two words, friend, could end my torment—but in vain! My fate shall remain misfortune until eternity breaks its long silence and the graves bear testimony for us!'

"'Is it this certainty, then, that can make you happy?'

"'Happy? Oh, I despair of ever being happy again!—but uncertainty is the most horrible damnation!' (After falling silent for a time, he recovered and continued sadly.) 'I wish he could see me suffer!— Can this loyalty that makes the misfortune of a brother make him happy? Should the living languish on account of the dead who can no longer enjoy?—If he knew of my agony. . . .' (And here he began to cry bitterly, pressing his face to my chest.) 'Possibly, yes, just possibly, he would lead her into my arms himself!'

"'But should this wish, then, be so impossible to fulfill?'

"'Friend! What are you saying?'—He looked at me, terrified.

"'Far lesser occasions,' I continued, 'have entwined the deceased in the fate of the living. Ought the entire temporal fortune of a person— a brother . . .'

"'The entire temporal fortune! Oh, that is what I feel! How truly you said it! My entire happiness!'

"'And the respite of a mourning family ought not be the suitable reason to call upon the forces invisible for aid? Certainly! If any earthly matter can justify disturbing the quiet of the blessed, can justify making use of a power . . .'

"'For God's sake, friend!' he interrupted me, 'no more of this. Before, I confess it, I had entertained such thoughts—I seem to recall that I told you of it, but I have rejected it now. It is nefarious and disgusting!'"

"Now you see," continued the Sicilian, "where this is leading us. I made every effort to dismiss the reservations of the knight, and in the end I succeeded. It was decided that the spirit of the deceased was to be summoned, whereby I made the condition that I would need fourteen days to prepare myself, as I said. When this time had passed, and my machines were suitably erected, I took the opportunity of a frightful evening, when the family was assembled about me as usual, to solicit their acquiescence, or actually, to guide them, such that they would make this request of me themselves. I had the most difficult time with the young baronness, whose presence was, nevertheless, quite necessary; but here, the fantastic flights of her passion came to our aid, and perhaps even a weak shimmer of hope that he, supposed dead, might yet live, and not appear in answer to the summons. Mistrust in the matter itself, doubt in my arts, was the only obstacle I did *not* have to struggle with.

"As soon as the family consented, the third day was appointed for the work. Prayers, which had to be said through the day to midnight, fasting, vigilance and mystical instruction, combined with the use of a still unknown musical instrument that I had found quite useful in similar cases, were the preparations for the solemn act, so successfully according to wish, that the fanatic enthusiasm of my audience enflamed my own imagination, and considerably enhanced the illusion which I had to achieve on this occasion. The awaited hour finally arrived . . ."

"I have guessed," said the prince, "who it is that you will now present us with, but continue, continue . . ."

"No, most gracious lord; the conjuring proceeded quite according to plan."

"But where is the Armenian?"

"Have no fear," the Sicilian answered, "the Armenian will appear in good time.

"I will not describe the entire process of deceit, which would take me too far out of my way in any case. Suffice it to say that it fulfilled all my expectations. The old marchese, the young baronness, along with her mother, the knight, and some other relatives, were present. You may well believe, that in the long time that I spent at this house, there was no lack of opportunity to make the most precise inquiries as to everything concerning the deceased. Various paintings I had found of him permitted me to give the apparition the most deceiving similarity, and, as I permitted the spirit to speak only in signs, his voice was certain not to arouse any suspicion. The deceased himself appeared in the clothing of a barbarian slave, a deep wound in his neck. You will note," said the Sicilian, "that I departed from the usual conjectures here, which held that he had drowned in the waves, because I had cause to hope that just the unexpected in this turn of events would do not a little to increase the crediblity of the vision, as, on the contrary, there seemed nothing more dangerous to me than a certain approximation to the natural."

"I believe this to have been correctly judged," said the prince, turning toward us. "In a succession of extraordinary phenomena, it seems to me, that it is precisely the *more probable* that would be disruptive. The ease of understanding a discovery would only debase the means applied to obtain it; the ease of inventing it would even give rise to suspicion; for, why take the trouble with a spirit if one intends to learn no more from him than what could have been brought forth without him, with the aid merely of common sense? But the surprising novelty and the difficulty of discovery is here at once the guarantor of the miracle by which it is obtained—for, who would cast doubt on the supernatural in a phenomenon, if that which is achieved cannot be achieved by natural forces?—But I have interrupted you," added the prince. "Tell your story to the end."

"I asked the spirit," he continued, "whether there were nothing left in this world that he would call *his*, and whether he had left behind nothing dear to him? The spirit shook its head three times, and stretched one of his hands to the sky. Before he went away, he slipped a ring from his finger, and it was found on the floor after his disappearance. As the baroness looked more closely, she discovered it was her engagement ring."

"Her engagement ring!" exclaimed the astonished Prince. "Her engagement ring! But how did you manage that?"

"I. . . it was not the real one, most gracious Prince. I had it . . . it was only a copy! . . . ."

"A copy!" repeated the prince. "But to make a copy you need the original, and how did you obtain that, as surely the deceased had never removed it from his finger?"

"That is quite true," said the Sicilian. "It was a very simple gold ring with the name of the young baronness, I think . . . but you have brought me quite out of my train of throught. . . ."

"What happened then?" asked the prince in a quite dissatisfied and ambiguous manner.

"Now everyone was convinced that Jeronymo no longer lived. From this day on, the family made his death known publicly, and established official mourning for him. The circumstance with the ring permitted even Antonie no longer any doubts, and this lent the suit of the knight all the more force. But the strong impression, which the apparition had made upon her, caused in her a dangerous illness, which would have dashed the hopes of her lover forever. When she had recovered, she insisted upon taking the veil, from which only the most vehement arguments of her father confessor, in whom she placed limitless confidence, were able to dissuade her. Finally, the combined efforts of the man and the family overcame her anxiety at acceding to the marriage. The last day of mourning was to be the happy day, at which time the old marchese intended to make even more festive celebration by bequeathing all his earthly possessions to his heirs.

"The day arrived, and Lorenzo received his trembling bride at the altar. The sun set, and a magnificent meal awaited the joyous guests in the brightly lit wedding room, a raucous music accompanying the gaiety. The happy old marchese wanted the entire world to share in his happiness; all entrances to the palace were open, and everyone was welcome. Among this throng now . . . ."

Here the Sicilian stopped short, and a shiver of expectation stayed our breath.

"Among the throng," he continued, "was one, who sat next to me, a *Franciscan monk*, as immobile as a pillar, tall and thin of stature, his face ashen pale, his serious and sad gaze fixed upon the bridal pair. The joy everywhere, laughing on all faces, seemed to pass him by, his manner remained unchangeably the same, like a marble bust among living figures. The extraordinary about him, which, as he had surprised me in the middle of the fun, and stood out so crudely against everything else happening, worked the more deeply upon me, left an indelible impression upon my soul, so that on that account alone I was able to recognize, in the facial lines of the monk, the physiognomy of the *Russian* (for you now well understand that he and your *Armenian* are one and the same person), something which otherwise would have been preposterous. I attempted, persistently, to avoid the eyes of this horrible shape, but involuntarily I returned to them, and found them unchanged each time. I toasted to my neighbor, he to his; the same curiosity, the same astonishment spread to everyone at the table; the conversation remained hanging; a general, sudden stillness; it did not disturb the monk. The monk was immobile, always the same, still fixing a serious and sad look upon the bridal pair. One of them, however, was apart: the young baronness alone found her grief once again in the face of the stranger, and hung, with a quiet delight, upon the only one among the company who seemed to understand, to share her anguish. Gradually, the assembly thinned, midnight had passed, the music began to still, forlorn; the candles flickered more dimly, only single ones burned; the conversation became quiet, whispering ever more quiet—and it became desolate, and even more desolate in the darkly lit wedding hall; the monk stood, immobile, always the same, his still and sad gaze fixed upon the bridal pair.

"The tables were cleared, the guests went to and fro; the family gathered in a small circle together; the monk remained, uninvited, in this smaller circle. I do not know why it was that no one wanted to speak to him, but no one spoke to him. The close female acquaintances gathered around the bride, who kept her gaze on the reverend stranger, begging, imploring; the stranger failed to respond.

"The men assembled in the same way around the bridegroom—an expectant stillness—'That we are so happy to be among each other,' offered the venerable marchese finally, the only one who seemed not to have noticed the stranger among us, or at least not to be amazed by him. 'That we are so happy,' said he, 'and that my son Jeronymo should not be here!'—

"'Have you invited him, and he stayed away?' asked the monk. It was the first time that he had opened his mouth. We all looked at him in terror.

"'Oh, he has gone where one remains for eternity,'" said the marchese. 'Reverend sir, you misunderstand me. My son, Jeronymo, is dead.'"

"'Perhaps he only fears to show himself in such company,' continued the monk. 'Who knows what he might look like, your son, Jeronymo!—Let him hear the last voice he ever heard!—Ask your son, Lorenzo, to call him.'"

"'What is this?' everyone murmured. Lorenzo's color changed. I do not deny that my hair began to rise.

"Meanwhile the monk had stepped up to the table where the gifts were laid, where he took a full wine glass and put it to his lips. 'To the memory of our dear Jeronymo!' he called out. 'Those who loved the deceased, do as I do.'

"'Wherever you may have come from, reverend sir,' said the marchese, 'you have named one very dear to me. You are welcome here!—Come, friends!' (whereupon he turned to us, and had glasses passed around), 'do not let a stranger shame us!—To the memory of my son, Jeronymo.'

"'I believe never was health drunk in such bad spirits.

"'One glass is still full—why does my son Lorenzo refuse to join us in this joyous toast?'

"Trembling, Lorenzo took the glass from the hand of the Franciscan—trembling he brought it to his mouth—'To my beloved brother, Jeronymo,' he stammered, and again trembling, put the glass down.

"'That is the voice of my murderer,' cried out a horrible form, that suddenly appeared in our midst, its clothes dripping with blood, scarred with ghastly wounds.

"As to the rest, do not ask me," said the Sicilian, all the signs of dread in his face. 'I had lost consciousness from the moment that I looked at the apparition, as did everyone else who was present. When we came to ourselves again, Lorenzo was in the throes of death; the monk and the apparition had disappeared. The knight, twitching terribly, was brought to his bed; no one but the priest and the venerable marchese, who would follow him to the grave in but a few weeks, was with the dying man. His confessions lie buried in the heart of his father, and no living person has ever learned them.

"Not long after these events, it happened that a well had to be cleaned out in the rear courtyard of the mansion, hidden by wild bushes, unused for many years; when the debris was cleared away, a skeleton was discovered. The house where this came to pass no longer stands;

the family line del M**nte is now extinct, and, in a cloister not far from Salerno, you may be shown the grave of Antonie.

"Now you see," continued the Sicilian, as he saw that we were still all mute and startled, and no one wanted to speak: "You now see whereupon my acquaintance with this Russian officer, or this Armenian, is founded. Now you may judge whether I have had cause to fear this creature, that has thrust itelf in my path twice in such a horrible manner."

"Answer just one more question," said the prince, standing up. "Have you spoken honestly about everything concerning the knight in your story?"

"I know not otherwise," said the Sicilian.

"So, you really thought he was a righteous man?"

"That I did, by God, I did," the other replied.

"Even when he gave you the ring?"

"What?—He gave me no ring.—I never said that he gave me a ring."

"Good," said the prince, as he pulled on the bell-rope, preparing to leave. "And the spirit of the Marquis of Lanoy?" he asked, coming back again, "the one the Russian had follow your spirit yesterday—do you think this one was a real and genuine spirit?"

"I can believe nothing else," answered the other.

"Come," the prince said to us. The prison guard came into the room. "We are finished," the prince told him. "You, my man," turning to the Sicilian, "you shall hear from me again."

When we were alone once more, I told the prince, "The question that you last put to the Sicilian, I would would like to ask you myself. Do you think that this second spirit was real and genuine?"

"I? No, no longer."

"No longer? Then, you once did?"

"I do not deny that I permitted myself to be caught up in the story for a moment, and that I saw something more than trickery in it."

"And I," I said, "I would like to see the one who, under these circumstances, could refrain from similar conjectures. But what reason do you now have to change your opinion? After what we have just learned about this Armenian, one's faith in his wondrous powers should have been strengthened, rather than diminished."

"What a good-for-nothing told us about him?" the prince interrupted in all seriousness. "For, hopefully, you no longer doubt that that is what he is. . .?"

"No," said I, "but should his testimony therefore . . ."

"The testimony of a good-for-nothing—assuming I had no other reason for casting doubt upon it—cannot hold its own against truth and common sense. Does a person who cheated and deceived me on numerous occasions, who has made deception his trade, deserve to be heard in a matter where the most sincere love of truth itself must purify itself first, in order to deserve credence? Does such a person, who likely never told the truth for its own sake even once, does one such deserve to be believed when he presents himself as a witness against human reason and the eternal order of nature? That would be as if I wanted to give a certified scoundrel full authority to lay suit against innocence itself, never sullied, never in ill repute."

"But what reason should he have to give a man such glorious testimony, one whom he has many reasons to hate, or at least to fear?"

"Even if I do not understand these reasons, should he, therefore, have fewer of them? Do I know in whose pay he lied to me? I confess, that I am still unable to see through the entire fabric of his deception; but he did the cause, on behalf of which he acted, a very infamous service by disclosing himself to be a fraud—and perhaps something far worse."

"The business with the ring does obviously seem to be somewhat suspicious."

"*It is more than that*," said the prince, "it is decisive. This ring— permit me to assume for the moment that the events he related in fact occurred—he received this ring from the murderer, and he must have been certain at that moment that it was the murderer; for who but the murderer could have taken the ring from the deceased, who certainly never took the ring from his own finger? Throughout the telling of it, he tried to convince us that he had himself been deceived by the knight, and that he believed he was deceiving the knight. What was the point of this subterfuge, unless he knew how much he had given away when he admitted his complicity with the murderer? His entire story is obviously nothing but a succession of inventions to string the few truths he saw fit to tell us alongside each other. And, for this I am to hesitate more, to accuse a good-for-nothing of an eleventh lie, after I have just caught him with ten on his lips, rather than permit the basic order of nature to be broken, an order in which I have yet to find even a single disharmony?"

"To that, I have no answer for you," I said, "but the apparition we saw yesterday remains, nevertheless, no less inexplicable."

"Inexplicable to me also," added the prince, "although I am sorely tempted to find a key to it."

"How?" I asked.

"Do you not recall that the second form, as soon as it had entered, went straight to the altar, took the crucifix into its hand, and stepped onto the carpet?"

"That is how it seemed to me. Yes."

388   FRIEDRICH SCHILLER: *Poet of Freedom*

"And the crucifix, as the Sicilian told us, was a conductor. Thus, you see that the form hurried to make itself electric. The stab which Lord Seymour attempted with the dagger could not but remain ineffective, because the electric shock paralyzed his arm."

"As for the dagger, that seems to be correct. But what about the bullet that the Sicilian shot at the form, and which we heard rolling slowly upon the altar?"

"Do you know for certain that it was the bullet shot from the pistol that we heard?—I do not even want to mention, that the marionette or the person who represented the spirit might have been quite well protected against bullets and daggers.—But reflect just a little upon *who* it was who loaded the pistols."

"That's right!" I said, and a light seemed to be shed upon the whole matter.—"The *Russian* loaded them. But this happened right in front of our eyes; how could he have deceived us then?"

"And why should he not have been able to do so? If you were already suspicious enough of this person, that you had thought it necessary to observe him? Did you investigate the bullet before he put it into the barrel of the gun, a bullet that could have been made of mercury or merely painted clay? Did you watch carefully to see if he really put the bullet into the barrel, and not merely let it fall into his hand? What convinces you—assuming that he really loaded the pistols—that he took the *loaded* ones with him into the other pavilion, and did not substitute another pair, which might have happened so easily, that no one would come upon the idea of observing him, and just as we were quite busy undressing? And is it not possible, that the apparition, at just the moment that it was hidden from us by the smoke of the gunpowder, let another bullet, at hand for an emergency, fall upon the altar? Which of each of these possibilities is the more impossible?"

"You are right. But the striking similarity of the form to your deceased friend—I also saw him with you quite often, and I immediately recognized him in the apparition."

"I too—I can only say that the deception was driven to the extreme. But, if this Sicilian, after just a few glances at my snuff-box, was able to give even his own portrait a vague similarity, that deceived you and me, why should the Russian not be able to accomplish this all the more? He had free use of the snuff-box during the entire meal, and had the advantage of being and remaining unobserved; and besides, it was to him that I confided who the portrait on the box was meant to be. And, add to that—as the Sicilian noted—that the most characteristic features of the marquis were just in such facial lines, that can be crudely imitated. What, then, is supposed to remain inexplicable in the entire apparition?"

"But the content of his words? The information about your friend?"

"What? Did not the Sicilian tell us that he had put a similar story together out of the little that he had asked of me? Does this not prove how natural it was to fall precisely upon this invention? Besides, the answers of the spirit sounded so oracularly dark, that he ran no danger of a contradiction. Assume that the creature of the Sicilian, the spirit, was both sagacious and discreet, only a little instructed concerning the circumstances—how far could this fraud *not* have been carried?"

"But consider, most gracious Prince, how vast the preparations of the Armenian for such a deception must have been! How much time he would have needed! How much time to paint a human head so true to that of another as we are here assuming! How much time to instruct the spirit so well as to be insured against any crude mishap! How much attention to the small details, those that either aid in the deception, or those necessary ones, which, because they could have been disruptive, must be taken care of! And now, consider that the Russian was not absent for more than half an hour. Could even the most indispensable precautions have been arranged in a mere half hour?— Truly, most gracious Prince, not even a theater writer, at a loss for the three unities of his Aristotle, would have encumbered such an act with so much action, nor would he have presumed his theater-play to enjoy such credibility."

"What? You think it simply impossible that all of these preparations could have been made in half an hour?"

"In fact," said I, "I think it as good as impossible."

"I do not understand this manner of speaking. Does it contradict all the laws of time, space, and physical effect, that such a skilled mind, as this Armenian so incontestably is, with aid of his creatures, possibly just as skilled, in the dead of night, observed by no one, equipped with all accessories such as a man of this trade would never be without, that such a person, favored by such circumstances, could bring about so much in so little time? Is it absolutely inconceivable, is it absurd, to believe that he, with aid of a few words, orders, or signals, that he could have his associates put far-reaching operations into motion with little effort?—And, may we permit something else, a pure impossibility, to be posed against the eternal laws of nature? Do you rather want to believe in a miracle than admit an improbability, rather overthrow the forces of nature than allow of an artificial and less probable combination of these forces?"

"Even if the matter at hand does not permit us to draw such bold conclusions, you must, nevertheless, grant me that it far surpasses our comprehension."

"I am almost tempted to argue even that point with you," said the prince with mischievous gaiety. "What if it turned out, my dear count, that he was working for this Armenian, not merely during and after that certain half hour, but over the entire evening and night? Reflect upon this: the Sicilian took nearly three full hours for his preparations."

"But that was the Sicilian, most gracious Prince!"

"And how do you intend to demonstrate, that the Sicilian did not have as much a hand in the second apparition as in the first?"

"What, most gracious Prince!"

"How do you intend to demonstrate that he was not the Armenian's chief accessory—in short, that both of them were conspiring with one another?"

"That would be hard to prove," I put in, rather amazed.

"Not as difficult as you think, dear Count. How? Are we supposed to assume, that it was merely accidental that these two persons met, at the same time, in the same place, for the purpose of such a strange, such an intricate assault upon one and the same person; that between their mutual operations, there was only accidentally such striking harmony, such collusion of action, well thought out, each for his own part; that the acts of one played into the hands of the other? Let us suppose, that one charlatan made use of the cruder device merely in order to provide the backdrop for the finer. Suppose the one was sent in advance, in order to determine the degree of credulity the other would have to take account for in my case; to spy out the accesses to my confidence; in order, by means of this attempt, which might have failed, without doing any damage to the rest of his plan, to familiarize himself with his subject; in short, in order to tune his instruments for the play. Suppose he did this, so that, while challenging my alertness on one side by design, keeping me vigilant on that side, he would lull me to sleep on the other side, the one more important to him. Suppose he made certain inquiries, and then desired, that the charlatan be made to account for that in order to divert attention from the real track?"

"What do you mean?"

"Let us assume, that he bribed one of my people, in order to obtain certain secret information—perhaps even documents—which would serve his purpose. My corporal is missing. What dissuades me from believing, that the Armenian had a hand in his disappearance? I might have found out the trick by accident; a letter might have been found, a servant might have gossiped. His entire reputation were ruined, had I found out the source of his omniscience. So, he pushes the charlatan into the game, necessarily, to make this or that assault upon me. He does not neglect to let me know of the existence and intentions of this person. Therefore, whatever I might discover, my suspicions were to fall upon no one but the charlatan; and the Sicilian would then take the credit for inquiries serving the Armenian's purpose. The charlatan, the Sicilian, was the puppet he let me play with, while he himself, unobserved, beyond suspicion, wove me into a net of invisible threads."

"Very good! But how are these, his supposed intentions, then supposed to rhyme with the fact, that he himself then helps to undo the deception, and discloses the secrets of his art to profane eyes? Must he not have feared, that once a deception were discovered to be so thoroughly groundless, a deception driven to such a high proximity to truth as the Sicilian's indeed was, that this would only weaken your credulity, and thus make his future plans all the more difficult?"

"What were the secrets he disclosed to me? None of them reliable enough for him to have wanted to exercise them on me. He lost nothing by their profanation—to the contrary, how much had he gained, were this apparent triumph over deception and charlatanry such as to make me secure and confident, if, by that means, he had succeeded in diverting my vigilance in the contrary direction, fixing my undetermined, wavering suspicion upon objects the farthest removed from the actual site of the assault? He might then have expected, that sooner or later I would seek the key to his magic in the very art of charlatanry itself, either acting from my own suspicions, or upon some external motivation. What could he have done better, than to have placed the two examples side by side, at once giving me the standard to judge by, and, by establishing artificial limits to my judgment, either increasing my estimation of him, or confusing my judgment of his own part in the plot. How many conjectures he cut short by this device! How many possible explanations upon which I might have fallen, he refuted in advance!"

"At least he worked considerably against himself by sharpening the eyes of the one he wanted to deceive, weakening your belief in miraculous powers by disclosing such an artificial deception. You are, most gracious Prince, yourself the best refutation of his plan, if, indeed, he ever had one."

"He may have been mistaken about me—but his judgment was not one bit less sharp on that account. How could he foresee that I would precisely remember that which could become the key to the magic? Was it his plan, that the creature he made use of should expose himself the *way* he did? Do we know that this Sicilian did not, in fact, overstep his authority by far?—With the ring, he certainly did.—And yet, it was especially this single moment which decided my suspicion against this person. How easily a finely honed plan can be disfigured by such a crude instrument. Surely, it was not his intention that the charlatan should trumpet his glory to us in the tone of a market-crier, that he should tell us a story so easily refuted upon the slightest reflection—what sheer audacity to claim, that his miracle-worker must cease discourse with men at the strike of twelve midnight! Did we not see him ourselves in our midst at this time?"

"Quite right!" I said, "He must have forgotten that!"

"It is in the character of this sort of people, that they exaggerate, and by going too far degrade that which a more modest and moderate fraud might have achieved to perfection."

"Nonetheless, I can still not convince myself, most gracious Prince, that this entire matter was only contrived. How could it be? The Sicilian's horror, the twitching, the fainting, the entire miserable condition of this person which made us feel pity—all of this, only a role he learned? I admit, that, though theatric charlatanry were driven ever so far, the art of the actor may yet be unable to have perfect command of the instruments of his own life."

"As far as that is concerned, friend—I saw *Richard III* by Garrick— and, were we sufficiently cool and unpreoccupied to be impartial observers? Were we really able to judge this person's condition, so overwhelmed by our own state of affairs, as we were? Besides, the decisive crisis, even that of a deception, is such an important event for the deceiver himself, that the *expectation* may easily lead to symptoms as violent *in him* as *surprise* produces in those *deceived*. If, in addition, you take into account the unexpected appearance of the officers of the court . . ."

"And they, most gracious Prince—how good that you remind me of it—would he have dared to have revealed such a dangerous plan before the eyes of justice, or to have put the loyalty of his own creature to such a test?—To what end?"

"Let him worry about that; he knows his own people. Do we know what secret crimes guarantee him the silence of these people?—You have heard what office he holds in Venice.—And, even if you account this to the other fables—how much would it have cost him to help this poor fellow who has no accuser outside of himself?

(In fact, developments confirmed the suspicions of the prince fully. When we inquired after the prisoner a few days later, we obtained the answer that he had disappeared.)

And you ask to what end? How else would he have been able to obtain such an improbable and infamous confession, the most essential point in the entire affair, than through such violence? Who else, but such a despondent person, one who has nothing to lose, could make up his mind to betray such humiliating information about himself? Under which other circumstances would we have believed him?"

"Everything granted, most gracious Prince," I finally said. "Both apparitions were frauds. The Sicilian was put up to telling us a fable, one taught him by his principal, both to a single purpose, mutually agreed upon, mutually aimed at this effect, and all of this is supposed to explain each strange and chance occurrence that has caused us no slight perplexity in this entire affair. That prophecy on St. Mark's Square, the first miracle opening the way of all the rest, this remains, nonetheless, unclarified; and, what does the key to the solution of everything else help us, if we must despair of the solution to this one?"

"Turn it the other way around, dear Count," he answered. "What do all the miracles prove, if I can prove that just one of them is a fraud? That prophecy—this I confess—that is still beyond my powers of comprehension. If *it* stood *alone*, had the Armenian ended his game with *that*, just as he began it—I confess, I do not know how far that could have taken me. But, in this *low* company of frauds laid bare, even this prophecy seems just a little suspicious to me. . . ."

"Granted, most gracious Prince! But it still remains incompehensible, and I demand of all our philosophers that they give us satisfactory information on this point."

"But should it really be so inexplicable?" the prince continued, after reflecting for a moment. "I am far from claiming the title of philosopher for myself, and yet I could be tempted to find a natural solution even to this mystery, or rather, to disrobe it of all appearances of the extraordinary."

"If you could do *that*, my Prince, then," as I made a face of incredulity, "*you* would then be the only miracle I would believe in."

"And, as proof," he continued, "of how little we are justified in taking refuge in supernatural forces, I shall indicate two different paths, over which we might get to the bottom of this affair, without doing violence to nature."

"Two paths at once! You are making me extremely curious, indeed."

"You read the more detailed news of the illness of my deceased cousin with me. He suffered an attack of cold fever, and fell into an apoplectic fit, of which he died. The extraordinary aspect of this death, I confess, occasioned me to ask the judgment of some physicians, and what I learned put me on the track of this work of magic. The illness of the deceased, one of the rarest and most horrible, has this most characteristic symptom, that during the fever, the patient falls into a deep sleep, from which he cannot be awakened, and, in the second part of the cycle, paroxysm kills the patient apoplectically. As these paroxysms repeat themselves with strict order and timing, the physician who has once made his judgment on the species of the illness is then perfectly capable of determining the hour of death. As is known, however, the third paroxysm of a three-day fever occurs on the fifth day of the illness—and a letter from ***, where my cousin died, takes just that long to reach Venice. If we assume, that our Armenian had some vigilant correspondents among the entourage of the deceased, that he indeed had a vital interest in obtaining information from there, that he had intentions upon me, for which this information aids him in promoting in me a belief in the miraculous and the appearance of supernatural forces—you then have a quite natural explanation for a prophecy which seems so inconceivable to you. Enough. You see, here, the possibility of a third person having given me word of a death which, at the very moment he was reporting it, occurred forty miles away."

"In fact, prince, you are combining things here which, taken singly, sound quite natural indeed, but can only be so combined by something itself no better than magic."

"Why? You shy away from the magical *less* than from that we are *seeking*, the uncommon? Once we concede, that the Armenian has an important plan, one in which I am either the target, or in which I am to be used as a means—and, must we not concede this, whatever judgment we make of him as a person?—then nothing is unnatural, nothing forced, which leads him to his goal over the shortest possible path. What shorter path to assure oneself of a person than the credentials of a miracle worker? Who would resist a man before whom the spirits themselves kneel? But, I grant you that my conjecture is fabricated; I admit I am not satisfied with it myself. I do not even insist upon its veracity, because I do not think it worth the trouble to make use of a fabricated and circumspect scheme, where mere accident suffices."

"What?" I interrupted. "It was supposedly a mere accident that . . ."

"Scarcely anything more!" the prince continued. "The Armenian knew what danger my cousin was in. He met us on St. Mark's Square. The opportunity invited him to dare a prophecy which, if it failed to hit its mark, was merely a lost word or two—but, if it struck true, might have the most important consequences. Success crowned the attempt—and only then might he have considered using the gifts of chance for an interconnected plan.—Time will clarify this secret, or perhaps not—but, believe me, friend" as he lay his hand on mine and assumed a very serious demeanor, "a person, before whom higher forces kneel, will have no need of charlatanry, or he will despise it."

Thus ended a conversation, which I have set down here in its entirety, because it demonstrates the difficulties to be surmounted with the prince, and because, as I hope, it will purify his memory of the reproach, that he fell blindly and unreflecting into the snare laid for him by a shocking deviltry. Not everyone—continues the Count of O**—who, in the very moment that I am writing this, perhaps looking down upon his weaknesses in mockery, and in the proud darkness of his own, untested reason, thinking himself justified in breaking the staff of damnation over him, I say that not everyone, I fear, would have withstood even this first test in such a manly fashion. If now, even after this fortunate preparation, you see him fall nonetheless; if you now find the black stroke, against whose ever so distant approach his good genius warned, coming to fruition in him, you will ridicule his folly less than you will be astounded at the immensity of the villainy that slew such well-defended reason.

Wordly considerations play no part in my testimony, for he, who should thank me for it, is no longer. His horrible fate is ended; his soul has long since cleansed itself upon the throne of Truth, the same before which mine too will long have stood, by the time the world reads this, but—forgive me the tears that fall, involuntarily, to the memory of my most dear friend—I write this down as a tribute to justice: he was a noble person, and would certainly have become an ornament to the throne by which he let himself be so deluded as to want to ascend it in crime.

BOOK TWO

Not long afterwards—the memoirs of the Count of O** continue—I began to notice significant changes in the prince's state of mind. Up to this time, the prince had avoided any strict examination of his faith, and was quite content to rarify the crude and sensuous notions of religion he had been raised with, by means of the better ideas he subsequently assimilated, but without investigating the foundations of his beliefs. He once confessed to me, that the objects of religion were always like an enchanted castle to him, one into which a person did not step without shuddering, and one was better off passing it by in respectful resignation, without running the risk of losing one's way in its labyrinths. A contrary inclination, however, drew him irresistibly to make investigations in this connection.

A bigoted, slavish education was the source of his fear; it was this, that had impressed his tender mind with images of horror, from which he was never able to free himself for as long as he lived. Religious melancholy was a hereditary disease in his family; the education given him and his brothers conformed to this disposition, thus making of them either fanatics or hypocrites. To suffocate all vitality in the child in stupefying strictures, was the most assured way to guarantee utmost tranquility to the royal parents.

Our Prince was haunted by dark and ghastly shapes his entire youth; joy was banned even from his play. All of his ideas about religion had something horrible about them; things dreadful and brutal were the first to take command of his lively imagination, and they made the most lasting impression. His God was an image of horror, a vengeful being; his worship, a slavish cowering, a blind submission, that suffocated all power and boldness. Religion dampened all of his childish, youthful inclinations, the which were given to explode all the more violently, because he was robust of body, and in flourishing health;

religion was at odds with everything his youthful heart yearned for; he never knew it as a blessing, rather only as a hostage to his passions. Gradually, a quiet rancor against religion caught fire in his heart, making for the most bizarre mixture of respectful faith and blind fear in his heart and mind—a repugnance for the Lord, before whom he felt an equal degree of horror and awe.

No wonder he grasped at the first opportunity to escape such a heavy yoke—but he fled like a bonded slave from his cruel master, carrying the feeling of his slavery with him into freedom. For this reason, because he had not renounced the beliefs of his youth in calm reflection, because he had not waited until his more mature reason was able to ease itself free, because he had fled like a refugee, while his Lord's rights to possession still held—for these reasons, after ever so many distractions, he always needed to return to Him. He had fled *with* his chains, and for that reason, was necessarily easy prey to every villain who discovered them. The course of this story will show, in case the reader has not already guessed as much, that such a villain did, indeed, appear.

The confessions of the Sicilian had left impressions in his heart with more significance than their object was worth, and the slight victory, that his reason had carried over this paltry deception, had remarkably increased his confidence in his powers. The ease, with which he was able to discover the fraud, seemed to have surprised even him. Truth and falsehood had not yet separated themselves so precisely in his mind for him not to confuse the pillars of the one with the pillars of the other rather often. Thus, the blow delivered to his belief in miracles shook the entire edifice of his religious faith. Its effect upon him was like that of an inexperienced person, cheated in friendship or love, because he had chosen badly, who now loses faith in those very emotions, because he had once taken fortuitous impressions for real and true qualities. A deception discovered made him suspicious of the truth as well, because the truth had, unfortunately, been proven with the same bad reasons.

He enjoyed this supposed triumph all the more, the greater the pressure, from which it seemed to liberate him, became. A skepticism blossoming in him from this point onward had no mercy, even toward things most worthy of reverence.

A confluence of events served to keep and fortify in him this state of mind. The solitude, in which he had previously lived, now ceased, and made way for a life of diversions of all kinds. His royal rank had been discovered. Hospitalities to be requited, the etiquette in conformity with his station, tore him, unnoticed, into the turmoil of the great outside world. His rank, as well as his personal qualities, opened the doors to the most spirited society in Venice; he soon found himself in contact with the most brilliant minds of the republic, scholars as well as statesmen. This forced him to expand the narrow horizons in which his mind had previously enclosed itself. He began to perceive the narrowness of his thinking, and to feel the need for higher cultivation of the mind. His old fashioned way of thinking, otherwise so advantageous, stood in disadvantageous contrast to the current mode of society, and his awkwardness in the most commonplace things often made him appear ridiculous—he feared nothing so much as appearing ridiculous. The unfavorable prejudice that clung to his fatherland seemed a challenge to him to refute it in his own person. There was, in addition, that peculiarity of his character, that he would shrink away from attentions paid him, if he thought they were due to his rank, and not to his person. He felt this humiliation especially in the company of persons of brilliant mind, persons who had triumphed over their origins of birth by virtue of their own personal merits. To see oneself set apart in such a society as a prince, shamed him deeply each time, because he unfortunately believed himself excluded from any competition, merely on account of his name. All of this together convinced him of the necessity to give his mind that cultivation that he had previously neglected, in order to catch up with that humorous and thinking world that he was so far behind.

To that end, he chose the most modern treatises, and devoted himself to the study of them with that seriousness with which he was accustomed to deal with everything he understood. But, the evil hand at work in the selection of these treatises permitted him, unfortunately, to fall upon only those, through which neither his reason nor his heart were very much improved. And here, too, his customary bent prevailed, drawing him with irresistible enticement toward all those things that are not to be understood. His attention and memory were devoted exclusively to such matters; his reason and heart remained void, while those compartments of his brain were filled with confused notions. The dazzling style of one author enraptured his imagination, while the subtlety of another entangled his reason. It was easy for each of them to subjugate his mind, a prey for those who forced themselves upon him with a measure of audacity.

One such treatise, passionately pursued for more than a year, had hardly enriched him with beneficent conceptions, but had, indeed, filled his head with doubts, the which, considering his determined character, inevitably soon found their unhappy way into his heart. In short—he had immersed himself in this labyrinth like a fanatic, with scores of articles of faith, and left it a skeptic, finally even a confirmed free-thinker.

Among the circles into which he had been drawn, there was a certain closed society, called the *Bucentauro*, which promoted the most

unrestrained license of opinions, as well as morals, under the guise of
a noble, reasonable freedom of thought. As there were a number of
priests among the members, and it even boasted the names of a number
of cardinals at its head, the prince was all the more moved to have
himself introduced into the society. Certain dangerous truths of reason,
he thought, could nowhere be better provided for, than in the hands
of such persons who were sworn to moderation by their positions, and
who had the advantage of having heard and tested the opposing party.
Here the prince forgot that *libertinism* of the mind and morals among
persons in these positions is all the more pronounced, because here
it finds no reins, and is not deterred by any such aura of sanctity as
often blinds eyes more profane. And this was the case in the *Bucen-
tauro*, most of whose members reviled not only their positions, but
humanity itself, through their execrable philosophy and corresponding
moral practices.

The society had its secret degrees, and, in the prince's favor, I
would like to believe, that he was never considered worthy of the
innermost shrine. He who entered this society, had to renounce his
rank, his nation, his religion, in brief, all conventional signs of differ-
entiation, and accept a certain position of universal equality for as long
as he lived. The selection of members was very strict, indeed, since
only exceptional qualities of mind opened the way. The society boasted
the finest manners, and the most cultivated taste, and it actually enjoyed
this reputation in all of Venice. This, as well as the appearance of
equality that prevailed within, drew the prince in irresistibly. A witty
company, the best of the scholarly and political worlds, all in all,
gathered together, as if at its center, concealed the danger of this
connection from him for a long time. When the spirit of the institution
gradually became clear to him, through the mask, or because the various
members grew tired of trying to conceal it from him any longer, the
retreat became just as dangerous, and false shame, as well as concern
for his own safety, forced him to hide his inner discontent.

Yet, mere familiarity with this sort of people and their habits,
although he did not imitate them, was sufficient for him to lose the
pure and beautiful innocence of his character and tastes. His under-
standing, with so little of firm knowledge, was unable to free itself from
the sophisms it had become entangled in, without outside aid, and
imperceptibly, this ghastly corrosive had gnawed everything away—
nearly everything, upon which his morality should have rested. He
shunned the natural pillars of happiness as sophisms which abandoned
him in decisive moments, and thereby he found himself compelled to
grasp at the first, arbitrary best thing tossed at him.

Perhaps the hand of a friend might have succeeded in holding him
back from this abyss in time—but, aside from my having become

acquainted with the inner nature of the *Bucentauro* only after the damage was done, an urgent matter had called me away from Venice at the very beginning of this period. Lord Seymour, too, a dear acquaintance of the prince, whose cool head resisted deception of every sort, and could have served him as a secure pillar without fail, left us at this time to return to his fatherland. Those, in whose hands I left the prince, were upstanding, but inexperienced, and in their religion, extremely limited people, who lacked both insight into the nature of evil, as well as authority with the prince. Against the insidious sophisms of the prince, they had nothing but the claims to authority of a blind and untested faith, and this was capable merely of irritating or amusing the prince; he overlooked them all too easily, and his superior mind soon coerced these defenders of the good into silence. The others, who subsequently commanded his confidence, did their utmost to sink him ever more deeply. When I returned to Venice the following year, how different everything was!

The influence of this new philosophy manifest itself in the prince's life. The more he was visibly successful in Venice, and won new friends, the more he began to lose his old friends. He pleased me less as each day passed; we saw each other seldom, and he was simply there less and less. The stream of the great world had caught him up. His doorstep was never empty when he was at home. One amusement gave way to another, one party to another, one rapture to another. He was the handsome one everyone vied for, the king and idol of all. As difficult as he once thought the grand competition in the previous style of his narrow life, now, to his amazement, he found it quite easy. Everyone was so obliging to him, every word from his lips so fitting, and, when he was silent, it bereaved the whole party. And this good fortune, which pursued him wherever he went, this universal success, made out of him something *more* than he actually was, because it gave him courage and confidence in himself. The elevated opinion he thereby obtained of his own worth, gave him faith in the exaggerated, and nearly idolatrous, worship bestowed upon him, the which, without this increased, and to a certain extent justified self-estimation, would necessarily have been reason for him to become suspicious. But now, this general acclamation was merely the enforcement of that which his own self-satisfied pride quietly told him—a tribute, as he believed, due him by rights. He would inevitably have escaped this noose, had one but granted him a few hours of calm, in which to compare his own worth with the images in the lovely mirror held up to him. His existence, however, was a continuous condition of drunkenness, a dizzying frenzy. The higher on the pedestal he was placed, the more effort he required to maintain this height; even in sleep, he had no rest. His weakness was seen through, and the passions set affire in him well assessed.

Soon, his honest companions had to do penance for their master's having become a great mind. The serious emotions and revered truths, to which his heart had once warmly clung, now became the objects of his derision. He sought now to avenge himself, for the pressures under which his delusions had so long held him, upon the truths of religion; but there was far more bitterness than joyous courage in his frivolity, for a voice in his heart, one not to be shunned, did battle against the giddiness in his mind. He began to change; he became moody. That most beautiful distinction of his character, his modesty, disappeared: flatterers had poisoned his excellent heart. The considerate delicacy of his manners, which had once led his companions to forget he was their master, now often gave way to an imperious, dominating tone, causing all the more pain, for being founded not upon the objective difference of birth, a matter easily consoled, but rather upon the insulting insinuation of his own elevated personality. Since, at home, he often aired considerations, which high society would never have permitted him to entertain, his own people seldom saw him but in a dark mood, complaining and unhappy, while he enlivened circles of strangers with a forced joviality. We suffered sympathetically, too, as he trod this path, but he did not hear the weak voice of friendship amidst the tumult into which he had been thrown, and was still too happy at this time to understand it.

At the very beginning of this period, urgent affairs required my presence at the court of my sovereign, affairs which I could not set aside, even for the most passionate interests of friendship. An invisible hand, which I discovered only much later, had discovered ways to throw my affairs there into disorder, and to spread rumors about me, which I had to refute by means of my personal presence. It was difficult for me to leave the prince, but the parting was all the easier for him. The bonds, which had bound me to him, had been loosened for some time. His fate, however, had awakened my entire sympathy; I therefore made Baron of F*** promise to stay in contact with me, providing information by letter, and he held to his promise most conscientiously. From this time onward, I was no longer an eyewitness to these events. You, my reader, will permit me to introduce Baron of F*** in my place, and to fill this gap with excerpts from his letters. Although the manner of presentation of my friend F*** is not always my own, I did not, nevertheless, want to change anything in his letters, and the reader will discover the truth in them with little effort.

Baron of F*** to Count of O***

First Letter

May 17**

Thank you, most honored friend, for permitting me to continue our friendship, which was my best joy when you were here, in your absence. There is no one here—you know that—with whom I would dare to discuss certain things; whatever you may have to say against it, I hate these people. Since the prince has become one of them, and since you have been torn away from us, I am forsaken in the middle of this populous city. Z*** takes it more lightly, and the beauties of Venice know how to make him forget the offences he must bear with me at home. And, what would he have to grieve about? He sees and requires no more of the prince than a master whom he finds every-where—but I! You know how I take the welfare and tribulations of our Prince to heart, and how much I have cause to do so. It is now sixteen years that I have been with him, that many years that I live only for him. I entered his service as a nine-year-old boy, and nothing has separated me from him since. I grew up under his eyes; long ac-quaintance groomed me to him; I have experienced all his adventures with him, adventures great and small. I thrive in his happiness. Until this unhappy year, I only saw my friend, my older brother, in him; I lived under his gaze as if in brilliant sunshine—nothing clouded my happiness. And all of this has now turned to rubble in this unsavory Venice!

Everything has changed since you left us. The prince of **d** arrived last week with a considerable entourage, giving our circle new, tumultuous life. Since he and our prince are so closely related, and are now on rather good footing with each other, they hardly leave each other's sides during his stay here, which—I have heard—ought to last until the festivities of the Ascension. They have made a good start; the prince has not caught his breath for ten days. The prince of **d** started off right at the top, and he always likes to do that, because he departs again quickly; the worst of it, though, is that he has also infected our prince, and, as he could not very well keep himself away, and given the special relationship between the two families, the prince felt he was called upon to contest the position of his own family. Besides, our departure from Venice is approaching in a few weeks, which will spare him the trouble of continuing this extravagant expense for much longer.

It is said that the prince of **d** is here on the business of the *** Order, whereby he flatters himself that he is playing an important role. Be assured that he immediately took possession of all of the prince's acquaintances. He was, especially, introduced into the *Bucentauro* with great pomp, since he always loved to play the witty mind and strong spirit, and insists upon being called Prince Philosopher by all of his correspondents, of which he has many in all parts of the world. I do not know whether you have had the good fortune to see him. A very promising exterior, busy eyes, the demeanor of a connoisseur of the arts, ostentatious readings, and acquired (permit me this word) nature; a princely condenscension to human feelings, attended by an heroic confidence in himself, and an eloquence sure to talk everyone else down. Who might fail to pay homage to a royal highness with such brilliant qualities? How the quiet, inarticulate, and basic values of our Prince will fare beside this towering excellence, the denouement must tell.

Much has changed in our accommodations over time. We have moved into a magnificent new house across from the new procurator, because our quarters in the Moor Hotel were too small for the prince. Our entourage has been enlarged by twelve people, pages, Moors, and the like—nowadays, just everything has to be large. You complained about the expenses when you were here—you should see us now!

Otherwise, our circumstances are the same as before, except that the prince, no longer held in check by your presence, speaks to us in monosyllables and, if that is possible, has become even frostier in his behavior. We see him little, except when he is dressing or going to bed. On the pretext that we speak French badly, and Italian not at all, he excludes us from his sundry company, which, as far as I am concerned, is no great insult; but I believe, that the truth of the matter is that he is ashamed of us—and that hurts me; we have done nothing to deserve that.

Of our own people (since you do want to know all the details), he uses the services, almost exclusively, of Biondello, who, as you know, was taken into his service after the disappearance of our corporal, and who has become quite indispensable to the prince now, in this new life style. The man knows everything in Venice, and he knows how to make use of everything. It is as if he had a thousand eyes, and could set a thousand hands into motion. He says he manages this with the help of the gondoliers. He has made him exceedingly useful to the prince for that reason, able to introduce the prince to all the new faces that turn up in this society; and the secret messages that he gives the prince have always proven to be correct. He speaks and writes Italian and French excellently, for which reason he has been promoted to the prince's secretary. But I must tell you about a trace of unselfish loyalty, indeed so seldom found in a person of this sort. Recently, a famous merchant from Rimini asked for an audience with the prince. The object of this visit was a peculiar complaint about Biondello. The procurator, his former employer, who is said to have been an eccentric priest, had lived in irreconcilable hostility to his relatives, who survived him. He placed his confidence exclusively in Biondello, to whom he was accustomed to reveal all of his secrets; the latter was made to swear to him upon his death bed, that he would keep these secrets and never use them to the advantage of his relatives; he was to be rewarded with a considerable legacy for his silence. As his last will and testament was opened, and his papers examined, there were considerable gaps and matters of confusion, about which only Biondello would have been able to provide clarification. The latter stubbornly denied, that he knew anything, left the sizeable reward to the heirs, and kept his secrets. The relatives made him immense offers, but all to no avail; finally, to escape their persistence, because they threatened to take him before the court, he entered the service of the prince. Now the main heir, the merchant, came to the prince, making even larger offers than those already made, in case Biondello should change his mind. But even the intercession of the prince was in vain. Biondello confessed to him, indeed, that he had been entrusted with such secrets, and did not deny that the deceased had probably gone too far in his hate against his family. "But," he added, "he was my good master and my benefactor, and he died trusting in my honesty. I was the only friend he left behind in this world—so much the less can I cheat him of his last wish." He let it be known at once, that this deference to the memory to the deceased would not do him much credit. Is that not fine and noble? You may well believe, that the prince did not insist very much upon making him waver in his laudable sentiment. This loyalty, so rare, that he showed his deceased master, won him the boundless confidence of the living one.

Live in good fortune, my dearest friend. How I yearn for the quiet life in which you found us here, and for which you so pleasantly re-compensed us! I fear my good times in Venice are past, and profit enough if the same is not true for the prince. The circumstances of his life are now such that he could not be happy for very long, or sixteen years of experience must be deceiving me. Live long.

*Baron of F*** to Count of O****

Second Letter

May 18

I never thought our stay in Venice could lead to anything good! He has saved a person's life, and I am reconciled with him. The prince was recently carried home from the *Bucentauro* last night, two servants, among them Biondello, accompanying him. I do not know how it happened, but the litter, that had been hastily put together, broke, and the prince found it necessary to go the rest of the way on foot.

Biondello went in advance; the route led through some dark, remote alleys, and since it was not long before dawn, the lamps were burning dimly, or had already gone out. They walked for perhaps a quarter hour when Biondello discovered he had lost the way. The similarity of the bridges deceived him, and instead of crossing at St. Mark's, they found themselves in the Sesture of Castello. It was in one of the remote alleys, with not a soul in sight; they turned around to orient themselves in the main street. They proceeded only a few steps, when a blood-curdling cry issued from an alley. The prince, unarmed as he was, ran to the area from which the cry had come. Three fearsome men were intent upon striking down a fourth, who, together with another man accompanying him, was but weakly able to defend himself. The prince appeared just in time to thwart the fatal stab. His own, and the calls of his servants so startled the assassins, who had expected no such surprise in such a remote spot, that they took flight after a few light blows from their man. Half unconscious and exhausted from the fighting, the wounded man fell into the arms of the prince; his attendant revealed, that the man the prince had just rescued was the Marquis Civitella, the nephew of the cardinal of A***i. As the Marquis had lost a great deal of blood, Biondello hurried, as fast as he could, to fetch a physician, and the prince took care to have him taken to his uncle's palace nearby, and accompanied him there himself. He then left quietly, without letting on who he was.

He was, nevertheless, betrayed by a servant, who recognized Biondello. The cardinal appeared at once the following moring, and proved to be an old acquaintance from the *Bucentauro*. The visit lasted one hour; the cardinal was deeply moved when he came out, with tears in his eyes, and the prince, too, was touched. The same evening, a visit was made to the patient, for whom the physician assured the best recovery. The coat, in which he had wrapped himself, had made the blows unsure, and had broken their force. Since this incident, not a day has passed upon which the prince did not either visit the house of the cardinal, or receive him in his own, and a strong friendship has begun to form between the prince and the house of the cardinal.

The cardinal is a venerable man of 60 years, majestic in appearance, full of cheer and health. He is thought to be one of the most wealthy prelates in the entire republic. He administers his immeasurable wealth youthfully and, while reasonably frugal, foregoes no worldly pleasure. This nephew is his sole heir, but it is said, that he is not always on the best of terms with his uncle. As little as the old man is an enemy of pleasure, the behavior of the nephew is said to exhaust even the greatest of tolerance. His libertine principles and unrestrainable manner of life, unfortunately supported by everything conducive to depravity and the titillation of sensuality, make him the terror of fathers, and the curse of husbands; it is even claimed, that he called this last attack upon himself, because of an intrigue he entered with the wife of the ambassador of ***, not to speak of other affairs, from which only the reputation and money of the cardinal were able to save him, and with considerable effort.

Except for this, the latter would be the most envied man in all Italy, becauses he possesses all that one could possibly wish for in life. With this one scourge of the family, fortune has revoked these gifts, and makes the enjoyment of his wealth loathsome, because of the omnipresent fear, that it will find no heir.

I have all of this information from Biondello. The prince has a real treasure in this man. He makes himself more indispensable as each day passes, and each day we discover some new talent in him. The prince became quite excited recently, and could not sleep. The night light was extinguished, and no amount of ringing could wake the chamber servant, who was pursuing his love affair outside of the house. The prince decided to get up and call one of his people. He had not gone far, when he heard pleasant music coming from a distance. He followed the sound as though entranced, and found Biondello in his room playing a flute, his companions sitting around him. The prince did not want to trust his eyes and ears, and ordered him to continue playing. With astounding ease, Biondello then extemporated upon the same melting adagio, with the most pleasing variations and all the detail of a virtuoso. The prince, who is an expert, as you know, claims he might well be heard in the best orchestra.

"I must let this person go," the prince said the next morning. "I am not capable of rewarding him as he deserves." Biondello, who overheard these words, came forward. "Most gracious Prince," he said, "if you do that, you shall deprive me of my best reward."

"You are destined for something better than to serve," said the Prince. "I must not stand in the way of your fortunes."

"Please, do not impose any other fortune upon me, most gracious Prince, than that I have chosen."

"And to neglect such talent!—No! I cannot permit it."

"Then permit me, most gracious Prince, to exercise it for the time being in your presence."

Preparations were immediately made to just that purpose. Biondello was given a room next to that of his master, where he lulled him to sleep and woke him up again, also to music. The prince wanted to double his salary, but he forbade it, declaring that the prince should deposit this intended gratuity as a capital, which he might need to draw upon shortly. The prince now expected, that he would soon come to ask for something, and whatever that might be, it was guaranteed in advance. Live well, dearest friend. I await news from K***n impatiently.

Baron of F*** to Count of O***

Third Letter

June 4

The Marquis Civitella, now fully recovered from his wounds, was introduced to the prince last week by his uncle, and has been following him ever since, like a shadow.

It turns out, that Biondello did not tell me the truth about this marquis, or at least, that he greatly exaggerated it. He is very charming in appearance, and irresistible in demeanor. It is impossible to dislike him; I was won over on the first glance. Imagine the most fascinating figure, carried with dignity and grace, a face full of spirit and soul, an open, inviting manner, an ingratiating tone of voice, the most fluent eloquence, the most flourishing youth, combined with all of the graces of the finest education. He has not a touch of that disdainful pride, that melancholy stiffness, which we find so unbearable among the rest of the *nobili*. Everything about him breathes youthful joy, benevolence, warmth of feeling. His excesses must have been greatly exaggerated, for never have I seen a more perfect, more handsome picture of health. If he is really so bad as Biondello tells me, he must be a siren no one can resist.

He was very open towards me from the outset. He confessed to me, in the most pleasant sincerity, that he does not stand in the best repute with his uncle, and that he might well have deserved it so. He is, however, seriously resolved to improve, and for that, he thanks the prince alone. At the same time, he hopes, through the prince, to be reconciled with his uncle, because the prince has influence over the cardinal in everything. Until now, he only lacked a friend and leader, and in the prince, he hopes to gain both.

The prince, for his own part, presumes upon all the rights of such a leader, and treats him with the vigilance and strictness of a mentor. But, just this relationship also gives the marquis certain rights with respect to the prince, rights he well knows how to make good on. He never leaves his side; he is at every party where the prince takes part; up to now, he has been considered still too young —his good fortune!— for the *Bucentauro*. Everywhere he goes with the prince, he entices him away with his fine manners, with which he knows how to keep the prince employed, and to attract him to him. No one, they said, has been able to tame him, and the prince would earn an inscription of thanks, were he to succeed in this herculean labor. I fear, however, that the leaf may turn, and the mentor may well heed the lessons of his pupil, a turn toward which circumstances seem to be heading already.

The prince of **d** has left, much to everyone's relief, my Prince not excepted. What I predicted, my dear O***, in fact happened. Between such contrary characters, with collisions so inevitable, it was impossible that they could stay on friendly terms for long. The prince of **d** had not been in Venice very long, when a regrettable schism arose in the intellectual world, putting our Prince in danger of losing the half of his former admirers. Wherever he let himself be seen, he found this rival, who possessed just that dose of cunning and self-serving vanity, to capitalize upon each small advantage that the prince allowed him. Since he commanded all kinds of petty tricks, the use of which the prince disdained, out of a feeling of noble dignity, it could not but turn out, that he had all the simpletons on his side, boasting of a game well worthy of his sort.*

The most reasonable thing were, not to have allowed oneself to be drawn into any competition with an opponent of this sort, and, a few months earlier, this had certainly been the game the prince had played. But now, he was already pulled too far into the stream, to be able to reach the other bank of the river once more so quickly. These vanities, if due only to circumstances, had taken on a certain value for him, and, even though he really despised them, his pride did not permit him to renounce them at a point, when his surrender were understood less as a voluntary decision, than a confession of defeat. The wretched back-and-forth of cutting diatribes from both sides came into it as well, and the spirit of rivalry, that excited his followers, had also taken its grip upon him. Thus, to defend his conquests, to maintain himself upon this slippery pedestal, to which the opinion of the world has assigned him, he believed it necessary to seize every opportunity to shine and engage, and this, in turn, was only to be achieved at a princely expense; perpetual parties and revelries, expensive concerts, presents, and gambling for high stakes. And, since this strange frenzy soon spread into the entourage and servants of both sides, who, as you know, are prone to be even more vigilant of the articles of honor than their masters, he had come to aid of the good will of his people with his generosity. A very long chain of misery, all of which the inevitable consequence of one single, rather unforgivable weakness, which the prince permitted to creep over him in such an unfortunate moment.

---

*Remark by Count of O***: As for the harsh judgment, which the Baron of F*** passes here, and in certain parts of the first letter, upon a certain Prince, everyone, who has had the good fortune of becoming better acquainted with this Prince, will agree with me, that it is exaggerated, and attribute it to the prejudiced mind of this young person.

We are, indeed, now rid of the rival, but what he has corrupted will not so easily be set aright. The prince's purse is exhausted; that which he saved in years of wise economy is gone. We must hurry to get out of Venice, if he is not to plunge into debt, against which he has been most cautiously on guard until now. Our departure is now firmly decided, just as soon as fresh money arrives.

Oh, might all of this expense have been incurred, if only my Prince could have had just a little joy in it! But he has never been less happy than now! He feels, that he is not what he once was—he is looking for himself, plunging into new diversions to escape the consequences of the old ones. One new acquaintance follows upon the other, pulling him ever deeper in. I do not see how this will turn out. We must get away—there is no other salvation here—we must leave Venice. But, dearest friend, still no word from you! How am I to explain this long, stubborn silence?

Baron of F*** to Count of O***

Fourth Letter

June 12

Thank you, dear friend, for the sign of your remembrance, that the young B***hl brought with him. But you speak of letters, ones I am supposed to have received? I have received no letters from you, not one line. What a detour they must have taken! In the future, dearest O***, if you honor me with letters, send them through Trient, to the address of my Prince.

We have finally had to take the step, dearest friend, that we had fortunately avoided up to now.—The money draft has not arrived, for the first time it has not arrived, just when we are most urgently in need, necessitating that we have recourse to a usurer, as the prince likes to pay for the secret somewhat dearer. The worst of this unpleasant impasse is, that it delays our departure.

It came to an exchange of words between myself and the prince on this occasion. The entire business went through Biondello's hands, and the Jew was there before I suspected anything. It weighed upon my heart to see the prince brought to such extremities, and awoke all my memories of the past, all horrors for the future, so that I may have looked somewhat sullen and moody when the usurer was finally gone. The prince, the more irritable after the event, in any case, walked up and down in his room in ill temper; the rolls still lay on the table, and I stood by the window, busily counting the window panes in the Palace of Procurators; after a long silence, he finally burst out.

"F***!" he began, "I cannot stand gloomy faces about me."

I said nothing.

"Why do you not answer me?—Do I not see that your heart is aching to vent your annoyance? And I want you to speak. You might otherwise believe the things of wisdom you keep from me are wonderful."

"If I am gloomy, most gracious Prince," said I, "it is only because I do not see you cheerful."

"I know," he went on, "that you no longer like me—and this for quite some time—that you disapprove of everything I do, that. . .what does the Count of O*** write?"

"The Count of O*** has written nothing to me."

"Nothing? Why do you deny it? You have poured out your hearts to each other, you and the Count! I know it quite well. But admit it to me. I do not want to interfere in your secrets."

"The Count of O***," I told him, "has still to answer the first of three letters I sent him."

"I have done the wrong thing," he continued, "have I not?"—As if playing a part.—"I should not have done it."

"I understand that this was *necessary*."

"I ought not to have gotten myself into this necessity?"

I said nothing.

"Of course! In my wishes, I ought never have dared beyond that, and beyond that, to become an old man just as I became a man! Just because I cast aside the sad uniformity of my former life, and looked around to see whether a source of pleasure might not open for me somewhere else, because I . . ."

"If it was an experiment, most gracious Prince, then I have nothing more to say—all the experience this has given you will not have been bought too dearly at three times the price. I admit, that it hurt me that the opinion of the world was to have decided the question of *how* you were to be happy."

"Good for you, that you can despise it, the opinion of the world! But I am its creature, and must be its slave. Everything to do with us princes is opinion. Opinion is our nurse and teacher in childhood, our legislator and lover in our adult years, our crutch in old age. If you take from us that which we have from opinion, then the very worst of the other classes of people are better off than we are; he whose fate helps him obtain a philosophy, receives consolation from this philosophy for his fate. A prince who ridicules opinion nullifies himself, like a priest who denies the existence of God."

"And, nevertheless, most gracious Prince . . ."

"I know what you want to say. I *am* able to trespass the circle that my birth circumscribed around me, but am I able to eradicate all of the illusory notions from my memory, which education and early habits implanted, and which a hundred thousand imbeciles among you have entrenched ever more firmly? Everyone actually were preferably what he is, but our existence is simply to *appear happy*. Because we cannot *be* that in your way, are we, therefore, not to be happy at all? If we can no longer draw joy immediately from its pure source, ought we not deceive ourselves with artificial enjoyment, ought we not be permitted to receive a slight recompense even from the hand that stole from us?"

"You would otherwise find it in your own heart."

"And if I no longer find it there? Oh, why are we talking about this? What does it matter if I have taken refuge in this tumult of the senses, to benumb an inner voice, which is the misfortune of my life, to silence this carping reason, which sears to and fro in my brain, like the swing of a sickle, and, with each new sweep, cuts off even another twig of my happiness?"

"My best Prince!"—He had stood up, and was pacing around the room in extraordinary excitement.

"If everything in front of me and behind me is swallowed up in an abyss, if the past lies behind me in dismal monotony, like a kingdom of fossils, if the future offers me nothing, if I see the entire compass of my existence closed into the narrow space of the present, who will blame me for taking this meagre gift of time, this moment, into my arms, passionate and insatiable, like a friend whom I see for the last time?"

"Most gracious Prince, you used to believe in a more lasting good . . ."

"Oh, make the clouds stop for me, and I will throw my glowing arms around them. What joy should I derive from making beings, who will be gone tomorrow (just as I will) happy?—Is not everything around me, in fact, in flight? Everything is pushing and shoving its neighbor away, hurrying to drink a drop of existence, and depart again, parched with thirst. Now, in the very moment that I take joy in my own power, a life coming to be is designated to be my destruction. Show me something that lasts, and I will be virtuous.

The Philosophical Dialogue*

"What was it that destroyed the beneficence, that was once the joy and guiding principle of your life? To plant seeds for the future, to serve a higher, eternal order. . . ."

*Translator's note: The *Philosophical Dialogue* was expanded by Schiller in editions that followed the original publication in the *Thalia*, Vol. 6, 1789, and continues as part of the fourth letter to the end of the letter. The form of the dialogue here is the most extensive version Schiller published.

"Serve! Certainly, to serve, as certainly as the most insignificant stone in the wall serves the symmetry of the palace that rests on it! But, also as a being to be consulted, one with whom to share joy? A delightful, kindhearted delusion of mankind! You want to devote your powers to it, this higher, eternal order? Are you, then, really capable of refusing to do so? What you are and what you have, you are and have only for its sake. If you have given that which you were capable of giving, that which you alone were capable of giving for its sake, that does not make you more than you are, and this higher, eternal order carries out the judgment. But who, then, is this Nature, this Order, against which I complain? No matter. If, like the Greek Saturn, it devoured its own children, it were still only itself, if it merely survived the second just past! An immeasurable tree in immense space. The wisdom and virtues of entire generations run like sap in its veins; centuries, and the nations drum their noise in them, fall like withered blossoms, like dried up leaves from its branches. Can you demand of it that which it does not itself possess? Can you, a ripple that the wind blows over the surface of the sea—can you demand, that a trace of your existence be secured on that surface?"

"World history already refutes this cheerless proposition. The names of Lycurgus, Socrates, Aristides have survived their works."

"And the useful man, who ploughs the earth—what is his name? Do you mourn a rewarding goddess, who is not *just*? You live in history, like mummies in balsam, to pass away with their history somewhat later."

"And this impulse to eternally lasting existence? Can or *may* its necessity vanish? Can there be something in the power, which corresponds to nothing in the effect?"

"Oh, this effect is the most important of all. Does not the jet of water in the cascade rise up with a force that could hurl it through an infinite space? But in the very moment of its rising, gravity pulls on it, air presses upon it, driving it, sooner or later, in a higher or lower arc, back to mother earth. To fall so late, it must rise with this mighty power—an elastic power needs also belong to it, like the human impulse to immortality, if the phenomenon of mankind is to make way for the necessity pressing upon it. I will concede the context, dearest friend, if you can prove to me, that this impulse to immortality in men is not consumed as completely with the temporal purpose of existence as the sensual drives are. Of course, pride seduces us to use power, which we have only *for*, only *through* necessity, against necessity itself, but would we even have this pride if there were no advantage to be drawn from it? Were this impulse a reasonable existent, it had as much joy in our philosophies as the general in the mischievousness of the young warriors, who promise to be heroes in battles someday."

"The thought only serves the moment? The whole is dead, and the parts live? The purpose is so common, the means so noble?"

"We ought never to have said *purpose* at all. To adopt your manner of expressing it, I derive this concept from the moral world, because here we are accustomed to call the consequences of an action its purpose. In the soul, indeed, purpose has priority over means; but, when their internal effects go over into the world outside, this order is reversed, and means are related to purpose like cause to effect. In this latter sense, I use the expression figuratively, but this need not have a disruptive influence on our present inquiry. If, in place of means and purpose, you say cause and effect, where is the difference between common and noble? What could be noble in the cause, other than that it brings about its effect? Noble and common merely denote the relationship in which an object stands *to a certain principle in our soul*— Thus, it is a concept applicable only within, not outside of our soul. You see, however, that you already assume as proven that which we first want to determine in our conclusions. Why else do you say of thoughts, in opposition to movement, that they are noble, than for the reason, that you assume the thinking-being to be the center point, to which you subordinate the succession of things, in advance? If you adopt my manner of thought, this ordering of rank disappears, the thought is effect, and the cause is movement, and a part of necessity, like the pulse-beat that accompanies it."

"You will never prevail with this paradoxical, unnatural doctrine. Nearly everywhere, with our own understanding, we are able to follow the purpose of physical Nature up into humanity. Where do we see this order reversed even once, subjecting the purpose of humanity to the physical world? And, how do you intend to unify this external determination with the impulse to happiness, which directs all of its efforts inwards, against external determinations?"

"Let us try it. To be brief, I must once again use your language. Let us assume, that moral phenomena are as necessary as light and sound; there must, then, exist entities so constituted as to be appropriate to this special function, just as ether and air must be constituted just so, and not differently, in order to be capable of that number of vibrations, which gives us the impression of color and sound. There must, therefore, exist entities which set themselves in motion, because the moral phenomena are based upon freedom; that, therefore, which, the original form supplies for air, ether, minerals, and plants, must here be maintained by an *inner* principle, with respect to which the inducement to movement, or the moving forces of this entity, are approximately in the relation of the moving forces of plants to the invariable type of their constitution. Just as it directs the merely organic

entity by means of an unchangeable mechanism, so it moves the think-
ing and perceiving entity by means of pleasure and pain."

"Quite right."

"We see, therefore, that the moral world is losing its previous
ordering, and is even coming into apparent strife with itself. The motive
forces establish a new center in each moral entity, a state within a
state, as though the general purpose had been completely forgotten.
All activities must incline themselves toward this center with a com-
pulsion like that exerted in the physical world by gravity. This entity
is constituted in itself, a true and real whole, and is formed to its center
just as the planet Earth became a sphere by means of gravity, and
continued to exist as a sphere. Up to this point, it seems to have
forgotten itself altogether.

"But we have heard, that this entity only exists to bring forth that
moral phenomenon, of which it was in need; the freedom of this entity,
or its ability to move itself, must, therefore, have been subordinated
to the purpose to which freedom determined it. If freedom wanted,
therefore, to also remain master of the effects it has caused, it would
have to become master of the principle according to which the moral
entity moves itself. So, what else could it do than to couple *its* purpose
with this entity to the principle by which it is governed, or, in other
words, to make its purposive activity the necessary condition of its
happiness?"

"That I understand."

"If the moral entity fulfills the conditions of its happiness, it thereby
enters once again into the plan of Nature from which it seemed to have
been separated by this distinctive plan, just as the planetary bodies
are made capable of describing eclipses by the fall of their parts toward
the center. Thus, through pain and pleasure, the moral entity expe-
riences only the relationship of this present condition to the condition
of his highest perfection, which, in turn, is identical with the purpose
of Nature. The organic entity neither has, nor requires, such a path-
finder, for it can neither approach closer to, nor separate itself from
the condition of its perfection by itself. The latter has the advantage
over the former in the enjoyment of its perfection, i.e., happiness,
but, with the former, there is also the warning, or if it deviates, the
suffering. If an elastic sphere were conscious of its condition, the pres-
sure of a finger pressing upon it would be so painful, that it would
return to the most beautiful roundness with a feeling of sensual plea-
sure."

"Its elastic force serves in the place of that feeling."

"But there is as little similarity between the rapid movement that
we call fire and the sensation of burning, or between the cubic form
of salt and the bitter taste of it, as between the feeling that we call

happiness, and the condition of our inner perfection that accompanies it, or the purpose of Nature which it serves. Both, we might say, are bound together by a coexistence just as arbitrary as the laurel wreath's relationship to the fact of a victory, or a scar from a burn to a dishonorable deed."

"So it seems."

"Thus, men need not be cognizant of the purpose which Nature carries out through them. Were a person to know of no other principle than that by which he governs himself in his own small world, were he to lay down the conditions of this, his small world, in pleasurable, self-serving delusions, as the law of Grand Nature—then by the act of serving his own structure, with him are Nature's purposes served.

"And can anything be more excellent than that all parts of the great whole promote the purposes of Nature only in remaining true to their own, that they must not *want* to contribute to the harmony, but that they *must* do so? This thought is so beautiful, so enticing, that one is moved by it alone to . . ."

". . .to grant it a mind, you want to say? Because the self- serving person would like to bring his species everything good and beautiful, because he were so pleased to have a creator in the family? If you give a crystal the ability to have ideas, its greatest world plan will be crystallization, and its godhead will be the most beautiful form of crystal. And must it not be so? If every individual sphere of water did not hold, so true and firm, to its center, an ocean would never have moved."

"But do you know, most gracious Prince, that, up to now, you have merely argued against yourself? If it is true, as you say, that man can not deviate from his center point, from where do you take your own arrogance to determine the course of Nature? How could you ever undertake to want to fix the rules according to which Nature acts?"

"Nothing less. I do not determine anything, I merely disregard what men have confused with Nature, what they have taken from their own breasts and pompously dressed her up with. What preceded me, and what will come after me, I see as two black, impenetrable curtains, hanging down on both sides of human life, curtains no mortal has yet lifted. Many hundreds of generations have stood with torchs in front of them, guessing and guessing what might be behind. Many see their own shadow, the forms of their passions, moving enlarged upon the curtain of the future, wincing and shuddering at their own images. Poets, philosophers and founders of states have painted the curtains with their dreams, pleasant or gloomy, depending upon whether the heavens over their heads were the more cloudy or clear; and, from a distance, the perspective is deceiving. Many charlatans exploit this general curiosity, and set fantasies into amazement with strange mummery. A deep stillness reigns behind this curtain, and no one who ever

gets behind it ever comes back to give answers—all that one hears is
a hollow echo of the question, as if one had called into a tomb. Everyone
must go behind this curtain, and they grasp it in their hands, shud-
dering, uncertain as to who might be standing behind it to receive
them; *quid sit id, quod tantum morituri vident.* Of course, there are
non-believers who claim that this curtain only drives men crazy, and
that no one has ever observed anything, because there is nothing behind
the curtain to be seen; but, to convince them, they are sent behind
the curtain in all haste."

"It was always a rash conclusion, if they had no better reason than
that they had seen nothing."

"Now you see, my friend, I am quite content not to want to look
behind this curtain—and it will certainly be wisest if I give up any
curiosity about it. But, by inscribing myself inside this untransgressable
circle, enclosing my entire being in the confines of the present, this
tiny bit, which vain thoughts of conquest had almost brought me to
ignore, becomes even more important to me. That which you call the
purpose of my existence concerns me no longer. I can not escape this
purpose, I cannot lend it assistance, but I know, and firmly believe,
that I must and do fulfill such a purpose. But the means which Nature
has chosen to fulfill its purpose with me, are all the more sacred to
me—it is everything that is mine, namely, my morality, my happiness.
Whatever else there is, I will never learn of it. I am like a messenger
carrying a sealed letter to its destination. The messenger is completely
indifferent to what the letter may contain—he has nothing to earn,
but the wage of a messenger."

"Oh, how impoverished you leave me standing here!"

"But where did we go wrong?" the prince exclaimed, grinning, as
he looked to the tables where the roles lay. "Then again, not so far
wrong!" he added, "for, perhaps, you will find me once again in this
new way of life. I, too, was unable to wean myself so quickly from
illusory wealth, unable to quickly divorce the pillars of my morality
and happiness from the sweet dreams, with which everything I had
lived for until then was so inextricably entwined. I yearned for the
thoughtlessness which makes the existence of most people around me
so tolerable. I welcomed everything that carried me away from myself.
I confess it to you: *I wanted to sink*, to destroy this source of my
suffering with the power to sink away."

I could not bear to have the discussion broken off at this point.

"Most gracious prince," I began again, "do I understand you right?
The final purpose of mankind is not within mankind, but outside? Man
only exists for the sake of his consequences?"

"Let us avoid this expression, for it leads us astray. Let us say,
that man exists because the causes of his existence were existent, and

because his effects exist, or, which amounts to the same thing, because the causes, which preceded him, had to have an effect, and the effects, which he brings forth, must have a cause."

"So, if I want to attribute a value to man, I can only do so according to the weight of the number and importance of the effects of which he is the cause."

"According to the *number* of the effects. We see, that an effect is important, merely on account of the larger number of effects it draws in its wake. Man has no other value than his effects."

"Therefore, that person, in whom the reason for numerous effects is contained, would be the more excellent person?"

"Incontestably."

"How can that be? Is there, then, no longer any difference between good and bad? Moral beauty is lost?"

"On that account, I have no fear. Were it so, I had immediately conceded that I have lost this contest with you. The feeling of the moral difference is something far more important to me than my reason— only then did I begin to believe in the latter, because I found it to be coherent with that imperishable feeling. Your morality needs something to support it, while mine rests upon its own axis."

"Does not experience teach us that the most important roles are often played by the most mediocre actors, that Nature consummates the most beneficial revolutions by means of the most harmful subjects? A Mohammed, an Attila, an Azurangzeb* are as effective servants of the universe as storms, earthquakes and volcanos are precious tools of physical nature. A despot on the throne, who brings distinction to his government each hour with blood and misery, would thus be a far more worthy member of your Creation than the farmer in his fields, just because he is more effective—Yes, the saddest aspect of this is, that he would then be the more excellent for the very reasons which make him the object of our disgust, which are all damnable.—He would lay claim to the name of being an excellent man to the degree, that he degrades himself to less than man. Depravity and virtue . . ."

"Look," exclaimed the prince, annoyed, "look how easily you are fooled by superficialities, how easily you concede my victory! How can you claim, that a life of destruction is an active one? The despot is the most useless creature in the state, because he binds the most active forces with fear and anxiety, and suffocates creative joy. His entire existence is one horrible negative; and if he lays his hands upon the most noble and sacred, life, and destroys freedom of thought . . . one hundred thousand people can not restore in a century that, which a Hildebrandt, a Philip of Spain laid waste within a few years. How can

---

Translator's note: The Mogul emperor of India, installed by the Jesuits.

you honor these creatures and perpetrators of destruction, by comparing them with those beneficient tools of life and fertility?!"

"I admit, that my examples are weak—but in place of a Phillip, let us put Peter the Great on the throne; now, you can not deny, that he is more effective in his monarchy than the private man, given the extent of his fortune, which determines the degree of excellence according to your system, because it is fortune that distributes the opportunities to be effective!"

"So, in your opinion, the throne were preemininently just such an opportunity? But tell me, if the king governs, what does the philosopher do in his kingdom?"

"He thinks."

"And when the vigilant philosopher sleeps, what does the vigilant king do?"

"He sleeps."

"Take two burning candles: one of them casts its light in a peasant's hut, the other in a magnificent room with gay and noble company. What will the two candles do?"

"They will cast light. But that speaks in my favor. Two candles, let us assume, that burn equally long and equally bright, and no one were able to distinguish them, were they exchanged in their places. Why shall the one be more excellent, merely because fortune favors it with the circumstance that it casts its magnificence and beauty in a brilliant room; why shall the other be worse for being condemned by fortune to making visible the poverty and grief in a peasant's hut? And yet, this necessarily follows from your proposition."

"Each is equally excellent, but has each also the same effect?"

"How is that possible? Merely because the candle in the larger room cast so much more light than the other? Merely because the one effected so much more joy than the other?"

"Just consider, that we are speaking only about the initial effect, not the entire chain of effects. Only the effect which immediately follows belongs to the immediately preceding cause; only so many parts of light-matter, immediately moved, set the burning candle vibrating. And what advantage is the one supposed to have over the other? Is it not possible to draw an equal number of rays from each center-point? And just as many out of the pupil of your eye, as out of the center of the earth? Break your habit of presupposing, that the great masses, which the understanding only comprehends as wholes, exist as wholes in the real world. The spark which falls into a powder magazine, explodes a tower, and shakes hundreds of houses, is still, for all of that, merely a spark, that ignited one tiny grain of powder."

"Very good, but. . ."

"Let us apply this to moral actions. We go for a walk, and we meet up with two beggars. I give one a piece of gold; you do the same for the other. My beggar gets drunk with the money, and, in this condition, commits a murder; yours buys a dying father something with which to strengthen himself, prolonging his life. Are we to say that I took a life, on account of the very same act through which you bestowed life? Nothing of the sort. The effect of my act ceased to be *my* act with its immediacy, just as yours did."

"But if my understanding surveys the succession of events, and only this survey determines me to act—if I give this beggar money, in order to prolong the life of a dying father, all of the consequences of the act are mine, if they happen as I conceived them."

"Quite right. But never forget that *one* cause can only have *one* effect. The entirety of the effect, which you brought forth, was to bring the money from your hand into the hand of the beggar. Of the entire, long chain of effects, this is the only one you can ascribe to yourself. The medicine has the effect of medicine, etc. . . . you seem pained by what I say. You think I am merely posing paradoxes. One single word were probably sufficient to reconcile us, but we want to find it in our conclusions."

"From what we have said up to now, I see that it follows, that a good deed is not to blame for its bad effects, and a bad deed is not responsible for its excellent effects. But from that, it also follows, that a good deed is not responsible for its good effects, nor a bad deed for its bad effects, and that both are, therefore, perfectly identical in their effects.—You had then to exclude the unusual case, in which the immediate effect is also the intended one."

"There is no such immediate connection, for an entire series of arbitrary events will insert themselves in between each effect outside of himself which a person brings forth, and the inner cause, or the will, even if these interceding events be merely muscular movements. So, you might as well admit at once, that both acts are equivalent in their effects, i.e., morally indifferent. And who will want to deny this? The stab of a dagger, that ends the life of a Henry IV and a Domitian are both the same act."*

"Correct, but the motive . . ."

"So, the motive determines the moral act. And of what do motives consist?"

"They consist of ideas."

"And what do you call ideas?"

Translator's note: Henry IV, King of France, assassinated by Ravaillac in 1610; Domitian, A.D. 51-96, a Roman Emperor.

"Inner acts, or activities of thinking beings, which correspond to external changes."

"A moral act is, thus, the consequence of an inner activity, which corresponds to external changes?"

"Quite right."

"So, if I say that ABC is a moral act, that is as much as to say, that a series of external changes, which constitute ABC, is preceded by a series of inner changes, abc."

"That is right."

"So, the acts abc were already concluded when ABC began."

"Necessarily."

"So, had ABC not begun, abc were, nevertheless, existent. Were morality contained in abc, it remains even if we efface ABC."

"I understand, most gracious Prince—and, this way, that which I took for the first member in the chain turns out to be the last. When I gave the beggar the money, my moral act was already completed, and its entire value, or lack thereof, decided."

"That is what I mean. If the consequences ensue as you conceived them, ABC follows abc, so that it was nothing more than a successful act. In this external stream of events, man has nothing more to say, nothing is his, but his own soul. From this, you will see, once again, that the monarch has no advantage over the private man, because the former is master of this stream just as little as the latter; for him, too, the entire kingdom of his effectiveness is merely within his own soul."

"But that changes nothing, most gracious Prince, for evil acts have motives, their inner activities, just as much as good ones, and we call them evil only on account of these motives. If you take the motives and purposes of a person in the sum of his activities, I still do not see how you can take morality out of his purposes, and we then return to my previous objections."

"Let us see. We agree that good and bad are predicates we attribute to acts only in the soul."

"That much is proven."

"Then, let us erect a wall which divides the external world and the thinking being, so that, on the outside, the particular acts appear indifferent, and, inside the soul, we name them good or bad."

"Correct."

"So, morality is a condition, one which can only be conceived inside the soul, but never outside of it, as, for example, honor, which is a condition only possible in civil society."

"Quite right."

"As soon as we conceive of an act as present in the soul, it appears to us then like a citizen of a completely different world, and we must judge it according to completely different laws. It belongs to its own totality, one which has its mid-point in itself, from which everything which is flows, against which everything it receives streams. This mid-point, or this principle, is, as we previously agreed, nothing but the inner drive to give effect to all its forces, which is the equivalent of achieving the highest proclamation of its existence. It is in this condition, that we presume the perfection of the moral being, just as we say that a clock is perfect, when all the parts, out of which the artisan constructed it, correspond to the effect, on whose account he constructed it, and just as we call a musical instrument perfect, when all of its parts participate to the highest degree in the greatest effect of which they are capable, and on whose account they were, thus, assembled. Now, the relationship, in which the activities of the moral being stand to this principle, we denote with the name of *morality*, and whether an act is morally good or morally evil depends upon whether it approximates or deviates from this principle, or whether it promotes or hinders this principle. Are we agreed?"

"Perfectly."

"Now, since this principle is nothing but the most perfect activity of all of the powers of a person, is a good act that in which more forces were active, and an evil one that in which less were active?"

"Here, most gracious Prince, let us pause a moment. Were your argument true, then a small good deed of mine stood far lower in the moral order than the years' long conspiracy of the Bartholomew Night, or the conspiracy of Cueva against Venice."*

At this point, the prince lost his patience. "When will I be able to make you understand," he began, "that Nature knows no whole? Combine those things that belong together. Was that conspiracy *one* act, or was it not, rather, a chain of hundreds of thousands of acts?— In fact, hundreds of thousands of deficient acts, against which your small good deed still has the advantage. The drive of human love was asleep in them, but alive in yours. But we are going astray. Where was I?"

"Your argument was, that a good act is one in which more forces are active, and vice-versa."

"And that an evil act is evil, on account of the lesser forces active in it, and vice versa."

"That I understand."

Translator's note: Bartholomew Night: the massacre of Huguenots in Paris on orders of King Charles IX and his mother, Catherine of Medici; Cueva: the name of the Marquis of Bedemar, who tried to topple the republic of Venice in 1608, known to Schiller from the *History of Remarkable Conspiracies*, written by Schiller's friend, Huber.

"Therefore, an evil deed only negates that which is affirmed in a good deed."

"Correct."

"I cannot say, therefore, that an evil heart is necessary to commit this act, as little as I can say, that a child, and not a man, is necessary to lift this stone."

"Quite true. I would rather say, that so much of a good heart must be lacking to commit this act."

"Depravity is, therefore, only absence of virtue, foolishness the absence of understanding, a conception approximately that of shadows or quietude."

"Quite right."

"Just as one can hardly say, that emptiness, quiet, or darkness exist, depravity can hardly exist in a person, or depravity at all, in the entire moral world?"

"That is evident."

"If there exists no depravity in a person, then everything, that is active in him is virtue, or is good, just as everything emits sound which is not quiet, and everything has light that does not stand in shadows?"

"That follows."

"Every act, therefore, which a person commits, is, by virtue of being an act, something good!"

"According to the line of argument we have followed."

"And, if we see a person do something evil, this act is precisely the only good thing we notice about him at that moment."

"That sounds rather strange."

"Let us make use of an analogy. Why do we call an overcast, foggy winter day sad? It is because we are adverse to a snowy landscape, *per se*? Nothing of the kind, for if we transferred it into summer, the snow were increased in beauty. We call it sad, because this snow and this foggy air would not exist had the sun shone to dissipate it, because it is incompatible with the incomparably greater enticement of summer. So, winter is something bad for us, not because it implies a dearth of pleasures, but because it precludes even greater ones."

"That is obvious."

"And the same holds for moral beings. We despise a person who flees, and thereby escapes death, not because we dislike the effective drive for self-preservation, but rather because he had surrendered less to this drive, had he possessed the more magnificent quality of courage. I can admire the bravery, the cunning of a thief who steals from me, but I call him depraved, because he lacks the incomparably more beautiful quality of justice. Thus, I may be amazed by an underaking that is an outburst of the craving for vengeance, held simmering over years, but I call it despicable, because it manifests to me a person who was capable, for years on end, of living without love for his fellow human beings. I walk over a battlefield reluctantly, not on account of the life decaying there before me—a plague or an earthquake might have devastated more, without irritating me—and also not because I do not think, that the power, the art, and the heroic courage, which laid these warriors low, are excellent—but rather, because this sight reminds me of so many thousands who lack humanity."

"Excellent."

"The same holds for the *degrees* of humanity. A skillful, evil deed, finely conceived, persistently pursued, courageously executed, has something brilliant about it, which often incites weak souls to imitation, for one finds so many great and beautiful powers come to fruition, in their full glory. And yet, we say these deeds are worse than those executed with less spirit, and we punish them more severely, because they manifest to us that lack of justice, that much more often, in their grander chain of motives. When such deeds are committed against a benefactor, our entire emotion is outraged on that account, because the opportunities in this case to set in motion the drive of love were the greater, and we make the discovery once again, that this drive has, thus, remained, that much more often, without effect."

"Clear and evident."

"To return to our question. You thus admit, that it is not the activity of forces which makes the depraved person depraved, but rather their inactivity."

"Perfectly."

"Motives, however, are such activities; so, it is incorrect to say, that an act is depraved on account of its motives. Nothing of the sort! The motives for such a deed are the only good in the act, it is only evil on account of the motives it lacks."

"Irrefutable."

"But we could have made this proof much shorter. Would the wicked person act upon these motives, if they did not guarantee him pleasure? It is *pleasure* alone, that sets the moral being into motion; and, as we know, only that which is good can provide pleasure."

"I am satisfied. It follows incontestably from this, that, for example, a person of brilliant mind and benevolent heart is only better than another of like qualities of mind and a less benevolent heart, because the former more approximates the maximum of inner activity. But another consideration occurs to me. If you assume a person of qualities of understanding, of courage, valor, etc., to the highest degree, and let him lack just that one quality, which we call a good heart—shall you prefer him to another, who has those qualities to a lesser degree, but this latter quality in its highest degree? Incontestably, the former is a far more active person than the latter, and, according to you, the activity of the powers determines the moral prize, so that you must judge in his favor, which contradicts the judgment we had otherwise made."

"My judgment were quite in agreement with that, without fail. A person, whose powers are active to a great degree, will also certainly possess an excellent heart, since that which he loves in himself, he cannot hate in another. If experience seems to contradict this, one has either judged too liberally of his understanding, or too limitedly of his moral qualities. A great mind, with a sensitive heart, stands as far above the brilliant scoundrel in the order of being, as the simple-minded with a soft, or better said, a feeble heart, stands below the latter."

"But one given to fantasies, and of the strong sort, is clearly more active than a common person of phlegmatic blood and a limited mind?"

"In such a phlegmatic and limited, common person, each power has its effect, because none is displaced by another. Such is a person in healthy sleep; the dreamer is like a frenzied maniac, throwing himself into convulsions, if the life forces stop at the most extreme arteries.— Do you still have objections?"

"Like you, I am convinced, that the morality of a person consists of the 'more' or the 'less' of his inner activity."

"Now recall," the prince went on, "that we undertook this entire investigation within the closed realm of the human soul, that we separated the soul from the succession of events in the outside world with a wall, and that we constructed the entire edifice of morality within the confines of the wall, and we never transgressed it. We found at once, that a person's happiness merges with his moral excellence, and, therefore, that the latter requires nothing more, that no pleasure is given to him in advance of a perfection yet to be achieved, as little as a rose that blossoms today should only become beautiful the following year, as little as a mistake at the piano should appear as a discord in the following piece. It were equally as inconceivable, that the glow of the sun should be present this afternoon, but the warmth only tomorrow afternoon, or that the excellence of a person should be in this world, but his happiness in another.—Is this now established?"

"I can think of no argument against it."

"The moral being is, therefore, perfect and circumscribed within himself, like that which, for the sake of differentiation, we call the organic, circumscribed by its morality, as this latter is by its composition, and this morality is a relationship completely independent of that which occurs outside of it."

"That is established."

"So, whatever might happen around me, the moral indifference remains."

"I suspected where you were headed, but . . ."

"Were there a Whole, ordered according to Reason, an infinite Justice and a Good, a lasting existence of the personality, an eternal Progress—this can not be derived from the moral world with any greater cogency than from the physical. To be perfect, to be happy, the moral being requires no court other than himself—and were he to expect one, this expectation, at least, cannot be founded upon a requirement of Reason. Whatever becomes of him must be as indifferent to him, as far as his perfection is concerned, as it is a matter of indifference to a rose, whether it blossoms in the desert, or in a princely garden, whether for the bosom of a beautiful woman, or for the worm that devours it."

"Is this comparison appropriate?"

"Perfectly, because I say explicitly to be *beautiful,* to be *happy there,* not to *exist!* That belongs to a new investigation, and I do not want to extend this discussion."

"But I cannot let you go yet, most gracious Prince. You have proven—and, it seems to me, most irrefutably so—that a person is only moral to the extent that he is active in himself, but you previously claimed, that he only has morality to have an effect outside of himself."

"You ought to say, that he only has effects outside of himself, because he has morality. Your *in order to* will confuse us. I cannot stand your *purposiveness.*"

"It amounts to the same thing. The idea is, that he contains the reason for most effects outside himself, only to the extent that he achieves the highest degree of his morality. You still owe me the proof of this."

"Can you not derive the proof yourself, from what we have already discussed? The condition of the highest inner effect of his powers, is this condition not the same, in which he can be the cause of the most effects outside himself?"

"*Can* be, but not *must* be, for have you not yourself admitted, that a good deed that remains without effect, loses nothing of its morality on that account?"

"Not merely admitted, I have insisted on it as most necessary! It is so difficult to dissuade you of the mistaken idea once it has taken hold of you. This apparent contradiction, that the external consequences of a moral act are irrelevant to its value, and that the entire purpose of its existence lies, nevertheless, in its external consequences, always confuses you. Assume that a great virtuoso plays for a numerous, but crude audience; an amateur comes in and steals the entire audience from him—which would you say is the more useful?"

"The virtuoso, of course, for he will delight other ears another time."

"And would he do so, did he not possess the art that was then lost, that he then practiced."

"Hardly."

"And will his rival ever bring forth the effect which he brought forth?"

"He not, but . . ."

"But perhaps a greater rival with his larger audience—is that what you want to say? Can you seriously doubt, that an artist, who knew how to enchant a circle of people with feeling, brilliant connoisseurs, has done little more than that amateur in his entire life? That *one* sensation he awoke in a fine soul elevated itself to deeds that later became useful for millions? That this sensation was, perhaps, the only link still missing in an important chain, and crowned a magnificent plan?—Even that amateur, I grant you, can make people happy—even the person who lost his moral crown will still have an effect, just as a fruit rotting on the tree can be a meal for birds and worms, but it will no longer be worthy of touching an enticing mouth."

"But let that artist play in a desert, live and die there. I say, his art gives him recompense; even where no ear hears his music, he is his own audience, and, in the harmonies he brings forth, he enjoys the even more magnificent harmonies of his being. But you cannot say this. Your artist must have listeners, or he has existed in vain."

"I understand you—but your hypothetical case can never occur. No moral being exists in a desert, where it lives and weaves and touches the bordering All. The effect it has—were it only this single one we know—could have been produced by only *this* being and no other, and it was capable of this effect only by virtue of its entire character. Even if our virtuoso played only *once*, you must grant me, that he must have been precisely *this* artist who he was, that in order to be this, he must have proceeded through so many degrees of practice and skill, and that his entire preceding life as an artist must, therefore, have participated in this moment of triumph. Was that first Brutus not useful for twenty years, because he played the imbecile for twenty years? His *first* act was the foundation of a republic, which still stands as the grandest in world history. And so, it were conceivable, that my *necessity* or your providence might have prepared a person for a certain act over an entire generation, which he only executes in his last hour."

"As probable as this sounds . . . my heart cannot accustom itself to the idea that all powers, all endeavors of a person are supposed to work only for his influence in this life. The great, patriotic statesman, cast from the rudder of the ship of state today, carries all knowledge gained, his practiced powers, his matured plans, into private life, where, abandoned, he dies. Perhaps there was merely the last stone to set in the pyramid that collapsed behind him, that his successor had to begin again from the bottom-most stone. In fifty years of life, did the years accumulate during his exacting administration of the realm solely for the sake of his inactive quietude of private life? You cannot tell me that he fulfilled his effectivness in this act of administration. If influence in this world were to exhaust the entire determination of mankind, his existence ceased with his effect."

"I refer you to the testimony of physical nature herself, where, you must admit, *she* only works for this life. How many seeds and embryos, which Nature constituted with so much artistry and care for future life, are dissolved once again into their elements, without ever surviving to develop? How does Nature gather them? An entire human race slumbers in each human pair, just as it did in the first—out of so many millions of mankinds, why does Nature permit only one to *unfold*? As surely as Nature also digests these destructive seeds, just as surely shall moral beings, to whom Nature seems to have bequeathed a higher purpose, also dissolve. To wish to fathom how Nature reproduces individual effects through the entire chain of events, would be childish arrogance. We frequently see that Nature drops the thread of an act or an event, and then picks it up again just as suddenly three centuries later; Nature submerges the arts and customs of the 18th Century in Calabria, perhaps to exhibit them again to a transformed Europe in the 30th century; she feeds healthy hordes of nomads for generations on the steps of Tartar, to send them south like fresh blood, just as she casts the sea over the coasts of Holland and Zeeland, perhaps to discover an island in America! Even in the individual, and in the small, such traces are not completely absent. How often the frugality of a father, long dead, performs wonders upon an ingenious son; how often was a life only lived, perhaps, to earn an inscription upon a tomb, only lived to light a fire in the soul of a descendant? Just because an infested bird dropped some seeds on its flight, a peasant people on a desert island harvests a bounty—and some moral seed is wasted on ever so fertile ground!"

"Oh, good Prince! Your eloquence incites me to take up the battle against you. You want to elevate your insensitive necessity to a position of grandeur, and you do not even wish to make a god happy with it. Wherever you find pleasure available, you find yourself a pleasure-seeking being—and yet, this infinite pleasure, this feast of perfection, is supposed to stand empty for eternity!"

"Strange!" said the prince, after considering for a long time. "That, upon which *you* and *others* found your hopes, is just that which has dashed all of mine—this supposed perfection of things. Were everything not so self-contained, were I able to see but a single, disfigured splinter, jutting out of this beautiful circle, that alone were sufficient proof for me, that immortality exists. Yet, everything I see falls back into this center, and the most noble thought we are capable of, is merely an indispensable mechanism for driving this wheel of ephemeral reality."

"I do not understand you, most gracious Prince. Your own philosophy passes judgment upon you; you are, truly, like the rich man who starves surrounded by his treasure. You admit, that a person contains in himself everything he needs to be happy, and that he can obtain this happiness only by means of that which he possesses, but you want to seek the source of your unhappiness outside of yourself. If you are right, it is impossible for you to even wish to strive beyond the confines in which you keep mankind imprisoned."

"That is the worst of it all, that we are only morally perfect, only happy, in order to be useful, that we enjoy our *labor* but not our *works*. A hundred thousand laboring hands carried the stones to build the pyramids—but the pyramids were not their reward. The pyramids delighted the eyes of the king, and the slaves were paid off with their livelihood. What does one owe the laborer, if he can labor no longer, or if there is nothing for him to labor upon? Or, what do you owe a person, if he is no longer useful?"

"He will always be useful."

"Always, even as a thinking being?"

Here we were interrupted by a visitor, and late enough, you might think. Forgive me, dearest O***, for this eternally long letter. You wanted to know all the details about the prince, and, in that, I have included his moral philosophy. I know that his state of mind is important to you, and what he does—I know—is only important to you for that reason. That is why I have written everything I could remember about the conversation so faithfully.

———————

*Remark by the Count of O****:* I too beg forgiveness of my reader for having so faithfully copied the Baron of F***. If the excuse he had in his friend is no excuse for me, I have another excuse, and the reader will have to accept it. That is, the Baron of F*** could not foresee the influence, which the philosophy of the prince could have upon future fate—but I *know*, and, for that reason, I have left everything as I found it. I assure the reader, who hoped to see ghosts here, that some are still to come; but the reader will see for himself, that they make a lot of fuss about such a disbelieving person as the prince of *** happens to be.

———————

In the future, I will relate a detail, which you will scarcely put in connection with a discussion such as this. Live well.

Baron of F*** to Count of O***

Fifth Letter

July 1

Since our departure from Venice is now rapidly approaching, we intend to use this week to make up for all the sightseeing of paintings and buildings, which one always postpones on an extended visit. In particular, we have been told to see the Marriage at Cana, by Paul Veronese, which is in the Benedictine cloister on the island of St. George. Do not expect me to describe this extraordinary work of art to you, for although I was, indeed, quite astonished by it, I did not find its impression pleasing. We had needed as many hours as minutes to take in a composition of one hundred and twenty figures, over thirty feet wide. What human eye can encompass such a complex whole, and enjoy the entire beauty that the artist lavished upon it in one viewing! It is a pity, that a work of such proportions, which ought to shine forth and be enjoyed by everyone in a public place, has no better fate than to please a number of monks in their reflectorium. Even the church of the cloister is no less worthy of a visit. It is one of the most beautiful in this city.

Toward evening, we were driven over to the Guidecca to spend a lovely evening in the enticing gardens. The company, not very large, soon dispersed itself, and Civitella, who had been seeking an opportunity to speak with me the whole day, drew me behind a hedge.

"You are the prince's friend," he began, "and reliable sources tell me, that he keeps no secrets from you. As I was going into his hotel today, a man came out, one whose business I know—and the prince was upset when I went to him."—I wanted to interrupt him.—"You can not deny it," he went on, "I knew my man, I took a good look at him—and, could it be possible? The prince is supposed to have friends in Venice, friends who are bound to him by blood and life, and yet the prince has been brought to such extremes as to avail himself of such creatures? Be honest, baron!—Is the prince in difficulty?—Otherwise, you obviously want to hide it. If I do not learn of it from you, I know my man, and every secret can be bought."

"Marquis . . ."

"Pardon me. I must appear indiscreet, not to be ungrateful. I owe my life to the prince, and, far more important to me than life, a reasonable employment of life. Shall I merely stand by, as the prince does things beneath his dignity? It is in my power to spare him that, but am I supposed to suffer it to occur?"

"The prince is in no difficulty," I said, "Some money that we expected to receive over Trient unexpectedly has not arrived. Accidentally, no doubt—or, still uncertain of his departure, one expects additional information from him. Such information has been dispatched, and until then . . ."

He shook his head. "Do not mistake my intentions," he said." It is not that I want to thus reduce the extent of my obligations to the prince—for that, all of my uncle's wealth were scarcely sufficient. My intent is to spare him even a single unpleasant moment. My uncle is quite wealthy, and I dispose of his wealth as though it were my own. A fortunate turn of chance gives me the only opportunity to do something useful for the prince, and it is in my power to do so. I know," he went on, "what delicacy the prince insists upon,—but this holds for both of us—and it would be magnanimous of the prince to grant me this small satisfaction, were it merely an apparent one, and make the burden of obligation, which weighs us down, the less felt."

He would not desist until I promised him I would do all that I could; I knew the prince, and had little hope. He said he was prepared to accept any conditions the prince might make, although he admitted, that it would hurt him very much, were the prince to treat him like a stranger.

We had wandered from the rest of the company in the heat of discussion, and we were just on our way back when Z*** came up to us.

"I was looking for the prince . . . is he not here?"

"We were just on our way to him. We suppose he is with the rest of the company."

"Everyone is there, but he is nowhere to be found. I do not know how we lost sight of him."

Here Civitella recalled, that it might have occurred to him to visit the adjacent church, which he had pointed out to him a short time ago. We started off to look for him there. From a distance we saw Biondello waiting at the entrance of the church. As we approached, the prince came rather hastily out of a side door; his face glowed, his eyes sought Biondello, who he called to him. He seemed to give him some order in an urgent tone, always looking toward the door, which had been left open. Biondello hurried into the church—the prince, without noticing us, pressed past us through the crowd, and hurried back to the party, arriving before we did.

It was decided to take supper in an open pavilion in the garden, where the marquis had arranged a small concert without our knowledge, and it was excellent. One young woman, a singer, especially enthralled us with her beautiful voice as well as her alluring figure. Nothing seemed to make any impression on the prince; he spoke little, and answered as though he were distracted, his eyes restless, looking in the direction from which Biondello would come; a great tumult seemed to be going on inside him. Civitella asked him how he had liked the church, but the prince had nothing to say. There was discussion of some remarkable paintings, but he had seen no paintings. We saw, that our questions were bothering him, and so fell silent. Hours passed, but Biondello still did not come. The prince's impatience grew and grew; he left the table early, and walked to and fro in a remote alley. No one could understand what might have happened to him. I did not dare to ask him the cause of such an odd turn; for a long time I have not dared presume such intimacies with him. I awaited Biondello's return all the more impatiently, hoping he might be able to resolve the paradox.

It was after ten o'clock when he returned. The news he brought the prince contributed nothing to making him more talkative. He excused himself from the party sullenly; a gondola was called for, and we soon rode back home.

There was no opportunity for me to speak to Biondello the entire evening, so I had to sleep on my unsatisfied curiosity. The prince had taken leave of us early, but a thousand thoughts running through my mind kept me awake. Over my bedroom, I heard him pacing back and forth; sleep finally overcame me. A voice awoke me late after midnight—a hand passed over my face; as I looked up, I saw it was the prince, standing in front of my bed, a light in his hand. He said, that he had been unable to sleep, and asked me to help him make the night shorter. I wanted to throw myself into my clothes, but he told me to stay where I was, and sat down in front of my bed.

"Something has happened to me," he began, "something, whose impression will never quit my soul. I left you, as you know, and went into the *** church, the one Civitella had made me curious about, as it had attracted me even from a distance. As neither you nor he were nearby, I went the few steps alone; I had Biondello wait for me at the entrance. The church was quite empty—a gruesome cold embraced me as I entered, leaving the sultry and bright light of day behind me. I found myself alone, in an immense vault, permeated by a solemn, tomb-like stillness. I positioned myself in the middle of the dome, and let the fullness of this impression engulf me. The grand proportions of the majestic construction gradually emerged before my eyes; I lost myself in contemplation of it. The evening bells rang above me, their ring echoing softly in the vault as in my soul. A number of altar pieces drew my attention from afar; I went nearer to look at them; without noticing it, I had wandered through the entire side of the church to the opposite end. Here one winds his way around a pillar, up some steps, and into an adjoining chapel, where a number of smaller altars and statues of saints were standing in the niches. As I stepped into the chapel from the right, I heard a tender whisper, like someone speaking softly; turning toward the sound, I caught sight of a woman's form two steps away from me . . . no! I cannot describe her to you! Horror was my first sensation, which soon gave way to the sweetest bewonder-ment."

"And this form, most gracious Prince—do you know for sure that it was something living, something real, not merely a painting, no face of your imagination?"

"Listen further . . . It was a lady . . . No! Never had I seen such a creature until this moment! Everything around me was dark; the sunset fell into the chapel through a single window; the sun shone upon nothing but this form. With the most indescribable grace, half kneeling, half reclining, she was cast before the altar, the most daring, most lovely, most exquisite contour, unique, inimitable, the most beautiful line of Nature. Her robe was black, enveloping the most alluring body, enclosing the most dainty arms, spreading in broad folds around her like a Spanish robe; her long, light blond hair, thrown in two tresses, loosened under its own weight and, falling out from under her veil, flowed in charming disorder broadly over her back —one hand lay upon a crucifix, and it in turn rested softly upon the other. But where do I find the words to describe that heavenly, beautiful face to you, there, like the soul of an angel, exuding the fullness of her allurement, as though reclined upon a throne. The evening sun played upon it, and its airy, golden hue seemed to surround it in artificial glory. Remember the Madonna of the Florentine—here she was, all there, right down to the irregular, so irresistible idiosyncrasies, that I found so attractive, so irresistible in the painting."

The matter of the Madonna, which the prince speaks of here, was this: shortly after you had departed, he became acquainted with a Florentine painter here, one who had been called to Venice to paint an altar piece for a church I do not now quite remember. He brought three other paintings with him for the Cornay Palace. They were of a Madonna, Heloise, one of them a nearly naked Venus—all three of exceptional beauty, each as valuable as the other, so that it was impossible to decide for one of the three. Only the prince was not a single moment undecided; the paintings had scracely been presented to him, when his attention was fixed upon the Madonna; we admired the genius of the artist in the other two, but, in this painting, the prince forgot the artist and his art to bask completely in the contemplation of the work. He was marvellously stirred; he could hardly tear himself away from the piece. The artist, in whom one saw that, in his heart, he approved of the prince's judgment, obstinately insisted upon not sep-arating the three paintings, and demanded 1,500 zechin for all three. The prince offered him half the sum for this one painting—the artist insisted upon his conditions, and who knows what might have happened if a resolute purchaser had not been found. Two hours later, and all three pieces were gone; we have not seen them since. This was the painting the prince now recalled.

"I stood," he continued, "I stood there, lost in her gaze. She did not notice me, she did not permit herself to be disturbed by my intervention, so deeply was she immersed in her devotions. She prayed to her God, and I to her.—Yes, I worshipped her; all these images of saints, these altars, these burning candles, had failed to remind me of it; now, for the first time, it took hold of me, that I was in a shrine. Ought I confess it to you? In this moment, I firmly believed in Him, who held her beautiful hand. I even read His answer in her eyes. Thanks to her devotions! She made Him real to me—I followed her through the entire expanse of His heavens.

"She arose, and only then did I come to myself again. In shy embarrassment, I stepped to the side, and the noise I made revealed my presence to her. The unsuspected proximity of a man must have surprised her, my impudence might have insulted her; but neither the one, nor the other, was to be found in the glance she cast upon me. Calm, indescribable calm, was in her eyes, and a kind smile played upon her cheeks. She descended from her heaven—and I was the first happy creature to offer itself to her benevolence. She was still poised on the last strain of her prayer, not yet returned to earth.

"There was now a stir in the other corner of the chapel. It was an elderly lady, who stood up just behind me from a church stool. I had not seen her until then. She was only a few steps away from me; she had seen all of my movements. This startled me. I cast my eyes to the ground, and the two others hurried past me.

"I saw them go down the long corridor of the church. The beautiful form was erect—what lovely majesty! What nobility in her gait! That which was, is no more—new graces, an entirely new phenomenon. They descended slowly. I followed from a distance, timidly, uncertain whether I ought to overtake them. Will she grace me with her gaze no more? Did she look at me as they passed by, and was I unable to raise my eyes to her? Oh, how this doubt tormented me!

"They are there, standing still, and I am incapable of moving my foot from the spot. The elderly lady, her mother, or whatever else she was, she notices the disorder of the beautiful hair, and busily sets it aright, giving her the sunshade to hold. Oh, how I wish that hair disorderly, and those hands clumsy!

"The toilette is complete; they approach the doors. I quicken my steps—half of the form disappears, then the other half—Only the shadow of her robes flying behind her—She is gone—No, she is coming again. She drops a flower, bends over to pick it up—She looks back, and—Is she looking for me?—Who else might her eyes seek among those dead walls? So, I was no stranger to her any longer—She left me behind, like her flower—Dear F***, I am ashamed to tell you how childishly I interpreted this look, which . . . Perhaps it was not even intended for me!"

As to this latter point, I believed I might reassure the prince.

"Strange," the prince went on, after a long moment of silence, "is it possible never to have known something, never to have felt its absence, and then, a few moments later, to be able to live only for this one thing? Can a single moment separate mankind into two so completely different species? It were as impossible for me to return to the joys and lusts of yesterday morning, as to the games of my childhood, since I have seen this form, since this image lives here, this vital, powerful feeling in me: You cannot love anything but that, and nothing else in the world will ever have any effect upon you!"

"Consider, most gracious Prince, in what an excitable mood you were as this apparition surprised you, and how many things conjoined to tense your imagination. Suddenly, out of the bright and glaring light of day, out of the throngs of the streets, plunged into still darkness—completely surrendered to sensations, which, as you admit yourself, excited the stillness and majesty of the place in you.—The more susceptible to beauty through study of beautiful works of art—And, in your opinion, alone and lonely at once—At once, right beside you, surprised by the figure of a woman in a place where you expected no witness—Surprised by beauty, as I gladly grant you, even intensified by advantageous lighting, a fortunate position, an impression of enthused devotion—What were more natural, than that your enflamed fantasy constructed something idealistic, something supraterrestrial?"

"Can fantasy produce something it never received?—And there is nothing in the scope of my imagination, with which I might possibly combine this image. It lies in my memory, entire and unaltered, just as it was at the moment of vision; I have nothing but this image —but you can offer me a world for it!"

"Most gracious Prince, that is love."

"Must it necessarily be a name under which I am happy? Love!—Do not degrade my emotion with a name that thousands of weak souls abuse! Who else has felt what I feel? Such a being has not even existed before now; how can the name exist before the emotion? It is a new, solitary emotion, newly arisen with this new, unique being, only possible for this being!—Love! Higher than love, of that I am certain!"

"You sent Biondello, doubtless to follow the trail of your stranger, to bring you news of her? That news did he return with?"

"Biondello discovered nothing—or as good as nothing. He found her still at the church door. An elderly, well-dressed man, who looked more like a native citizen than a servant, appeared to guide her to a gondola. A number of beggars formed a line as she passed, and left her once more satisfied. Upon this occasion, said Biondello, there appeared a hand, upon which precious stones glitter. She discussed something Biondello was not able to understand with the woman attending her; he claimed, that they spoke Greek. As they had a good way to walk before they reached the canal, something of a crowd of people began to gather; the extraordinary nature of the sight brought everyone passing to a standstill. No one knew her—but beauty is a born queen. Everyone reverentially made way for her. She let a black veil fall over her face, half covering her robe, and hurried to the gondola. Biondello kept the gondola in sight along the entire canal of Guidecca, but the crowd prevented him from following it further."

"But he saw the gondolier well enough to be able to recognize him again?"

"He was certain he would find the gondolier; but he is no one of those with whom he usually has to do. The beggars he asked could tell him nothing more than that the Signora had appeared here every Saturday for some weeks now, and always divided a piece of gold among them. It was a Dutch dukat, that he exchanged and brought to me."

"So, a Greek woman, and apparently of some rank, at least of some wealth, and benevolent. That ought to be enough to know for now, most gracious Prince—enough, and almost too much!

"But a Greek woman, and in a Catholic church!"

"Why not? She may have given up her faith. Moreover—it is always something mysterious—Why once a week? Why only Saturdays in this church, when it is usually deserted, as Biondello tells me? —This issue will have to be decided by next Saturday at the latest. But, until then, dear friend, help me span the time! But in vain! Days and hours take their tempered steps, and my desire has wings."

"And when this day arrives—what then, most gracious Prince? What should happen then?"

"What should happen?—I will see her. I will discover where she lives. I will learn who she is.—Who she is?—What do I care about that? What I *saw* made me happy, so I already know everything that can make me happy!"

"And our departure from Venice, set for the beginning of next month?"

"Could I have known in advance, that Venice still held such a treasure for me?—You are asking me, as though I were still living as I did yesterday. I tell you, that I am, and want to be, only from today on."

I now believed, that I had found the opportunity to hold the marquis to his word. I made it understood to the prince that his prolonged stay in Venice could not be borne, given the weakened condition of his finances, and that, if he prolonged his stay beyond the date agreed upon, he could not expect much by way of support from his court at home. I thereupon learned something which had been kept secret from me until then: that his sister, the governing *** of ***, was paying him, in secret, considerable sums, to the exclusion of his other brothers, and that she would gladly double them, were the court ever to abandon him. This sister, a pious religious fantast, as you know, believed herself to have no better use for the large savings made at a very limited court than to give them to a brother, whose wise benevolence you know, and whom she ardently worshipped. I have known, and indeed for some time, that there was a very certain relationship between the two, and that they exchanged letters; but, since the prince's previous expenses could be paid from the known sources, it never occurred to me, that he had hidden sources of aid. It is, thus, evident, that the prince had other expenses which he likewise kept secret from me, and they still are; and, to judge from his character, these expenses are surely none but those that do him honor. And, could I have flattered myself to have found out what they were?—Following this discovery, I felt so much the less permitted to hesitate in revealing the marquis' offer to him—which, to my no slight amazement, was accepted without any difficulty. He gave me warrant to arrange the matter with the marquis in whatever manner I saw fit, and to pay off the usurer at once. He would write to his sister without delay.

It was morning as we parted. As unpleasant as this incident is and must be to me, for more than one reason, it is most vexing, that he threatens to prolong our stay in Venice. I expect far more good than bad from this burgeoning passion. It is, perhaps, the most powerful means to pull the prince down from his metaphysical dreaming, back to ordinary humanity: The passion will, I hope, have the usual crisis, and, like an artificial sickness, take the old away with it as it goes.

Live well, dear friend. I have written all this down for you while the event was still fresh. The mail is leaving immediately; you will receive this letter with the previous one in *one* day.

Baron of F*** to Count of O***

Sixth Letter

July 20

This Civitella is the most obliging person in the world. The prince had just left me recently, when a note from the Marquis arrived, recommending the matter to me with the utmost urgency. I sent him a promissory note in the name of the prince for 6,000 zechin at once; it came back in less than half an hour, along with double the sum in notes and cash. The prince agreed to this increase of the sum in the end; but he insisted that the promissory note, only extended for six weeks, would have to be accepted.

This entire week was spent inquiring after the mysterious Greek woman. Biondello set all his machines into motion, but everything was in vain. He did manage to find the gondolier, but nothing more was to be extracted from him than that he had ferried the ladies to the island of Murano, where they boarded two lorries that were waiting for them. He had thought they were English, because they spoke a foreign language, and paid him in gold. He did not know their attendant either; he thought he might have been a mirror maker from Murano. Now, at least, we knew we were not to look for her in the Giudecca, and that, in all probability, she was at home on the island of Murano; but the misfortune was, that the description that the prince gave of her was of no use to a third person who might otherwise have recognized her. Just that passionate attentiveness with which he had entangled his first sight of her, prevented him from actually seeing her; he had been blind to everything to which others would have paid special attention. After hearing his description, one was more tempted to seek her in Ariosto or Tasso than on a Venetian island. Furthermore, the inquiries had to be made with considerable caution, in order not to excite offensive attention. Since Biondello was the only one, besides the prince, who had seen her, at least through the veil, and would thus be able to recognize her, he searched everywhere she might be suspected to be at the same time; this poor man's life over the whole week consisted of nothing but continuously running through all the streets in Venice. No researches were spared, especially in the Greek church, but all with the same miserable success; and the prince, whose impatience grew with each dashed expectation, finally had to console himself to wait for the next Saturday.

His discontent was horrible. Nothing amused him, nothing was capable of capturing his attention. His entire being in hectic motion, he was lost for all company, and the malaise intensified in his loneliness. He was never more besieged by visitors than in this week. News of his pending departure had made the rounds, and everyone thronged by. These people had to be entertained to keep their suspicious attentions away from the prince; *he* had to be entertained to distract his mind. In this distress, Biondello fell to gambling, and, to keep at least the masses away, he played high. He hoped to awaken at least a transient taste for the game in the prince at the same time, one over which he would always have command, as to take it away again, as well as to suffocate the prince's fanciful passion. "The cards," said Civitella, "have saved me from many a folly that I was about to commit, and even recompensed me for some I have committed. The calm, the composure, that a pair of beautiful eyes cost me, I have often regained at the gambling table, and never have women had more power over me, than when I needed money to gamble."

I leave aside to what extent Civitella was right—but the medication we had fallen upon soon began to become even more dangerous than the malaise it was intended to alleviate. The prince, who only knew how to give the game the same fleeting enticement by wagering the utmost, soon found no limits any longer. He had lost his balance. Everything he did took on passionate form; everything happened with that most impatient impetuosity that ruled in him now. You know how indifferent he is towards money; here it became an absolute insensibility. Pieces of gold ran like water through his hands. He lost almost without interruption, because he played without paying even the slightest attention to the game. He lost vast sums, because he played desperately. —Dearest O***, I write this with my heart pounding—in four days, the 12,000 zechin, and more, were lost.

Do not cast blame upon me. I blame myself enough. But could I have prevented it? Did the prince listen to me? Could I do anything but complain? I did what was in my power. I cannot find myself guilty.

Civitella, too, lost a considerable sum; I won some 600 zechin. The prince's unprecedented bad luck caused a stir; he was even less able to leave the game now. Civitella, in whom one saw, that he was glad to oblige, advanced him the sum. The hole has been plugged, but the prince owes the marquis 24,000 zechin. Oh, how I yearn for the savings of the pious sister!—Are all Princes like this, dearest friend? The prince behaves no differently than if he had just bestowed a great honor upon the marquis, and the marquis—at least he plays his role well.

Civitella sought to console me, that just this excess, this extraordinary bad luck, was the most powerful means to bring the prince to reason. The money is no loss to him. He supposedly does not feel the loss, and would place three times as much at the prince's disposal at a moment's notice. Even the cardinal gave me assurance, that his nephew's attitude was correct, and that he would answer for him on all accounts.

The saddest of it all was, that this immense sacrifice did not achieve its intended effect at all. One might have thought the prince would at least play with interest. Nothing of the sort. His thoughts were far away, and the passion that we wanted to suppress, seemed only to feed itself upon his misfortune in the game. When a decisive blow ought to have occurred, and everyone was pressing around his gaming table, full of expectation, he sought the eyes of Biondello, to steal some news he might have brought. Biondello never brought anything—and the prince's hand always lost.

By the way, the money went into needy hands. Certain excellencies, who, as the wicked world tattles, carry their frugal midday meals home from the market themselves, entered our home as beggars, and left it decently well off. Civitella pointed them out to me. "You see," he said, "how it is to the advantage of so many poor devils, that the prince is not in his right mind! But I like that. It is princely and kingly! A great man must make others happy, even in his aberrations, and, like the flooding steam, fructify neighboring fields."

Civitella thinks fine and nobly—but the prince owes him 24,000 zechin!

The Saturday so yearned for finally arrived, and the prince could not be held back from going into the *** church immediately after noontime. He went into the same chapel where he had seen his stranger for the first time, but in such a way that he would not be noticed immediately. Biondello had orders to stand watch at the church doors, and to strike up an acquaintance with the lady's attendant. I had taken it upon myself to take a seat in the same gondola in the guise of an unsuspecting passerby on the return trip, to follow the track of the stranger, should all else fail. In the identical place where, according to the testimony of the gondolier, she had disembarked the previous times, two lorries were rented; superfluously, the prince had the officer of the chambers, von Z***, follow in a separate gondola. The prince himself wanted to revel entirely in the look of her, and, if possible, to try his luck in the church. Civitella stayed away altogether, for he had too low a reputation among the women of Venice for his interference not to make the lady suspicious. You see, dearest Count, it was not due to our preparations, that the beautiful stranger eluded us.

Never have more passionate desires been entertained in any church than in this one, and never were they so horribly disappointed. The prince persevered until past sunset, his anticipation stirred by every sound approaching his chapel, by every creaking of the church doors, a full seven hours—and no Greek woman. I tell you nothing of his state of mind. You know what a hope disappointed is—and one for which alone one had lived seven days and nights.

*Baron of F*** to Count of O****

Seventh Letter

July

The prince's mysterious stranger reminded Marquis Civitella of a romantic experience he had some time ago, and, to entertain the prince, he was disposed to tell us about it. I relate it to you in his own words. But the lively spirit with which he is capable of garnishing everything he says is lost in my presentation of it.

"Last Spring," Civitella said, "I had the misfortune to have incited the Spanish ambassador against me, who, in his seventieth year, had committed the folly of wanting to marry, all for himself, an eighteen-year-old Roman girl. His vengeance pursued me, and my friends advised me to escape the effects of such by taking timely flight, until such time as either the hand of nature or an amicable settlement might have liberated me from this dangerous enemy. As it was too difficult for me, however, to entirely abandon Venice, I took up residence in a remote quarter of Murano, where I lived in a house under an assumed name, days keeping myself hidden, and devoting the nights to my friends and pleasures.

"My window looked out upon a garden which adjoined the wall of a cloister on the West, but on the East protruded like a small peninsula into the lagoon. The garden had the most charming design, but was infrequently visited. Mornings, when my friends left me, I was in the habit of spending a few moments at the window before going to sleep, watching the sun rise over the gulf, and then to bid her good-night. If you have never had the pleasure, most gracious Prince, I recommend this site, perhaps the most exquisite in all Venice, to savor this magnificent phenomenon. A scarlet night over the depths, and a golden mist announces the sun's epiphany from afar, at the edge of the lagoon. The heavens and the sea lie in waiting, brimming with anticipation. Two winks, and there she is, full and perfect, and all the waves burn—it is a tantalizing performance!

"One morning, as I am about to abandon myself as usual to the delights of this scene, I suddenly discover, that I am not the only witness present. I believe I hear human voices in the garden, and as I turn toward the sound, I see a gondola landing at the waterside. In a few moments, I see people come forth into the garden, with slow steps, walking together, strolling up the path. I see that it is a man and a woman, who have a small negro with them. The woman is dressed in white, a diamond sparkling on her finger; more I cannot discern in the twilight.

"My curiosity is stirred. Quite certainly a rendevous and a loving pair—but at this place, and at such an entirely unusual hour!—For it was scarcely three o'clock, and everything lay still, veiled in dim twilight. It seemed a novel notion to me, fit for a sketch to a story of romance. I wanted to await the conclusion.

"I soon lost sight of them in the caverns of foliage in the garden, and it was to be a long time before they reappeared. A pleasant singing meanwhile filled the air. It came from the gondolier, who in this way shortened the time in his gondola, and whose song was answered by a comrade from the neighborhood. They sang stanzas from the Tosso;

time and place lent their own harmonious voices thereto, and delightfully the melody echoed in the stillness.

"Meanwhile, day had broken, and objects became more clearly recognizable. Hand in hand, they walk up a long promenade and often remain standing, but they have turned their backs to me, and their way takes them further away from my apartment. From the decorum of their gait, I judge that they are of distinguished position, and, from their noble and angelic statures, that they possess extraordinary beauty. They seemed to speak little, the lady, however, more than her companion. They seemed to take no notice at all of the theater of the sunrise, which just now enveloped them in sublime splendor.

"Just as I fetch my telescope, and train it upon the two, to bring this singular occasion as close to me possible, they suddenly disappear into a side path, and a long time passes before I gain sight of them again. The sun has now risen entirely, they come very close underneath me and look straight at me . . . what a heavely form I see! —Was it the play of my imagination, was it the magic of the light? I believed I saw a supraterrestrial being, and my eyes flew away, struck by blinding light.—So much grace attending so much majesty! So much spirit and nobility together with so much flourishing youth! It is in vain that I try to describe it to you. Before this moment, I had never known beauty.

"Their conversation causes them to linger near me, and I have the muse to abandon myself to the wonderful contemplation of them. Hardly do my glances fall upon her companion, even her beauty is powerless to tear my eyes from him.

"He seemed to be a man in his best years, somewhat lean, and grand and noble of stature—but no human brow has yet exuded so much spirit, such elevation, so much of the divine. I myself, although secure against discovery, was incapable of withstanding the penetrating gaze, which shot forth, like lightning thrown from under the dark eyebrows. A calm, stirring sadness was about his eyes, and a trace of benevolence around his lips softened the grim seriousness that overshadowed the entire face. But a certain cut of the face, which was not European, combind with a garb, composite of many fashions, but with a taste no one will imitate, bold and fittingly selected, gave him an aura of peculiarity, which, to no slight degree, increased the impresssion of his entire being. Something wild in his look might have led one to suspect he was a fantast, and yet his bearing and exterior decorum told of a man the world had educated."

Z***, who, as you know, just has to blurt out everything he thinks, could not hold himself in any longer at this point. "Our Armenian!" he cried out. "Our Armenian, and no one else!"

"What sort of Armenian, if one might ask?" queried Civitella.

"Has no one told you of the farce yet?" said the prince. "But no interruptions! I am beginning to become interested in your man. Continue your story."

"There was something incomprehensible in his behavior. His look rested significantly, with passion, upon her when she looked away, and fell to the ground when their eyes met. Is this man out of his mind, I thought. Were I he, I would want to linger an eternity and contemplate nothing else.

"Once again, the shrubbery stole them from me. I waited for a long time, a very long time, to see them re-emerge, but to no avail. I discovered them, at last, from another window.

"They stood before a pier, at a certain distance from each other, each deeply lost in thought. They may have been standing in this position for a considerable time already. Her open, tender eyes rested upon him, searching, and seemed to lift each germinating thought from his brow. He, as if he did not feel sufficient courage to receive it first hand, furtively sought her image in the mirroring tide, or stared at the dolphin spraying water into the basin. Who knows how long this silent game might have lasted, had the lady been able to sustain it? With the most charming graciousness, that beautiful creature went to him, and took one of his hands, which, with her arm around his neck, she led to her mouth. That cold person let it happen, indifferently, and her gesture of love went unrequited.

"But there was something about this that stirred me. It was the man that stirred me. A powerful emotion seemed to work in his breast, an irresistible power, drawing him toward her, a hidden arm tearing him away. This struggle was a calm, but painful one, and the danger so beautiful at his side. No, thought I, he is undertaking too much. He will, he must submit.

"At a small wink from him, the negro disappears. I now expected a scene of the most sentimental sort, a kneeling apology, a reconciliation sealed with a thousand kisses. Nothing of all of that. This incomprehensible person takes a sealed package from a portfolio, and gives it into the hands of the lady. Sadness draws over her face as she sees it, and a tear glitters in her eye.

"After a brief silence, they move apart. An elderly lady, who had kept her distance from them the whole time, and who I discover now for the first time, walks toward them from a side path. They walk off slowly, the ladies in conversation with each other, while he takes the opportunity to remain behind. He walks, then stands, indecisively, then walks again, his staring gaze toward her. He disappears suddenly into the shrubbery.

"The ladies, walking ahead, finally look around. They seem upset not to find him. He does not come. My eyes help them search the entire garden. He is not there. He is nowhere to be found.

"Suddenly, I hear something make a noise on the canal, and a gondola shoves off from the bank. He is in it, and I restrain myself with effort from shouting it out to her. Now it was evident—this was a farewell scene.

"She seemed to *suspect* what I *knew*. She hurries to the bank, more quickly than the other is able to follow. Too late. The gondola flies away as fast as an arrow, only a white cloth fluttering afar in the breeze. Soon thereafter, I see the two women cross over, too.

"As I awoke from a brief slumber, I had to laugh about my delusion. My fantasy had continued this story in my dreams, and now the truth, too, became a dream. A girl, alluring like a virgin from paradise, who strolls before daybreak in a remote garden, in front of my window, with her lover, a lover who can think of no better use for such an hour, to me this seemed to be a composition, which only the fantasy of a dreamer could dare, and excuse. But the dream had been too beautiful not to renew it as often as possible, since my fantasy had populated it with such enthralling creatures. A number of inclement days following this morning banished me from the window, but the first clear evening drew me, involuntarily, toward it. Imagine my amazement, when, after a brief search, the white robe of my stranger came shimmering toward me. It was she. She was real. I had not merely dreamed.

"The matron of the previous encounter was with her, leading a small boy. All the places, still special to her from the previous time, on account of her companion, were visited in turn. She tarried especially long at the basin, and her eyes, affixed, seemed to seek in vain the beloved image.

"Had this supreme beauty overpowered me the first time, today she affected me with a more tender power, a power which was no less strong. Now I had perfect freedom to contemplate the divine image; the amazement of the first encounter made way, imperceptibly, to a sweeter sentiment. The glory about her vanished, and I see in her no more than the most beautiful of all women, she who sets all my senses aglow. In this moment it is resolved. She must be mine.

"As I consider, whether to go down and approach her, or, before I dare that, to find out more about her, a small portal in the cloister wall opens, and a Carmelite monk exits through it. Upon hearing the noise he makes, the lady leaves her place, and I see her stride, her steps lively, toward him. He draws a paper from his breast which she eagerly seizes, and vivid joy seems to fly into her face.

"In this precise moment, my usual evening visitor drives me from the window. I scrupulously avoid the window, for I begrudge anyone else the conquest. I have to hold out a full hour in this distressing impatience, until I succeed to remove the burdensome fellow at last. I hurry back to my window, but everything has vanished!

"The garden is entirely empty as I go down to it. No boat in the canal any longer. Nowhere a trace of people. I know neither where she came from, nor where she went. As I wander around aimlessly, peering everywhere, something white in the sand glitters at me from a distance. I approach it; it is a piece of paper, folded in the form of a letter. What else could it be, than the letter that the Carmelite brought her? 'Happy find!' I call out. 'This letter will reveal the entire secret to me, it will make me the master of her fate!'

"The letter was sealed with a sphinx, without inscription, written in code; this did not deter me, however, for I know how to decipher codes. I copied it quickly, for it was to be expected, that she would soon miss it, and would come back to look for it. If she did not find it, it would needs be proof to her, that the garden had been visited by others, and this discovery could easily dissuade her from ever coming back. With what worse calamity could my hopes be dashed?

"That which I suspected happened. I was hardly finished wih my copy, when she appeared once again, with her former companion, both of them searching anxiously. I affix the letter to a piece of shale that I pry loose from the roof, and let it fall to a place she must pass by. Her joy upon finding it recompenses me for my generosity. With a sharp, inspecting look, as though she wanted thereby to espy the sacriligious hand that might have touched it, she examined the letter from all sides; but the satisfied air, with which she tucked it away, proved that she was utterly without malice. She left, and a backward glance of the eye bid farewell to the protecting gods of the garden, who had so faithfully guarded the secret of her heart.

"Now I hurried to decipher the letter; at last, I succeeded with English. Its content was so peculiar to me that I learned it by heart."

—

I am being interrupted. The conclusion another time.

Baron of F*** to Count of O***

Eighth Letter

August

No, dearest friend. You are unfair to the good Biondello. Your suspicions against him are surely unfounded. I would not vouch for any other Italian, but this one is honest.

You think it strange that a person of such brilliant talents and such exemplary behavior should degrade himself in the position of a servant, were it not that he supposedly entertains secret intentions thereby, and, for that reason, you consider, that these intentions must be suspicious. Why? Is it really such a novelty, that a person of mind and merits seeks to oblige a prince who has it in his power to make his fortune? Is it dishonorable to serve him, or anything of the sort? Does Biondello not make it clear enough, that his devotion to the prince is of a personal nature? He has indeed confessed, that he has a plea dear to his heart: this will undoubtedly explain the entire mystery. He may well still have secret intentions, but might these not be innocent ones?

It astonishes you, that, in the first months, and that was when we still had the pleasure of your presence, this Biondello kept all the great talents hidden, those that he now permits to to see the light of day, and that previously he in no way drew attention to himself. That is true, but where had he the opportunity, at that time, to excel? The prince required no one of his sort as yet, and it was necessary, that chance reveal the rest of his talents.

But he recently offered a proof of his devotion and honesty, one that dashes all your doubts to the ground. Secret inquiries had been made into the prince's lifestyle, his acquaintances and relationships. I do not know who it is with such curiosity. But listen.

Here in St. George, there is a public house, where Biondello frequently goes in and out, he may have a lover there, I do not know. He was also there some days ago; he finds a group of people together, attorneys and officials of the government, merry comrades and acquaintances of his. They are surprised, they are happy to see him again. The old acquaintance is renewed, each tells the story of his life up to the present moment, Biondello, too, is to provide an account of his own. He does so in few words. They wish him well in his new employment, they have already heard tell of the splendid lifestyle of the prince of ***, of his generosity especially toward people who know how to keep a secret, his relationship to the cardinal A***i is world renowned, he likes to gamble, etc. Biondello, is taken aback—They joke with him, that he is being so secretive; they know, that he is the agent of the prince of ***; the two attorneys take him into the center of the room; the bottle is diligently emptied—they force him to drink; he apologizes, because wine does not agree with him, but he drinks in order to pretend to be drunk.

"Yes," one of the attorneys said at last, "Biondello knows his trade; but he has not completed his apprenticeship, he is only half a master."

"What do I still lack?" asked Biondello.

"He understands the art of keeping a secret," said the other, "but not yet the other art, that of betraying a secret to advantage."

"Might there be a buyer?" asked Biondello.

At this, the other guests withdrew from the room, he remained with his two people in a tête-à-tête, who now came out with the offer.

To be brief, he was to provide them information about the prince's relationship to the cardinal and his nephew, betray the source of the prince's money, and hand letters written to the Count of O*** over to them. Biondello put them off to the next time, but he was unable to draw out who had engaged them. To judge from the magnanimous offers made him, the inquiry must have come from a very rich man.

Yesterday evening, he revealed the entire incident to the prince. The latter was initially inclined to have them arrested in short order, but Biondello made objections. One would have to set them free again, in any case, and he would thereby have put his entire credit with this type of people, perhaps even his life, in danger. These sorts of people band together, all stand for one; he said he had rather have the High Council of Venice itself for an enemy, than be denounced as a traitor among these people, and he were of no use to the prince any longer, once he had lost the confidence of this class of people.

Again and again, we tried to guess from whom this might have come. Who is there in Venice, who could have an interest in knowing what the prince's income and expenses are, what he has to do with the cardinal A***i, and what I write to you? Or, is this Armenian stirring again?

Baron of F*** to Count of O***

Ninth Letter

August

The prince is swimming in ecstasy and love. He has his Greek once again. Just listen, how this came about.

A stranger, who came from Chiozza, and told a great deal about the beauty of this city on the gulf, made the prince curious to see it. Yesterday, we satisfied it, and, to forgo all constraints and expenses, no one but Z*** and I, in addition to Biondello, were to accompany him, and the prince wanted to remain unrecognized. We found a boat just departing, and booked seats. The company was quite mixed, but unimportant, and there was nothing special about the ship.

Chiozza is built upon driven piles, like Venice, and is said to number approximately 40,000 inhabitants. There is little nobility to be found, but in every third person one meets a fisherman or seaman. Those who wear a wig and a coat are rich; a cap and a cloak are the signs of the poor. The city is beautifully situated, but then, one must never have seen Venice.

We did not tarry long. The ship's master, who had other passengers, had to be back in Venice on time, and nothing held the prince in Chiozza. Everyone had already taken his place in the ship when we arrived. We took a room for ourselves, because the company had made itself so troublesome on the first leg of the trip. The prince inquired who else was on board. A Dominican was the answer; and some ladies returning to Venice. The prince was not curious to see them, and went immediately to his room. The Greek woman was the subject of our conversation on the way from Venice, and again on the return trip. The prince passionately recalled her appearance in the church, plans were made and cast aside; the time passed, as though in a moment; before we knew it, Venice lay in front of us. Some of the passengers went on shore, the Dominican among them. The ship's master went to the ladies, who, as we now learned, were only separated from us by a thin board, and asked where he was to dock. On the island of Murano, was the answer, and the house was named. "The island of Murano!" cried the prince, and a thrill of presentiment seemed to fly through his soul. Before I was able to answer him, Biondello burst in. "Do you know in what company we are travelling?"—The prince sprang to his feet.—"She is here! She herself!" Biondello continued. "I have just come from her companion."

The prince rushed out. To him the room had become too small, in this moment the whole world had been too small. A thousand sensations raged in him, his knees trembled, his face alternately flushed and paled. I trembled with him, in anticipation. I cannot describe this condition to you.

We stopped in Murano. The prince leaped to shore. She came. I read in the prince's face, that it was she. Her look left me no doubts. I have never seen a more beautiful form; the prince's description fell far short of reality. A glowing flush drew over her face as she came into the prince's view. She must have heard our entire conversation, nor could she doubt, that she had been the object of the same. She cast a significant glance at her companion, as if to say: There he is! And then, in embarrassment, cast her eyes downward. A narrow plank, upon which she had to walk, was laid from the ship to the shore. She seemed anxious as she set foot on it, but less, as it seemed to me, because she feared to slip, but rather beause she was unable to walk upon it without aid, and the prince was already reaching his arm to help her. Necessity won out over her doubt. She accepted his hand, and was on shore. The tumultuous state of mind of the prince made him impolite; the other lady, who expected the same service, he forgot— what had he not forgotten at this moment? I at last extended her this service, which deprived me of the prelude to a discussion that had begun between my Prince and the lady.

He still held her hand in his—out of distraction, I think, and without himself knowing it.

"It is not the first time, Signora, that. . . that. . . that. . . ." He could not say it.

"I ought to remember," she lisped.

"In the *** church," said he.

"In the *** church," she said.

"And today, had I imagined . . . you, so close . . ."

Here she softly withdrew her hand from his. He was quite apparently confused. Biondello, who had meanwhile spoken with the servant, came to his aid.

"Signor," he began, "the ladies have called for lorries; but we returned sooner than they expected. There is a garden nearby, where you may tarry long enough to escape the throng."

The proposal was accepted, and, you might well imagine how willingly on the side of the prince. They stayed in the garden until evening. We, Z*** and I, managed to entertain the matron, so that the prince was able to converse, undisturbed, with the young lady. You may gather, that he well knew how to make use of the moment from the fact, that he was given permission to visit her later. He is there now, or as I am writing to you. When he returns, I will learn more.

Yesterday, when we returned, we found the expected money from our court, but accompanied by a letter which set the prince aflame. He is being called back, and in a tone to which he is not at all accustomed. He sent a reply of similar tone at once, and will remain. The bills of exchange are just sufficient to pay the interest on the money he owes. We are anxiously awaiting a letter from his sister.

*Baron of F*** to Count of O****

Tenth Letter

September

The prince has broken with his court, all of our resources there have been cut off.

The six weeks, after which the prince was to have paid the marquis, had already elapsed some days, but still no money, neither from his cousin, of whom he again, and most urgently, demanded a grant, nor from his sister. As you can well imagine, Civitella sent no reminder; the prince's memory, however, was all the more faithful. The answer from the governing court arrived yesterday afternoon.

We had just concluded a new contract on account of our hotel, and the prince had publicly declared his prolonged stay. Without saying a word, the prince gave me the letter. His eyes sparkled, I read the contents on his brow.

Can you imagine, dear O***? In ***, one is informed of everything concerning the prince here, and slander has woven a ghastly web of lies out of it all. It had been learned, with disapproval, so it says, that the prince has for some time begun to disavow his former character, and to adopt a behavior quite contrary to his previous laudable way of thinking. It is known, that he chases women and gambles most extravagantly, plunging himself into debt, lends his ear to visionaries and conjurers, that he has suspicious relations with Catholic prelates, and maintains a court too expensive for his rank as well as his income. It even says, that he is about to make this highly objectionable behavior complete with an apostasy to the Catholic Church. To cleanse himself of the latter accusation, it is expected that he return without delay. A banker in Venice, to whom he is to deliver an account of his debts, has instructions to satisfy his creditors *immediately upon his departure,* for, under these circumstances, one does not consider it wise to deliver money into his hands.

What imputations, and in what a tone! I took the letter, read it through once again, I wanted to find something in it to soothe him; I found nothing, it was utterly incomprehensible to me.

Z*** now reminded me of the secret inquiry tendered to Biondello some time ago. The time, the context, and the circumstances cohered. We had wrongly ascribed the inquiry to the Armenian. Now the secret of its origin was out. Apostasy!—But, in whose interests can it be, to so horribly and crudely slander the prince? I fear this is the hand of the prince of ***d***, who wants to accomplish our Prince's departure from Venice.

The latter still said nothing, his eyes, staring, fixed ahead of him. His silence made me anxious. I threw myself at his feet. "For God's sake, most gracious Prince," I cried out, "do not decide to do something violent. You should, you shall have complete satisfaction. Leave the matter to me. It is beneath your dignity to answer such accusations; but *you* must permit *me* to do it. The slanderer must be named, the eyes of *** must be opened."

It was in this condition that Civitella found us, asking in amazement after the cause of our dismay. Z*** and I were silent.

The prince, however, who for some time had been used to make no differentiation between himself and us, still too strongly agitated to listen to wisdom at the moment, ordered us to show him the letter. I hesitated, but the prince tore it out of my hand and gave it to the marquis himself.

"I am your debtor, marquis," the prince began, after the latter had read the letter through in astonishment, "but do not let that upset you. Give me just twenty days more, and you shall be satisfied."

"Most gracious Prince," exclaimed Civitella, deeply moved, "do I deserve this?"

"You did not send me a reminder; I acknowledge your delicacy, and thank you. In twenty days, as I said, you shall be fully satisfied."

"What is this?" Civitella asked me in dismay. "How does this cohere? I do not understand."

We explained what we knew. He was beside himself. The prince, he said, must insist upon satisfaction; the slander was scandalous. He swore, meanwhile, to make use of his entire capital and credit, without limit.

The marquis had left us, and the prince had still not spoken a word. He paced up and down the room in agitation; something extraordinary was working in him. He stood still at last, and murmured to himself through his teeth, "'Wish yourself good luck,' he said, 'at nine o'clock he died.'"

We looked at him in horror.

"Good luck," he continued, "Luck. I ought to wish myself good luck—Is that not what he said? What did he mean by that?"

"Where do you get that idea?"

"I did not then understand what the man wanted. Now I understand him—Oh, it is unbearably hard to have a Lord above one!"

"My dearest Prince."

"Who can let us feel it!—Ha! It must be sweet!"

He paused. His mood terrified me. I had never seen him like this.

"The most miserable among the people," he started up again, "or the next Prince upon the throne! It is the same thing. There is only *one* difference between people—obey or rule!"

He looked into the letter again.

"You have seen the person," he went on, "who permits himself to dare write me this. Would you greet him on the street, if fate had not made him your master? By God! There is something great in a crown!"

He went on in this vein, and then came speeches I shall never dare entrust to any letter. But upon this occasion, the prince revealed something to me, which caused me no slight amazement and horror, and which can have dangerous consequences. We have been grossly mistaken up to now, as concerns the familial relations at the *** court.

The prince answered the letter at once, although I tried to prevent it, and the manner in which he did it permits us no hope of an amicable settlement.

You will be curious, dearest O***, to finally learn something definite about the Greek lady; but it is just in this regard, that I am still unable to give you satisfying answer. Nothing is to be had from the prince, because he has been drawn into the secret and, as I suspect, has had to swear to keep it. But, that she is *not* the Greek lady we took her for, that much is out. She is German, of the most noble family. A certain rumor I have come across says, that her mother is very high, and she herself is the progeny of an unhappy love, about which there is a great deal of talk in Europe. Secret persecution by a powerful hand, according to this word, has forced her to seek refuge in Venice, and this is also the reason for her seclusion, which made it impossible for the prince to determine where she was. The veneration with which the prince speaks of her, and the deference he observes toward her, seem to lend force to these suspicions.

He is bound to her with a fearsome passion, one that grows as each day passes. In the beginning, his visits were sparingly permitted; but in the second week, the separation was shortened, and no day passes now when the prince is not there. Entire evenings vanish without our seeing him, and if he is not in her company, it is *she alone* who occupies his attentions. He walks around as if in a dream, and none of the things which interested him previously, are even able to snatch his fleeting attentiveness.

Where will it end? I shudder for the future. The break with his court has placed my Prince in a degrading dependancy upon one single person, upon the Marquis Civitella. He is now master of our secrets, our entire fate. Will he always think so nobly as he now manifests himself to us? Will this good disposition last, and is it wise to grant one person, even the most excellent, too much importance and power?

A new letter has been sent to the prince's sister. I hope to be able to report success to you in my next letter.

Continuation by the Count of O***

But this letter never arrived. Three full months passed before I received news from Venice—an interruption whose cause was only too well elucidated in the subsequent course of events. All letters from my friend were held back and suppressed. One can easily judge my dismay when, at last, in December of this year, I received the following letter, which mere accident brought to my hands (because Biondello, who was to have delivered it, fell suddenly ill).

"You do not write. You do not answer—Come, Oh come on the wings of friendship. Our hopes are gone. Read the enclosed. All our hopes are gone.

"The wounds of the marquis are said to be fatal. The cardinal is stewing revenge, and his assassins are seeking the prince. My Prince, Oh my unhappy Prince!—Has it come to this? Unworthy, dreadful fate! Like vile creatures, we must hide ourselves from assassins and thieves.

"I am writing this to you from the *** Cloister, where the prince has found refuge. Just now he is lying on a hard bench next to me, sleeping—Oh, the slumbers of the most deadly exhaustion, which will only strengthen in him the feeling of his suffering. Over the ten days that she was ill, there came no sleep into his eyes. Traces of poison were found. Today she will be buried.

"Oh, dearest O***, my heart is torn asunder. I have experienced something that will never be extinguished from my memory. I stood before her death-bed. She departed like a saint, and her last words were exhausted in guiding her beloved on the way she strode to heaven— Our steadfastness was shaken, the prince alone stood firm, though he suffered her death three times over, he maintained sufficient strength of mind to deny the pious fantansy of her last request."

In the letter was the following:

"*To the prince of ***, from his sister*.
"The only sacred church, which has made such brilliant conquest in the prince of ***, will not also permit him to look for means to continue the lifestyle to which she thanks this conquest. I have tears and prayers for an errant one, but no benevolence any longer for an unworthy one.

Henriette ***"

I took the coach at once, traveled night and day, and in the third week I was in Venice. My haste was no longer of any use. I had come to bring consolation to an unfortunate; I found one fortunate, who no longer required my weak assistance. F*** lay ill, and could no longer speak when I arrived; I was brought the following note from his hand. "Go back where you came from, dearest O***. The prince needs you no longer, nor me. His debts are paid, the cardinal reconciled, the marquis recovered. Do you remember the Armenian who distressed us so last year? In *his* arms you will find the prince, who has been hearing the first mass for five days."

I pressed nonetheless, to see the prince, but I was refused. I heard the scandalous story at last at the bed of my friend.

Principles of The Schiller Institute

1. The purpose of the Schiller Institute is to counterpose to the multiple tendencies toward decoupling Western Europe from the United States a positive conception for the maintenance and revitalization of the Western alliance. Its members commit themselves to the idea of returning to the spirit of the American Revolution, the German Classics and the Liberation Wars against Napoleon, and to proceed from that basis to find solutions to the present problems.

2. The Schiller Institute sees as its task to newly define the interest of the Western alliance, namely in the humanist tradition of Nicolaus of Cusa, Leibniz and William Penn, and to work for a more just world order in which national sovereign republics are united as a community of principle of mutual help and development. The members of the Schiller Institute regard themselves as world citizens and patriots alike, in the sense that Friedrich Schiller used these notions.

3. It is not without reason that the Western alliance has been afflicted with the present crisis. To elaborate those causes of the crisis and to redesign the areas of positive collaboration are included tasks of the Institute.

4. The Institute shall carry the name of Schiller because no one has combined the idea of republican freedom and the idea of poetical beauty more effectively than Friedrich Schiller. For Schiller as for the members of this Institute, the greatest work of art is building political freedom.

SCHILLER INSTITUTE MEMBERSHIP

Sign me up as a member of the Schiller Institute.

- ☐ $1,000 Lifetime Membership
- ☐ $ 500 Sustaining Membership
- ☐ $ 100 Regular Annual Membership
- ☐ $ 25 Students, unemployed, senior citizens

Name _____

Street _____

State _____ Zip _____

Phone ( ) _____

Make checks payable to:
Schiller Institute, Inc.
1612 K St., N.W., Suite 300, Washington, D.C. 20006   (202) 955-5938